Garland Studies in

THE HISTORY
OF AMERICAN
LABOR

edited by

STUART BRUCHEY
Allan Nevins Professor Emeritus
Columbia University

THE NEW LABOR RADICALISM AND NEW YORK CITY'S GARMENT INDUSTRY
Progressive Labor Insurgents in the 1960s

LEIGH DAVID BENIN

Routledge
Taylor & Francis Group
LONDON AND NEW YORK

First published 2000 by Garland Publishing, Inc.

Published 2018 by Routledge
2 Park Square, Milton Park, Abingdon, Oxon OX14 4RN
52 Vanderbilt Avenue, New York, NY 10017

First issued in paperback 2018

Routledge is an imprint of the Taylor & Francis Group, an informa business

Library of Congress Cataloging-in-Publication Data is available
from the Library of Congress.

Benin, Leigh David
The new labor radicalism and New York City's gament industry :
progressive labor insurgents in the 1960s / by Leigh David Benin
p. cm.— (Garland studies in the history of American labor)
Includes bibliographical references and index.
ISBN 0-8153-3385-4 (alk. paper)

ISBN 13: 978-1-138-97710-5 (pbk)
ISBN 13: 978-0-8153-3385-2 (hbk)

Dedicated to the Memory of

Marcia Herman Benin
and
Robert Milton Benin

Lovers of Justice and Learning

Contents

vii

Introduction

THE FOCUS OF THE PRESENT STUDY

This study examines how Progressive Labor, an antirevisionist offshoot of the Communist Party USA, attempted to revolutionize the labor front in New York City's garment industry during the 1960s. An ideologically driven group, whose founders were loyal to Stalinism and attracted by Maoism, Progressive Labor set out in 1962 to become the vanguard of the American working class. However, PL—most of whose several hundred members were students, intellectuals and professionals—is primarily known for the factional role that it played in Students for a Democratic Society, the largest radical organization in the United States during the 1960s. The Worker–Student Alliance, PL's caucus in SDS, championed the cause of working-class revolution. Although most SDSers, who identified with the New Left's reliance on students or minorities, never embraced PL's faith in the American working class as an agency of radical social change, PL gained enough supporters for its pro-worker strategy to precipitate a disastrous split in SDS in 1969.

Progressive Labor was not only the first of the newly organized radical groups in the 1960s to advocate a working-class strategy, but the first to turn its members into workplace organizers. Thus, while PL was vociferously urging students to support working-class revolution, it also sought to validate its pro-worker stance by winning workers at the point of production to communism. Therefore, although most large-scale radical actions in the 1960s were campus based and we primarily know PL as an important player in the factional wars that led to SDS's disintegration

Introduction

at the end of the decade, this study focuses on PL's historical experience in the labor field, an arena in which PL's activities were not entirely insignificant, and which PL regarded as a proving ground for the theories it advanced within SDS. A historical analysis of PL's labor organizing, even in one venue, provides a useful vantage point from which we can reevaluate the theoretical debate within SDS over agency (the social basis for radical social change). To what extent did PL's experience with on-the-job organizing confirm its sanguine view of contemporary American workers' revolutionary potential? To what extent did PL's practice at the point of production justify the party's enormous self-confidence as an aspiring labor vanguard? By looking at PL's attempt to revolutionize the labor front, this study illuminates the seldom examined labor agitation of 1960s' radicals, as well as the little explored radical element in the labor movement of the period.

During the 1960s and 1970s, public and service sector unions were more dynamic than unions in the industrial sector, including the ILGWU, and PL's predominantly college-educated base generally played a greater role in public and service workers' unions than in unions of industrial workers, where PL had few members. However, PL relied primarily on the revolutionary potential of industrial workers, especially "super-exploited" Blacks, Hispanics, and, in feminized industries, women. Because PL was headquartered in New York City, this study focuses on PL's organizing efforts in the city's industrial heartland, the garment industry, whose large number of minority and female workers were represented by the International Ladies' Garment Workers' Union, the city's biggest and most influential labor union.

Progressive Labor's roots were in New York City, which had a strong union and radical tradition, including a history of labor radicalism. A labor town, New York was also the headquarters of the CP, whose internal disputes in the late 1950s and early 1960s led to the creation of PL. Progressive Labor's new communists partially rejected their CP training, but they also attempted to perpetuate the CP traditions that they valued, including a communist struggle to control the needle trades dating back to the 1920s. For the most part, Jewish men who were either immigrants themselves or the children of immigrants led the city's garment industry, the ILGWU and PL. Their own responses to exploitation and anti-Semitism (capitalist enterprise, socialist unionism, and communist revolution, respectively) informed their approach—at a time of rising radical, labor, civil rights, and feminist ferment—to the city's newest garment workers, Black and Hispanic women. Examining the PL-led insurgency in the ILGWU informs our understanding of New York City during the 1960s and the ILGWU's attempt to cope with changes in the garment workforce as the industry's decline in New York threatened to devastate the union.

Thus, this study of PL's attempt to revolutionize the labor front in New York City's garment industry during the 1960s enhances our knowledge of Progressive Labor, contemporary student and labor radicalism, and New York City, especially its largest industry and major labor union.

PROGRESSIVE LABOR AND STUDENT RADICALISM

Progressive Labor emerged as an antirevisionist offshoot of the Communist Party USA in 1962. Progressive Labor's leaders expressed frustration with what they considered to be the CP's defensive stance during the anticommunist purge under Truman and Eisenhower, and bitterness at the party's anti-Stalinism following Khrushchev's denunciation of Stalin in 1956. They found the Communist Party of China's increasingly vociferous critique of Soviet revisionism persuasive. Over the course of twenty years, from 1962 to 1982, PL read international events and reflected on its own practice, and discovered what it considered to be the logical implications of antirevisionism. In attempting to progressively purify communism of revisionist errors, that is, concessions to capitalist ideology and power, it evolved a pure and simple communism that was utopian in character.

Progressive Labor believed that it could persuade the American working class to make a revolution for egalitarian communism. Indeed, unless PL could gain significant working-class support for its revolutionary communism, the egalitarian society it envisioned would remain a *utopia*. Its CP training and increasingly radical antirevisionism shaped PL's approach to labor organizing. Progressive Labor's leaders believed that American workers were more militant and much more open to communist ideas than the CP acknowledged, and they were determined to prove it in practice at the point of production by leading militant struggles and advocating communist politics. But PL's organizing within New York City's unions during the 1960s and 1970s is terra incognita to almost everyone except the relatively small number of people who were directly involved, that is, the new communist insurgents, the management and union officials whom they assailed, and the rank-and-file union members whom they aspired to lead.

However, scholarly works on the new radicalism of the 1960s, which have focused almost exclusively on student radicalism, do discuss the role that PL played in the breakup and ultimate demise of SDS, the biggest and most influential mass organization produced by the New Left. Students for a Democratic Society, parented by the democratic socialist—and anticommunist—League for Industrial Democracy, and the Progressive Labor Movement, started by ex-CPers, were both founded in the summer of 1962. Although the emergence of SDS's new leftists and the PL's new communists reflected the demise of the CP as the most important center of American radicalism, they adopted divergent paths toward the renewal of American radicalism. While SDS's *Port Huron Statement* expressed hope that peace forces would permeate important decision making centers, PL's new communists advocated laying siege to the edifice of Cold War liberalism in the name of an anti-imperialist crusade.

However, between 1962 and 1965, SDS responded to the Kennedy and Johnson administrations' escalation of the Vietnam War by becoming increasingly radical.[1] In April 1965 the two hundred delegates to the Progressive Labor Party's founding convention interrupted their proceedings to carry anti-imperialist banners in SDS's march in Washington, which attracted an unprecedented 25,000 anti-Vietnam War protesters. Students for a Democratic Society, which was not committed to a distinct ideology, was gaining a mass following. In 1966 Progressive Labor dissolved its small student antiwar front, the May Second Movement, and advised its members to join SDS to promote its own distinctly ideological approach to revolutionary politics.[2]

Students for a Democratic Society, influenced by contemporary leftist intellectuals who doubted the revolutionary potential of industrial workers in advanced capitalist countries, attempted to build a countervailing power from below by organizing the poor into "community unions."[3] By contrast, PL differentiated between the labor establishment and rank-and-file workers. While PL ridiculed labor leaders as the junior partners of American capitalism, it argued that rank-and-file workers would become a revolutionary force if genuine communists provided them with leadership. Progressive Labor organized the WSA faction of SDS to counteract SDSers' antiworker biases and gain control of SDS. In 1968 the WSA organized the SDS Work-In, which sent SDSers into the workplace to politicize workers.[4] The general strike in France that year lent credence to PL's pro-worker campaign, which was gaining adherents among radical students who were frustrated by their inability to end the Vietnam War and reshape American political culture. The WSA, however, was "expelled" from SDS in 1969 by a temporary alliance of two other revolutionary SDS factions, the Revolutionary Youth Movement II and the Weathermen. The WSA claimed to be the "real" SDS and continued to operate as SDS until PL dissolved it in the early 1970s.

The fracturing of SDS was followed by two decades of post-mortem analyses, for the most part by PL's New Left critics. They deplored the renewed currency in the latter half of the 1960s of the Old Left's insistence on Marxist-Leninist discipline, belief in the imminence of revolution, and reliance on the working class; and they lamented the failed promise of New Left innovations, such as participatory democracy, cultural criticism, expressive politics and reliance on students or minorities. Within this general framework, these analysts differed about why SDS failed.[5]

However, all of them faulted PL for its allegedly destructive role in SDS. "PL helped to Marxize SDS," former SDS leader Todd Gitlin wrote, "and PL fattened, parasitically, as Marxism and then Marxism-Leninism became SDS's unofficial language."[6] The portrayal of PL as the scourge of the student movement (emerging from obscurity to achieve fifteen minutes of fame as SDS's destroyer and then dwindling into an irrelevant fringe group) is far from adequate. The characterization of PL as Old Left, Stalinist and Maoist, even if substantially accurate, does not constitute a substantive analysis of the party's ideas and actions; and noting that students became radicalized by the late 1960s, or that PL possessed disciplined cadres, does not fully explain what enabled PL to build a significant SDS caucus oriented toward working-class revolution, or why PL, rather than some other Old Left group, was able to do it. Progressive Labor's importance in the story of SDS's collapse suggests the need for a comprehensive examination of PL. A better understanding of PL would, undoubtedly, make the rise of revolutionary politics—and the rise of PL—in SDS more comprehensible.

PROGRESSIVE LABOR AND LABOR RADICALISM

The present study, however, does not propose to scrutinize PL to clarify matters that principally have to do with the student movement. The purpose here, rather, is to illuminate the least understood aspect of the new radicalism, that is, radicals organizing in the workplace. The schism in SDS centered on the debate over what stance students should take toward workers. Moreover, thousands of former student radicals of various political persuasions became workers during the 1960s and 1970s, entering a workforce that showed signs of renewed spirit.

The resurgence of student radicalism at the end of the 1950s and the beginning of the 1960s coincided with an upsurge of labor ferment. The labor movement had been relatively quiescent for almost fifteen years after the immediate postwar strike wave subsided—in part, due to the anticommunist crusade that devastated labor's Left.[7] Beginning in the early 1960s, a number of liberal and leftist labor intellectuals observed what they regarded as depressing signs of ossification in the labor movement.[8] But there was also evidence that labor ferment was on the rise. A major spurt of new organizing among public, service and professional employees offset declining union membership rolls in the heavily organized manufacturing sector of the Northeast and Midwest. The worker militancy that facilitated union organizing also led to rank-and-file revolts against established union leaders. This wave of insurgency crested from the late 1960s to the early 1970s. Moreover, radicals sometimes played a leading role in rank-and-file insurgencies, especially in unions of college-educated workers in health, education and welfare. This reinvigorating of the labor movement induced a sense of optimism in leftist labor intellectuals.[9]

However, by the end of the 1970s, the tide of worker militancy had subsided and the unions were clearly on the defensive vis-a-vis employers. Again, labor intellectuals attempted to explain, and suggested ways to reverse, organized labor's evident decline.[10] To some extent, these writers addressed the resurgence of labor radicalism in the 1960s, but barely mentioned PL's role in this movement.[11]

From its inception in the early 1960s, however, Progressive Labor aspired to be the vanguard party of the working class. To be sure, PL saw students and bourgeois intellectuals as potential allies of working-class revolution. But before, during and after its involvement in SDS, PL attempted to bring its revolutionary communist ideas to workers at the point of production. While PL never became the vanguard of the working class, it unquestionably was in the vanguard of the industrializing movement of the new radicals.

PROGRESSIVE LABOR IN NEW YORK CITY'S INDUSTRIAL HEARTLAND

Progressive Labor played an active role in labor unions across the United States, but PL was headquartered in New York, where this small Marxist-

Leninist party had its largest base. In view of PL's relative strength in New York, which had a strong radical tradition, a diverse workforce, a dynamic labor movement and national political importance, the city is a good focus for a study of PL's approach to winning the hearts and minds of American workers.

New York City deserved its reputation as a union town. By 1945, unions had organized much of New York's labor force and played an important role in the city's political life. Despite important exceptions, White working-class men dominated both the membership and leadership of New York's labor movement. However, changes in demography, patterns of employment and unionization in the postwar period altered the composition of the labor movement and, eventually, its leadership. The city's large number of Black and Hispanic immigrants found employment in unskilled and semiskilled occupations, women increasingly found employment at various levels, and the boom in higher education and public sector employment brought many college graduates into the workforce. Unions of public, service and professional employees in New York enjoyed a major growth spurt from the early 1960s to the mid-1970s, bringing a large number of Blacks, Hispanics, women and the college-educated into the city's labor movement.[12] The diversity of New York and its labor movement raised issues of race, class and gender that both unions and labor radicals could not afford to neglect.[13]

New York City also has a strong radical tradition. During the 1930s and 1940s, the Communist Party's largest chapter was located in New York. The anticommunist crusade of the 1940s and 1950s devastated the CP, but New York became an important center of resurgent radicalism, including labor radicalism, in the 1960s and 1970s. Even though New Left students wrote off organized labor as a force for radical change, some new radicals—PLers not the least among them—did attempt to influence unionized workers, and student radicals' interest in labor rose in the late 1960s as worker militancy increased. Moreover, because college-trained workers in health, education and welfare unionized during the 1960s, New York's labor movement was peppered with radical intellectuals. They offered alternative visions of unionism and alternative solutions to New York's urban crisis, mobilizing rank-and-file militancy in support of their positions. They were not mere gadflies buzzing around the house of labor, but posed a threat to employers, union leaders and public officials, who often collaborated to defend the liberal consensus in labor relations and public policy. The labor radicals' struggle against entrenched institutional power ran like a red thread through the fabric of labor relations in New York during the 1960s and 1970s.[14]

College and university students, intellectuals and professionals, as well as a growing number of college-educated workers, such as case-workers, teachers and hospital technicians, comprised the vast majority of PL's membership. Not surprisingly, then, there were many more PLers in such New York unions as the Social Service Employees Union, the United Federation of Teachers, Hospital and Nursing Home Workers Local 1199 and the Committee of Interns and Residents than in any union of industrial workers in the city. Generally, PL had a more palpable impact on unions representing the college-educated than on unions in the city's industrial sector.

None of the unions representing public and service employees, how-ever, were as important to PL as the imperious ILGWU, which repre-sented the bulk of the garment workforce. In order for tiny PL, which had only a few hundred members in New York, to win garment workers to its brand of communism, it would have to take on not only the garment in-dustry but the staunchly anticommunist ILGWU, the largest institution in New York City's garment center and one of the most politically influ-ential organizations in the city. This was a case of David going forth to slay Goliath.

However, PL saw chinks in the ILGWU's armor. The defeat of New York's labor leftists occurred at a time when garment, still the city's major industry, was employing an increasing number of Blacks and Hispanics, especially women, in low-paid positions. Liberals and radi-cals faulted the ILGWU for failing to adequately defend the interests of its newest members, whose marginalization in a declining industry con-tributed to the emergence of New York as an increasingly divided city. By contrast, in health care, which was replacing garment as the city's major industry, Local 1199's CP-trained leadership, which had survived the anticommunist crusade, won significant gains for egregiously ex-ploited minority women by merging the crusading spirit of the contem-porary civil rights movement with militant unionism.

Filled with revolutionary optimism, PL attempted to turn the ILGWU, which faced daunting challenges, into a school for commu-nism. This was an expression of PL's confidence in the industrial work-ing class and a crucial test of its class analysis. Progressive Labor believed that winning industrial workers to communism was a vital com-ponent of its revolutionary mission. From its inception in 1962, when PL set out to rebuild a labor Left, initially in New York City, it focused on the garment industry and the ILGWU's alleged racism. The auto and steel industries might be more important nationally, but in New York City, where PL was headquartered, garment was still the key industry. Progressive Labor aspired to be a working-class party, but especially a party of, by, and for the industrial workers, whom PL envisaged as the backbone of the coming social revolution and new social order; and PL saw low-paid Black, Hispanic, and female garment workers as potentially the key revolutionary force in New York City because they suffered from racism and sexism, as well as economic exploitation.

If PL could not organize a communist base among oppressed Black and Hispanic industrial workers in New York City, where the party had its biggest chapter, and where party leaders could give close supervision to on-the-job organizers, then where could PL expect to succeed? Even when PL's activities in other New York industries looked promising (for example, in the hospitals during the 1970s), PL continually renewed its commitment to building a communist base in the garment industry. Moreover, despite the breadth of PL's labor organizing over two decades, and the periodic changes in PL's line and practice during that period, the experience of the party's garment organizers in New York during the late 1960s was, in most important respects, representative of the experience of PL's labor organizers generally. Therefore, New York's garment industry during the 1960s is a good focus for a study of PL's attempt to revolutionize the American labor front.

Historical accounts of radicalism and labor in the 1960s and 1970s have largely left unexplored the struggles waged by the new generation of labor radicals, including PLers, who became politically active during these decades. Because New York City was a center of resurgent labor radicalism and served as PL's center, it offers abundant material for a study of the new labor radicalism and PL. Focusing on PL's labor activities in New York City's garment center, where PL hoped to build a communist base among workers in the city's largest industry, is a useful vantage point from which to assess PL's theory and practice in the labor field. This study provides: (1) a needed survey of PL's development during the 1960s and 1970s; (2) an opportunity to reassess PL and its pro-worker stance based on the labor organizing that the party regarded as crucial to its development as the vanguard of the American working class; (3) a picture of PL's part in the resurgence of labor radicalism during the 1960s and 1970s, especially in New York City; (4) a view of the ILGWU from the vantage point of its PL critics at a time when the union was confronted by ethnic, racial and gender changes in the garment workforce, and the industry's decline in New York City; and (5) instructive case studies of new communist labor insurgencies in the industrial field.

STRUCTURE OF THE WORK

Considering the fact that there is no scholarly history of the Progressive Labor Party, this study begins with a survey of PL (Part I), which examines the origin of PL (Chapter 1), the development of its antirevisionist theory (Chapter 2) and its labor organizing practices during the 1960s and 1970s (Chapter 3).

Part II considers PL's organizing activities in New York City's industrial heartland, examining the party's critique of the ILGWU (Chapter 4); the political apprenticeship of one of PL's leading organizers in garment trucking (Chapter 5); the PL-led work stoppages in garment trucking, involving members of Local 102, ILGWU (Chapter 6); the PL-led wildcat strike at Figure Flattery, which involved members of Local 32, ILGWU (Chapter 7); and the anticommunist purge that followed the Figure Flattery strike (Chapter 8).

Acknowledgments

Many people contributed to the completion of this work, but none more so than Dr. Daniel J. Walkowitz, Director of Metropolitan Studies at New York University, whose patient support and insightful critiques, over many years, were indispensable. I am also deeply indebted to other members of the faculty, past and present, of the Department of History at New York University's Graduate School of Arts and Science, especially to the late Dr. Albert U. Romasco, the late Dr. Warren Dean, Dr. Michael Lutzker, Dr. David M. Reimers, Dr. Susan Ware, Dr. Nikhil Pal Singh and Dr. Paul Mattingly. My research would have been impossible without the invaluable assistance I received from the dedicated and very knowledgeable staff of the Tamiment Library–Robert F. Wagner, Jr. Labor Archives, especially Jane Latour. Richard Strassberg of the Labor Documentation Center at Cornell University and Walter Mankoff of the Research Department at UNITE gave me very useful advice, as did Kitty Krupat, Jon Bloom, Joe Doyle, Dr. Richard Weisberg, Dr. Ursula Schoenheim, Susan and Iris Grodinger, Ted Krulik, and Dr. Gerald Meyer. I am grateful to Edward Lemansky and Felipe DeJesus for agreeing to be interviewed, and to Milton Rosen, the late Mortimer Scheer, Walter Linder, Edward Lemansky, Harvey Mason and many others for helping me to understand Progressive Labor's perspective and history. The book could not have been completed without Henrie Benin's careful reading of the manuscript and the technical assistance that Jeff Simon so generously provided. I also thank Marisa Schwartz, Victoria Fensterer and Laura Benin for their help with the manuscript. I could not have gotten through the slow, and sometimes painful, process of thinking through the issues this book addresses without more than a little help from very good friends; I especially value many soul-saving talks with Laszlo Berkovits, Dr. George Kaysen and Robert Pope. There is no way to sufficiently thank my wife, Janet Benin, and my daughter, Laura Benin, for the years they patiently endured my preoccupation with this project; and I thank my extended family and friends as well for their unfailing patience and support. But no one who assisted me is responsible for the errors in this book; all of its many faults are attributable to me.

List of Abbreviations

AFL-CIO	American Federation of Labor–Congress of Industrial Organizations
APU	Acion Patriotica Unitaria
CCNY	City College of New York
CIA	Central Intelligence Agency
CORE	Congress of Racial Equality
CPC	Communist Party of China
CPSU	Communist Party of the Soviet Union
CPUSA or CP	Communist Party of the United States
CUNY	City University of New York
FBI	Federal Bureau of Investigation
FOUR	Federation of Union Representatives
FUPI	Federacion de Universitarios Pro Independencia
GPCR	Great Proletarian Cultural Revolution
HUAC	House Un-American Activities Committee
ICC	Interstate Commerce Commission
ILGWU	International Ladies' Garment Workers' Union
InCAR	International Committee Against Racism
KKK	Klu Klux Klan
M2M	May Second Movement
MYAC	Monroe Youth Action Committee
NAACP	National Association for the Advancement of Colored People
NEP	New Economic Policy
NLR	*New Left Review*

OEO	Office of Economic Opportunity
PL	Progressive Labor
PL	*Progressive Labor Magazine*
PLM	Progressive Labor Movement
PLP	Progressive Labor Party
RR I	*Road to Revolution*
RR II	*Road to Revolution II*
RR III	*Road to Revolution III*
RR IV	*Road to Revolution IV*
SBI	State Bureau of Investigation
SDS	Students for a Democratic Society
SDS-LP	Students for a Democratic Society–Labor Project
SNCC	Student Non-Violent Coordinating Committee
SWP	Socialist Workers Party
UAW	United Automobile Workers
WAC	Workers Action Committee
WAM	Workers Action Movement
WPA	Works Progress Administration
WSA	Worker–Student Alliance

THE NEW LABOR RADICALISM AND NEW YORK CITY'S GARMENT INDUSTRY

PART I

Reinventing American Communism

An Overview of Progressive Labor
in the 1960s and 1970s

CHAPTER 1

Antirevisionism in Action
The Origin of the Progressive Labor Party, 1956–1965

This chapter discusses Progressive Labor's formative period, from the late 1950s and early 1960s, when PL's future leaders were dissident members of the Communist Party USA, to the creation of the loosely organized Progressive Labor Movement in 1962, and finally to the formation in 1965 of the Progressive Labor Party, a Marxist-Leninist vanguard party organized along democratic-centralist lines.[1]

COMMUNIST PARTY DISSIDENTS

Progressive Labor, which quickly transformed itself between January 1962 and April 1965 from a magazine into a political party, emerged from the acrimonious internal disputes that plagued the embattled and disintegrating Communist Party USA of the late 1950s.[2] In August 1961 the CPUSA removed Milton Rosen and Mortimer Scheer from party leadership, as New York State labor secretary and Erie County chairman, respectively, because of their disagreements with the party's strategy and tactics. Four months later, the party expelled them for engaging in "secret factional activities." They had, the CP alleged, "crassly violated the Leninist principles of democratic centralism" and become a "center of disruption."[3] After being expelled from the CP, they founded *Progressive Labor*, which subsequently justified their actions as "strictly within the guidelines of democratic centralism," and accused the CP's national leadership of having feared "inner-party ideological struggle."[4]

This quarrel about which side had violated mutually accepted rules of engagement governing inner-party warfare reflected deep political divisions between the belligerents. The CP leadership accused the "handful of disrupters in New York headed by Milt Rosen" of having a "sectarian and dogmatic outlook."[5] Contrarily, PL portrayed its founders as former leaders of the CP's "new Left" who had been expelled by the CP's "revisionist" national leadership.[6] In the charged language of party polemics, where adversaries quickly became enemies, combatants wielded epithets such as *revisionist* and *sectarian* like knives in a street brawl.[7] This may seem like a tempest in a teapot, but the belligerents believed, as did Lenin, that the fate of the world's working class depended on the outcome of such disputes in obscure revolutionary circles.[8]

Progressive Labor traced the roots of this rancor to the "grave internal crisis" that rocked the CPUSA following the repudiation of Stalinism by the Twentieth Congress of the Communist Party of the Soviet Union in 1956.[9] In the principal dispute that divided the CPUSA, the defenders of ideological orthodoxy, led by Eugene Dennis, the general secretary, and especially William Z. Foster, the chairman, defeated the reformers, led by John Gates, editor of the *Daily Worker*.[10] Progressive Labor regarded the defeated reformers, who criticized the CPUSA for being sectarian, as "right-wingers." However, from PL's pro-Stalin perspective, the victorious Foster-Dennis forces were "centrists," rather than genuine leftists, because they "never defeated the revisionists' class collaborationist program" and "never repudiated the 20th Congress of the CPSU."[11] Ironically, PL's future leaders had developed their political ideas during the Cold War, when Foster's policies, which he later characterized as "left-sectarian," guided the CPUSA.[12] In important respects, PL reenacted in the 1960s and 1970s Cold War imperatives initiated by the Foster leadership in the late 1940s and early 1950s.[13]

Progressive Labor self-importantly characterized the CP's "leading industrial cadres in Buffalo, New York," who later founded PL, as the "the Left."[14] Progressive Labor was proud of its working-class origin. Within communist circles, belonging to the proletariat bestowed social status and political authority.[15] However, the CP, unwilling to concede this advantage to PL's future leaders, accused them of being tainted by petit bourgeois backgrounds or influences—a stinging rebuke.[16] For its part, PL disparaged as "petit bourgeois sectors" the disappointed reformers who left the CP "in droves," especially in New York State, where 50% of the party's membership lived.

These defections created a leadership vacuum that allowed Milt Rosen, a relatively young steel worker and leftist industrial leader in the Buffalo CP, to become the CP's Upstate New York organizer. When the

House Un-American Activities Committee attacked the CP's industrial base in Buffalo in 1957, anticommunist union leaders, according to PL, initiated numerous firings. Progressive Labor claimed that co-workers usually defended CPers who were open communists, enabling them to retain their jobs. In any case, the CP organization in Buffalo survived and Rosen was elected labor secretary of the New York State CPUSA. This promotion apparently emboldened Rosen, who now had an opportunity to implement his ideas statewide in the CP's most important state.[17]

Rosen's revival of CP street rallies in New York City's garment district, "for the first time in many years," was emblematic, PL later reflected, of its future leaders' determination to "openly bring the banner of socialism into the working-class movement." They were just as determined to oppose what they considered to be fundamental concessions to capitalist hegemony in the United States and internationally. For example, they sat out the 1960 presidential election, refusing to back John F. Kennedy even though the CP supported him as the lesser-evil candidate.[18] After Kennedy's election, they concentrated on fighting his administration rather than the "Ultra-Right," which the CP regarded as representing the "most dangerous elements" in American society.[19] Rosen and Scheer believed that the CP's preoccupation with right-wing extremists diverted workers from fighting the "main sources of monopoly power which control the state apparatus."[20] They also rejected the CPUSA's contention, which conformed to the line of Khrushchev's CPSU, that "war is not inevitable and that peaceful coexistence is possible." The CPUSA retorted that Rosen's group was in accord with the Albanian party, whose leaders "support the methods and practices of the Stalin cult."[21]

The relative political strength of these opposing outlooks within the CP was decisively tested at the party's 17th national convention in 1959. Milt Rosen and Mort Scheer failed to win seats on the party's national committee.[22] As PL subsequently saw it, the newly elected general secretary, Gus Hall, had "maneuvered" to put "well known revisionists" from New York into national leadership. The Hall leadership's victory over the "political delinquents" in New York set the stage, PL believed, for their expulsion.[23]

According to the CP, following the defeat of his national committee candidacy at the CP's 17th convention, Milt Rosen "organized and continued an active opposition to the basic policy decisions of that convention." As a result, he was removed from "all his posts" by the New York State party committee. His response, the CP charged, was to engage in factionalism.[24] In December 1961 the CP leadership accused Rosen's group of having held an "anti-party faction meeting." According to the CP, the "disrupters" did not deny the charge, but refused to "recognize the authority of the party to inquire into the matter" and "disavowed the party." They were "unanimously expelled" by the CP's New York State leadership.[25] PL later surmised that Gus Hall had expelled the "new Left cadres" because he, unlike his "ideologically weak" left-wing opponents, who were unaware of the international roots of the CPUSA's "revisionism," was cognizant of the developing Sino-Soviet split and fearful of "large-scale defections" to the Chinese side. Whatever the merit of this supposition, PL affirmed that twelve "comrades," representing thirty-five communist workers, and fifteen communist students who were influenced by the Cuban Revolution, met under Rosen's leadership that December and made the fateful decision to build a new communist party.[26]

It is unlikely that Gus Hall was excessively disturbed by the defection (or expulsion) of Rosen's group. In view of the collapse of the CP, whose membership declined from 20,000 to 5,000 in the late 1950s, the loss of thirty-five Stalinist workers and fifteen pro-Castro students did not significantly reduce the party's forces.[27] On the contrary, from the Hall leadership's point of view, the removal of Rosen, Scheer and other incorrigible Stalinists, who allegedly had formed a disruptive and potentially dangerous faction, strengthened party unity, enabling the CP to defend itself against government attacks and pursue its policies unhindered by internal dissension.[28] For his part, Rosen undoubtedly agreed with the sentiment expressed by Foster that "It is better to have fifty true members than 50,000 people who are not genuine communists." Rosen forfeited only five thousand CP "revisionists" to preserve a core of fifty "revolutionary" communists. However, Rosen would have to demonstrate in practice that this sacrifice was justified.[29]

While Progressive Labor never made the "absurd claim" that it was the "first true communist party in history," it did consider itself to be the CP's successor as the standard-bearer of communism in the United States.[30] As the CP's self-appointed heir, PL intended to preserve all that was truly revolutionary in the CP's past, while expunging the elements of revisionism that it had inherited from its CP training. However, when PL's future leaders resolved to build a new communist party, admittedly an "enormous" task, the CP was still around and, although greatly diminished in size, was still much larger than the diminutive group that coalesced around Milt Rosen. Clearly, PL and the CP would be competing for recruits and influence in the same political market. However, PL's future leaders, who had, while still members of the CP, sharply criticized its "revisionist" policies, now decided to remain mute on the subject of the CP. They argued that "concentrating on fighting the old communist party" was a "sectarian trap" that had destroyed other groups of ex-CPers. They decided to use all their meager resources to "get off the ground" by developing a "revolutionary program with a mass line" and building a "new working class base."[31]

PROGRESSIVE LABOR AND THE LABOR MOVEMENT

To begin the process of building a new working-class base for their brand of revolutionary politics, Rosen's small band of ex-CPers published *Progressive Labor* in January 1962. The new magazine's editors wanted to reach workers new to communist ideas, rather than engage in polemics with the CP. They avoided communist jargon in favor of a language familiar to trade unionists. From its inception, *PL*'s editors identified themselves as trade unionists "at present or in the recent past" and proclaimed that *PL*'s "main purpose" was to "assist, in whatever way it can, the forward progress of the American labor movement." Hence, they chose the name *Progressive Labor*. By emphasizing their common identity and commonality of interest with other trade unionists, by placing themselves, in other words, squarely within the trade union camp, *PL*'s editors attempted to gain a hearing for their more heterodox views—principally, their advocacy of socialism. Not surprisingly, they presented socialism as the culmination of trade-union aspirations.[32]

The new *PL* magazine began its lead article, modestly entitled *For An Alternative Labor Policy*, by declaring, "The trade union is the only instrument the American worker has with which to protect his job, his working conditions, and his general welfare."[33] The CP ridiculed this formulation as flatly "anarcho-syndicalist," and an indication of how far Rosen's group had "already traveled from the party and Marxism-Leninism." The CP affirmed that trade unions were the "elementary organizations of the working class—their most important mass bodies," but warned workers to be mindful of "the political party of the working class—its vanguard—which is the highest type of working class organization—an indispensable instrument for labor's advance on immediate issues and for the achievement of socialism."[34]

Progressive Labor's editors believed in the essential role of a vanguard party, but found themselves in an awkward and, presumably, frustrating position.[35] The CP had expelled them, but they were not yet able to form a new party. While still members of the CP, they had rejected "Hall's political line," which, in their view, was to "bury the party in the labor movement."[36] Now, with no party of their own to promote, and hoping that the labor movement would provide fertile ground for building a new party, they rhetorically buried their not-yet-dead former party, the CPUSA, and praised labor as a mass movement. *Progressive Labor* lauded organized labor for its "historic role" as a "force for progress" and asserted that "any serious progress" required the "positive role of the labor movement," which *PL* regarded as the "pivotal force in American society."[37]

After assessing the labor movement's past accomplishments and intrinsic importance to the struggle for social progress, *Progressive Labor* identified "one of its basic weaknesses" as the "virtual absence of a socialist outlook." *Progressive Labor* recalled the anticommunist witch hunts of the late 1940s and 1950s, which saw "thousands of progressive and socialist-minded individuals" driven out of the labor movement, "labeled, smeared and vilified" for opposing the labor leadership's "support for the Cold War abroad and collaboration with big business at home."[38] While blaming the Cold War crusade against communism for depriving organized labor of socialist leadership, *PL*'s editors were unwilling to explicitly credit the CP, their former party, with having been, as the CP claimed, in the "forefront of the struggle to build the modern labor movement." They also refrained from mentioning their own commitment to communism and considerable record as CP trade-union cadres.[39]

If they were reticent about their political backgrounds, they were unreserved in their criticism of the labor establishment. *Progressive Labor* accused AFL-CIO leaders of adhering to the policies of big business, and estimated that there were "no more vocal or enthusiastic supporters of the status quo than these junior partners of mid-century American capitalism." Under their leadership, *PL* thought, the labor movement, despite the "fondest hopes of millions," awakened by the AFL-CIO merger in 1955, had "stagnated to the point of retrogression" and was in a "state of crisis."[40]

Progressive Labor was optimistic, however, that in a "world moving rapidly to Socialism," the American worker would "fight for his due, making radical changes in his union, in government, and in the economy, to guarantee a life of security." *Progressive Labor* was confident because, it observed, American workers respond to "good militant leadership" and have often "taken on the companies, their own union leaders and the government all at once to preserve their economic standards and working conditions."[41] For *PL*, the remarkable militancy exhibited by American workers in innumerable reform struggles revealed their capacity to fight for a radical transformation of American society. *Progressive Labor* implied that if workers were willing to fight so hard for even a small slice of the capitalist pie, they would fight even harder for the whole pie—but only if they were enlightened by socialists. *Progressive Labor*'s policy statement recognized that labor required socialist leaders, but glossed over the qualitative difference between an extremely militant struggle for economic demands and a revolutionary struggle for state power. Even so, *PL*'s editors offered to provide the labor movement with the socialist leadership that it was lacking. *Progressive Labor* suggested that although reformist trade unions had won partial and temporary gains for workers, rank-and-file trade unionists could, ultimately, realize their aspirations for a decent life only through socialism. Striving for socialism was the essence of the "alternative labor policy" that *PL*'s editors offered to organized labor. Implicitly, *PL*'s editors also offered themselves as an alternative to the AFL-CIO's reformist leadership.[42]

In this first major policy statement, *PL* presented its Marxist-Leninist vision of the symbiotic relationship between communists and trade unionists in a trade-union language that it primarily aimed at organized workers, but which addressed communists as well. *Progressive Labor*'s editors, who subscribed to Lenin's belief that workers were incapable of arriving at socialist consciousness without help from communists, and who viewed themselves as the nucleus of a new communist party, offered to serve the interests of American workers by leading them to socialism.[43] However, if workers needed communist leadership, as *PL* claimed, albeit in veiled language at this juncture, communists certainly needed a substantial working-class following to accomplish their goals. *Progressive Labor*'s editors believed that they could not lead a socialist revolution in the United States without the support of millions of workers, especially rank-and-file trade unionists in the nation's highly organized basic industries.[44] Thus, if *PL*'s editors claimed that trade unionists needed socialists, they also implied the converse—that socialists needed trade unionists.[45] This was the subtext of *PL*'s praise for organized labor as a "force for progress." If no serious progress could occur, as *PL* argued, without the "positive role of the labor movement," then socialism, the embodiment of progress, could certainly not be achieved without labor support. *Progressive Labor* aimed this correlative message in its appeal for an alternative labor policy at communists who disdained organizing for socialism within reformist labor unions.[46]

There was asymmetry as well as symmetry in *PL*'s envisioned symbiosis between communists and trade unionists. While *PL*'s editors were acutely aware that they needed support from organized workers, there is little evidence that rank-and-file union members were searching for socialist leadership. Nevertheless, *PL* insisted that many workers responded positively to such leadership when they came across it. So, *PL* thought that even if workers were not socialists, they were open to the overtures of socialists. *Progressive Labor* believed that workers' essential willingness to struggle for self-improvement would draw them toward *PL*'s militant leadership and socialist program.[47]

However, *PL* still had the burden of selling itself and socialism to organized workers. It was not at all certain that unionized workers, in pursuing their rational self-interest, would necessarily ally with *PL* and confront their employers, union leaders and government, as *PL* suggested. *Progressive Labor* was sanguine about the future of socialism in America, and confident about its own future as well. Whether *PL*'s optimism was well-founded, and whether its idealizing of working-class people and demonizing of AFL-CIO leaders would strike a responsive chord in unionized workers, remained to be seen. *Progressive Labor*'s analyses and leadership remained to be tested.

THE PROGRESSIVE LABOR MOVEMENT

Progressive Labor's clarion call for a socialist solution to labor's problems and sweeping attack on the AFL-CIO leadership was as bold as its refusal to discuss openly its communist orientation was timid, at least in view of *PL*'s subsequent insistence on broadcasting its communist identity. However, there was no good reason to suppose that any policy statement by *PL*, a new publication whose editors were relatively obscure, would have an impact on the labor movement, or even be noticed beyond a limited circle of leftists. Talk was cheap, but action required organization. To begin their journey out of the political wilderness and toward the promised land of egalitarian socialism, *PL*'s editors gathered their modest forces. Fifty delegates from eleven cities met in New York City's Hotel Diplomat in July 1962 to form the Progressive Labor Movement.[48]

At this meeting, according to PL, the "Right" proposed creating an educational association and the "Left" called for founding a Leninist party immediately. The leadership argued that while the working class needed a democratic-centralist vanguard, the foundations for building a new revolutionary communist party were lacking. Milt Rosen's political report called for the achievement of four key tasks: developing a revolutionary Marxist-Leninist program; initiating militant mass struggles; building a base of support among "young workers and students"; and establishing a network of clubs and a collective leadership. The Progressive Labor Movement, as the name implied, would be "loose in form" and would use the principles of "flexibility and persuasion to develop united action and policies." Rosen concluded his report by urging PLMers to "Organize, organize, organize."[49]

THE TRADE UNION SOLIDARITY COMMITTEE
FOR HAZARD MINERS

The newly formed Progressive Labor Movement, eager to emerge from its obscurity, participated in four "nationally significant struggles," which focused a surprising degree of attention on the small organization (and formed the basis of PLP's narrative of its prehistory as an activist movement). The first was on behalf of coal miners, members of the United Mine Workers of America, in the Appalachian Mountain Region of Kentucky, Tennessee and West Virginia. In the winter of 1962–1963 the miners were engaged in what PL described as a "bitter all-out strike" against "inhuman working conditions and starvation wages." According to PL, the sight of "black and white miners united side by side and armed had sent the local bosses and politicians into a frantic rage." When PLM's leaders learned of the strike, several months after it began, they sent one of PLM's southern organizers to Hazard, Kentucky, the strike's center. There, he interviewed Berman Gibson, a rank-and-file leader of the strike. A cable from Hazard to PLM headquarters in New York City read, "RELIEF NEEDED DESPERATELY . . . HUNGRY BABIES CRYING. . . ." In response, PLM's Wally Linder, an ex-CPer who was president of his local union's railroad lodge, organized the Trade Union Solidarity Committee for Hazard Miners, which collected food, clothing and funds for the striking miners. This committee also raised funds for a mimeograph machine that enabled striking miners to publicize their views, and it organized a mass meeting in New York City that enabled Gibson to address a sympathetic audience of more than one thousand people. While PLM praised and supported rank-and-file miners, it disparaged United Mine Workers of America leaders, whom it accused of trying to "break the strike."[50]

Progressive Labor, which saw itself as the conscience of the working class, regarded strike support as an essential ingredient of working-class solidarity. By supporting striking Kentucky miners, whose militancy was legendary, PL undoubtedly gained a degree of legitimacy as a leftist labor organization, although how much is difficult to determine. The strike's impact on PL's esprit, however, was evident. By supporting the Hazard strike, young urban intellectuals in PLM, who were imbued with Marxism-Leninism, gained a living connection with the historic battles waged by Kentucky miners, that is, with heroic working-class struggles that represented an authentic tradition of American radicalism. The greatly suffering Hazard miners were part of the "other America" that socialist Michael Harrington described, and their enormous courage and determination embodied the working-class militancy that PL relied on to carry forward the struggle for socialism. In PL's view, the miners' strike confirmed PL's picture of American workers; the strike confirmed both the need for socialism and the possibility of winning it.[51]

However, according to PL, Gibson and other rank-and-file leaders, succumbing to the increasingly intensive anticommunist campaign being waged against PLM, broke with their new communist allies and accepted support from liberal and social-democratic sources instead. After many more months, the strike petered out. Despite these disappointments, PLM's actions on behalf of the coal miners' strike spoke louder than all the words in *For An Alternative Labor Policy*. Whether PLM was being supported or attacked, it was starting to be noticed.[52]

THE STUDENT COMMITTEE FOR TRAVEL TO CUBA

The Progressive Labor Movement soon gained greater attention. Following the Cuban Missile Crisis of October 1962, which brought the world to the threshold of nuclear war, PLM unfurled its "HANDS OFF CUBA!" banner in the galleries of the United Nations. When President Kennedy declared an economic boycott of Cuba, which included a U.S. State Department ban on travel to Cuba, PLM declared that it would break the ban. The Progressive Labor Movement selected seventy-five American students, out of five hundred applicants, to travel to Cuba at the invitation of the Cuban Federation of University Students, which paid for the trip. When the Canadian government blocked PLM's publicly known plan to travel to Cuba through Canada, PLM secretly rerouted the trip through Czechoslovakia. In June 1963 fifty students landed in Castro's Cuba, crashing the "Kennedy curtain."[53]

When the PLM-led student group returned from Cuba in August 1963, U.S. immigration officials at Idlewild (Kennedy) Airport began invalidating their passports. After the passports of the first five students were stamped *invalid*, however, the remaining students refused to submit their passports. The stalemate that ensued lasted two and one-half hours, only ending when they were allowed through with their passports intact. Nevertheless, the State Department subsequently declared that the remaining passports were invalid as well. This skirmish over passports was only the prelude to bigger battles.[54]

Late in the summer of 1963, members of PLM's Student Committee for Travel to Cuba and PLM leaders, including Milt Rosen and Mort Scheer, were called before the House Un-American Activities Committee, and subpoenaed by a federal grand jury in New York. From PLM's perspective, HUAC's investigation of PLM revealed the Kennedy administration's fear of losing public favor. "The frantic attack now being directed by the Kennedy Administration and its stooge Un-American Committee," a PLM press release asserted, "clearly shows their fear of the rising tide of resentment in this country against the Administration."[55] In addition, *PL* accused the committee of racism. "HUAC, headed by Dixiecrat Congressman Willis from Louisiana and a band of southern racists," PL charged, "didn't dare subpoena any of the Negro students who took part in the trip (Willis would not like the American people to hear slave state Louisiana compared to the new Cuba free of Jim Crow)."[56]

At the HUAC hearings on 12 and 23 September, PLM witnesses were politically outspoken and uncooperative, refusing to testify about others. Members of PLM packed the galleries and supported witnesses with sustained outbursts of applause, provoking Chairman Willis to call on the police for assistance.[57] For example, the *New York Times* reported that when "Katherine [Catherine] Jo Prensky" was asked whether she was a member of PL's Student Committee for Travel to Cuba, she replied:

> I am. I joined it because, as a Socialist organization, it can put down racism and will see to it that truly representative people are elected to Congress. We are against the barring of Negroes from voting and . . .[58]

At this point, the *Times* reported, she was "drowned out by another outburst of applause and stirrings within the audience," which led to another intervention by the police.[59] According to one of PL's detractors, the "rowdy outbursts led to a riot."[60]

By the second day of hearings, PLM sensed that its tactics were working:

HUAC had had it. By the middle of the afternoon, Committee Counsel Nittle was so nettled he was forgetting to ask the witnesses their addresses and the names of their lawyers. Willis had turned whiter than even he would like to be, and his hand jumped nervously to the gavel at every sound.[61]

Besides rattling HUAC, there were indications that PL was also gaining the moral high ground. The Committee to Uphold the Right to Travel, in San Francisco, received a letter from the philosopher Bertrand Russell, which was printed in *Progressive Labor*:

> The students who traveled to Cuba exercised an elementary right. . . . The further persecution of them by the semi-literate paranoids who compose the Unamerican activities Committee is a credit to the students and an added instance of American tyranny. Finally, the brutality of the police completes the picture and displays the true character of the persecutors and their assumptions.[62]

Smelling victory, and despite threats from anti-Castro Cubans, PLM held a "victory rally" at New York City's Town Hall on 15 September. Progressive Labor's disruption of the HUAC hearings was very different from the timidity that CPers had exhibited before HUAC just a few years earlier.[63] Progressive Labor congratulated itself on the difference in political temperament between American communism in the 1950s and the *new communism* of the 1960s:

> But the key element in the student's victory—in Washington, in Town Hall, in the eyes of the world—has been their forthright declaration of their political opinions. *They have not been afraid to say what they believe!* They did not take advantage of the Fifth Amendment to avoid discussing politics in a public forum. Those who were members of the Progressive Labor Movement said so and said why.[64]

This was very different from PL's reticence about communism in *For An Alternative Labor Policy*.

Despite PLM's sense of having triumphed over HUAC, the federal grand jury, on 27 September, indicted four students on various charges stemming from the Cuba trip. Defiant, PLM sent an additional eighty-four students to Cuba in 1964. Nine more indictments followed, and there were numerous contempt citations besides the thirteen indictments.

Some of the indicted PLMers faced possible prison sentences of up to twenty years. However frightening the possible consequences, PL greeted the government's charges as a badge of honor.[65] Phillip Luce, one of those indicted, declared, "These indictments are simply another attempt by the government to frighten us from sending young Americans to the 'forbidden land.' "[66]

Progressive Labor's defiance of the United States Government and support for the Cuban Revolution bolstered PL's membership. Many radical students, including PLM's student cadres, identified with Castro's romantic rebellion. After the legal battle reached the United States Supreme Court, all the charges were dropped and the travel ban was broken. Most important to PL, "many students joined PLM" and "PLM began to emerge as a new vigorous force in the emerging new left in the U.S." That PLM could not recruit militant coal miners in Hazard, but recruited students through its Cuba trips, prefigured PL's future pattern of recruitment.[67]

THE MAY SECOND MOVEMENT

Students were the focus of a third PLM national campaign in 1964. In March of that year, Milt Rosen's call for a nationwide mobilization on 2 May to protest "U.S. aggression" in Vietnam "electrified" five hundred students and faculty members attending a conference on socialism at Yale University. After the conference "overwhelmingly" approved Rosen's proposal, the May Second Committee was formed under PLM's leadership. On 2 May 1964, according to PL, "thousands" marched and rallied in "numerous cities across the country" in the "first" national anti-Vietnam War demonstration. Over one thousand people rallied at 110th Street and Central Park West in New York City to demand the "immediate withdrawal of all American troops from Vietnam." Afterward, six hundred protesters marched to Times Square and the United Nations, in what PL proudly claimed was "the largest single demonstration against U.S. intervention in Viet Nam to be held in this country so far." On the heels of this success, PLM formed the May Second Movement, a national "anti-imperialist" peace organization that hundreds of young people joined.[68]

Although the May Second Movement's subsequent antiwar protests in New York resulted in numerous arrests, the organization expanded its activities against the Vietnam War. Demonstrations in New York City's Times Square in August 1964, called by M2M to protest the U.S. bombing of North Vietnam, violated a police ban and resulted in the arrest of forty-seven people "on charges ranging from disorderly conduct to resisting arrest and felonious assault." Writing in *PL*, PLer Jerry Weinberg alleged that the New York police and the federal government were trying to "destroy our movement against the war in Vietnam before our influence grows among young people throughout the country"; he concluded that "police brutality is a real thing in New York." Some veterans of PLM's Cuba expeditions became leaders of M2M, which issued "hundreds of thousands" of leaflets, organized demonstrations, initiated Vietnam teach-ins in universities across the country, and launched the Free University as an off-campus alternative to the "bourgeois educational system."[69]

Even though M2M popularized opposition to "U.S. imperialism" in Vietnam and attracted many students, PL believed that three principal weaknesses—drugs, sectarianism and racism—prevented it from emerging as a powerful mass movement. Despite these weaknesses, which PL outlined to explain M2M's failure to develop into a mass movement, PL credited M2M with helping to move the peace movement from a pacifist to an anti-imperialist perspective.[70]

THE HARLEM REBELLION

If M2M failed to make fighting racism a central issue, racism, nevertheless, became a major focus for PLM in 1964. In the summer of 1964, Black resentment against racism erupted in the form of a major ghetto rebellion in Harlem, New York. The uprising was sparked by the police shooting, on 16 July, of fifteen-year-old James Powell. The Progressive Labor Movement's Harlem Defense Council circulated thousands of posters that read, "Wanted For Murder, Gilligan the Cop" and bore a picture of the officer involved; and PLM's rally and march on 25 July defied Police Commissioner Murphy's temporary ban on such activities in Harlem. William Epton, vice-chairman of PLM, and attorney Conrad Lynn, who characterized the ban as "illegal and a violation of the Constitution," were arrested and charged with disorderly conduct and unlawful assembly. Fifty people were handed *John Doe* injunctions, signed by District Attorney Hogan and Mayor Wagner, enjoining them from engaging in political activity in Harlem.[71] Progressive Labor's new newspaper, *Challenge*, commented that the "big-money boys downtown are running scared. . . . They have seen the writing on the bloodstained walls of Harlem."[72]

On 5 August a Manhattan grand jury (known as the Second August Grand Jury) indicted Epton for inciting to riot and for violating a 1902 New York State law against anarchist conspiracy. His indictment was part of a concerted assault on PLM activists. On 13 September five PLMers were arrested in predawn raids and charged with perjury and criminal contempt of the grand jury. On 21 December subpoenas were issued to additional PLM activists. The imprisonment, on 27 January 1965, of PLMer Elinor Goldstein, a City College of New York student, who was sentenced to thirty days for civil contempt of the grand jury, drew attention to the substandard conditions that prevailed in New York City's Women's House of Detention. There were additional subpoenas, contempt citations, arrests and sentences, some as late as January 1966, and the New York City Board of Education fired Mrs. Vivian Anderson, a Harlem school teacher, subsequent to her release from prison.[73]

International attention focused on Epton's defense, drawing support from various progressive quarters around the world. This support was founded on the issues of dissent and civil liberties, not PLM. Carl and Ann Braden wrote, "We join in protest against the use of nullified laws, or any other kind of laws, to punish people for expressing their opinions." The writers Jean Paul Sartre and Simone De Beauvoir protested the "persecution of Bill Epton." The philosopher Bertrand Russell claimed that were he in New York, he too would be guilty of trying to overthrow the New York State government. Epton also received support from the Mississippi Freedom Democratic Party, the Vietnam Day Committee, Cheddi Jagan of British Guiana and the National Liberation Front of South Vietnam, among others. However, Epton was eventually convicted. He faced up to twelve years in prison and a $6,000 fine. When he was sentenced to one year in prison on all counts, he addressed the court and, what is more important, the court of public opinion.[74] He ended his lengthy speech, entitled *We Accuse*, by declaring:

> You may put me in your jail, but you cannot stop the march of my people towards freedom and liberation, and in the final analysis, when the last and most important voice is heard—it will be the voice of the people who will make the ultimate judgment, not on me, but on the U.S. government and those who carry out its policies.[75]

The courtroom was "moved to cheers" by Epton's "fiery speech" and then cleared by order of the judge, at which point one hundred people began picketing outside the courthouse, PL reported.[76]

Progressive Labor's activities in Harlem were later investigated by the House Un-American Activities Committee, which held hearings on "Subversive Influences in Riots, Looting, and Burning" in 1967, by which time urban riots, or "ghetto rebellions," had broken out in numerous cities.[77] Committee Chairman Edwin E. Willis, of Louisiana, charged that "subversive elements played a major and probably the key role in precipitating the Harlem riot of July 1964." Willis concluded that of the various organizations that acted to inflame the community, Progressive Labor "clearly" played the "most important role." Those who charged that outside agitators sparked Black rebellions could avoid coming to grips with the role racism played in such explosions. Progressive Labor tried to have the best of two worlds. To win adherents among rebellious Blacks and White radicals, PLM claimed credit for the militancy it had shown both before and after the Harlem rebellion, but to defend Epton and other PLMers against the serious charges that were brought against them, the organization denied actual responsibility for the rebellion.[78]

Progressive Labor claimed that it had recruited "a few of the rebel fighters," but was frustrated that it had not even gotten the names, addresses and phone numbers of the "hundreds of young people" who had come to its Harlem headquarters during the rebellion or participated in various PLM-led protests. The Progressive Labor Movement's organizational ineptitude was damaging, but years later the Progressive Labor Party estimated that PLM's support of "progressive" Black nationalism had been even more deleterious to PLM's recruitment efforts in Harlem. As PLP subsequently viewed it, PLM's decision to keep the great majority of its membership, who were White, from doing political work among Black workers, disunited the antiracist struggle and prevented PLM from raising the "revolutionary class consciousness of the hundreds of thousands of young militants who admired PLM for daring to give some leadership to the rebellion."[79] The Progressive Labor Party, which stepped away in the late 1960s from what it saw as its earlier "illusions about Black nationalism," argued that loyalty to the "international working class had to replace narrow allegiance to a nation or a grouping within a nation."[80] However, after PL adopted an antinationalist line in the late 1960s, it fared no better in recruiting Black workers, and lost some of its Black leaders, including Bill Epton.[81]

Just as PLM gained student adherents through its Cuba trips but did not win Kentucky coal miners through its solidarity campaign, it recruited many more student antiwar protesters through M2M than Harlem rebels through the Harlem Defense Council. In laying the foundation for a vanguard party of the proletariat, then, PLM was acquiring a small base that was mainly made up of White students, albeit, White students who invested their hopes for a socialist revolution in the working class, Black as well as White.[82]

ROAD TO REVOLUTION

Whatever their shortcomings, PLM's national and local campaigns did succeed in attracting into its ranks what the journal *PL* called a "relatively large number of revolutionary-minded young workers." However, if PLM had several hundred members, they were mainly young, White students, intellectuals and professionals.[83] Nevertheless, PLM congratulated itself for having initiated "militant mass struggles," recruited "new forces" and built a "network of clubs and a collective leadership." To develop a "revolutionary Marxist-Leninist program," Rosen's remaining condition for founding a party, PLM's National Coordinating Committee published the *Marxist-Leninist Quarterly*. The new journal's lead editorial castigated revisionism as a "dangerous and self-defeating folly," but also suggested that PLM did not seek a war with other leftist groups:

> We do not want to enter into a fratricidal war with the CPUSA . . . nor with the SWP [Socialist Workers Party], nor with any other socialist group. . . . We seek only a frank exchange of differences and, whenever possible, a coordinated struggle against the imperialist enemy.[84]

Looking back at this apparently contradictory stance, PL's leadership ruefully observed, "we declared that we were ready to fight revisionism, but unwilling to fight revisionists." This contradiction, the intensifying polemics between Chinese and Soviet communists, and a circle of new members and friends who were demanding to know more about PLM's ideological and political differences with the CP and its view of the Sino-Soviet debate, impelled PLM to declare its position on revisionism within the communist movement.[85]

Resisting the CP's "revisionist" leadership had led to the defection or expulsion of PL's future leaders from the CP in late 1961. The Progressive Labor Movement's decision in late 1963 to openly "fight revisionists" foreclosed the possibility of alliances with its close ideological competitors, precluding a "coordinated struggle against the imperialist enemy." For communists, there were both inspiring and problematical precedents for this position. The Bolsheviks in Russia, who had waged an uncompromising polemical struggle against their Menshevik rivals and other leftist groups, were able to seize control of the Russian Revolution.[86] However, in the early 1930s, Soviet-directed German communists vied with their social-democratic rivals (whom they called *social-fascists*), giving Hitler, tragically, his opportunity to seize power. Progressive Labor, filled with revolutionary optimism, was more sympathetic to the hard line promulgated by Stalin in the early 1930s than his subsequent retreat, which PL believed had begun in 1935, when the Seventh Congress of the Communist International adopted its *United Front Against Fascism* line.[87]

The entire socialist camp in the U.S. during the 1960s was tiny, but PLM expected to develop a mass base for its own approach to socialist revolution.[88] With a few dramatic actions under its belt and aware that radicalism was gaining currency, at least among students, PLM decided to break away from the small socialist pack. Two years before, engaging in polemics with the CP would have been aimed at detaching committed communists from the "old party," a course of action that PL had rejected as "sectarian," but now PLM directed its antirevisionist struggle at newly radicalized young people. Convinced that its own line was correct and would prevail, PLM was willing to risk alienating other socialists. In any case, preserving the integrity of its revolutionary line and building a new party, even a very small one, to advance that line took precedence over winning popularity in the short run. Progressive Labor did not want to gain political victories at the expense of its communist principles, believing, in essence, that it was *better to be right than president.*[89]

Thus, PLM abandoned its policy of peaceful coexistence with the CP. On 23 October 1963 Milt Rosen gave a report on revisionism to PLM's National Coordinating Committee. In March 1964, after much discussion and revision, PLM published the report in the form of a 126 page pamphlet entitled *Road to Revolution.*[90] It declared:

> Two paths are open to the workers of any given country. One is the path of resolute class struggle; the other is the path of accommodation, collaboration. The first leads to state power for the workers, which will end exploitation. The other means rule by a small ruling class which continues oppression, wide-scale poverty, cultural and moral decay and war.[91]

On PL's road map of revolutionary politics, one was either traveling toward socialist salvation or heading for capitalist damnation. There was only one route to socialism, which PL mapped out by applying the science of Marxism-Leninism (Dialectical and Historical Materialism).[92] Those who strayed from this path were necessarily on the wrong track. Progressive Labor believed that the forces arrayed against revisionism would be triumphant, but as its antirevisionist animus spurred PL onward over the next twenty years, its road to socialism became an increasingly lonesome road.[93]

Progressive Labor claimed that it was revolutionary, while the CP was revisionist.[94] Progressive Labor proudly proclaimed that *Road to Revolution* represented a "devastating ideological assault on the old 'C'P.'"[95] In this pamphlet, PL defined its raison d'etre: "From the earliest days of the communist movement in the United States to the present, revisionism and its political manifestation, class collaboration, has been the chronic weakness." The CP's "revisionism," PL's leaders argued, while usually identified with individual leaders such as Jay Lovestone, Earl Browder and John Gates, "permeated the entire fabric of the party."[96] Many "genuine communists," including PLM's leaders, had tried and failed to transform the CP into a revolutionary party. "The total penetration of the C.P. leadership" by ruling class ideology was a significant defeat for the working class, but one from which, PL affirmed, it could recover. So long as there was class struggle, PL observed, there would be a revolutionary force. It predicted that as a result of U.S. imperialism's developing contradictions, "a new revolutionary party will arise in this country stronger than ever."[97] However, despite continuing recruitment, PL remained much smaller than the CP, which had dwindled to a small fraction of its own former size.[98]

The struggle against revisionism was not confined to the United States. "A great debate has broken out in the international movement," PL announced. The outcome of this debate would, PL predicted, "determine to a great extent the character of the class struggle in every country in the world." This was not "merely a political debate but a matter of life and death for millions of people." In this crucial contest of ideas, PL sided with the Chinese communists against their Soviet rivals.[99]

In the past, PL affirmed, the Soviet Union had been a "beacon to all workers." The Soviets' "unyielding anti-imperialist line and their generally correct application of Marxism-Leninism made it possible to defeat imperialism time after time, encouraging hundreds of millions to take the road to socialism and freedom." However, the Twentieth Congress of the CPSU was a "crystallization of developing revisionist trends." Progressive Labor acknowledged that Stalin had fostered the growth of bureaucracy, and PL admitted, "Many innocent people, or people with differences which could have been worked out in the course of principled ideological struggle, were wrongly killed." This admission was a gross understatement of Stalin's transgressions. However, PL argued that the CPSU was throwing out Stalin's contributions, which PL believed were the primary aspect of his career, and perpetuating his "grievous errors." Progressive Labor argued that Khrushchev had attacked Stalin to negate Marxism-Leninism—which "Stalin had defended and developed"—and promote his own "revisionist" line, that is, a policy of peaceful coexistence with imperialism, the doctrine that war was not inevitable, a policy of avoiding local wars (because they might lead to nuclear war), the idea that there could be a peaceful transition to socialism in democratic countries, and "unprincipled" power politics in relation to bourgeois nationalist governments.[101]

On the other hand, PL credited the Communist Party of China with taking up the fight against Soviet revisionism as early as 1956. The Chinese communists, according to PL, fought for the correct line, that is, the need for a dictatorship of the proletariat, the idea that every state is the instrument of class rule, the need for a revolutionary seizure of state power, the preservation of peace by exposing and opposing imperialism, and the struggle to unify the world communist movement around a revolutionary line, rather than a policy of peaceful coexistence. Progressive Labor defended the Chinese communists against the charge that they were disuniting the world communist movement. They were engaging in "open and sharp struggle with the Soviet leadership" because they recognized, PL argued, that Khrushchev's policies were "rapidly undermining the stability and revolutionary potential of the international movement." Moreover, they were aware that a "disarmed movement is an open invitation to the imperialists to intensify aggression and oppression against all people." Clearly, the causes of the Sino-Soviet split were complex. Even so, PL was now openly and uncritically committed to the Chinese camp.[101]

THE PROGRESSIVE LABOR PARTY

Road to Revolution established PL's basic ideological identity and its adoption allowed PLM to transform itself into the Progressive Labor Party in April 1965.[102] The preamble to PLP's constitution, messianic in tone, demonized the United States:

> The great American dream of "life, liberty and the pursuit of happiness" has been turned by a ruthless regime into a nightmare of death,

destruction and the pursuit of dollars. . . . In the remotest corner of the earth, the initials U.S.A., which once stood for hope, have replaced the crooked cross of Nazi Germany as the symbol of tyranny and death. . . . Yet there is another U.S.A: . . . the U.S.A. of the men and women who sweat in factories to produce goods, of the housewives who struggle to keep the homes and raise the children, of the students, artists and honest intellectuals who want desperately to create new beauty for life and not bombs and billboards for death. . . . This U.S.A., beaten down time and again, deceived and denied, is still ready to organize and to resist.[103]

If the United States was the moral equivalent of Nazi Germany, as PL hyperbolically claimed, then PLers were as morally obligated to resist as Germans had been under Hitler.

Progressive Labor recognized that the fight for socialism would be "long and hard" because the established powers, the "kings, queens and bishops of modern finance and their political pawns," would use "every form of force and violence in their desperation to hold onto their stolen billions." Yet, PL was confident that "from the very flames our fight—the fight of all honest working people, students, housewives and intellectuals of our country and the world—a new society shall be built—in which our children, our children's children, and the billion billion children to come will never be forced to hunger for food or shelter or love—a new society without exploitation of man by man, a society, a nation, a world of revolutionary socialism." To achieve this end, the preamble concluded, "we here resolve to give our every energy, our resources, and our lives." Thus, the idealistic participants of PL's founding convention were pushed toward revolution by the moral necessity of resisting a Nazi-like regime and pulled toward revolution by an inspiring vision, millenarian in spirit, of a secular utopia.[104]

However, to realize its extensive goals PL needed organization. Now that PL was a communist party, and no longer a mere movement, its leaders sought to employ Lenin's system of democratic centralism to maintain party discipline. "Democratic centralism," the constitution explained, "unites leaders and members in bonds of mutual confidence and trust, while developing an iron discipline far stronger than military discipline, since it is based on voluntary association, not on fear; on understanding, not command."[105] This was an idealized picture of democratic-centralist parties. In practice, they exert enormous social pressure to ensure discipline; and once in power, employ coercive measures to punish and intimidate recalcitrant members.[106] The road to revolution was paved with good intentions, but for communists, expansive goals, that is, the salvation of a "billion billion" children, could justify any sacrifice by friends or enemies.

Progressive Labor introduced an egalitarian element into its hierarchical structure of power, one that went beyond simple rhetoric. Members of the "entire party" were to engage in "criticism and self-criticism" to combat "certain habits" concerning racism, sexism and ethnocentrism that, the party affirmed, would put a "stranglehold" on its full potential. Progressive Labor was adamant:

> As communists we cannot tolerate in ourselves or in our comrades any form of racism, or male supremacism. Male supremacist attitudes, which limit the full participation of women, and racism are among the most effective ideological weapons of the ruling class, and we must struggle constantly against divisions on the basis of race, national origin and sex.[107]

This stand was progressive, but a commitment to self-criticism and the politics of inclusion did not diminish the power and influence enjoyed by PL's leaders due to the party's hierarchical structure. "Clubs," the party's basic units, were organized "on a shop, industry, community or functional basis, or by school." For rank-and-file party members, the club was the center of party activity. The bi-annual National Party Convention was to be the party's highest authority, but in practice, the Steering Committee of the National Committee, which led PL between National Committee meetings, held the reins of power within PL. The party would establish local or statewide intermediary bodies when it needed them. In any case, the decisions of higher bodies were binding on lower bodies, and members could be reprimanded, suspended or expelled for violating decisions of their club or a higher body, or for "endangering the security of the organization." On 18 April 1965 this plan of organization was adopted unanimously by the two hundred people who attended PL's founding convention, which also elected a national committee of twenty, headed by Milt Rosen as chairman, and Mort Scheer and Bill Epton as vice-chairmen.[108]

Milt Rosen hailed PL's transition from a movement into a party as a blow against revisionism, but warned his followers that they were in danger of making "idealist" errors. His report to the convention declared:

> The development of the PLM and now the PLP is an expression of the fact that the class struggle in our country continues in full. It is also a

> serious setback to revisionism. Revisionism no longer has a clear field
> in our country. Revolutionary ideas are being put forward and tested in
> life. . . . Ideological struggle, debate and examination is the life-blood
> of our party. . . . Without this debate we would quickly become a ster-
> ile sect. . . . Our victory becomes inevitable only when we rid our-
> selves of idealism, and master dialectical materialism.[109]

By *idealism*, Rosen meant an unrealistic belief in the power of ideas to
transcend the limits imposed by material reality. The intellectual problem bequeathed to PL's new communists by Marxism-Leninism involved
avoiding revisionism without falling into idealism. It originated in the
tension between communism's utopian goals and communists' commitment to adopt realistic policies to advance those goals. Rosen believed
that revisionists, in the name of realism, had relinquished revolution and
become reformists. However, PLers faced the contrary danger, Rosen
suggested, of ignoring reality in their pursuit of revolutionary goals and
becoming sectarian. Rosen's recent past as a leftist insurgent in the CP
suggests that he was somewhat uncomfortable restraining the sectarian
impulses of his followers, but their youthful adventurism ran counter to
some of his CP-bred sensibilities, which he retained despite his leftist in-
clinations.[110]

Whether PL could maintain a viable tension between its own revolutionism and the prevailing reformism in American society remained to be
seen. Finding realistic policies to advance its utopian goals would not be
easy. Learning from history and PL's own practice would not be the scientific process that democratic-centralist theory promised and that PL
expected, but a matter of historical interpretation that filtered experience
through an ideological prism. Progressive Labor never questioned its
basic ideology, that is, the revolutionary potential of the working class,
the necessity for a Leninist party, and the ultimate triumph of egalitarian
socialism. In practice, PL regarded these doctrines as unfalsifiable.

As the convention ended, PLP's vice-chairman, Mort Scheer, was
undaunted by the problems facing PL. The party, he declared, would
have to defeat "left-sectarianism" and "all manifestations, subtle or otherwise, of white supremacy" within its own ranks, and party members
would have to master Marxism-Leninism and organize in the workplace,
not just on campus or in working-class communities. However, he was
inspired by the turnout of thirty thousand for SDS's antiwar demonstration in Washington, which PLers had left their convention to join. He estimated that thirty million Americans already opposed the Vietnam War
even though "it's only hundreds of American youth at this point that have

been killed by U.S. imperialism." Estimating that tens or hundreds of thousands might be killed, he anticipated a "radicalization of the peace sentiments of the American people." The convention adjourned singing the *International*.[111]

Milt Rosen and Mort Scheer, expelled from the CP three years earlier, had taken their first steps toward reinventing American communism. At the end of the 1960s, PL declared, "The emergence of our party and its ideas among the more militant class-conscious workers is the most significant political development of the past 25 years." No one outside PL was likely to believe that. Why should they? It was presumptuous for a still tiny, fledgling organization to make such a grandiose claim. But PL ascribed great power to its revolutionary ideas. The party was convinced that if it brought these ideas to the working class, ideas which PL had rescued from the jaws of revisionism, they would attract a mass following and transform the world. However, when PL failed to attract a mass working-class following or change the world to any great extent, its ideas became increasingly utopian.[112]

CHAPTER 2

Purifying the Communist Movement and Searching for Utopia

Progressive Labor in Theory, 1965–1982

PLers viewed their participation in mundane struggles at the point of production as part of a world-saving crusade, and regarded every such fight as a test of their communist theories and revolutionary mettle. Progressive Labor's strategy and tactics on the labor front reflected the party's developing analysis of the revolutionary process and changing vision of the communist future it anticipated. Because PL's commitment to antirevisionism guided its approach to organizing on the job, the present chapter discusses the development of PL's theory of communist revolution.

ROAD TO REVOLUTION II

Road to Revolution, which justified the formation of the Progressive Labor Party, was not the end of PL's ideological journey, but only the beginning; it was the first of four consecutively numbered policy statements that bore the same title. Appearing between 1964 and 1982, they delineated PL's march toward pure and simple communism.[1] Whatever else one can say about PL, it took ideas seriously. If its political line was not the only thing for PL, it was by far the most important thing. Furthermore, if "Acting like a communist presupposes thinking like one," then understanding PL's actions requires examining the party's conception of its communist enterprise.[2]

Road to Revolution II, adopted on 17 December 1966, reaffirmed the fundamental stance of *RR I*, but went further toward demonizing Soviet communism and idealizing Chinese communism. *RR II* declared,

"Within the Soviet Union the essence of capitalism has been restored." Charging that a "crop of millionaires" had arisen within the Soviet Union, PL concluded that the "spirit of capitalism has swept the Soviet hierarchy and the overlords of industry which it represents."[3] The roots of revisionism in the Soviet Union, PL thought, went deep; Soviet leaders had emphasized material development, but had neglected the ideological development of the "millions."[4]

Contrarily, the Communist Party of China, through its Great Proletarian Cultural Revolution, was "elevating ideas, man's dialectical and creative thought, into an invincible force." Progressive Labor, envisaging "700,000,000 Chinese steeped in revolutionary ideology," concluded that whenever revolutionary ideas are adopted by the masses, they become an "invincible" material force. The Cultural Revolution assumed "historic proportions" because it was pointing the way for the "revolutionary process everywhere." As a fraternal communist party, PL praised its Chinese mentor: "We have great confidence that by utilizing the thought of Mao Tse-tung [Mao Zedong] the experienced and tested CPC will succeed in its new historic endeavor."[5]

ROAD TO REVOLUTION III

Given Progressive Labor's enthusiastic endorsement of Chinese communism, it is not surprising that some people referred to PLers as "Mao's Marauders."[6] By 1967 the Chinese communists considered PLP the only revolutionary Marxist-Leninist party in the United States.[7] However, PL's alliance with the CPC was short-lived. When Mao Tse-tung ended the Cultural Revolution and embarked on "ping-pong diplomacy" with the United States, PL reconsidered its support of Maoism.[8] In November 1971 PL published *Road to Revolution III*, which reinterpreted China's recent history and repudiated the CPC.[9]

Mao had avowedly launched the GPCR to combat a "small handful of capitalist-roaders," who comprised no more than five percent of the party's cadres. However, PL sided with left-wing Cultural Revolutionists, who charged that China was already in the hands of a "red bourgeoisie," and that ninety percent of the party's leading cadres were part of this oppressor class, which used the People's Liberation Army to maintain itself in power.[10] According to PL, millions of Chinese students and workers supported these left-wing communists. Progressive Labor praised them as the genuine Left in China, but the CPC eventually condemned them as counterrevolutionary.

Examining Chinese politics between 1947 and 1968, PL discerned a cyclical pattern in which the Left, supported by Mao, advanced, Mao restrained the Left from breaking completely with "bourgeois ideas," and the Right successfully counterattacked. Thus, the rise of a "red bourgeoisie" was the result of a series of struggles between the Left and the Right in which the CPC's Mao leadership "swung back-and-forth periodically between these two groups and, most importantly, refused to break decisively with the Right."[11]

Progressive Labor's account of China's response to events in 1958–1959 is a case in point. According to PL, the Chinese Left supported the communes established under the Great Leap Forward, which introduced the free supply of grain, and other communal measures, "so that the principle of distribution 'to each according to his needs' was no longer a distant goal separated from the present by a long process of economic development, but a living reality." However, the CPC leadership, according to PL, saw the Great Leap primarily as a "production drive" rather than as a way of "opening up the transition to communism." Thus, when production declined, it abolished the free supply of grain and reinstated income differentials based on productivity.[12] In criticizing the CPC for this retreat from communist ideals, PL glossed over the very serious production problems that attended the CPC's experiment. However, there can be no distribution without production. The economic failure of the Great Leap, multicausal as it may have been, jeopardized CPC rule and discredited, for the time being, such innovations.[13] Nevertheless, the reversal of China's leftward leap, in PL's view, was a regrettable victory for the Right, which held sway from 1960 to 1966.[14]

Ironically, the Chinese communists had published their polemics against Soviet revisionism during this period. In *RR I* and *RR II*, PL had sided with the CPC, but now asked, "Why would China's new 'red' bourgeoisie feel it necessary to defend the ideology of Marxism-Leninism against the changes the Russians were advocating?" The immediate cause, PL thought, was the Soviet Union's refusal to provide China with a nuclear arsenal. In a deeper sense, PL alleged, the CPC sought a "Left" cover for its counterrevolution, and aspired (presumably, for geopolitical reasons) to lead the worldwide anti-imperialist united front.[15]

Progressive Labor was convinced that it had discovered something even more damaging to Chinese communist credibility, namely, that Mao Tse-tung's version of Marxism-Leninism "contained a number of ideas which led inexorably to bourgeois restoration." The CPC could not expose the real roots of Soviet revisionism, PL argued, because it could not acknowledge its own revisionism; its own policies were part of the problem. For example, the Chinese Revolution of 1949, according to PL, "threw imperialism—especially U.S. imperialism—into a panic," but the Chinese revolutionaries "never broke with the old policy of concessions to the so-called 'progressive' bourgeoisie." To PL, Mao's policy of New Democracy, which made serious concessions to the nationalist bourgeoisie, "was nothing more or less than the Chinese version of the NEP," that is, Lenin's New Economic Policy, which had permitted some private enterprise in order to rebuild the Soviet Union's economy after the devastating Civil War of 1918–1921 and the Bolshevik experiment with War Communism. These "tactical retreats," PL argued, were unprincipled concessions that paved the way for a restoration of bourgeois rule. Progressive Labor supposed that such historic triumphs of communism as the Bolshevik Revolution, Soviet victory in the Anti-Fascist War (WW II) and the Chinese Communist Revolution could have been achieved without Lenin's NEP, Stalin's United Front Against Fascism and Mao's New Democracy, policies that these communist leaders believed were made necessary by the backwardness of the masses and the power of the bourgeois classes. But PL would not justify major concessions to capitalism.[16]

As PL saw it, the Mao cult compounded the damage done by Mao's revisionist errors because the idealization of Mao undermined China's genuine Left. Provoked by the resurgence of the Right in China during the early 1960s, the Chinese Left had counterattacked by initiating the Cultural Revolution. Progressive Labor praised the GPCR for attacking China's "red bourgeoisie" and wanting Chinese socialism to emulate the Paris Commune of 1871. However, this Left made a key error, PL scolded, "when it failed to separate itself ideologically and organizationally from Mao." Mao's enormous prestige enabled him to co-opt and undermine the Cultural Revolution. The Left was defeated, PL alleged, because it "tolerated and in some cases encouraged the anti-Marxist Mao cult." PL attacked such cults:

> The myth of leaders' infallibility has been a millstone around the neck
> of the communist movement for decades. . . . In the final analysis, we
> must decide once and for all who is the prime motive force in history—
> individuals or the masses.[17]

Khrushchev, PL alleged, had "attacked the Stalin cult from the right, in order to discredit Marxism-Leninism and secure political power for the new Soviet bourgeoisie." By contrast, PL maintained that it was attacking the cult of the personality from the left, to serve the masses and win socialism.[18]

Progressive Labor criticized personality cults for taking "political power out of the hands of the masses." At the same time, PL reaffirmed its commitment to the idea of a democratic-centralist party, albeit, one based on "criticism and self-criticism by all party members and leaders." Self-criticism would prevent the party from persisting in egregious errors, and safeguard the party from corruption. In PL's view, then, a self-critical, collectively led party would empower the proletariat to fight the bourgeoisie, but would not threaten to disempower the masses politically. The party sword, in other words, did not cut both ways, or if it did, the masses would be shielded by the party's own commitment to collective self-criticism. However, what if the party, despite sincere efforts at self-correction, went bad? What could the masses do then?[19]

China was the case at hand. In PL's portrait of China's Cultural Revolution, Mao, the supposedly "infallible" leader, allied with leftist mass organizations against the CPC's right wing, and then with these rightists against the Left. The inability of the Chinese Left to question their "infallible" leader's swing to the right underscored the problem of personality cults, and PL took measures to oppose the development of one within its own movement.[20] Progressive Labor did not want to imitate the personality cults that had arisen in the Soviet Union, China and other communist countries. But although PL criticized the CPC for not making a thorough analysis of the development of errors in the international communist movement, it failed to admit the possibility that, for structural reasons, power in countries ruled by democratic-centralist parties tends to concentrate in the hands of one individual despite sincere efforts to the contrary.[21]

While PL opposed cults centered on an "infallible" leader, a phenomenon that "appeared down through the ages," it still believed that state power should be vested in "a revolutionary working-class party directly tied to the masses and controlled by them."[22] Thus, influenced by Mao's populism, PL pictured a vanguard party controlled by the masses. However, ruling communist parties have felt entitled to control the masses—for their own good—through persuasion and, if necessary, coercion. Unaided by a powerful figure such as Mao, it seems improbable that the masses could control one of these self-assured, powerful bureaucracies.[23]

Leninist doctrine claimed that the democratic-centralist party, by applying the science of Marxism-Leninism and relying on its ties to the masses, was the advanced detachment of the working class, and, although not infallible, was far more able than the masses to choose the correct path to communism.[24] Despite its view that the CPSU, the CPC and the CPUSA had become revisionist, PL did not question the necessity for a vanguard party or doubt its own ability to gradually rid itself of the errors that had caused revolutionary parties with ties to millions to succumb to revisionism. In other words, PL opposed the cult of the leader because uncritical belief in the leader undermined the party's ability to function collectively in the interest of the masses. But if PL opposed the cult of personality, it still upheld the cult of the party. To PL, there did not seem to be any other choice, for without a party there would be no practical way to place the distilled experience of millions of revolutionary workers, gained through enormous sacrifice, at the service of the still exploited and oppressed masses. Progressive Labor was not going to throw out the baby with the bath water; PL would combat revisionism, but not abandon the idea of a communist party.[25]

Nevertheless, communist parties, in PL's view, continued to abandon genuine communist principles. By 1971, besides the CPSU, other European communist parties and the CPC, PL had written off as revisionist the communist parties of North Korea, North Vietnam and Cuba as well. Apparently, fewer and fewer people were traveling down the road to revolution.[26] However, PL remained optimistic:

> We have no reason to bemoan our fate or to pity ourselves for being the only ones with these 'way out' ideas. The ideas we hold did not fall from heaven, nor do they belong to us exclusively. We know that millions in China hold them. Many other groups and individuals around the world either share some of these ideas or are open to them. In the final analysis, everyone is open to them. . . .[27]

The communist party was the conscience of the working class, but if it became corrupted by revisionist errors, as many parties had been, there was no reason to despair, PL maintained. Inevitably, the inexperienced communist movement had made serious errors, but was learning from its mistakes. Particular parties might fail, but the working class would succeed in the end. The working class was eternal, and infallible in the sense that the contradictions of capitalism would compel it to create a new and improved vanguard party when that became necessary.[28] That is how PL harmonized its populism, its romantic faith in the masses with its fervent "party-mindedness"—its Leninist elitism.

Nevertheless, from PL's point of view, the defeat of the Cultural Revolution in China was an enormous setback for the international working class, and for Progressive Labor, whose antirevisionism had been informed by Chinese communism for more than a decade. Progressive Labor began its career by giving uncritical support to Mao, by glorifying him as the paladin of the antirevisionist cause, and wound up by demonizing him as the saboteur of the Cultural Revolution, and by charging that his policies had been flawed from the beginning. Although PL never gained the degree of prestige from its association with CPC that the CPUSA had gained from its identification with the CPSU, PL did gain a certain amount of self-confidence, and legitimacy in radical circles, from its Chinese connection. By breaking with the CPC, PL gave up a powerful patron. The party would have to rely on its own resources, but it was free to follow the leftist instincts that had drawn it to Maoism, undeterred by the burdens of power that preoccupied Mao.[29] Progressive Labor conceived of communist theory, like communist revolution, as a work in progress, and concluded, "The ideas in this report by no means constitute the final word on the subject."[30]

ROAD TO REVOLUTION IV

A little more than a decade later, PL took what it believed to be one more giant step to the left. In the spring of 1982, the party published *Road to Revolution IV: The Fight For the Dictatorship of the Proletariat.* Borrowing an image from Sir Isaac Newton, but employing it with less humility, PL proclaimed, "This new document stands on the shoulders of our party's other major documents, published over the past twenty years." *RR IV* continued PL's examination of the errors that "led to the restoration of capitalism in the Soviet Union and China and the destruction of the old communist movement as a force for revolution."[31] More interested in evoking Marx than Newton, PL entitled its new document *A Communist Manifesto, 1982.* Progressive Labor called for a mass communist party, the immediate abolition of the wage system after the revolution, and the building of communist, not socialist, economic relations under the dictatorship of the proletariat.[32]

This, Progressive Labor's *great leap forward*, was a leap of faith. Twenty years earlier, in 1962 (which was only forty-five years after the Bolshevik revolution), PL, plausibly optimistic, had seen a "world moving rapidly to socialism."[33] At that time, communist parties ruled the Soviet Union, China and about a dozen other countries in Europe, Asia and

Africa; the Cuban Revolution was still fresh and inspiring; there were communist-led anti-imperialist struggles in the Third World; and radical-ism was on the rise in the U.S.[34] However, by 1982 PL had written off the old communist movement as hopelessly corrupt. If existing communist regimes no longer deserved to be called *communist*, as PL implied, it was also true that no communists whom PL saw as *genuine* (PL and like-minded extreme-left splinter groups in various countries) were close to seizing power. Despite its fifteen minutes of fame during the 1960s, and its ideological innovations, PL had failed to win anything approaching a mass base for its ideas. The world had moved rapidly away from social-ism, and would soon move even farther.[35]

Progressive Labor now moved away from socialism as well, but toward communism, not capitalism.[36] Progressive Labor operated on the principle "When defeated, move to the left."[37] Communism, in PL's judgment, had been defeated every time it made concessions to capital-ism. "Every compromise made by communists to capitalism," PL com-plained, "ended in disaster." Communists typically justified these concessions as tactical retreats that aided the forward march of commu-nism, but to PL, they simply paved the way for further retreats and ulti-mate defeat for communism. Progressive Labor opposed several hallmark policies of the world's communist parties as unnecessary re-treats from communism, namely, (1) Lenin's New Economic Policy, be-cause it reintroduced capitalism into the Soviet economy, (2) Stalin's United Front Against Fascism, because it sought alliances with bour-geois democracies, (3) Mao's New Democracy, because it allowed the nationalist bourgeoisie to share power, (4) the communist movement's support for alliances with bourgeois nationalists in the anti-imperialist struggle, because these nationalists invariably turned on their communist allies, and (5) the CPUSA's policy of sacrificing revolution for reform, because it undermined the party's revolutionary will.[38] Progressive Labor now added socialism to its list of unprincipled concessions to capitalism, and declared, "Our members and friends will tolerate no more retreats from the basics of Marxism-Leninism, from communism."[39]

However, neither Marx nor Lenin believed that a communist revolu-tion could immediately institute communist economic relations. Both Marx's *Critique of the Gotha Program* and Lenin's *The State and Revo-lution* suggested that socialism, in which each receives according to his work, was a necessary stage on the way to communism, in which each receives according to his needs.[40] Progressive Labor acknowledged that these authoritative communist leaders regarded socialism as a necessary concession to the political backwardness of the masses.[41] However, PL argued that socialism, rather than preparing the way for communism, had paved the way for a restoration of capitalism. In 1982 PL paraphrased Mao to illustrate what Mao's Cultural Revolution had emphasized—that ideas are powerful. Modifying Mao's famous dictum that "All power flows from the barrel of a gun," PL declared, "Political power grows less from the barrel of a gun than from the ideology of the worker holding the gun." "Inequality," PL predicted, "will open the door first to differences, and then to classes, and finally to defeat." Progressive Labor based this dire prediction on its reading of history. In previous socialist societies, according to PL, the perpetuation of economic privilege sabotaged the struggle for egalitarianism. The revolutions in Russia and China that had established socialism were subsequently "reversed." These countries were now "capitalist societies with new bosses."[42]

Why was socialism so corrupting? Progressive Labor believed that it had discovered the roots of revisionism in the pernicious role of privilege:

> Past socialist societies retained privilege, which quickly found its way into the party. Some party members and many leaders were often better off than others. This practice made many workers cynical, by perpetuating the bosses' anti-communist lie that all power corrupts.[43]

Progressive Labor proposed to guard against the corrupting influence of power by foreclosing the possibility of privilege. It declared, "Our party fights for egalitarian communism and an immediate end to the wage system after the revolution." Communist distribution would eliminate the "material incentive for the emergence of new bosses corrupted by all sorts of privilege." Apparently, PL perceived power as corrupting if, and only if, it served as a means of attaining privilege—and not if it was sought solely for its own sake.[44]

Nevertheless, great revolutionaries, as PL acknowledged, had warned that attempting to institute a communist economic system right after the revolution would jeopardize proletarian rule.[45] The party proposed a solution to this dilemma. If past communist revolutions, which had seized power with a small communist base and then made "necessary" concessions to the "backwardness" of the masses, were guilty of "opportunism," as PL claimed, then the answer was to begin spreading the idea of communism now, to "start now to build a base among all workers." If millions of workers were won to communism before the revolution, then the revolutionary regime could establish a communist society immediately. Progressive Labor painted a compelling portrait of the revolutionary process it envisioned: "When the revolution and its communist ideas triumph, the party will already have won countless millions to launch a communist society, with no retreats to capitalism."[46]

However, could "countless" millions be converted to communism before the revolution? The Progressive Labor party was encouraged by its reading of the revolutionary past:

> History proves that workers want a life free from capitalist exploitation, and that, much to the bosses' dismay, they will fight to the death for it. . . . From the caves of Yenan in China to the battle of Stalingrad in Russia, workers proved that they could fight and work together in a communist manner.[47]

These examples of collective sacrifice on a grand scale bolstered PL's confidence in the working class. However, PL presented little evidence to prove its unprecedented claim that a mass communist base—sizeable enough to sustain a communist economy in the immediate postrevolutionary period—could be created under capitalism. This claim strained credulity, and PL's own recruitment record was dismal.[48] However, PL envisioned its communist millennium being ushered in by an imperialist apocalypse. "We will have to rebuild a society severely disrupted by a third world war," PL noted flatly, and asked, "Why should we keep any of capitalism's deadly trappings in the process?"[49] In 1982 predicting an eventual nuclear war between the United States and the Soviet "Evil Empire" was pessimistic, but plausible; anticipating that communism could be constructed in the aftermath of the ensuing nuclear holocaust was excessively optimistic.[50] Essentially, PL argued that communism was necessary and, therefore, inevitable. In other words, reality was not rational, but what was rational would eventually be realized.[51] For PL, believing otherwise meant surrendering to an intolerable system. Revolutionary optimism was the only moral option. There were, in PL's philosophy, no other alternatives to the horrors of capitalism. Convinced that people wanted to be "productive in a non-alienated way," Milt Rosen asserted, "Communism will offer this to the human race, and I believe that the human race can, and will, choose this over the false promises inequality and selfishness offer, which always lead to exploitation, war and misery for the overwhelming majority."[52]

However desirable and inevitable egalitarian communism might be, PL did not imagine that it would arise spontaneously. Only a prolonged revolutionary struggle waged by the international working class—led by PL—could create "an egalitarian, communist society under the dictatorship of the proletariat." Progressive Labor immodestly proclaimed, "The only solution is communist revolution under the banners of the Progressive Labor Party." However, to achieve its aims, this revolution would have to be international in scope. "Only world-wide communism," PL affirmed, "offers workers, soldiers and students an alternative to the misery of capitalism." For PL, however, communist internationalism no longer meant fraternal relations between independent national parties, but one party for the workers of all nations. Dismissing national differences, PL boldly asserted, "The workers of the world need only one communist party, and only one communist strategy."[53]

Progressive Labor believed that its overall strategy, which included the idea of one worldwide communist party, uniquely served the interests of the international working class. The establishment of various national communist parties was a concession to the bourgeois notion of nationalism and undermined communists' commitment to proletarian internationalism, which PL considered of paramount importance. Summing up its adamant opposition to nationalism, PL declared:

> Workers in one part of the world are not different from or better than workers in another. Nationalism creates false loyalties. Workers should be loyal only to other workers, never to a boss. We endorse the revolutionary slogan: "Workers of the world, unite!"[54]

The party was determined to root out nationalism from the communist camp by turning itself into a new type of communist international. The CPSU had once abetted revolution around the world through the parties of the Third Communist International, which it controlled. Progressive Labor was prepared to dispense with pretenses and openly organize for international revolution in its own name, that is, without hiding behind a facade of seemingly independent allies. However, the CPSU had gained enormous resources and even greater prestige as the first proletarian party to seize state power.[55] By contrast, PL was a very small party with few resources, few significant accomplishments and only a very modest reputation.[56]

Nevertheless, Progressive Labor was confident that it had the right ideas and was prepared to run with them. Milt Rosen, an apostle of Leninism, summed up PL's leadership role as a vanguard party: "The job of the communist party—PLP—is to grasp what is good for the working class as a whole and then to make certain that it is carried out."[57] Progressive Labor believed that its democratic-centralist structure, which enabled the party to both develop and implement its line collectively, facilitated the development of dedicated leaders, which both PL and the working class required to establish an egalitarian communist utopia. Progressive Labor affirmed:

> Within the party at all times and within society at large after the revolution, the role of central leadership is decisive. The working class requires a general staff that places the victory of communism above all other goals and that fights to make the party the leader of society.[58]

Progressive Labor argued that the party, as the necessary means to an essential end, deserved power commensurate with the enormity of its mission. Progressive Labor conceived of itself as the indispensable leadership of the working class—before, during and after the revolution—and believed that it should become the exclusive center of power in postrevolutionary society. "Throughout the process of seizing, holding and expanding revolutionary power," PL insisted, "workers need only one leading force—the communist party." Progressive Labor envisaged that after it led workers in a revolution to smash the bourgeois state, it would be the exclusive center of political leadership and exercise political power directly, dispensing altogether with a separate governmental apparatus. "After the revolution," PL anticipated, "workers and their allies will not need a government separate from the party." A government would be superfluous, PL reasoned, either because it "would be a rubber stamp for the workers' mass party, or it would represent enemies of communism." Progressive Labor disdained to disguise or dilute the power it anticipated having. For PL, there were only two kinds of political leadership, the party and its enemies. The first should rule openly and the other not at all. So PL proposed that the party, "composed of tens of millions of workers," lead society. Essentially, PL's principle was "All power to the party."[59]

Lenin had turned Marx's proletarian dictatorship into a dictatorship of the proletarian party.[60] Progressive Labor went even further, envisioning a postrevolutionary society run by the party leadership according to democratic-centralist principles. *RR IV* explained that the working class would have an opportunity to discuss party directives before being compelled to carry them out. Afterward, the party would evaluate the results:

> After the leadership has guaranteed full and open discussion of policy, every party member and worker must develop the discipline to accept

and carry out the collective decision. Even those who disagree must hold
to this discipline. The effort to put party decisions into action must be
united everywhere. Later we can see clearly the rightness or wrongness
of decisions, and, if need be, make adjustments or scrap them. In this
way, both majority and minority viewpoints will get a serious hearing.[61]

Like Plato, PL envisioned a utopia in which hierarchy and discipline cen-
tralized political power in the hands of philosopher kings. It is impossible to imagine the leadership of such a ruling party not being able to
impose its will on the party membership, or the party unable to impose
its will on the masses.[62] Nevertheless, PL justified concentrating power
in the party by arguing that only the party could spread the ethos of communist egalitarianism—which Plato had prescribed for the political and
military elites—to the masses.[63]

This centralization of power in the party, making it "the ultimate organizational expression of working class power, in addition to its primary role as political and ideological leader," evidently "worried some
people" in PL who feared that the party would become "a new ruling
class." These PLers wanted postrevolutionary society to be a democracy,
in which the party respected the will of a mass electorate, and in which
the masses had "some sort of institutional protection against the party,
some sort of institutional system of checks and balances against the party
becoming corrupt." Given PL's long history of antirevisionism, it is not
surprising that PLers were keenly aware of the tendency of communist
parties, no matter how well-intentioned they were, to constitute themselves into a new ruling class.[64]

However, PLP's chairman, Milt Rosen imagined a future in which
there would be no institutional restraints on PL's authority as a ruling
communist party, which meant that he envisioned the party leadership's
future power as unlimited. Rosen, contrary to the impression created by
the party's sanguine predictions, was probably realistic about PL's
doubtful prospects for achieving state power soon. With the revolution a
distant prospect, it is unlikely that he anticipated personally exercising
the far-reaching powers that he hoped PL's leadership would eventually
enjoy. Nevertheless, his portrayal of the communist future was self-serving
inasmuch as it enhanced all PLers' sense of self-importance and emphasized the overarching importance of PL's leaders. In any case, Rosen
reminded pro-democracy PLers of *RR IV*'s doctrine that under communism, all authority would be vested in the party—because any dilution of
party power would retard the thoroughgoing transformation of society
along communist lines:

. . . [*RR IV*] says explicitly that the leadership, the party, wants to encourage direct working-class transformation of the society and direct
working-class leadership of the society, but that, when push comes to
shove, in an ultimate sense, the power of the society should rest in the
hands of the party, rather than in the hands of a non-party group, or
some sort of coalition between the party and non-communist forces.[65]

Rosen implied that all communists would be in PL or support it, and that
nonparty groups would necessarily be less competent advocates of egalitarian communism than PLP. In other words, PL was so self-confident
that it had mastered the problem of revisionism that it could no longer
imagine the legitimacy of leftist mass organizations arising to combat
party corruption—not if the party in question was PLP. In *RR III*, PL had
praised such mass organizations for having initiated the GPCR's campaign against China's "red bourgeoisie." With its adoption of *RR IV*, PL
now believed that it possessed a political line that substantially inocu-
lated it against revisionism, obviating the need for the revolutionary
masses to ever seek organizational expression outside PLP.[66]

Progressive Labor's party-mindedness, the Leninist elitism it
learned from Stalin, triumphed over its former flirtation, under the influence of Mao, with populism.[67] The populist element remained, however,
in PL's perspective of becoming a mass party, a party of millions. The
party believed that it would be able to create a communist economy in
the immediate postrevolutionary period precisely because it expected to
recruit millions of politically enlightened people before the revolution.
Progressive Labor believed that it could have the best of both world's, a
disciplined party organized along Leninist lines that approached a nu-
merical strength typically associated with significant electoral parties.
Unfortunately, PL offered no evidence that millions of people could be
won to revolutionary politics in a stable society, and its own meager
record of recruitment strongly suggested the contrary.[68]

For Rosen, formal democracy opened the door to privilege, and was,
for that reason, an obstacle to achieving equality of condition, which he
regarded as more profoundly democratic. Moreover, formal democracy
would politically empower the economically privileged. Paradoxically,
then, PL believed that political centralism insured decisions that bene-
fited the vast majority, while formal democracy jeopardized the welfare
of the masses. It seems that for PL, recruiting millions to the party in the
prerevolutionary period did not insure that the masses, if given the
chance, would vote for communism. [69]

Although PL perennially expressed confidence in the masses, it understood that most people were not yet ready to adopt a communist way of life.[70] PL believed that it would have to control political power for an indefinitely long time to win the masses to communist ideals. Marx had anticipated that the proletarian dictatorship would wither away after a time, but PL was not prepared to say how long that would take.[71] Milt Rosen didn't know for sure, but surmised:

> Perhaps more than 200 years and less than a million. No one knows and no one can begin to imagine what life will be like after a hundred, a thousand, ten thousand years of communist economic relations.[72]

Progressive Labor, then, anticipated a universal and, for all practical purposes, an eternal party dictatorship, a secular theocracy run by the elect of history to establish heaven on earth. In PL's totalitarian vision, a relatively small collective of communist leaders, abetted by millions of communists, would control the entire earth indefinitely, using their power to wipe out the age-old culture of oppression and create a new type of human being.[73]

THE LOGIC OF ANTIREVISIONISM

It took Progressive Labor twenty years of wrestling with the problem of communism to draw out the logical implications of its antirevisionist critique—to arrive at and bluntly state this vision of Leninist elitism informed by Maoist idealism and populism. Why was communism so problematic for PL? Communism is a mixture of insoluble elements, utopianism and political realism. Unlike his utopian socialist predecessors, Marx did not construct a detailed model of communist society, but *discovered* the concrete historical processes that would produce a revolutionary proletariat to bring about communism. Lenin elevated the importance of revolutionary intellectuals in this process; leading a disciplined proletarian vanguard, they would use their intelligence and will to push history in its appointed direction. Within this Leninist context, policy determinations by communist leaders became all important. Leninists, who combined utopian aspirations with a tough-minded determination to recognize and maximize any opportunity to advance the communist cause, were continually faced with difficult choices that required making realistic assessments. For Leninists, underestimating what could be achieved was a right-wing error, and they denounced defeatist strategies as "revisionist." Conversely, attempting to overreach objective limits was left-wing "adventurism" and a sign of "sectarianism." Because the stakes were high for the working class and for the communists themselves, communists could not have taken their disputes over policy more seriously or argued among themselves more bitterly.[74]

In Progressive Labor's estimate, the perennial failure of the communist movement was revisionism and a red thread of antirevisionism ran through PL's ideological march to the left. Progressive Labor was inspired by communist ideals and the achievements of the great communist revolutions, but disappointed and frustrated by the corruption of communist regimes—the extent to which they retreated from communism's utopian goals.[75] Unwilling to give up on communism as a practical ideal, PL looked for the roots of revisionism and found them in *unnecessary* concessions to capitalist power and ideas. Progressive Labor's leaders thought that they could emulate past communist triumphs without making the compromises that had undermined the commitment of communist leaders to achieving an egalitarian society. They elevated the utopian side of communism over its realistic quest for power. Like Frederick Douglass, PL was committed to struggle, but PL's banner might have read, "There can be no progress without principle." So PL progressively stripped communism of everything that smacked of unprincipled compromise, and became progressively sectarian and politically inert.[76] However, from PL's perspective, adopting revisionist policies or abandoning the communist paradigm meant conceding the future to capitalist exploitation, imperialist war and fascist oppression.[77]

Progressive Labor defeated capitalism on paper, but not in the real world, where American capitalism, although challenged in the 1960s by militant Black rebellions, a massive antiwar movement, a cultural revolution among young people, and, to a lesser degree, an upsurge in worker militancy, was resilient and remained essentially stable.[78] As the radical surge of the 1960s ebbed in the 1970s, and PL's expectation of a rising tide of revolution gave way to its predictions of war and fascism, PL stuck to its ideological guns and became even more insistently sectarian—preaching its utopian vision to an increasingly conservative society.[79] Contrary to *American exceptionalists*, who favored accommodating communist policy to American realities, PL believed in its moral superiority and the transforming power of its revolutionary ideas.[80] Progressive Labor proposed utopian communism in the world's most successful capitalist country, revolution in a society with a demonstrated capacity for reform, collectivism in a highly individualistic culture, dictatorship in a nation committed to formal democracy, atheism in a very religious country, antiracism and antinationalism in a racially and ethnically divided society, ideological purity in a culture renowned for philosophical pragmatism, proletarian internationalism in a nation of patriots, industrial working-class leadership in a post-industrializing society, left-wing extremism in a nation moving rightward, anti-imperialism in the heart of an informal American Empire and egalitarianism in the land of opportunity. By opposing so much in American life—the good, the bad and the neutral, PL distanced itself from the vast majority of Americans, and reduced the effectiveness of its criticisms. However, for PL, capitalist culture was a seamless web of exploitation, oppression, racism and war.[81]

When PL confronted its frustrating failure to become more than a marginal aspect of American political life, it pursued the logic of its analysis, and moved further leftward. Progressive Labor did not believe that its marginalization disproved its most fundamental beliefs, which it regarded as unfalsifiable in the near future. Conditions would eventually change, and when what it saw as the contradictions of capitalism inevitably asserted themselves, PL would be there to assume leadership of the working class. Like Christianity or capitalism, neither of which became ascendant in a day, the transition to communism was a historical process that would take time, perhaps hundreds of years. Progressive Labor maintained that it had set the stage for communism's next advance by purifying communist theory of its revisionist errors, and by building a small but devoted following to spread the word, which would eventually be welcomed by millions. Determined to hold the banner of revolution aloft in a society that was, at least for the time being, decidedly nonrevolutionary, PL was on the horns of a dilemma. Ultimately, PL solved the contradiction between its revolutionary utopianism and the pragmatic reformism that predominated among American workers by being defiantly sectarian and anticipating a crisis-ridden future that would be more conducive to its revolutionary communist mission.[82]

Progressive Labor began in 1962 by opposing some of the concessions to capitalism that important communist leaders had sanctioned, and by calling on PLers to organize as open communists. By 1982 Progressive Labor's antirevisionism had developed into the doctrine that millions could be directly won to making a revolution for the immediate abolition of the wage system and the establishment of a PL-run egalitarian society. But throughout PL's development, its strategy and tactics on the labor front reflected the party's faith in the transforming power of its ideas.

CHAPTER 3

Reform, Revolution, and the Search for the Working Class
Progressive Labor in Practice, 1962–1982

Progressive Labor's leadership was proud of having marked out the road to revolution and confident that its ideological innovations were progressively purifying communism of the revisionist errors that had sidetracked communists from their goal of an egalitarian society. However, PL's political line was only a road map; traveling down the road to revolution required fighting the bosses and their allies every step of the way—and fighting them in what PL's leaders considered a revolutionary communist way. The present chapter will discuss the problems PL encountered as it attempted to put its antirevisionist line into practice.

FIGHTING FOR REFORMS AND RAISING REVOLUTIONARY POLITICS

Angry at the myriad crimes it ascribed to capitalism, inspired by its utopian vision and bolstered by democratic-centralist discipline, PL plunged into the class struggle during the long, tumultuous decade of the 1960s, which began at the end of the 1950s and did not end until the mid-1970s.[1]

This was an era in which militant reform struggles abounded, involving one segment after another of American society: the southern civil rights movement started to make headway in the latter half of the 1950s; the student movement picked up momentum in the early 1960s; the antiwar movement mushroomed after 1965; ghetto rebellions raged in the mid-to-late-1960s; a strike wave peaked in 1970–1971; the environmental movement burst into public consciousness at the same time;

44

and the feminist movement continued to gain strength into the mid-1970s. The masses were in motion, and PL looked forward to turning the reform tide into a tidal wave of communist revolution led by the working class. In 1970 PL optimistically predicted, "Though workers hung back in the sixties, they will soon take over leadership of the emerging mass movement."[2]

Even in view of the multifarious mass movement of the 1960s, it is incredible that Progressive Labor, an organization whose membership probably never exceeded fifteen hundred, and which had far fewer members for most of this period, could have intervened in so many situations, raised so many issues, launched so many campaigns, caused such a stir, and provoked so much criticism.[3] In sum, PL was the soul of aggressive political activism. The Progressive Labor Movement's solidarity campaign for Kentucky miners, Cuba trips, antiwar demonstrations, and controversial role in the Harlem rebellion presaged PLP's future activism, its commitment to bold action and militant struggle.[4] *Struggle* became a byword in PL; the party boldly proclaimed, "The main thing in life is the class struggle."[5]

Yet, activism was not an automatic consequence of subscribing to PL's visionary goals; the opposite was often the case. Evidently, a considerable number of PL members resisted becoming engaged in reform struggles. Some even argued that since any reform could be co-opted by the ruling class, party members would only confuse people by participating in these reform activities.[6] Student radicals had grown increasingly frustrated as the 1960s drew to a close; impatient with the pace of reform, they were in a hurry to get to the revolution.[7] Moreover, it is not surprising that many zealous, young PL members believed that their involvement in reform activities would slow down or even sidetrack the revolutionary process. Progressive Labor's leadership had quit the Communist Party, complaining that the CP had become addicted to reform at the expense of revolution, and that reform had supplanted revolution as the CP's mission. Progressive Labor tacitly admitted that American capitalists had taken the wind out of the sails of revolution by enacting reforms, but blamed the CP for acquiescing in the process.[8] If "right opportunism" was the main weakness of the communist movement, as PL's leadership argued, then movements dedicated to reforming American society might represent a serious threat to the aspirations of American revolutionaries.[9]

However, whether reform was primarily a threat to the revolutionary cause or an opportunity to spread the revolutionary message depended on how one looked at it. Progressive Labor's leadership, which did not reject all its CP training, was convinced that despite the risks involved, reform activities represented a unique opportunity to proselytize for socialist revolution. Milt Rosen suggested that communists could serve the cause of revolution by introducing "revolutionary consciousness into the struggle for reforms." They could use reform victories to illustrate that "the strength of the working class is limitless."[10]

In the unprecedented social turmoil of the late 1960s, PL's chairman slyly suggested to PLers, "We ought to ask ourselves what issue is being fought over today that isn't a reform." The answer, of course, was none. He urged party members to "start at the level people are at, with the issues that concern them."[11] The point seems so obvious that it is curious that he felt the need to make it. However, Rosen was addressing a membership that was, for the most part, acclimated to the overheated political atmosphere of the radical student movement. In the summer of 1969, when Rosen's *Build a Base in the Working Class* was first published, the party's campus cadres were making their infamous bid for power in Students for a Democratic Society, whose leadership and activist element, at least, had turned to revolution.[12] Most PLers, in other words, had learned their political ideas and their political style on campus, where revolutionary ideology had expanded the political spectrum.

However, it was otherwise among industrial workers, the vast majority of whom had barely been touched by the radical political ideas that pervaded American campuses.[13] It was one thing to employ revolutionary rhetoric to win radical students to PL's perspective of working-class revolution and quite another to awaken working-class people to their revolutionary potential. The party's leadership warned that while winning workers to fight for socialist revolution was PL's ultimate goal, party organizers would have to begin by addressing their fellow workers' immediate demands. Rosen rhetorically asked PLers, "in a shop would you start with wages and conditions or the war and socialism?" Party leaders warned their young followers that while ending the war in Vietnam and fighting for socialist revolution were closest to their hearts, they could not win workers to their cause with the brash political style that they had learned on campus. To transpose their revolutionary political consciousness into the working-class movement, ex-students would have to "introduce revolutionary and anti-imperialist ideas into immediate struggles, and show the interrelationship."[14] That would take time and require skill as well as patience on the part of young PLers, whose commitment to revolution partly reflected youthful impatience with the scope and pace of reform.[15]

To illustrate his view that revolutionary ideas should be raised within the context of reform struggles, PL's chairman told the story of a party member who had been working for six years, had consistently fought on shop issues and been elected shop steward. Because he had established a reputation as a fighter, Rosen argued, he was able to raise anti-imperialist ideas on the job and at union meetings, and even talk to "some workers" about socialism. However, if he had not been known as one who "produces against the boss in the immediate class struggle," Rosen warned, he would have been politically "dead," and unable to prevent the "boss or the union mis-leaders" from "red-baiting him out of his job." Rosen's warning, which reflected his own experience as a CP steelworker in Buffalo, was a measure of the political distance that he perceived between the world of student radicalism and the less ideologically expansive working-class world into which PL's ex-students were beginning to venture.[16]

Therefore, Rosen urged PL members to fulfill their responsibility as revolutionists by becoming active in reform struggles:

> . . . we participate in (and help launch) reform-type struggles in order to raise the struggle to the next highest level. This IS the job of a revolutionary. Not raising the struggle is opportunist. Not participating in most reform struggles is sectarian. Both help the enemy.[17]

He believed that by fighting militantly for reforms PLers could differentiate themselves from collaborationist union leaders and "fake" leftists, and attract militant workers to the party's revolutionary cause. Progressive Labor's chairman estimated that the militancy of American workers was stronger than their anticommunism.[18]

If *Build a Base in the Working Class* outlined PL's basic organizing strategy, *Road to Revolution III* reiterated the importance of engaging in the immediate struggles that preoccupied workers:

> . . . most workers are not ready to launch a socialist revolution now. They are ready to fight like hell on many immediate grievances. To abstain from these fights would be to reduce socialism to an abstraction. There would be no way to win people to the need for socialist revolution, and to show how the fight for reform by itself can never solve workers problems. . . . Our party won't grow if it doesn't initiate struggles, if it doesn't stand in the forefront of all struggles, and if it doesn't build united fronts with those who are prepared to join with us on specific issues and sets of issues.[19]

By participating in reform struggles, the party suggested, PLers could connect the idea of socialist revolution to the immediate concerns of their fellow workers, that is, they could raise socialist ideas in a concrete and emotionally compelling way. To do so, PLers would have to insinuate their socialist message into shop struggles as they unfolded, that is, strike while the iron was hot. Wally Linder explained:

> We are not describing a "two-stage" struggle; that is, a communist's role is not to first participate in a trade union fight and "later" turn it into a revolutionary one. Rather, the struggle for revolutionary ideology must go on all the time, throughout the fight for so-called trade union demands. That is the only guarantee that turns will be made.[20]

However, it was difficult to bring up controversial and potentially divisive issues in the heat of battle. Members of PL might very well be reluctant to raise their controversial ideas on the job, especially in the midst of shop struggles, because they feared antagonizing bosses, union leaders and, probably most important, anticommunist fellow workers.[21]

Not surprisingly, fighting for reforms did not necessarily lead to the fruitful political discussions between PLers and their fellow workers that the party envisaged. Progressive Labor's organizers in the workplace often tended, the party charged, to avoid struggling politically with their fellow workers; either they preached revolution to workers at a distance, without becoming involved in their struggles or lives, or they integrated themselves into the shop struggles, and sometimes even into the lives, of their fellow workers but failed to raise their own revolutionary politics. In either case, the party complained, these young PL organizers were giving in to their fear of anticommunism and betraying a lack of confidence in the working class.[22] In sum, they were not fulfilling Milt Rosen's prescription for building a *political* base in the working class. Rosen admonished PL's young politicos, "Developing close personal-political ties with our fellow workers, is one of THE MOST POLITICAL THINGS WE CAN DO, provided, of course, it goes along with the raising of our line, the party's program."[23]

However, when PL organizers functioned in an exemplary manner—forming personal relationships with fellow workers and introducing revolutionary politics into the shop struggles that they led—individual workers, and occasionally several at the same time, were recruited to the party. Nevertheless, PL made no political breakthroughs; its roots in the working class remained shallow. This was true even when PL-led reform struggles assumed significant proportions, which they sometimes did.[24] Participation in the immediate struggles of workers, during this decade of varied and intense reform movements, helped to justify PL's self-image as the vanguard party of the working class, and undoubtedly contributed to the party's modest growth. However, PL was only able to recruit a tiny fraction of the considerable number of workers who participated in party-led reform activities over the years.[25]

Progressive Labor's experience organizing in the workplace indicates that workers were more willing to accept the open participation of communists in their reform struggles than those who vaunted the anti-communism of American workers acknowledged. A considerable number of PLers who were open about their communist politics became shop stewards, and a few were even elected to union leadership.[26] PL's leaders were correct in maintaining that it was possible for skillful PL organizers to function openly as communists in numerous workplaces and unions. However, PL's poor recruiting record also shows that workers were less willing to become revolutionists than PL's leadership had optimistically anticipated. Apparently, recognizing the reform capabilities of individual communists was very different from subscribing to their revolutionary program.[27] Although PL's leadership criticized the efforts of its on-the-job organizers to promote the party's message and recruit workers, PL never questioned the revolutionary message or the revolutionary potential of the American working class.[28]

LEFT-CENTER COALITIONS

To increase its influence among working-class people, PL perennially created various *front* groups for those who did not support the goal of socialist revolution but who were willing to work with the party for specific reforms.[29] Progressive Labor did act in its own name, especially when highly political issues were involved, but the party usually created new formations to promote the reforms that it supported.[30] These front groups ranged from short-lived ad hoc committees, formed to address immediate issues, to more permanent rank-and-file caucuses, created to displace established union leaders, and finally to national organizations such as the Workers Action Movement and the International Committee Against Racism, which were dedicated to achieving long-range reform goals.[31]

Progressive Labor hoped that these organizations would draw militant workers into the party's political orbit, and that workers who were attracted by the reform activities of these groups would come to know and respect PLers, assimilate their ideas and eventually join the party. Most of PL's recruits did participate in PL-led reform movements before they joined the party. To that extent, these organizations served PL's purpose.[32]

However, none of these *left-center coalitions*, that is, coalitions between the party (the Left) and militant workers (the Center), ever developed into mass organizations.[33] The issues they raised had the potential to garner mass support. The Workers Action Movement, for example, campaigned for "30 hours work for 40 hours pay" as a way of addressing the issue of unemployment. The International Committee Against Racism, which succeeded WAM as the party's national left-center coalition, advocated multiracial unity in the fight against all aspects of racism. Although both of these organizations initially gained a hearing far beyond PL's immediate base, they eventually settled into being no more than *PL-and-friends* groups, that is, PL by another name.[34]

Why did PL's left-center coalitions fail to fulfill their initial promise to become mass organizations? Ironically, PL was afraid that they would become reformist Frankenstein's monsters beyond the party's control. Progressive Labor feared that if they became mass organizations under the leadership of militant workers, either the party would be absorbed by them and relinquish its revolutionary mission or they would advocate unprincipled compromises that the party would be compelled to publicly condemn. To prevent either of these things from happening, PL insured its control of these organizations, pushed them to the left and publicly acknowledged playing a prominent role in them.[35]

Believing that it understood the requirements of the class struggle better than militant workers, PL insisted that the Left must lead the Center; otherwise, these reform movements would, the party warned, eventually embrace class collaboration, as the labor movement had done.[36] The party protected itself from being pulled to the right by pushing its left-center coalitions so far to the left that they endorsed all PL's positions except socialist revolution.[37] Furthermore, acting on the old adage that "The best defense is a good offense," the party protected its front organizations from red-baiting by underscoring its leadership role in them.[38] However, by restricting the membership of its left-center coalitions to those who were willing to identify openly with PL and follow its lead, the party insured that these PL-led groups would not develop into mass organizations.[39] Even worse, preoccupation with front groups inhibited PLers from integrating themselves into existing mass organizations.

When it moved even further left, PL questioned the usefulness of such organizations. They had not developed an independent leadership, and they softened PLers politically by requiring them to act as reform leaders. Furthermore, these front groups were not politically influential and had produced few recruits for PL.[40] In sum, fearing that its left-center coalitions might become reformist monsters, PL did not allow them any independence. Consequently, when the party decided to disband these front groups, there was no genuine Center around to protest.[41]

PARTY ACTIVISM

However, whether Progressive Labor acted in its own name or through PL-led reform organizations, the party never doubted that active participation in the class struggle was essential to its purposes; urged on by their leaders, PLers plunged into the arena of reform struggles.[42] They organized on campuses and jobs, in high schools and communities, and even in the U.S. armed forces. They were active in over a score of cities during the 1960s and 1970s, but principally in New York (where PL maintained its headquarters), Boston, Philadelphia, Chicago, Detroit, Houston, San Francisco, and Los Angeles.[43]

Progressive Laborites initiated or joined a host of struggles, for the most part small, but sometimes big, around a plethora of local, national and international issues. They opposed racism, sexism, anti-Semitism, fascism, police brutality, deportation of undocumented workers, Apartheid in South Africa, imperialism, the Vietnam War, ROTC recruiters, bourgeois politicians, budget cuts, evictions, sweatshops, unjust firings, unemployment, bad contracts, union sell-outs, and all other forms of exploitation and oppression. They met, discussed, debated, handed out leaflets, petitioned, rallied, protested, demonstrated, marched, picketed, organized unions and reform movements, filed grievances, led work actions, walkouts and strikes, ran for office, defied legal sanctions, heckled racist professors and physically assaulted KKKers and Nazis.[44]

Progressive Labor's actions usually attracted some supporters, and occasionally quite a few of them, considering the party's small membership.[45] However, PL was not deterred from acting just because it lacked support. As the self-chosen conscience of the working class, the party felt the need to act in an exemplary manner.[46] So even if almost no one responded to its call to action, which happened often enough, PL went on, sometimes acting virtually alone. Nevertheless, the party kept its members in continual motion, and mustered a modest number of supporters for most of its numerous activities.[47]

THE PARTY PRESS

The vast majority of PL's activities were only reported in the party's press, principally its newspaper, *Challenge*, subtitled "The Revolutionary Communist Newspaper."[48] "Our newspaper, *Challenge*," PL declared, "strives to present the unconditional truth of class struggle so our class can learn from experience how to win."[49] Like Lenin, PL put great store in the party press, which it hoped would rally revolutionary workers to PL's cause.[50] *Challenge* began publication in March 1964 as a monthly, became a biweekly by the early 1970s and a weekly by the mid-1970s. When PL waged an all-out campaign, at the end of the 1960s and the beginning of the 1970s, to increase the sale of its newspaper, which sold for ten cents, the party reported that circulation reached 100,000. But the paper's circulation dropped dramatically as the decade progressed.[51]

Progressive Labor distributed its newspaper in a variety of ways. The party made some efforts to place its literature in newsstands, but *Challenge* was principally sold by PLers—on campus and at antiwar demonstrations, on the street and in housing projects, at party rallies and on marches, at plant gates and in front of union halls, and on union picket lines and on the job, when PLers could manage that. Hundreds of thousands of people may have at some point held a copy of *Challenge* in their hands, and even read some of it, but many fewer people read the paper more than once, and fewer still read it consistently for an extended time. This group, which probably numbered no more than ten thousand at any one time—and was usually much smaller—was composed of subscribers and people who knew PLers personally and bought the paper from them on a regular basis. Therefore, only a very limited number of people were aware of PL's activities.[52]

Those who bought *Challenge* could read in its pages PL's ongoing self-narrative, in which the party was the protagonist of a deepening revolutionary drama. The sixteen pages of the 16 October 1971 issue of *Challenge*, for example, contained numerous articles which delineated PL's view of important events and reported on the party's participation in the class struggle: "Attica: Workers' Unity Spells Bosses' Doom"; "Seattle Rank & File Printers' Caucus Organizing Fight for 4 day Week"; "'*Not gonna be shut up*'—GE Workers Beat Anti-communist Attack by IUE"; "Detroit Auto Workers Roll Over UAW Boss & Nationalist Flunky to Picket Nixon"; "Storm Welfare Office, Win Checks; Fight vs. Cuts Gains"; "Boston H.S. A Prison; Slave Labor, Racism, Cops; Student-Teacher Unity Could Rout Rulers"; "Ft. Ord Ripe for Rebellion; March

Against Racist Attack On Black GI"; "Drive to Dump Liberal Harvard's Nazi Theorist"; and "Temple SDS'ers Put Racist Univ. On Trial in Fight Against Expulsion."[53]

This partial list of headlines from a typical issue of *Challenge* is more than sufficient to indicate the paper's extreme-left point of view, orientation toward militant workers, exaggerated and inflammatory language, penchant for demonizing bosses and idealizing workers, assertive and excessively optimistic tone, sometimes paranoid style, and preoccupation with PL's activities and constant overestimation of PL's importance (predictable in a party organ).[54] In defending *Challenge* against the charge that it used jargon, the party maintained that words such as *imperialism* and *bosses* empowered workers in the class struggle.[55] In sum, "The Revolutionary Communist Newspaper," in a "militant, partisan style and tone," portrayed the world as a seething cauldron of class struggle that PL was in the process of vigorously stirring into a maelstrom of revolution.[56] Milt Rosen, who often claimed that the "all-mighty dollar" was the "bosses' flag," hoped that *Challenge* would become the "flag of the working class."[57]

Whether the *bourgeois* press failed to report PL's generally small-scale actions because they were not newsworthy or because actions carried out by left-wing extremists constituted news that was *unfit to print*, not surprisingly, the vast majority of what PLers did was only reported in *Challenge*.[58] However, PL's actions occasionally attracted the attention of the mainstream press. For example, when PL's Worker-Student Alliance caucus of Students For a Democratic Society, the nation's most important radical student organization, vied with its revolutionary rivals at the SDS national convention in 1969, splitting the organization, PL became news nationally.[59] Even incidents that brought PL only local press attention sometimes had national implications. For example, when PL's Workers Action Movement led a sit-down strike at Chrysler's Mack Avenue Plant in August 1973, provoking officials of the United Automobile Workers to physically attack the strikers, it was front-page news in the *Detroit Free Press* and the occasion for pointed criticism of the national UAW leadership.[60]

CONFRONTATIONAL POLITICS

However, despite brief moments in the limelight, PL generally remained an obscure organization. But in the arenas where PL was active, it invariably provoked heated controversy. Progressive Labor evinced controver-

sial ideas and employed militant tactics. Revolutionary politics, PL believed, mandated a militant approach to the class struggle, and militancy
would appeal to potentially revolutionary workers. Furthermore, militancy could generate publicity, and achieve immediate results that were
otherwise beyond the capability of a small party. A tiny organization, PL
shouted to be heard at all.[61]

For all these reasons, PL employed a variety of aggressive tactics:
violating injunctions, heckling racist professors and budget-cutting
politicians, handing out *Nazi of the Year* awards to startled public figures,
throwing an egg at New York's mayor, Ed Koch, disrupting budget hearings, sitting-in, calling wildcat strikes, picketing bosses' homes, storming the headquarters of the New York Central Labor Council, assaulting
the Klan and the Nazis and resisting arrest. These *exemplary* actions,
typically carried out by PL and its close friends, but sometimes involving
people who only had a peripheral relationship with the party, ranged
from deadly serious street battles with Nazis to exercises in street theatre
and media-grabbing stunts that had only symbolic significance.[62]

Not surprisingly, confrontational politics provoked counterattacks:
investigations, firings, loss of union membership, arrests, beatings,
shootings, a bombing and civil lawsuits. Progressive Labor regarded the
reprisals that its *more militant than thou tactics* garnered as confirmation
of its vanguard role. Audacious actions that provoked attacks on the
party by the *class enemy* dramatized PL's revolutionary mission and sub-
stituted for accomplishments that required a broad base of support,
which were generally beyond the party's reach because of its limited
numbers, extreme-left rhetoric, elitism, abrasive style, outright temerity
and outrageous tactics. Revolutionary PL was much better at creating
dramatic political gestures than it was at building effective and enduring
political coalitions for achievable reforms.[63]

Although PL was more interested in building a constituency for revolution than in achieving even worthwhile reforms, revolution was not
on the political agenda of the American working class during the long
decade of the 1960s. So while PL intended to use reform fights to win
workers to revolution, most of the party's limited number of working-
class supporters wanted to use revolutionary communists in PL to enhance their own struggles for reforms.[64] The party feared that while it
was trying to increase revolutionary consciousness among workers,
its working-class allies were propagating reformism within the party.[65]
Progressive Labor withdrew from reform struggles when continued
involvement in them seemingly threatened the party's commitment to

revolution. Progressive Labor kept marching down its road to revolution during the long decade of the 1960s, but few workers followed. The party was still a self-appointed general staff in search of a working-class army.

REEVALUATING REFORM AND REVOLUTION

By the mid-1970s, the national reform tide had ebbed; the level of struggle among both students and workers had dramatically declined, and PL saw portents of war and fascism. In 1975 PL organized a militant May Day march of about 2,500 people through South Boston, a White working-class enclave, to protest against an ongoing campaign of racist violence aimed at preventing the integration of South Boston High School through court-ordered busing. The party warned, "The racist movement in Boston is a trial balloon for coast-to-coast fascism."[66]

Because PL had recruited more members through its antifascist May Day march in Boston than it had been gaining through its many reform activities, the party leadership reevaluated the relationship between fighting for reforms and raising revolutionary politics. Reflecting on that march, PL's leaders noted, "It was then and around other May Days that the most workers have seen the need to join the party and build for a revolution, not simply stick to reforms."[67] Reassessing its practice, the party leadership found that PL was leading a double life: "While the line has constantly moved to the Left, we have found ourselves applying far too much of our time and thinking to building militant reform struggle rather than revolution." There was, PL's leaders discovered, a widening gulf between the party's increasingly left-wing political line and its still largely reformist practice.[68]

To trace the roots of this contradiction, the party leadership recounted the history of PL's efforts to bring communism to the working class. Between 1962 and 1965, the Progressive Labor Movement "reasserted the public role of communists," but at the Progressive Labor Party's founding convention, there was only one trade union club, which had four members. Beginning in 1965, the party sent some ex-students into industry to become union activists but played down their affiliation with PL (allegedly, to prevent them from committing sectarian suicide). By 1968 the party considered this industrial *colonizing* effort to be a failure and ended it. Between 1969 and 1971, PL pushed the sale of *Challenge* at plant gates, raising circulation to 100,000 by the summer of 1970. However, when a wave of wildcat strikes swept the country in 1970–1971, the party was compelled to recognize the degree to which it was isolated from militant workers. In 1971–1972, PL members, who were now working on jobs appropriate to their educational level, became active in their unions, forming caucuses and other union oriented formations. In 1972 the party established the Workers Action Movement to fight for "30 hours work for 40 hours pay" and "re-develop the Left inside the labor movement." By December 1974, however, PL was chagrined to find that the party had become submerged in WAM. Turning to the left again, PL began a drive to build a mass party, and dissolved WAM. In August 1975 PL began to concentrate on building communist *fractions* in the unions. In sum, alternately turning toward reform and revolution, the party had zigzagged down its road to revolution for over a decade.[69]

Progressive Labor's leadership touted having put forward communist ideas and the party in a mass way but came to the conclusion that despite its last turn to the left it was still trying to win workers "first to militant reform and then to revolution," a two-stage approach to revolution that it had already rejected "in theory."[70] The party now warned its members that "unless we FIT THE REFORM STRUGGLE INTO REVOLUTIONARY POLITICS AND NOT VICE-VERSA, no matter what we say, we will become a revisionist party, that is, a party that accommodates itself to—and works within the framework of—the capitalist system." [71] In other words, PL reasoned that if its practice did not become revolutionary, then its line would become reformist.

What did making revolution primary mean in practical terms? To PL it meant making the size of its annual May Day march a barometer of the party's progress toward building a mass base for communism:

> Putting revolution primary and reform struggles secondary means building for something like May Day all year round. It means building a communist base who we can go to about participating in such an important party activity. Otherwise May Day will get smaller and smaller.[72]

Progressive Labor insisted that making revolution primary did not mean abandoning the reform struggle, but it did mean participating in reform struggles primarily to point out the faults of capitalism and the virtues of communism, and to convince workers of the need for revolution and the party.[73]

Progressive Labor had not been able to recruit more than a modest number of workers during the long decade of the 1960s, when the reform movement was at high tide. Now, PL concluded that, rather than having been too sectarian in this period, it had been too opportunistic. The party suggested that its members would have recruited many more workers if they had concentrated less on leading reform struggles and drawn more communist lessons for their fellow workers. Rather than trying to gain workers' confidence by fighting for reforms, PLers would now primarily preach communist politics to those who would listen. In other words, now that workers and students were less inclined to participate in militant reform struggles, PL, making a virtue of necessity, would be less inclined to compromise its politics, and squander its meager resources, to foment or tactically lead such struggles. Instead, PL would concentrate on proselytizing those who were already open to a direct political approach.[74]

If Progressive Labor's faith in the revolutionary potential of American workers was justified, and the objective situation was worsening, pointing to war and fascism, as PL believed it was, then there might be reason to hope that "the future of revolution was never brighter," as PL claimed.[75] However, if objective conditions did not push workers in a revolutionary direction, it was absurd to think that PL could pull them there in any significant numbers by preaching communism more vigorously, that a revolutionary PL tail could wag a reformist or quiescent working-class dog. Barring a crisis, and perhaps even then, PL was committing itself to remaining a revolutionary sect. Despite its dream of becoming a mass party, PL undoubtedly preferred being a revolutionary sect waiting for the "inevitable" crisis of capitalism, than a party like the CP, which it regarded as reformist, that is, *communist* in name only. In any case, there was an intrinsic relationship between remaining small and remaining pure. Progressive Labor had revived May Day, to be sure, but none of its May Day marches ever attracted more than a few thousand participants nationally.[76]

Progressive Labor's ongoing attempts to discover the "correct" relationship between reform and revolution assumed that communists could place revolution on the agenda of the American working class. However, contemporary American workers seemed deaf to the siren call of revolution. The conditions for working-class revolution were far more complicated and illusory than PL admitted. No policy innovations by PL could have created the social, economic and political conditions needed to generate a ground swell for communism or produce the number of revolutionary workers that PL hoped for and anticipated. Even if PL had achieved an "ideal" balance between reform and revolution, enabling it to become more deeply rooted in the working class without compromising its commitment to revolution, a revolutionary situation would not have occurred. Since the party could not produce the conditions for a revolution, and was not prepared to abandon its version of left-wing communism, there was nothing left to do but make policy changes within the confines of its chosen paradigm that might produce marginally better results in the real world. In any case, making adjustments in policy renewed the party's sense of purpose and enhanced its sense of control.[77]

TURNING STUDENTS TOWARD WORKERS

From its beginnings in 1962, PL's problematic pattern of recruitment suggested that there was a gap between its theory of revolution and American social reality. Progressive Labor could not counter the social forces that shaped its development as a party of the college educated, but from the start it kept trying to do so by turning students toward workers and into workers. Progressive Labor's illegal student trips to Cuba in 1963 and 1964, and anti-Vietnam War demonstrations between 1964 and 1966 enabled PL to garner a modest base of students.[78] Progressive Labor's first industrial organizers in New York City's garment district were veterans of both PL's Cuba trips and the May Second Movement. Their involvement in blue-collar unions was emblematic of the dilemma that PL faced regarding recruitment.[79]

Progressive Labor had set out in 1962 to lead American workers in a struggle for socialism. But PL recognized that the working class, "because it had little or no political consciousness, doesn't necessarily conceive itself as that class which will be the key, the instrumental class, in bringing about revolutionary socialism in our country."[80] Students were far more receptive to political radicalism than workers, but radical students, intellectuals and professionals were disillusioned by their observation of union corruption and misleadership, and the "prevalence of bourgeois ideology among large sections of the working class." These radicals did not understand "the historic role of the working class, by virtue of its relation to production." As early as 1963, PL was arguing that a "continuous fight must be waged" for the idea that the working class is the "main class on which to rely to smash the power of imperialism."[81] Progressive Labor was primarily attempting to persuade students to have confidence in the revolutionary potential of workers because only students were interested enough in revolution to listen.

Radical students who found PL's pro-worker stance persuasive accounted for most of PLM's modest growth during the early 1960s. Milt Rosen estimated that among the approximately two hundred people who attended the PLP's founding convention in April 1965 there were no more than "a baker's dozen" who had "some tangible relationship to the working class." Wally Linder estimated that there were only four who worked for a living and went to work every day.[82] But PL's leadership was patient. "At this early stage," the recently founded PLP wrote in 1966, "our party, like most new-born revolutionary parties, has a large percentage of intellectuals and members of middle-class background."[83] Nevertheless, PL aspired to be a party of the working class. To alter PL's social basis, that is, to transform the party from a student-based to a working-class organization, its recruitment pattern would have to change.[84]

Progressive Labor was founded by an alliance between Stalinist industrial cadres in their late-thirties, who had been politically trained by the CP's Foster-led Left during the dark days of the Cold War, and pro-Castro CP students, who were inspired by new revolutionary currents.[85] Thus, PL leaders such as Milt Rosen and Mort Scheer bridged the gap between the heroic CP-led labor struggles of the 1930s and the youth rebellion of the 1960s.[86] These former industrial cadres provided youthful rebels with a Marxist-Leninist vocabulary and the guiding voices of veteran revolutionaries. Progressive Labor's leaders rejected C. Wright Mills forceful advice to the New Left to abandon its "labor metaphysic," that is, its "unrealistic" faith in the working class as the agency of radical social change, which he dismissed as a legacy of Victorian Marxism.[87] Instead, PL trained its student cadres to steer the amorphous rebellion of their generational cohorts toward an alliance with workers, that is, PL's students were delegated to connect PL's leaders to contemporary workers by building a new working-class base for revolutionary communism.[88]

Progressive Labor's attempt to convince students that "workers will fight with guns-in-hand to defend their fundamental class interests" began dramatically in the winter of 1962–1963 with the Hazard Miners' Solidarity Campaign, a national effort to aid very militant coal miners, whose strike centered in Hazard, Kentucky.[89] Progressive Labor then carried the notion that students could radicalize workers into the heart of the radical student movement. In April 1965 PL and its May Second Movement joined SDS's massive anti-Vietnam War demonstration in Washington, D.C.; and that winter, PL dissolved M2M, persuading approximately one thousand of its members to join SDS, which became the most important radical student organization in the United States, attaining as many as 70,000 members.[90]

Progressive Labor then formed the Worker-Student Alliance faction of Students for a Democratic Society to win SDS to its working-class orientation, and, in the process, to win control of SDS.[91] The student-worker rebellion in France in 1968 lent credibility to PL's claim that workers were potentially revolutionary. Many politically frustrated American radicals were persuaded that workers might become, as the WSA argued, an agency of radical social change. As PL later saw it, at the very least, paying "lip service" to the need for unity with workers suddenly became fashionable among radical students. The party was contemptuous: "By the end of the sixties everyone and his brother 'saw the need' for workers. . . . We in PL sarcastically called 1968 The Year of the Worker."[92]

Even so, in the summer of 1968, PL's WSA organized a summer work-in, which sent scores of students into factories to radicalize workers and proletarianize themselves, a campaign that paralleled Mao's cultural revolution.[93] By 1969 the WSA was strong enough to fight for control of SDS, precipitating an irreparable, and much lamented, split in that organization. The WSA, which had constituted a majority at SDS's 1969 convention, carried on for several years. It used the name *SDS* and engaged in a number of noteworthy activities, including support for striking General Electric workers during the winter of 1969–1970.[94] However, when the size of PL's SDS dwindled to PL's immediate base in the early 1970s, the party abandoned the name *SDS*, reorganizing its students, and eventually its workers, into the International Committee Against Racism, which academics associated with PL had founded in 1971 to combat resurgent racist theories in academia. While PL became notorious for the controversial role it played in dividing SDS, the party was primarily interested in attracting a working-class following. That, after all, was PL's ostensible purpose in building the WSA.[95]

TURNING STUDENTS INTO WORKERS

Progressive Labor made progress during the 1960s in winning some radical students to the notion of working-class revolution. However, at its 1965 founding convention, PL had vowed to become a party primarily made up of workers. Progressive Labor maintained as one of its fundamental theses that "the working class, especially its industrial segment, is the key force for revolution in the U.S." By early 1969, however, the party's national committee was asking, ". . . whom have we been recruiting?" The answer was, ". . . mainly teachers, welfare workers and students, independent radicals and professionals." As an increasing number of student radicals entered the workforce, the number of college-educated workers in PL also increased. While the committee was gratified to have these workers in PL, it bemoaned the party's failure to recruit industrial workers, "except in rare instances." If the party could not win industrial workers, the committee argued, then "the whole thesis of the role of the working class breaks down, assuming that objective conditions are favorable to their being won." However, the objective conditions, the committee believed, were "certainly ripe and full of class struggle out of which workers can be recruited to our party."[96]

Ironically, the committee claimed that the source of the problem was the party members. "There is a gap—a subjective gap—between our party and the industrial workers," PLP's national committee declared. Rather than relinquish its fundamental thesis of working-class revolution, the party pointed the finger of blame at its college-educated membership for not recruiting industrial workers: "It is we who have not been equal to the task." Progressive Labor had grown quantitatively in the unions, but because the party lacked a base among industrial workers, it was not "qualitatively changing into a working class party." This situation appeared dangerous to PL's national committee, which believed that continuing to have a mainly middle-class membership would undermine the party's commitment to working-class revolution. The national committee warned that the party could "either begin to lose membership and/or easily become moribund like the revisionist CP."[97]

Progressive Labor's students would have to overcome the subjective barriers that separated them from workers, especially industrial workers. The antiworker prejudices of the party's college-educated cadre, the leadership argued, constituted the principal obstacle to recruiting workers. For example, the party's middle-class members were willing to tackle the shortcomings of potential recruits from middle-class backgrounds, such as living a bohemian life. "But if workers," PL's leaders charged, "run around with other women (or men) or drink heavily, or 'watch TV all the time,' or any other aspect of life that ruling class ideology engenders in workers—a wall gets set up between our members and these workers which not only rules them out 'for the foreseeable future' as party recruits, but tends to prevent us from talking (or doing) politics with them because they are somehow beyond our rigid (middle class) specifications of who can join the party."[98] These were the sorts of dilemmas that arose from the contradiction between the theory to which PL was committed, that industrial workers would lead a socialist revolution in the United States, and the evident fact that it was the new generation of college students, graduate students, intellectuals, semiprofessionals and professionals that, among White Americans at least, constituted the social basis for the new radicalism.[99]

However, Progressive Labor remained faithful to the idea of blue-collar radicalism, pinning its highest hopes on Black workers. By the late 1960s, PL noted that "currently in the U.S. Black workers are a decisive factor within the industrial working class."[100] In PL's estimate, for example, at least thirty-five percent of the workforce in the strategically and economically important auto and steel industries was Black, and that in some plants Black workers comprised a majority.[101] The fight against racism was "fast becoming the burning question in every major trade union and community struggle now taking place," PL was encouraged to observe.[102]

Progressive Labor calculated that "Wage differentials between Black and white workers each year amount to $22 billion," and argued that U.S. imperialism thrived on the "super-profits derived from the 'racial inferiority' thesis it has drummed home into both Black and white workers"—so much so that "Exploitation and systematic robbery of Black workers at home is the most profitable and most vital domestic business of U.S. imperialism."[103] It followed that U.S. imperialism would "never grant equality to Black workers," and that the "ability of the working-class to reject racism" was "crucial to its ability to end class oppression."[104] Progressive Labor saw its own ability to recruit Black workers as a reflection of its capacity to win White workers "away from racism and to a class line." The party concluded that "for the working class to emancipate itself and all oppressed people, for it to eventually seize state power as a class, with a Marxist-Leninist party in its vanguard, the racism that splits the working class must be buried."[105]

Moreover, Progressive Labor regarded racism as the "Achilles' heel" of American capitalism, and Black workers as the most revolutionary sector of American society.[106] In 1962, in its first major policy statement, "For an Alternative Labor Policy," *PL*, after pointing to the exploitation of "Negro" workers by American monopolies and the persistence of Jim Crow practices in both industry and organized labor, suggested, "The Negro worker and his special relationship to the entire Negro Freedom Movement can bring to the labor movement a new quality of struggle, can infuse the labor movement with his revolutionary vitality, and can therefore tend to move the whole labor movement along."[107] By 1969, after five years of ghetto rebellions that began with the Harlem uprising of 1964, PL declared, "Black rebellions represent the most advanced aspect of class struggle in the U.S. at the present time," and have "shaken the ruling class as have no other events in the past 30 years."[108]

Twenty-two million Black Americans, ninety-five percent of whom were workers, could "play their historic role in the defeat of imperialism," only if they were led by Black workers, who brought a "special militance and class understanding to the working-class movement at the point of production." Black trade union caucuses had even "drawn tens of thousands of white workers into militant class struggle."[109] In addition, PL observed that even though Black workers constituted only ten to fifteen percent of the population, "their presence—and militancy—in such vital areas of the economy as basic industry, the key unionized sectors, and key industries in big cities, gives them a far greater importance than their numbers suggest; in fact, a decisive importance." Their importance could be seen in New York City where Black and Hispanic workers made up only twenty-five percent of the population but were "a majority, or near it, in mass transit, sanitation, garment, post office, welfare department, and are sizable minorities in teamsters, railroad, longshore, distribution and city government." These workers could, PL suggested, "bring the city's politicians and their bosses to their knees."[110]

Progressive Labor firmly believed that Black workers were extremely militant and strategically important—a key force for revolution. Clearly, PL was not only keenly interested in recruiting Black workers, but believed that prevailing conditions favored their recruitment. Nevertheless, the party had only sporadic success in recruiting Black workers, only slightly more success than it had with White industrial workers. Initially, PL professed to be unconcerned about mainly attracting young, college-educated Whites. However, the stark contrast—social, racial and ethnic—between PL's actual base and the Black and Hispanic workers whom PL regarded as crucial to the revolutionary process became an important problematic for PL.

How could PL become rooted in those segments of the population that theoretically possessed the greatest capacity for revolution? Having confidence in Black workers and believing that its political line was correct, except for concessions during the 1960s to progressive Black nationalism, PL examined the social, ethnic and racial prejudices that prevented its members from recruiting Black and Hispanic workers.[111] "People who come from middle class or student backgrounds," the party leadership argued, "acquire a special brand of racism over and above the brand developed by white workers, a certain class snobbishness that is

directed against all workers but that becomes a racist attitude when it involves Black workers." The ongoing struggle to overcome these prejudices within the party became a major theme of PL's internal life, and a
central issue in PL's trade-union organizing.[112]

Progressive Labor also recognized that sexism oppressed women
and compounded the effects of racism; both were aspects of class oppression. "Women," PL observed, "have always been a specially exploited section of the working class." The capitalist class exploited
women by "barring them from certain types of work, paying lower
wages for work similar to men's, and by using them as a special 'reserve'
force against militant male workers." In addition, there was a "systematic
ideological campaign to place women socially, politically and economically beneath the status of the male population in general." Progressive
Labor recalled Frederick Engels' observation that "within the family, he
is the bourgeoisie, and she is the proletariat."[113]

However, Black women were worse off than White women because
they faced "super-exploitation as workers who are Black, together with
the additional burden of being women." Since Black women were the
most oppressed part of the population, they would, by PL's logic, fight
back the hardest and were, therefore, the "most potentially revolutionary
section of the working class." According to PL, Black women had recently "taken leading roles in the fight for better housing, welfare,
against police brutality and drug addiction." To undermine their struggle,
the ruling class was promoting male-supremacist ideas to divide and
conquer Black men and women, who would, PL was confident, defeat
these "splittist tactics of the enemy."[114]

Progressive Labor envisioned the U.S. working class being led by
"communist Black workers," especially Black women.[115] However, despite its recognition of the leadership potential of Black women and the
divisive role of sexism, PL did not give nearly as high a priority to fighting sexism within the party as it did to combating racism and antiworker
biases. While PL did eventually increase the number of women in party
leadership positions, it remained a male-dominated organization that relied on the male-dominated workforce in heavy industry to spearhead the
revolution. The women's movement mushroomed during the latter 1960s
and early 1970s, and women comprised a sizable percentage of PL's
membership. Therefore, it is not surprising that the issue of sexism
within the party was continually raised by PLers during the 1970s. But
PL was very slow to respond to these criticisms, missing a historic opportunity to play a more progressive role regarding the issue of sexism in
American society.[116]

Ultimately, PL found it difficult to recruit industrial workers, whether Black or White, whether men or women.[117] Party leaders devoted considerable energy to "struggling" with PL's youthful members, who were mainly students, intellectuals and professionals, to overcome their prejudices against workers, especially industrial workers. Negative attitudes toward workers took many forms, but they all amounted, PL thought, to lack of confidence in the revolutionary potential of the working class. Arguably, this "lack of confidence" was merely a realistic assessment and not a prejudice. The party leadership admitted that the workers exhibited a "low level of class-consciousness," but maintained that, "it is precisely our job—to bring class-consciousness into the workers' movements; to win political leadership of the working people." Progressive Labor did not blush at assigning its middle-class members the task of bringing working-class consciousness to workers.[118]

To facilitate their mission, the party urged its young college-educated members, many of whom came from working-class families (and may have been conflicted about their class status), to defeat the middle-class influences on their lives. Doing so, the party claimed, would enable them to overcome the "contradiction between workers and themselves and develop full working class relations with many potential revolutionary workers."[119] Young, college-educated PLers, who opposed social barriers and longed for a sense of community, were willing to wrestle with their "anti-working class prejudices." Urging these PLers to emulate workers' lives to win them to socialist revolution might facilitate PL's sought-after metamorphosis into a working-class party, but asking college-educated PLers to proletarianize themselves—so that they could recruit *real* proletarians to PL—underscored PL's problematic position as a predominantly middle-class party striving to become a party of industrial workers, whose interests it already claimed to represent.

Moreover, there was a moralistic tone to PL's criticism of its college-educated cadres. Defeating the middle-class influences that prevented them from forming close relations with workers would enable young PLers, the party ventured, to become "real people."[120] Progressive Labor's suggestion that the insubstantial lives of college-educated youths could become well grounded through close ties with workers— *the salt of the earth*—smacked of romantic populism and introduced an element of personal salvation into the party's discourse. Progressive Labor, which idealized the working class and demonized the middle class, blamed middle-class PLers for being who they were—as though being middle-class were a kind of original sin that required middle-class PLers to be baptized in a river of criticism and self-criticism—so that they could be born again purged of "middle-class influences" in a communist Great Awakening. Progressive Labor's moralistic tone was calculated to turn its middle-class cadres into guilt-ridden missionaries who could awaken workers to their true revolutionary selves.

To facilitate their assimilation into the working class, PL urged its young members to alter their bohemian appearance and lifestyle. Progressive Labor attempted to turn its middle-class members into imitation workers—a sort of sociological alchemy—so that they could build a working-class base. For PL, this tactic was not only unrealistic but occasionally produced comic or grotesque results—students who temporarily became caricatures of the workers they hoped to recruit. Ironically, as young PLers began to look more like workers of the 1950s, young workers were beginning to ape the bohemian styles of contemporary students. However, PL's attempt to reinvent itself socially was born of an ideological necessity. Progressive Labor tried to effectuate the metamorphosis of students into workers to turn itself into an authentic working-class party and, thereby, save its theory that American workers were revolutionary.[121]

If the main struggle within PL was between "complete dedication to the working class," on the one hand, and "middle-class self-interest" or "bourgeois individualism," on the other, the party, nevertheless, relied on the money, training, morality, idealism, guilt, asceticism, missionaryism, romanticism, rebelliousness and utopianism of its young, middle-class members. Ironically, if PL could have thoroughly transformed them into industrial workers, even militant ones, they would have been less likely to remain in the party. In actuality, PL sought to encourage middle-class romanticism about the masses, and to discourage middle-class snobbishness toward individual workers. Radicals who learned to love the working class as an abstraction, and who also learned not to look down on the flesh and blood workers whom they met, might become dedicated and effective organizers of a new working-class base for PL.[122]

Their own will to revolution made young radicals receptive to PL's pro-worker rhetoric. The suffering of the masses could justify revolution, and the masses could, if they were won to doing it, move the world; but middle-class PLers also had their own motivations for rebelling. They wanted to remake the world in their own rational and ethical image by replacing the bourgeoisie as the cultural and political elite. As a revolutionary vanguard, intellectuals could overturn illegitimate authority and mold in their own image the misruled and misguided masses. By attempting to lead a working-class revolution, PLers could identify with workers but remain superior to them. In practice, they generally trusted themselves to lead the revolution more than they trusted the real workers whom they knew, who were at a double disadvantage because they were not imbued with PL's ideology and lacked the academic training of PL's college-educated cadres. "Serving" workers by convincing them to follow PL also served the purposes of middle-class radicals, who saw workers as a means to their own revolutionary ends.[123]

In a revolutionary society, they might have succeeded; for example, intellectuals had captured the leadership of spontaneous revolutionary mass movements in Russia and China. However, PL's revolutionary line had little appeal for American workers during the 1960s and 1970s; and PL's efforts to turn its middle-class members into effective working-class organizers, even if much more successful, would probably not have succeeded in turning PL into a party of the proletariat. Beyond a certain point, blaming party members for being too middle-class probably kept them from realistically assessing the working class and PL's political line, and served to control them through guilt. Since the party line and the working class were both above suspicion, party members became the scapegoat for PL's understandable frustration at remaining a predominantly middle-class political phenomenon in working-class garb.[124]

However, PL was able to get a sizable number of young, middle-class radicals to take the American working class seriously enough to attempt to organize them for communist revolution. In this regard, PL was first among the radical groups that emerged during the 1960s and 1970s. Some of results are worth examining. The second part of the present study will examine PL's attempt to build a communist base in New York City's garment industry during the 1960s.[125]

PART II

New Communists in an Old Anticommunist Union

Progressive Labor and the
International Ladies' Garment Workers'
Union in the 1960s

CHAPTER 4

New Communists Challenge Old Socialists
Trespassing on "Dubinsky's Plantation," 1962–1966.[1]

Progressive Labor first tested its approach to building socialism within the labor movement in New York City's garment district.[2] Even before founding *Progressive Labor*, Milt Rosen—then, the Communist Party's New York State labor secretary—revived the CP's practice, in abeyance for many years, of holding open communist street rallies in the city's garment district; and for twenty years after its founding, PL continually tried to gain a following among the city's garment workers.[3] This chapter discusses the reasons for PL's perennial interest in garment workers, the conditions that prevailed in New York City's garment industry during the 1960s, PL's critique of the International Ladies' Garment Workers' Union, and the party's first attempts to influence garment workers.

PROGRESSIVE LABOR'S PREOCCUPATION WITH GARMENT

The garment industry loomed large in the economy of New York City. Until the 1960s, when public and service sector employment took precedence, the garment industry was New York City's largest employer, public or private, employing hundreds of thousands of workers. Historically, it was the city's economic engine.[4] Their numbers alone suggest that garment workers were strategically important, but from PL's Marxist perspective, their importance was greatly magnified by the fact that, besides manufacturing garments, they produced *surplus value*, the lifeblood of capitalism.[5] They would lead the revolution to overthrow the capitalist system and usher in the new socialist era.[6] If individual garment shops, in this fragmented and highly competitive industry, were small, they were, nevertheless, concentrated in the garment district, where tens of thousands of garment workers converged daily in the heart of the city.[7] The garment district was New York City's industrial heartland. A PL-led insurgency of significant proportions in the city's garment industry would constitute a communist "fifth column" in the economic capital of what PL termed "U.S. imperialism."[8]

New York City's economic importance nationally and internationally as a major producer of goods and services, a corporate headquarters and a commercial and financial center cannot be overestimated.[9] New York was also of paramount importance in the United States as a cultural, intellectual and political center. This was especially true for the American Left. New York City was certainly the single most important center of American communism.[10] Progressive Labor, which drew its initial strength mainly from elements of the New York State CP, established its headquarters in the city. To PL's leaders, an organizing breakthrough among garment workers in New York City would lend credence to their policies, build confidence in their leadership and put their tiny party on the political map.[11]

THE IMPERIOUS AND MUCH HONORED ILGWU

To win garment workers to its communist outlook, PLers would have to confront a formidable opponent. David Dubinsky's International Ladies' Garment Workers' Union was one of the oldest, biggest, richest and most politically powerful unions in the country. Founded in 1900, the ILGWU had 450,000 members in the mid-1960s and commanded enormous financial resources.[12] In addition, the ILGWU had fostered the unification of the American Federation of Labor and the Congress of Industrial Organizations after their twenty-year rivalry, and ILGWU leaders sat on the AFL-CIO's highest councils.[13] If the garment district was the industrial heartland of New York City, it was also true that the city was the birthplace of the ILGWU and "still its heartland."[14] The ILGWU was certainly the largest union in the New York City Central Labor Council, and as co-founder of the Liberal party, David Dubinsky, longtime ILGWU president, exercised "great political clout" in New York.[15] As Herbert Hill, who was labor secretary of the National Association for the Advancement of Colored People, expressed it, "The ILGWU is the largest union in the largest manufacturing industry in New York, the world's largest city."[16]

The ILGWU, which had organizational strength, financial resources, labor connections and political influence, was not only demonstrably powerful in New York City, and nationally, but was widely considered a quintessential progressive union as well. In 1951 the philosopher John Dewey elucidated the ILGWU's remarkable record of achievements: significantly advancing the living standards of its members; effectively settling industrial disputes; establishing model social welfare projects; engaging in widely admired research, educational, recreational and cultural activities; and being "in the very vanguard of labor and civic forces in the battle for progressive labor and social legislation and for increased democracy in every aspect of our common life." If that were not enough, the ILGWU fought for democracy abroad as well. Dewey attributed these achievements to David Dubinsky's "courage, vision and innate genius for organization."[17]

Labor columnist A. H. Raskin was not exaggerating when he reported that "Honors and monuments piled up around David Dubinsky."[18] After serving twenty years as an executive officer of the ILGWU, for example, Dubinsky was lavishly praised by high-ranking labor leaders, politicians and intellectuals. William Green, who succeeded Samuel Gompers as AFL president, wrote glowingly of David Dubinsky: "No one can adequately appraise the value of the service he has rendered in the promotion of the economic, social and industrial interests of the membership of the International Ladies' Garment Workers' Union."[19] President Harry S. Truman lauded the ILGWU's president: "David Dubinsky is a man of vision, integrity and courage."[20] The League of Industrial Democracy congratulated Dubinsky: "Under the inspiration of your leadership, . . . the ILGWU has become one of the nation's most powerful and socially visioned unions."[21] Walter Reuther, president of the United Automobile Workers, was convinced that these laudatory assessments of Dubinsky would stand the test of time: "When historians come to weigh the worth of the great men of this crucial era in human history, I am certain that they will award David Dubinsky a high rank among the humanitarians of our time."[22]

Seventeen years later, a group of historians, although not entirely uncritical, nevertheless lived up to Reuther's expectation that their profession would hold Dubinsky in high regard. Not long after his retirement, a collective appraisal of Dubinsky appeared in a special supplement to *Labor History*.[23] J. B. S. Hardman, intending to analyze rather than praise Dubinsky, observed that "The Dubinsky literature is already massive and, in the main, so highly laudatory, that there would be little to add in praise of his widely recognized merits." Even so, Hardman did praise him as an "outstanding leader in the real sense of the term, a man endowed with many leadership qualities."[24] Philip Taft agreed: "Dubinsky's influence in the general labor movement was based on a solid record of achievements as a leader in a difficult industry."[25] Joel Seidman estimated that "It is difficult to separate the achievements of the union during the third of a century that Dubinsky served as its president from the personality of its leader."[26]

The character of Dubinsky's leadership was the product of a dynamic tension between two disparate elements of his personality, which Seidman identified as an idealistic humanitarianism, stemming from his socialist background, and a pragmatic will to action. Adapting idealistic goals to a pragmatic context, Dubinsky assumed his historic role as the quintessential, and much lauded, progressive among reformist trade union leaders. "His administration," according to Seidman, "marks the transition from radicalism to practical liberalism, from rejection of the existing economic order to efforts to reform it, from ideological unionism on the left of the American labor movement to a central position in its progressive wing."[27] Jack Barbash, as well, approved of the ILGWU's transformation under Dubinsky's guiding hand. "The major change," according to Barbash, "has been in the evolution of the union from a protest movement—'a cry of pain' as Durkheim once said about socialism—to a going concern." Barbash applauded the "naturalization" of the union's radicalism from a "doctrinaire socialism essentially European in its origin . . . to a 'social unionism' more responsive to the indigenous forms of the labor problem."[28]

By gaining economic concessions from employers and labor law reforms, the labor movement, created in a spirit of rebellion against established powers and sanctioned ways of thinking, historically served to integrate alienated workers into the capitalist system, and in the United States, a nation of immigrants, to assimilate foreign-born workers to American norms.[29] The ILGWU, founded by radical Jewish immigrants, was emblematic of this process of domesticating radicalism, which could not have occurred without an expandable economy, conciliatory companies, enlightened government officials and workers willing to accommodate themselves to prevailing power arrangements to gain critically important reforms and acceptance within the larger society. The historians writing in *Labor History*'s special supplement observed that labor leaders, along with business directors and politicians, were instrumental in bringing about an accommodation between capital and labor, and they applauded David Dubinsky, a prominent exponent of "practical liberalism," for the key role that he played in opposing radicalism within the labor movement and consolidating labor support for a program of progressive reform.[30]

PROGRESSIVE LABOR OPPOSING
THE ILGWU LEADERSHIP

Progressive Labor detested Dubinsky's progressivism precisely because the ILGWU leader was committed to reforming capitalism, rather than fighting for socialism. Nothing could have been more antithetical to PL's hope and expectation that the struggles of trade unionists would culminate in a fight for socialism than Dubinsky's belief that "unions need capitalism like a fish needs water." For Dubinsky, who had been a "Socialist soapbox speaker in his early union days," socialism was only a stage in his development toward capitalism.[31]

Dubinsky was emblematic of everything that PL detested in the AFL-CIO leadership. His long history of "class collaboration" and staunch anticommunism, and his prominence among labor supporters of Cold War liberalism placed him high up on PL's list of hated AFL-CIO "bureaucrats."[32] Whether in his early socialist or later capitalist period, Dubinsky was an adamant opponent of communism. In 1957 Max Danish, who had been editor of *Justice*, the ILGWU's "militant publication," credited Dubinsky with more than thirty years of "unrelenting resistance to Communism throughout the needle trades' domain."[33] Dubinsky was a member of the ILGWU's general executive board during the 1920s, when the union was embroiled in a developing civil war between communists and their opponents. According to Danish, the communist bid for power in the needle trades' unions during the 1920s came "perilously close to success" in the ILGWU.[34] Their defeat was engineered by members of the ILGWU's general executive board, including its youngest member, David Dubinsky. He had already defeated the "Stalinites" in his own local, the Cutters' Union, turning it into an "anti-Red bastion" in the ILGWU's successful resistance to communist domination. This defeat of the ILGWU's communists during the 1920s, Danish argued, was historically important as the "first deterring point in the Moscow-directed invasion of the American labor movement." Later, as the ILGWU's secretary treasurer and president, Dubinsky "led in checkmating every Communist ruse or stratagem to reinfiltrate the women's garment workers' organization."[35] At the outset of the Cold War, Dubinsky issued "A Warning

Against Communists in Unions," in which he declared, "The Communists commonly refer to themselves as 'the vanguard' of labor, yet nothing could be further from the truth—they have disrupted many unions with their rule-or-ruin tactics and have left in their wake many saddened and disillusioned people, destroyed businesses and blasted hopes."[36] The ensuing expulsion of communist unions from the CIO in the late 1940s was a necessary precondition for the merger of the AFL and CIO in 1955, which Dubinsky helped to facilitate.[37]

"Small wonder," Danish mused, "that Dubinsky has over the years been the pet hate of the domestic Reds and their comrades abroad, who rarely mention his name without frothing at the mouth."[38] Progressive Labor was no exception to this rule. It missed no opportunity to castigate his policies as ILGWU president and vilify him personally. Although the animus behind PL's demonizing of Dubinsky undoubtedly reflected its antagonism toward his resolute anticommunism, PL attacked him for what it considered equally egregious errors that were more likely to be of concern to its potential working-class base.

The first of two articles by Milt Rosen decrying low wages in New York City appeared in the first issue of *PL* in January 1962. Rosen, sounding themes that would echo through PL's garment organizing for the next twenty years, laid the blame for the city's low wage problem at the doorstep of David Dubinsky's ILGWU, which Rosen accused of racism.[39] The ILGWU opposed minimum wage legislation in both New York City and New York State because it believed that a citywide or statewide minimum wage would hasten the industry's flight to areas with even lower wages. Teamsters' Union Joint Council 16 also complained that "the ILGWU has a vested interest in the perpetuation of exploitation, low-wage pockets, and poverty in New York City."[40] Joint Council 16's legislative director, Nicholas Kisberg, declared that New York City would soon qualify for the title "Sweatshop Capital of the World," and blamed the leadership of both the ILGWU and the Amalgamated Clothing Workers of America.[41]

Using Bureau of Labor Statistics figures cited by Kisberg, Milt Rosen pointed out that the average weekly wage earned by New York City's production workers was $84.36, dramatically lower than the $118.88 a week earned on average by production workers in the city of Detroit. He also alleged that the garment industry, which was New York City's largest industry, employing 300,000 workers, bore the primary responsibility for depressed wages among the city's production workers. Wages in the garment industry had increased only seven percent in the twelve years between 1948 and 1960, while the cost of living had risen thirty-three percent. To further dramatize the inadequacy of the wages earned by the city's production workers, Rosen called attention to the testimony given by James Dumpson, New York City Welfare Commissioner, in public hearings held at City Hall in February 1960. According to Dumpson, there were at least 375,000 people in New York City whose incomes were below the public assistance level. The most damning aspect of this dreary statistic was that most of the workers receiving supplementary public assistance were Black and Puerto Rican.[42]

Milt Rosen's second article on low wages in New York City, which appeared in the March 1962 issue of *Progressive Labor*, focused on the role of racism and the culpability of David Dubinsky in keeping the city's wages at a substandard level. "Jim Crow practices in the labor movement," Rosen charged, "are a big factor in the overall deterioration of the labor movement and its inability to achieve even its own modest goals." He blamed the labor movement for ignoring tens of thousands of unorganized Black and Puerto Rican workers, even after Local 1199's organizing success in New York City's voluntary hospitals had proved that these workers were "ready, willing and able to fight for their economic conditions."[43] Rosen's attack on racial segregation within the labor movement reflected both his training in the CP, which traditionally opposed racism in American society, and his appreciation of the antiracist struggle that was gathering momentum at the time.[44] Local 1199's organizing success among low-paid Black and Hispanic hospital workers, highlighted by Rosen, reflected the CP background of 1199's leaders, which enabled them to channel the animating spirit of the civil rights movement into militant trade unionism.[45]

Despite their profound political differences, the ILGWU, Local 1199 and *PL* were led by *men*.[46] If the labor movement largely ignored unorganized Black and Hispanic workers, Rosen ignored the equally compelling fact that organized labor, and *PL*, were male dominated.[47] The vast majority of both hospital workers and garment workers were women, and although they had decisively demonstrated their militancy in both industries, they were consistently disempowered by an almost exclusively male labor leadership in both the ILGWU and Local 1199.[48] Although highly critical of the labor movement's racism, *PL*'s male editors were less sensitive to the destructive role of sexism in the house of labor, and in their own movement.

For Rosen, the heart of New York City's low wage problem was the garment industry, and labor's biggest malefactor was the ILGWU's president, David Dubinsky. Rosen blamed Dubinsky for "being a willing partner in maintaining the incredibly low wage levels that exist in large sections of the industry." In the immediate post-World War II period, Rosen reminded his readers, New York workers were "among the highest paid and best organized in the country." While Rosen did not credit Dubinsky with having won these high postwar wages, he did blame Dubinsky for New York City's fall from grace as an exemplary labor town during the fifteen years that followed. Rosen concluded that "Dubinsky's policies remain the chief obstacle" to greater militancy by the AFL-CIO's New York City Central Labor Council.[49]

THE NEW YORK GARMENT INDUSTRY CRISIS, 1950–1960

To avoid being trampled by a stampede of runaway shops, the ILGWU committed itself to a strategy of keeping wages down in New York City to dissuade garment manufacturers from relocating to low-wage areas outside the city. The ILGWU's Charles Zimmerman threatened to resign from the Central Labor Council if it endorsed a New York City minimum wage of $1.50.[50] In the end, New York City garment workers were caught between the rock of runaway shops and the hard place of low wages. They were unable to escape either of these evils, which especially affected Black, Puerto Rican and female garment workers.[51]

Compared to other industries, garment industry wages had contracted during the fifteen years before Rosen's *PL* articles were published. Sociologist Robert Laurentz, whose study of ethnic and racial conflict in New York City's garment industry was critical of the ILGWU, observed that "immediately after postwar reconstruction had terminated, the New York garment industry began its gradual, irreversible decline." Laurentz found that wages in the garment industry declined "markedly" compared to wages for all manufacturing, and that this relative decline in garment wages was most dramatic for the highest-paying garment trades. He identified a variety of industry practices that inhibited the rate at which garment industry wages rose. Garment manufacturers shifted from skilled to semiskilled labor processes, used nonunion subcontractors, and relocated to low-wage areas outside the city—increasingly, to underdeveloped countries, where wages were extremely low. By 1961 the ILGWU's research director, Lazare Teper, complained that garment manufacturers' increasing tendency to produce abroad was "equivalent to a 'runaway shop' situation on an international scale."[52]

In response to this runaway shop situation, the ILGWU sanctioned the deskilling of the labor process in New York City's garment industry. This defeatist tactic, designed to save jobs and prevent the erosion of the union's membership rolls, had problematic results. Deskilling in the coat and suit industry, for example, contributed to ethnic, racial and gender stratification because it coincided with the influx of tens of thousands of Black and Puerto Rican women into the city's garment industry during and after the Second World War.[53] Thus, relocation was partially abated at the expense of semiskilled Puerto Rican and Black women who were supplanting Jewish and Italian craftsmen. They were denied the opportunity of advancing to more skilled jobs within their trade and the wages in their industry declined dramatically compared to the wages for all manufacturing. Thus, while the coat and suit trade had given Jewish and Italian workers, especially men, an opportunity to advance within the garment industry and in New York City's social structure, the trade became "nothing more than an embellished dead-end" for Puerto Rican and Black workers, especially women. Laurentz concluded that the ILGWU's overwhelmingly Jewish leadership was guilty of complicity in the development of this emerging system of "racial stratification" in New York City's garment industry.[54]

Dubinsky's progressivism had elicited support from an earlier generation of upwardly mobile Jewish and Italian garment workers. They had climbed out of the Great Depression of the 1930s under Dubinsky's leadership. Consequently, his approach to unionism remained unassailed, except by the Left, until the immediate postwar period.[55] However, as the conditions under which garment workers labored worsened, Dubinsky's ways looked less attractive to the ILGWU's new generation of economically marginalized Black and Puerto Rican members. They were trapped in dead-end, low-wage jobs. Besides being subjected to deteriorating real wages, Black and Puerto Rican garment workers were relegated to the bottom of a stratified labor force. Their employment possibilities were limited by discriminatory employer practices that dovetailed with the prejudices of the ILGWU's exclusive ethnic (Jewish and Italian) locals, which controlled the high-paying skilled crafts. In the context of the growing civil rights movement, the ILGWU's progressivism would be called into question by these rank-and-file members of the ILGWU, who experienced, in the words of the NAACP's Herbert Hill, "a profound sense of alienation and rejection from American society." Progressive Labor utilized Hill's analysis of the ILGWU to advance its own political agenda. But criticism from such mainstream sources as the NAACP would prove much more disturbing to the Dubinsky leadership than PL's shouts from the extreme left.[56]

CONGRESS INVESTIGATES THE ILGWU;
ANTIRACISM A WEDGE FOR PL

During the postwar era, opposition to racism within the ILGWU had gained momentum.[57] However, charges of racism by ILGWU members against the union's leadership did not gain a public hearing until prominent external critics interceded. In 1961 the NAACP's labor secretary, Herbert Hill, filed a complaint with the New York State Commission Against Discrimination alleging that Cutters' Local 10 had discriminated against Ernest Holmes, a New York garment worker, by refusing to admit him into membership even though he was employed as an assistant cutter. The commission found that there was "probable cause" to credit his allegation against Local 10, whose leadership threatened to seek vindication in the courts. Holmes finally agreed to drop the discrimination charge in exchange for Local 10's promise to assist him in becoming a qualified Local 10 cutter.[58]

According to Herbert Hill, the Holmes' case precipitated the congressional investigation of the New York City garment industry that was initiated in July 1962, soon after Rosen's PL articles appeared and just as the Progressive Labor Movement was being founded.[59] This investigation into the extent of discrimination, exploitation and corruption in the garment industry and the ILGWU was conducted by Congressman Herbert Zelenko's subcommittee of the House Committee on Education and Labor, chaired by Harlem Congressman Adam Clayton Powell. The ILGWU's leaders attempted to undermine their inquisitors' credibility by charging that their investigation was politically motivated, that Powell and Zelenko were retaliating against the ILGWU because the Liberal Party, its political ally, had declined to endorse them for another term of office.[60] Even if Powell's motives were suspect, there were still compelling reasons for inquiring into racism in the garment industry. Milt Rosen, who believed that "racism was rampant in the garment industry," and who held no brief for either Dubinsky or his congressional critics, accused Zelenko of holding hearings as a "last ditch effort" to "make a play for the Negro and Puerto Rican Vote" in the Twenty-third Congressional District, where many of the 130,000 Blacks and Puerto Ricans who worked in New York City's garment industry lived. However, despite the hearings, or because of them, Zelenko was defeated in the Democratic primary election by reform candidate William Fitts Ryan.[61] Gus Tyler, the ILGWU's education director, boasted that "Hundreds of ILGWU members—of whom a majority were Negroes and Puerto Ricans—threw themselves into a primary campaign to defeat the man who headed the Congressional investigation of Hill's charges."[62]

However, Zelenko's alleged inability to conduct the hearings effectively was of greater concern to Milt Rosen than the congressman's suspect motives for holding them. According to Rosen, Zelenko allowed the ILGWU's wily president, David Dubinsky, who was the main witness, to turn two months of hearings, during August and September 1962, into a "virtual fiasco" and a "farce."[63] By all reports, Dubinsky had his inquisitors by the tail. Stanley Levey, on page one of the *New York Times*, credited Dubinsky with having given a "virtuoso performance" at a subcommittee hearing. While conceding that the ILGWU was "not without sin," according to Levey, "Mr. Dubinsky, alternately roaring like a wounded lion or laughing like a pleased child, gave little ground."[64] A page one article in the *New York Herald Tribune* on the same day simply asked, "Dubinsky: Who's on Trial?"[65] John D. Pomfret later reported in the *New York Times*: "The subcommittee held hearings for four days in August. Observers said they believed Mr. Dubinsky fared better than Mr. Zelenko."[66]

As the hearings continued into September, Dubinsky maintained his aggressive stance. According to the *New York Daily Mirror*, Dubinsky "gave a convincing demonstration" of "how to confound a Congressional investigating committee." The *Mirror* explained how Dubinsky dominated the proceedings: he "took charge at the outset and turned the members of the House Labor Committee into a rapt audience for his performance. . . . He gesticulated, shook his fingers at the Congressmen, sometimes interrupted them and occasionally chuckled with satisfaction."[67] At one point, the *New York Times* reported, the ILGWU's president even offered to assume official control of the hearings from Livingston Wingate, the subcommittee counsel "who was fruitlessly interrogating him." An audacious Dubinsky told Zelenko, "I'll frame the questions for him. I'll ask the questions, and I'll give all the answers too."[68] For Rosen, however, Dubinsky's audacity did not adequately explain his ability to emerge from the hearings as "a martyr and the best friend the Negroes and the Puerto Ricans ever had." Rosen argued that the hearings were necessarily an exercise in hypocrisy because exposing Dubinsky "would get at the heart of the low wage situation in New York City—wages built on racist practices that guarantee millions in profits for New York bosses," who dominated the politicians conducting the hearings.[69]

However, some important issues were raised during the course of the investigation. The ILGWU had, for reasons of both expediency and racism, developed a Jim Crow setup in combined Local 60-60A. The highly paid members of Dress Pressers' Local 60, who were White, earned three times as much as the overwhelmingly Black and Hispanic membership of Local 60, who worked as shipping clerks. The NAACP charged that the ILGWU had belatedly organized the shipping clerks to prevent a rival union from gaining access to the garment industry, but made the clerks an appendage of Local 60 to prevent the election of the first Black to the position of local manager in the ILGWU.[70] When asked at the congressional hearings how many Blacks held an office higher than that of business agent in the 450,000 member ILGWU, Dubinsky shot back, "That's an unfair question. . . . Ask me how many Americans I got on my executive board." When he was no longer able to avoid answering, he admitted that not one Black held high office, but explained that this was "due to their failure to put themselves forward."[71] On another occasion before the subcommittee, Dubinsky, replying to an inquiry about the lack of Black and Hispanic representation on the ILGWU's general executive board, opposed the notion that "a man should be a union officer because of his race, color or creed," and affirmed, "He should be an officer on his merits, ability, character." Thus, Dubinsky implied that among the tens of thousands of Black and Hispanic men and women in the ILGWU there was not a single one qualified to be an executive officer.[72]

ILGWU "RACISTS" VERSUS "ANTI-SEMITIC" CRITICS

Although the congressional investigation had little immediate impact on the garment industry and the ILGWU, it ruptured the almost seamless web of public praise for the ILGWU's progressivism and encouraged further criticism of the contemporary ILGWU's policies, stirring a continuing controversy—in which Progressive Labor avidly participated.[73] Herbert Hill's testimony, which was excluded from the Congressional Record, started a controversy that took on a life of its own. Hill, besides being the NAACP's labor secretary, was a special consultant to Congressman Adam Clayton Powell's House Education and Labor Committee, whose subcommittee was investigating discrimination in the garment industry and the ILGWU. After members of the subcommittee stopped Hill from reading his prepared testimony into the Congressional Record—because it was not a factual statement, but "opinions, conclusions and characterizations"—he circulated it through the facilities of the NAACP.

As a result, Hill's statement became the basis of a serious rift between the NAACP and the ILGWU. Dubinsky asked the subcommittee to censure Hill for circulating his charges of discrimination against the ILGWU as testimony even though the subcommittee had not officially accepted his allegations.[74] In a letter to Powell, Congressman Burleson, Democrat of Texas, whom PL labeled a "Dixiecrat," contended that because Hill worked for the NAACP, which lobbied the United States Congress, his employment by Powell's committee "was obviously a conflict of interest." Burleson threatened not to honor pay vouchers for Hill and six other committee aids. However, in a letter to Burleson, Bishop Stephen Gill Spottswood, chairman of the NAACP's board of directors, endorsed Hill's employment with the Powell committee.[75]

Hill's *suppressed* statement found its way into the pages of the October 1962 issue of *Progressive Labor* in a lead article by Milt Rosen entitled "I.L.G.W.U.: Jim Crow and Dubinsky Rule." Rosen praised Hill for having done "consistent excellent work on exposing racism in the unions, Government, and industry." "Hill's work," Rosen wrote, "has consistently panicked racists of all kinds as he gets and publicizes the facts that are generally irrefutable."[76] What were Hill's *facts*? He charged that despite the ILGWU's public image, "carefully nurtured for many years by a very extensive and well-financed public relations campaign," Black and Puerto Rican members of the ILGWU were "discriminated against both in terms of their wages and conditions of employment and in their status as members of the union." Locals 10, 60 and 89, which controlled access to high-paying and stable jobs, Hill complained, were "lily-white." He also questioned the ILGWU's unwillingness to charter the "almost entirely black and Puerto Rican" Local 60A, which was combined with the "all-white" Pressers' Local 60. Hill charged that this peculiar arrangement was set up by the ILGWU leadership to prevent the almost certain election of a Black or Puerto Rican as local union manager. As a result of these and other ILGWU practices, all the general executive board members, vice-presidents, and local managers were White. In addition, Hill alleged that the ILGWU refused to allow its two locals in Puerto Rico to elect their own leadership.[77]

Hill also cited the Holmes' case and accused Moe Falikman, Local 10's manager, of refusing to select "non-whites" for training programs that would lead to membership in his local. In locals where there was a "major concentration of non-white workers," wages were "only a few cents above the bare minimum required by law," Hill alleged. Thus, Blacks and Puerto Ricans, with "no mobility," were trapped in "sweatshops." Hill connected this *unassailable fact* with the "fact that Negro and Puerto Rican members of the union," despite their significant numbers, "are excluded from top policy making positions." In an industry permeated by "an atmosphere of venality and corruption," he charged, the "real corruption, the real dry rot . . . is to be found in the discriminatory racial practices which victimize tens of thousands of Negro and Puerto Rican wage earners and their families."[78]

Not everyone agreed that Hill's facts were *irrefutable* or *unassailable*. Lester Granger, in the *Amsterdam News*, for example, wrote, "Regardless of Hill's motives, the 'facts' presented in his report were so sleazy that any ILGWU spokesman could tear them apart."[79] Gus Tyler, the ILGWU's education director, attempted to do just that. When Hill's statement appeared in the quarterly journal of socialist comment *New Politics*, it drew a sharp reply from Tyler in a subsequent issue of the same journal.

In "The Truth About the ILGWU," Tyler put Hill's charges "in perspective." Although the ILGWU did not "put a racial or religious tag on dues-payers," he estimated that the union had tens of thousands of "Negro and Spanish-speaking" members, who were "relative newcomers" to the ILGWU. The union admitted "all races, creeds and colors to its skilled craft locals, the cutters and pressers." The presence of two hundred Blacks and Hispanics in Cutters' Local 10 represented an "impressive demonstration of integration" in a trade with a small turnover rate and declining employment opportunities. Pressers' Local 89 was not "lily white," as Hill had charged, but simply "pure Italian." Black dress pressers, who worked in the same shops and under the same contract belonged to Local 60, which conducted its business in English. The union ran "extensive training and placement programs, especially for newcomers, and 90% of those being trained as skilled operators were Negroes and Puerto Ricans." The leadership of the ILGWU local in Puerto Rico was entirely Puerto Rican except for the manager, a "state-side man" who was appointed only after a Puerto Rican director of organization turned down the job. The ILGWU had an "unusual leadership training program" that aimed at developing leadership "reflective of the composition of the industry and the union." Union facilities were thoroughly integrated throughout the country, and the ILGWU was a recognized "force in civil rights movements."[80]

Tyler provided, with a few notable exceptions, detailed, although not necessarily persuasive, answers to Hill's individual charges. He denied, for example, that the mostly Black and Hispanic Shipping Clerks' Local 60A deserved to be called "Jim Crow" any more than the all-Black Sleeping Car Porters' Union deserved that infamous label. Tyler bristled at the suggestion that the ILGWU had refused to grant Local 60A a separate charter to prevent the election of a Black local manager. No single ethnic group constituted a majority of the Local 60A membership. However, more telling to Tyler, was Hill's assumption that the local's membership, however constituted, would cast a "racial" vote. He pointed out that the predominantly gentile American Federation of Labor had elected Samuel Gompers, a Jew, as its president for more than thirty years. More recently, the predominantly Protestant United States had elected John F. Kennedy, a Catholic, as president. Even more pointedly, however, Tyler called attention to the fact that the NAACP had chosen a "white Jew as its labor secretary." Tyler made the malice behind this observation evident when he accused Hill of using anonymous sources to smear the union. "To characterize a union or any body of humans by the anonymous smear," Tyler argued, "—the great mark of McCarthyism, of the anti-Semite, of the white racist, of the bigot—is hardly 'evidence.' This is the lynch spirit."[81]

Hill later realized that charging the ILGWU with racism would elicit "anguished cries of 'anti-Semite,' " a charge "too obscene, too rotten to permit a dignified comment." Hill had anticipated that his analysis of the ILGWU would be "met with the fury with which any powerful and entrenched bureaucracy retaliates when challenged." However, he did not foresee the "viciousness and hysteria" of the ILGWU leadership's personal attacks against him, culminating in the charge, made "publicly and in corridors," that he was "a Jewish anti-Semite, a kind of McCarthyite, and in the camp of the Birchites." Even more incredible to Hill, a member of the ILGWU staff allegedly informed various congressmen and other public officials that Hill was "a Communist stirring up racial strife, an anti-Semite, etc."[82]

Why was the Dubinsky leadership striking out "so wildly" and with "such malevolence" at him? Hill attributed this "grotesque" reaction to "a sense of guilt among those who have led the ILGWU from what it was yesterday to what it has become today." Characterizing the ILGWU's *progressive* label as no more than a "nostalgic hangover," Hill argued that the contemporary ILGWU no longer possessed the qualities of militancy, internal democracy and social vision suggested by the word *progressive*.[83]

Hill was not alone in believing that the ILGWU no longer deserved its progressive reputation. Union activist and labor analyst Paul Jacobs acknowledged that the ILGWU was for a long time "one of America's most far sighted and socially conscious unions," but he argued that "the corrosive effects of institutionalized power have eaten away at the idealistic underpinnings which once marked it in a very special way." Jacobs, who was proud to have been an ILGWU organizer, delineated his critique of the contemporary ILGWU in an article entitled "David Dubinsky: Why His Throne is Wobbling," which appeared in *Harpers Magazine* in December 1962. Jacobs described two "ugly quarrels" that revealed "deep dissatisfaction" with the union. According to Jacobs, Dubinsky used "every legal, financial and organizational resource of the ILGWU to smash" the Federation of Union Representatives, a group of ILGWU organizers, business agents and educational directors formed in 1959 to seek a collective bargaining agreement with the ILGWU. Jacobs traced Dubinsky's dictatorial style and irrational fear of FOUR factionalism to the traumatic battle against the communists in the 1920s, in which Dubinsky had played a decisive role.[84]

Even uglier than the FOUR controversy was the quarrel over Hill's allegations of ILGWU racism, charges which Jacobs, to some extent, supported. Jacobs decried the relative decline of garment wages, which were "often not more than the federal minimum wage," as well as the possibility that "Negroes and Puerto Ricans were being barred from locals that controlled the more highly skilled jobs." However, for Jacobs, the "tragedy" of the ILGWU was that "the leaders do not understand the membership of 'their' union." He explained, "A far deeper cultural empathy and common tradition exist today between the Jewish ILGWU leaders and the Jewish employers—many of them former garment workers themselves—than exist between the leaders and the members." This cultural gap was reflected in the union's contributions, which Jacobs alleged were disproportionately given to Jewish organizations, an allegation that the ILGWU denied.[85]

The *Jewish Daily Forward,* which Jacobs characterized as a "rightwing social-democratic paper, intimately attached to Dubinsky and the union," declared that, "Two Jewish young men, Hill and Jacobs, spread anti-Semitic poison against the ILGWU and against President Dubinsky." Tyler's response to Hill was circulated by both Harry Fleischman, Director of the American Jewish Committee's National Labor Service, and Emanuel Muravchik, National Field Director of the Jewish Labor Committee. A memorandum by Muravchik alleging that the NAACP's criticism of the ILGWU "contributes to anti-Semitic feelings" was answered by Roy Wilkins, the NAACP's executive director. Wilkins affirmed that Hill was employed to "maintain anti-discrimination work in the employment field as his top and only priority." Wilkins emphasized that Hill's loyalties were not divided: "He is not for trade unions first and Negro workers second." An angry ILGWU vice-president, Charles Zimmerman, resigned from the NAACP's Legal Defense Fund in retaliation for Wilkin's support of Hill, who was also supported by the Negro American Labor Council. The ILGWU rounded up support from various influential quarters, including the Black union leader A. Philip Randolph, the socialist Norman Thomas and the New York City Central Labor Council.[86]

This dispute revealed the potential for a serious rift in the alliance between Blacks and Jews in New York City.[87] Apparently, there already was a breach between Jews who were primarily worried about anti-Semitism and those for whom the victimization of Blacks and Hispanics was of greater concern (perhaps because in the minds of some American Jews, Blacks and Hispanics, as social outcasts—the *other* against which many White Americans defined themselves—were surrogates for Jews). However, the consciences of most Jews were probably divided to some extent between being troubled by racism and fearing anti-Semitism. In view of their own history as victims of discrimination, Jewish leaders were, understandably, sensitive to the suggestion that they were impli- cated, even if inadvertently, in racism, and especially sensitive to such charges made by fellow Jews. By victimizing others, Jews would sacri- fice their right to scorn anti-Semites, and lower the social barriers to their own persecution. Moreover, with a large and growing Black and Puerto Rican membership, the ILGWU leadership also had practical reasons for being concerned about Hill's charges. Undoubtedly, the ILGWU hurled charges of anti-Semitism at Hill partly to deflect criticism from itself.[88]

For Jews such as Hill and Jacobs, who viewed Blacks and Puerto Ri- cans as the chief victims of discrimination, the charge that they were Jewish anti-Semites was obviously wounding and infuriating, as it was meant to be. Jacobs admittedly had worried that referring to the "Jewish aspect of the ILGWU's role" would be interpreted as anti-Semitic, but decided that it was "intellectually correct" to go forward. However, he was emotionally shocked when he received "horrible mail" from anti- Semites congratulating him for exposing "the role of Jews in running the unions." He learned "how uneasy we still are about Jews in America—all of us Jews and Christians alike." Jews who inadvertently played into anti-Semites' hands by accusing Jewish leaders of racism might very well feel guilty. Thus, Jews on each side of this controversy could be conflicted.[89]

However, PL's Jewish leaders gave no indication that they perceived a contradiction between resistance to racism and opposition to anti-Semi- tism. As communists, they viewed capitalism as the cause of these twin evils. Communists saw society as mainly divided into two antagonistic so- cial classes, a hegemonic capitalist class and an exploited working class, rather than in terms of ethnicity, race, and gender. Anti-Semitism, racism and sexism were aspects of capitalist ideology that served to exploit workers, deflect their anger, and destroy the unity that was crucial to their fight for progressive reforms and ultimately for socialist revolution.[90] PL's Jewish leaders gave no indication that they were conflicted about their conclusion that anti-Black racism was the "main tool the ruling class has to divide the working class," and more crucial to combat than any other divisive doctrine. In view of the deep roots of racism in America and the titanic, inspiring and increasingly radical struggle being waged by Blacks against racism at the time—a struggle which polarized public opinion—this was a realistic assessment. The party rarely mentioned anti-Semitism, which had declined in the United States since the Second World War.[91]

Nevertheless, the subtext of Progressive Labor's principled opposition to racism was its palpable anti-Nazi animus.[92] Clearly, one did not have to be Jewish to hate Nazism, whose tens of millions of victims were of many nationalities and religions. However, in view of the Holocaust, it is worth noting that most of PL's leaders were Jewish. For some of them, World War II was a living memory. Milt Rosen, for example, served as an infantryman in the U.S. Army in Italy.[93] In declaring war on "U.S. imperialism" in 1965, the newly founded PLP declaimed, "In the remotest corner of the earth, the initials U.S.A., which once stood for hope, have replaced the crooked cross of Nazi Germany as the symbol of tyranny and death."[94] This implied channeling anger at Nazi anti-Semitism into the fight against American racism. Members of PL could only preserve their moral integrity in America by fighting racism, that is, by refusing to be *good Germans*. Progressive Labor believed that Nazism, the most virulent form of anti-Semitism, like all forms of fascism, was a product of decaying capitalism; and communists had defeated fascism, ending its concomitant genocidal practices.[95] In the United States, combating anti-Black racism was an integral aspect of socialist revolution. To those who were incensed by anti-Semitism and racism, PL promised that socialist revolution would annihilate all forms of discrimination.[96] Given their assessment of American society and sense of revolutionary priorities, then, PL's Jewish leaders, impelled as they were by intense anti-Nazi sentiments, focused much more on fighting racism than on combatting anti-Semitism.[97]

TRESPASSING ON "DUBINSKY'S PLANTATION"

Milt Rosen began his critique of the ILGWU's new contract with the jobbers' and contractors' associations in 1964 by declaring, "Two hundred thousand Negro and Puerto Rican garment workers in New York are going to be working under slave-like conditions on 'Dubinsky's Plantation' for at least the next three years." By portraying New York City's garment center as an antebellum slave plantation and Dubinsky as its master, Rosen created a powerful image that rhetorically collapsed the century that separated Blacks from their historical roots in slavery and the many miles that separated them from their origins in the rural South. In other words, Rosen equated their current condition as *wage slaves* to their former condition as chattel slaves. Rosen's rhetoric resonated with the strong antiracist animus aroused by the civil rights rebellion that had begun in the deep South and spread to northern cities, including New York. The movement rapidly became more militant as it progressed. Only four and a half years elapsed between the first sit-in, which took place in Greensboro, North Carolina in February 1960 and the first of the 1960s ghetto rebellions, which erupted in New York.[98]

In the summer of 1964, only a few months after Rosen's article appeared, Black resentment against racism in New York City erupted in a major ghetto rebellion in Harlem, which was sparked by the police shooting of fifteen-year-old James Powell. Thousands of posters, reading "Wanted For Murder, Gilligan the Cop" and bearing a picture of the officer involved, were circulated by the PLM's Harlem Defense Council, and a PLM rally and march defied Mayor Robert F. Wagner, Jr.'s temporary ban on such activities in Harlem. "The big-money boys downtown are running scared," PL's newspaper *Challenge* observed; and added, "They have seen the writing on the bloodstained walls of Harlem."[99] William Epton, who had been a member of the Negro American Labor Council, and other PLM leaders were indicted by a Manhattan grand jury for inciting to riot and for violating an old New York State law against anarchist conspiracy. Progressive Labor's activities in Harlem were later investigated by the House Committee on Un-American Activities, which held hearings on "Subversive Influences in Riots, Looting and Burning" in 1967, by which time ghetto rebellions had broken out in numerous cities.[100] The committee chairman, Edwin E. Willis of Louisiana, concluded that "subversive elements played a major and probably the key role in precipitating the Harlem riot of July 1964." Willis also concluded that of the various organizations that acted to inflame the community, Progressive Labor Party "clearly" played the "most important role." Although they were bitter antagonists, HUAC and PL shared—for different reasons—the same inflated sense of PL's importance. Progressive Labor sought to gain a reputation for militant antiracism and HUAC needed to justify its investigations by discovering a communist threat to law and order.[101]

To PL, some of the frustrations that created the context for that rebellion may have originated in what Rosen called the "twin evils of low-pay and racism" in the garment industry, which the ILGWU's new contract in the dress industry did "nothing" to alleviate.[102] Milt Rosen's characterization of Dubinsky as the slave master of a garment plantation was meant to widen the breach that, according to Paul Jacobs and Herbert Hill, existed between the ILGWU leadership and the union's Black and Hispanic members. Because the ILGWU was not a garment manufacturer, the plantation analogy seems inapt, but the union was a "major regulatory force" in the garment industry, and its single most powerful institution.[103] Rosen's plantation metaphor implied that PL would play the part of abolitionist in the garment center. However, to do so meant discrediting the liberal ILGWU's ties to the existing civil rights movement, whose nonviolent philosophy PL disparaged. Rosen scoffed, ". . . racist Dubinsky sends checks to the integration movement (particularly CORE) in a new kind of protection racket (I'll protect your racket if you protect mine)." Rosen was confident that "Despite these checks, Negro and Puerto Rican garment workers will find the ways and means to organize themselves—to introduce the revolutionary fervor of the Freedom movement into the industry, paving the way for the destruction of Dubinsky's plantation."[104]

Progressive Labor, inspired by Black militancy, tried to introduce its own kind of revolutionary fervor into both the civil rights movement and the garment district. Two of the five colonizers whom PL sent into New York City's garment district had previously been sent to Monroe, North Carolina to carry on, after their own fashion, the work of Robert F. Williams, a Black nationalist who had broken with the nonviolent NAACP to advocate armed self-defense. He subsequently fled to Cuba in August 1961 to escape kidnapping charges.[105] Even though PL's brief mission to Monroe failed to achieve lasting results there, the five PLers who participated in the project gained valuable organizing experience. However, until two of them became garment workers in the latter part of the 1960s, PL relied on its periodicals and street orators to reach garment workers with its message.

Milt Rosen, who had written PL's first articles on the garment industry, found the ILGWU's new three-year contract in the dress industry, signed in 1964, contemptible. According to Rosen, before the new contract, the majority of garment workers had been averaging $56 a week, making them "just about the lowest-paid production workers in any industry in the country." However, the new contract only provided a "big ol' average pay raise of about $6.00 a week—spread out over three years." Given the ten to twelve per cent increases in prices and taxes that Rosen expected, this "raise" would lead to a decline in real wages for the majority of garment workers. In contrast, the cutters, whom Rosen characterized as the "lily-white princes of the industry," were slated for a $14 a week raise, which he thought was "really nothing to brag about, except that it's so much better than the Negro and Puerto Rican workers will get." Besides, the contract provided no guarantee of a minimum yearly wage and no protection against speed-up or seasonal layoffs. Rosen also accused the ILGWU of maintaining low wages by allowing shops to leave the central garment market and then failing to organize them, even when they moved no farther than Brooklyn or the Bronx. "Somehow," a contemptuous Rosen concluded, "Dubinsky, militant red-baiter—and 'protector' of the workers all over the world who are being 'threatened by the communist menace'—cannot protect garment workers five miles away in Brooklyn, despite the ILGWU's multi-million dollar treasury."[106]

The first issue of the Progressive Labor Movement's newspaper, *Challenge*, carried an article by Milt Rosen attacking President Lyndon B. Johnson's visit to New York City, on 6 June 1964, to honor President Dubinsky of the ILGWU. Two days before Johnson addressed the ILGWU at the High School of Fashion Industries, PL held a rally at Thirty-eighth Street and Eighth Avenue, in the heart of the crowded garment district. The mainstream press did not cover PL's small garment rallies, but Rosen reported in *Challenge* that "hundreds of workers listened and were in agreement with the need to set up a rank-and-file caucus to begin the hard job of returning the union to the hands of the workers." One hundred workers signed petitions issued by PL's Garment Rank-and-File Committee, which called for "action to end low wages, racism, unemployment and sweatshops in the garment industry." On the day of Johnson's speech honoring Dubinsky, PL distributed four thousand leaflets calling the ILGWU leader the "leading racist in New York."[107]

According to Rosen, Johnson's audience that day was composed of a "collection of political stooges," which included Mayor Wagner, "George (I've never been on strike in my life) Meany," and "ILGWU pie-cards mixed with hundreds of white, high-paid, old-time ILGWU members in their sixties." This remark, which one could consider anti-White, anti-Semitic and ageist, was directed at the ILGWU's ageing labor aristocracy of highly skilled Jewish and Italian tailors and cutters. Even though the majority of the ILGWU's membership was Black, Puerto Rican and female, the ILGWU's highest paid crafts were dominated by White men, as was the ILGWU's top leadership. Rosen did not mention the gender of the participants, but it seems probable that most were male, even though the ILGWU's membership was predominantly female. In any case, Rosen disbelieved Johnson's declaration that "We will continue the hundred year struggle to give every American—of every race and color—equal opportunity in American society." Rosen scoffed, "What made Johnson's words appear more phoney and arrogant than usual was the virtual absence of Negro and Puerto Rican workers from the meeting." As for the honoree, Rosen denounced his "jim crow, boot licking policies," which made "New York the 20th lowest major city in wages in the country." Dubinsky's fight against poverty, Rosen thought, amounted to a "fight for poverty" that Johnson was preparing to emulate in a "war on the poor." Rosen did not share Johnson's optimistic view that racism was being progressively diminished by liberal reforms. In his article, which appeared just five weeks before the Harlem rebellion erupted, Rosen observed, "Every Negro and Puerto Rican Neighborhood is like an armed camp as the people begin to fight the slumlords and the police."[108]

When there were no major events to report, *Challenge* carried stories about individual garment workers whose experiences, in PL's view, showed that the ILGWU was guilty of complicity in the industry's maltreatment of its members. One such case, reported by PLer Steve Martinot, involved a sixty-eight-year-old unemployed female garment worker, whom Martinot called Mrs. Blum. She was forced to seek employment when the ILGWU raised the requirements for retirement from twenty years with the union and five years of consecutive work to twenty-five years with the union and ten years of consecutive work. She found a union job sewing hems on dresses with a felling machine, which was her skill area. The job paid $65 a week. However, when she arrived for work, the employer informed her that she would also be required to do some pinking, and that she would be paid at the rate for pinkers, which was only $50 a week. Three months later, the employer proposed that she go on unemployment insurance and work part-time off the books. Even though all the other workers in the shop had accepted this arrangement, Mrs. Blum refused. She told Martinot, "I'm no parasite, and I don't cheat anybody." Her part-time work as a machine feller ended shortly thereafter when she was unable to comply with her employer's request to do hand felling. After thirty-two years in the ILGWU, she was again seeking employment to qualify for a union pension. To Martinot, a union that would let this happen "certainly isn't the fighting organization a union should be."[109]

Another case of alleged wrongdoing by the ILGWU came to the attention of Wally Linder, PL's labor secretary. An older woman who had "helped to organize" the ILGWU explained how frustrated she was that the business agents of Embroiderers, Pleating and Allied Crafts Local 66 would "join the bosses to fight the workers." The ILGWU's contracts required that work during the slow season be shared equally among the workers in each shop. However, when she returned to her shop sometime after being laid off, she "found people working." Her employer told her that he would keep whom he wanted. When she complained to union officials, they accepted the employer's answer that she "smoked and talked" too much. On her next job, she was fired after complaining about the shop's employment of a nonunion worker. The forelady told her that the nonunion employee was none of her business. Union inaction forced her to sit out the season collecting unemployment checks. When union officials finally dealt with her case, they accepted the employer's "lies" that she "made mistakes that never existed." The union asked her, "Why do you want to work in a place where you're not wanted?" The "fiery old garment worker" concluded her story, by waving "her hand in disbelief." To Linder, the "frustration in her eyes" reflected her discovery that she now had "two bosses to fight: the one who owns the shop and the ILGWU union 'leader' who sees to it that no one interferes in the boss' running of that shop." Linder concluded, "It is pretty obvious that nowhere is a rank-and-file revolution needed more urgently than in the sweatshops of Seventh Avenue."[110]

Progressive Labor presented these carefully chosen anecdotes as emblematic of a pattern of collusion that it believed existed between garment employers and ILGWU officials. In painting a broad picture of poverty and racism in New York City's garment district, PL's Wally Linder dubbed David Dubinsky "The King of Hell." Borrowing a theme from Michael Harrington, Linder argued that "The area bounded by 34th and 41st Sts. and 7th and 9th Aves. contains some of the worst examples of concentrated poverty anywhere in the United States." Workers earning only $50 a week "pushing dress racks through streets or manufacturing garments inside sweatshop lofts" were, according to Linder, "at the bottom of the heap on which a $400,000,000 'union' empire has been built, a veritable plantation headed by 'boss-man' Dubinsky." Linder estimated that if the minimum wage in New York were raised to $1.50 per hour, "at least 100,000 workers in the garment center would get a wage increase." Moreover, the primary victims of this "super-exploitation" were the more than 125,000 "Negro and Puerto Rican" workers employed in the New York garment industry. Linder argued that Herbert Hill's charge that

"Negroes and Puerto Ricans" were barred from the high-paying crafts could easily be verified. "Just walk into shop after shop in the garment center," he suggested, "and try to find one in the cutting rooms." While President Johnson, the New York City labor movement and the press all acclaimed Dubinsky, "tens of thousands of Negro and Puerto Rican workers," Linder concluded, "are forced to work at sub-standard wages, with no job security, no paid vacations, and absolutely no say in union affairs."[111]

Even well written articles were more likely to be read if they emanated from an organization with a presence in the garment center. Before PL was able to send colonizers into the garment shops, it relied on street rallies to attract the attention of garment workers. The size and intensity of these rallies depended on the issues that were being addressed. Progressive Labor linked the ongoing concerns of garment workers about their wages and working conditions to the broader political issues of the day. For example, on 28 July 1964, in the immediate aftermath of the Harlem rebellion, PL's Harlem Solidarity Committee called a noon-time rally at the corner of Eighth Avenue and Thirty-eighth Street. Mark Shapiro reported in *Challenge* that more than 1,000 people listened to various speakers "attack the mayor and his whole police state apparatus." Milt Rosen's lead-off speech called for the dismissal of police chief "Bull" Murphy, the arrest and prosecution of "killer-cop" Gilligan, open grand jury hearings, dismissal of the injunction restraining PLM, the Harlem Defense Council and the Community Council on Housing from demonstrating in Harlem, and impeachment of Mayor Wagner. Shapiro affirmed that despite anticommunist heckling and other disruptions, "Loud applause and a virtually unanimous show of hands" indicated that workers supported each of Rosen's proposals.[112]

At another anti-injunction rally on 5 August 1964, a crowd of garment workers lined both sides of the street to hear various PL speakers, while "police and detectives wandered up and down in front of them." Milt Rosen declared, "When you fight the bosses and their set-up, they bring their courts to break you." *Challenge*'s editor, Fred Jerome, sarcastically claimed that the "big money boys never do anything wrong." He accused the ruling class of habitually blaming their victims, whether slum dwellers or Vietnamese peasants, for their own crimes, and angrily concluded, "The dollar buys freedom from guilt." Milt Rosen, alluding to the Nazi era, concluded by declaring, "This week it's Progressive Labor; next week it's the unions and the people."[113]

The following summer, on 15 June 1965, dozens of garment work-

ers listened to Milt Rosen allege that the same people who were exploiting them in the garment shops were responsible for bombing workers in
Santo Domingo and Vietnam. He also charged that New York City's
Wagner administration was indicting Harlem PL leader Bill Epton because he exposed their plans to "stifle the protest of the ghetto with police clubs and bullets." *Challenge* reporter Felipe DeJesus, who
addressed the crowd in Spanish, was applauded when he asked, "Where
were Johnson's marines when Trujillo was slaughtering thousands of
Dominican workers?" DeJesus charged that the United States had landed
20,000 troops in the Dominican Republic to protect the interests of corporations such as the United Fruit Company. "But," he added, "they
don't lift a finger to raise the wages of Puerto Ricans here or on the island. And meanwhile Dubinsky makes a pile on our backs." Citing the
"complete sellout of the garment workers at the recent Miami Beach
convention of the ILGWU, where Dubinsky's salary was raised to
$31,000 and the workers' dues hiked 50c a month," Wally Linder called
on garment workers to form rank-and-file committees to overthrow the
Dubinsky regime. Progressive Labor promised to become a regular presence in the garment center.[114]

Two weeks later, on 29 June 1965, even "bigger crowds" of garment
workers gathered to hear PL speakers at the party's "bi-weekly noon-
hour street meeting at 38th St. and 8th Ave." Even if everyone on the
street, normally crowded at midday, stopped to listen, PL speakers would
only be heard by a tiny percentage of the garment workforce. However,
Challenge was encouraged by the response of garment workers, who
"leaned out of garment loft windows and stopped at all four corners to
listen." They heard Bill Epton, Harlem candidate for the New York State
Senate, denounce New York City police officers who were picketing City
Hall that day to protest the creation of a civilian review board. "Those
cops," Epton charged, "who don't want any investigation into their criminal acts, are walking around City Hall with members of the American
Nazi Party." When the police later attempted to clear the crowded sidewalks, the Harlem Defense Council's David Douglas told his listeners
not to be intimidated, and alleged that the police "didn't want them to
hear the truth." Felipe DeJesus pointed out that "while the government
spends millions of the workers' tax dollars to build bases in Puerto Rico
aimed at stifling people's revolutions in Latin America, it doesn't lift a
finger to raise the minimum wage in New York above $1.25."[115]

The following summer, PL held a garment rally to protest the attempted assassination of civil rights leader James Meredith. Attracting

only forty people did not deter PL or dampen its enthusiasm. Progressive Labor linked its condemnation of "Johnson's war of aggression in Vietnam" to his "protection of Southern racists." Two independent candidates for Congress, Hal Levin and Leslie Silberman, who were running on a "U.S. get out of Vietnam" platform, addressed the small crowd. Levin observed that the "Democratic Administration drops napalm on Vietnamese and at the same time is allied with Southern racists who kill Black people." Calling on his audience to defend their democratic rights, he defiantly declared, "No tinhorn racist cowboy from Texas will stop us!" Silberman asked, ". . . how can a government that is responsible for the burning of babies in Vietnam with napalm bombs protect freedom here at home?" After highlighting anecdotal evidence that people were "on the move," she proclaimed, "We won't be stopped until we can determine our own destiny." Jim Houghton, director of the Harlem Unemployment Council, proposed, "The answer to those who conduct a war of genocide, to racism, to poverty in the ghettos and to the rotten sweatshop conditions right here in the garment center—the answer to all these reactionary policies of the same government is for the rank and file to organize ourselves against them."[116]

As the rally continued, PL speakers took the microphone. These included Felipe DeJesus, the new editor of *Desafío*, the Spanish language version of *Challenge*, and PL's two leading spokesmen, Milt Rosen and Bill Epton. The rally was held shortly after David Dubinsky retired, ending his long tenure as ILGWU president, but DeJesus still used the name *Dubinsky* as an epithet to disparage the ILGWU leadership.[117] He proclaimed, "The 40,000 Puerto Rican garment workers are a tremendous potential force right here in New York to fight for their own organization and throw out the Dubinsky-type misleaders who sit on our backs." Rosen declaimed, "The kind of 'freedom' that gunned down James Meredith is the same kind of 'freedom' that garment workers had to vote for a union president to replace Dubinsky—none at all." "How then can they bring 'freedom' to Vietnam?" Rosen rhetorically asked. He concluded by enjoining, "Not a drop of workers' blood for the bosses' dirty profits in Vietnam!" Epton warned his listeners that the "open, public gunning down of James Meredith, like the public murder of James Powell two years ago, is meant to create terror among the people, that this will happen to you if you 'step out of line.'" He advised, "What we must fight for is a socialist society where we determine what happens to our lives, not the rich bosses who send us to fight their dirty imperialist war in Vietnam." Progressive Labor concluded by renewing its perennial pledge to return *regularly* to discuss the issues and to "help organize against the conditions under which we all suffer."[118]

However, PL's street rallies were hardly likely to transform the garment center soon, even if they were as well attended and enthusiastically greeted by garment workers as PL—imbued with revolutionary optimism—claimed. Progressive Labor's hopes for a more immediate labor revolution in garment had quickened, though, when District 65, Retail, Wholesale and Department Store Workers' Union organized a march of four thousand workers through the garment center on 28 April 1965. The editors of *Challenge* were inspired: "The sight of thousands of workers, organized and unorganized, black, white and Puerto Rican, marching through the garment center in a demonstration demanding higher wages, unionization, decent working conditions and an end to discrimination could send shudders down the backs of the bosses and their servants in City Hall." However, neither District 65, which had a thirty-year history of organizing in the garment center, nor any other union had challenged the "corruption and intense exploitation" that, according to PL, dominated "Dubinsky's plantation."[119]

Progressive Labor argued that to defeat the "unholy alliance" between the garment employers and the ILGWU, it would be necessary to attack all the conditions that constituted the status quo in garment: slave wage levels; blatant discrimination; sweetheart contracts; racketeers; the "'extra-special' exploitation of more than 100,000 women"; ghetto housing and school conditions; "reactionary labor 'leaders'" in New York City's Central Labor Council, one-third of whose membership belonged to the ILGWU; and the "policies of the 'liberal' Democratic City Administration." Progressive Labor recognized that challenging all these egregious conditions would be extremely difficult: "To buck such a gang up is admittedly no small job. These conditions mean billions in profits for the bosses and banks." However, PL estimated that it could be done if District 65 mobilized all its members, especially in garment, in a "shop-by-shop organizational campaign" that would involve constant picketing, support from other unions, such as the teamsters, and unity with the Black and Spanish-speaking communities. In a messianic mood, PL envisioned that such a campaign would "speed a new alliance" and "drive the corporate money-changers out of their Wall Street temples and reclaim our City for the working people on whose toil and sweat the whole world turns."[120]

However, District 65 refused to organize such a fight, *Challenge* alleged, on the grounds that it could not "organize within Dubinsky's 'jurisdiction.'"[121] Progressive Labor praised the District 65 contract, which gave several thousand 65ers a $15 wage increase, promises of training and upgrading for "Afro-American" and Puerto Rican workers, and other benefits as well. While the members of District 65, who handled piece goods headed for dress and cloak manufacturers, would not grow rich from their $95 a week wage—and in some cases as much as $125—they were doing considerably better than the tens of thousands of unorganized workers and those within the ILGWU's jurisdiction who earned from $40 to $50 a week. District 65ers had made a good start, *Challenge* believed, but to really make New York a union town, which District 65 had advocated, it would be necessary for "honest, rank-and-file trade unionists to organize the non-union and victimized sections of the garment center." To those who believed that it couldn't be done, *Challenge* recalled the District 65 members who "fought the bosses, the goons, the cops, the anti-labor laws and the phoney politicians back in 1937—and organized the CIO in the garment center." Progressive Labor hoped to do something similar.[122] Small cadres had rallied small numbers, but PL—driven by the unflagging conviction that it spoke for all the workers—ignored smallness, seeing hundreds as a wedge to open further organizing doors. However, PL's garment center organizing would depend on the commitment and competence of a few carefully chosen cadres.

CHAPTER 5

The Making of a Communist Trucker

The Political Apprenticeship of a Progressive Labor Colonizer in Garment Trucking, 1940–1966

Progressive Labor's attempt to establish a communist beachhead within New York City's garment industry began in earnest in the mid-1960s. It sent a few of its best organizers to get jobs in New York City's garment center to lead garment workers in struggle at the point of production and recruit them to the party. The success of PL's strategy in garment depended in part on the quality of these college-educated, twenty-something, White, male party organizers. What experiences prepared these young PLers to become communist *colonizers* in New York City's garment industry?[1] This chapter examines the backgrounds of two PL garment colonizers, particularly the political apprenticeship of PL's leading garment organizer, Edward Lemansky.[2]

IRREGULAR GARMENT WORKERS

Lemansky and his fellow colonizers were able to get work in what the party characterized as the strategically important garment trucking industry—where "tens of thousands of mainly black and Latin workers" formed the "bulk of the work-force" that was the "life-blood of the city's largest industry." If thousands of drivers, mechanics, helpers and rack pushers "were to go on a unified city-wide strike," PL suggested, "the whole garment industry would collapse." As PL viewed it, Black and Hispanic garment truckers were racially oppressed and economically exploited workers whose revolutionary potential could be realized through PL's leadership. Progressive Labor envisaged leading them in a shut-down of New York City's major industry.[3]

Focusing on what it regarded as awful working conditions in garment trucking, PL was sanguine about the possibility of organizing a major strike. *Challenge* painted a vivid picture of the life of garment truckers:

> Sloshing through rain-soaked streets, dodging the densest all-day commercial traffic in the U.S., "drinking-in" the fumes of thousands of cars and trucks, hoisting hand trucks laden with hundreds of pounds of packed cartons from street to curb, running metal racks packed with dresses, coats, etc., outdoors in heat, cold and sleet, driving trucks that make 40 or more stops a day in a 50 to 60-hour week, with failing brakes, no heaters, defective lights—all to take home as low as. . . .[4]

If the garment industry was New York City's industrial heartland, it was these garment truckers—working hard under uncomfortable and dangerous conditions for relatively low wages—who formed the "fast and cheap" transportation system that linked thousands of small garment shops together into the city's major industry.[5]

However, even if PL was correct in believing that there were ample reasons for garment truckers to rebel and bring the "billion-dollar" garment industry "crashing down," that did not guarantee that they would rebel or that PL would be able to lead the rebellion if it occurred. Unlike PL's organizers, garment workers depended on their hard, low-paying jobs in the garment center in order to survive. As a PL garment trucker passionately put it, "The garment district in New York is where the poor go when they're down and out, and need a job, any kind of job, it doesn't matter how bad, how miserable, how degrading, as long as they can make a few bucks."[6] Consequently, even if garment truckers were as angry as PL supposed, they were likely to assess the risks of rebelling differently than PLers who took jobs as garment truckers solely for the purpose of fomenting a rebellion, and whose own real life prospects were not circumscribed by conditions in the garment industry.[7] Even though party organizers were able to light a surprising number of brush fires in their shops (which both employers and union officials scrambled to put out), the notion that they could ignite a major rebellion in garment trucking was probably unrealistic and could be construed as paternalistic.

Ironically, PL initiated its campaign to organize garment workers for communist revolution among garment truckers, who, arguably, were not garment workers at all. The ILGWU's president, David Dubinsky, an acknowledged authority on New York City's garment industry, affirmed before Congress, "They are teamsters, they are not regular garment workers."[8] Although Dubinsky made this remark to distance himself and the ILGWU leadership from the allegedly questionable practices of Local 102, the ILGWU's local for garment truckers in New York City, there was some truth in it.[9] Garment truckers, *Challenge* admitted, did not fit the "usual image" of garment workers "manipulating the intricate moves of a sewing or cutting machine, following designs and patterns of dresses or suits or children's clothing, pressing garments with steam irons, or putting together the various parts of garments sewn by others."[10] In fact, PLer Felipe DeJesus, who led a major strike of factory workers in New York City's garment center, flatly denied that garment truckers were garment workers.[11] Even so, *Challenge* maintained that garment truckers were as "essential to the finished product" as other garment workers.[12]

However, even if garment truckers formed an essential link in the chain of garment production, they were atypical garment workers in at least one important respect. In a largely feminized industry marked by a sharply defined sexual division of labor, garment trucking was an almost exclusively male domain.[13] Progressive Labor's stories of struggle in garment trucking during the late 1960s all but ignored the plight of female garment workers.[14] The party had condemned sexism at its founding convention in 1965, but the male orientation of PL's campaign in garment trucking undoubtedly diminished PL's impact on the predominantly female garment workforce.[15] Progressive Labor missed an important opportunity to express the concerns of doubly-disempowered female garment workers, who were employed by men and represented by the male-dominated ILGWU.[16]

Moreover, PLers were atypical workers in garment trucking in at least three respects: they were White, college-educated and communist. As a handful of left-wing communists, they would have constituted a tiny political minority in any workforce, but unpopular politics was not all that divided them from other garment truckers. As in other sections of the garment industry, there was evidence of ethnic and racial stratification in garment trucking. The great majority of the garment trucking workforce was comprised of Blacks and Hispanics, who were employed as relatively low-paid rack pushers and helpers. White workers were concentrated in the relatively higher-paid job categories of driver and mechanic. As drivers, PL's young, White organizers, therefore, were part of garment trucking's "labor aristocracy."[17] However, the "super-exploited" helpers and pushers, according to PL's labor theory, were potentially the most rebellious element in the industry.[18] Bridging the social and ethnic or racial gap between higher and lower-paid workers in their industry became an important problematic for PL's cadre in garment trucking.[19] Finally, given the expanding job market for college graduates during the 1960s and the relatively modest pay range in garment trucking, there probably were few people with a higher education driving trucks in the garment center. Aspiring to become effective industrial organizers, PL's college-educated colonizers in garment trucking tailored their rhetoric to the linguistic norms (as they perceived them) of their less-educated co-workers.[20]

FROM ANTIOCH COLLEGE TO GARMENT TRUCKING

Progressive Labor's campaign in garment trucking in the latter 1960s initially depended on the efforts of two young men who had become friends at Antioch College, Steve Martinot and Ed Lemansky. At Antioch, they had been politically active in civil rights struggles and had become increasingly radical. Martinot and Lemansky subsequently joined Progressive Labor Movement in New York City, gaining experience as communist organizers under PLM's tutelage. Both played a leading role in many of PLM's major off-campus campaigns during the 1960s.[21]

Steve Martinot was one of the three "public leaders and spokesmen" chosen by PL for its first student trip to Cuba, which was scheduled for December 1962, but did not occur until June 1963. Young PLers who travelled to Cuba, including Martinot, were called before the House Un-American Activities Committee. Along with several others, Martinot was indicted by the federal government for traveling to Cuba himself, and for conspiring to send others.[22] Moreover, Phillip Abbott Luce (who was similarly indicted, and later informed against PL) alleged that in the spring of 1963, Martinot and two other "premature [PL] revolutionaries" had taken a "truckload of guns" and clothing to striking miners in Hazard, Kentucky.[23] In July 1964 Martinot wrote the first in a series of articles "to describe and expose the conditions of the workers in the garment market and the garment shops of New York" for PL's new newspaper, *Challenge*.[24] Soon afterward, he was indicted for criminal contempt by a Manhattan grand jury in connection with PLM's role in the Harlem Rebellion of July 1964.[25] In an article entitled "Students and Liberalism," which appeared in the October 1965 issue of *Progressive Labor*, Martinot argued:

Thus, the great contradiction facing today's intellectuals is that in seeking as individuals to participate in humanity's great struggle toward fulfillment through knowledge, they find themselves hamstrung by the purposes and power of those who run society, and to whom they must eventually sell themselves, as they have been taught. Seeking to obtain unity with the whole of society, they find themselves only further isolated from the truth they seek, imprisoned in myth and reality.[26]

To solve this contradiction between the "highest goals men can strive for" and the need to "earn a living," Martinot became a revolutionary communist garment truck driver.[27]

THE EDUCATION OF AN INDUSTRIAL COLONIZER

Ed Lemansky's route to PL began at an early age. A *red diaper baby*, he was raised in Brooklyn, New York in the 1940s and 1950s by parents who did not openly discuss their membership in the Communist Party. Nevertheless, he absorbed important messages that permeated the progressive political atmosphere of his parental home, "notions, ideas, passions, and feelings" that were "in the air." He learned, for example, that racism was bad, that you had some responsibility for people other than yourself, and that you were expected to do something. During the nine years that intervened between his graduation from high school in 1957 and his employment in the garment trucking industry in 1966, Lemansky studied in Ohio, England and Michigan, and worked for PL in North Carolina, Cuba and New York.[28]

In 1957, when he went to Antioch College, twenty-five percent of whose student body hailed from New York City, Lemansky encountered many students who came from a political background similar to his own.[29] Like him, they were attracted by Antioch's liberal or progressive policies, such as the opportunity for members of the opposite sex to visit each other's dormitory rooms, and the possibility of participating in the governance of the college. However, Antioch did not always applaud the results of student influence over college policy. During their yearlong tenure in office, for example, Lemansky and three other elected student representatives on Antioch's Student Personnel Committee prevented the college from expelling any students. Lemansky also led a successful campaign to stop the college from administering loyalty oaths required by the National Defense Education Act.[30]

The atmosphere at Antioch was both bohemian and politically progressive. Antioch was on a quarter system and students alternated between full-time study and full-time work.[31] Bohemian men at Antioch grew a *quarter's worth of hair* during their quarters of full-time study, only getting a haircut before beginning their quarters of work. Haircuts also became the focus of an important civil rights struggle. A ten-year struggle to desegregate two segregated barber shops in Yellow Springs, Ohio culminated in 1960. Although only a handful of Antioch students were Black, one third of the student body belonged to the NAACP. Antioch students joined students from two Black colleges nearby to demonstrate in support of an NAACP boycott. Lemansky and other progressive students at Antioch were *doing* something about racism.[32]

There were also explicitly leftist activities on campus. A socialist discussion club, which invited Michael Harrington and other well-known leftists to speak at Antioch, attracted students such as Lemansky (and Stephen J. Gould, a red diaper baby from Queens, New York, who impressed fellow leftists by reporting that he had read all three volumes of Marx's *Capital*).[33] Lemansky was primarily impressed by speakers from the Socialist Workers Party.[34] He was also an enthusiastic admirer of the Cuban Revolution, which he believed embodied the ideals that he had learned at home. When the SWP organized a chapter of the Fair Play for Cuba Committee at Antioch, he "signed up right away."[35]

However, the turning point for Lemansky occurred in the spring of 1961. He was a visiting student at Oxford University's Ruskin College, which had been set up by Fabian Socialists for the benefit of British workers (whose tuition was sponsored by the British Labour Party). While at Ruskin, Lemansky was impressed by fellow students, and stirred by front-page stories in the British press about the Freedom Rides that were challenging segregation in the American South.[36] Like many other Americans in England at that time, he participated in "tremendous" protest demonstrations against the Bay of Pigs invasion of Cuba.[37] He also joined the tens of thousands who participated in the yearly Peace March at Aldermaston, where he encountered the full spectrum of the British New Left.[38] While he "thrilled" at reading the seminal New Left journal, *New Left Review*, Lemansky rejected its criticisms of the Cuban Revolution because he felt that "Fidel could do no wrong."[39] He also rejected *NLR*'s criticisms of Stalin, "who everybody hated."[40] By the time he returned from England, Lemansky considered himself to be a left-wing socialist or Marxist, and he saw the proletariat as the engine of social change—of revolution.[41]

During his senior year, Lemansky became friends with fellow student Steve Martinot, who guided his reading of leftist books and periodicals. Among other things, Lemansky read Ernesto "Che" Guevara's *Guerilla Warfare*, W. E. B. Du Bois' *John Brown*, the independent Marxist journal *Monthly Review* and various works by Mao Tse-tung.[42] Martinot convinced Lemansky that the Chinese, rather than the Soviets, were the world's true revolutionaries, the "true torch bearers of the international communist movement." By the time he graduated from Antioch, Lemansky was a Maoist but not yet a political activist.[43]

Until his senior year, Lemansky had studied government, but changed to sociology with the help of Everett K. Wilson, head of the Sociology Department at Antioch.[44] During his senior year, he studied sociology exclusively; a *B* student overall, he earned straight *A*'s in his new major. To maintain his student draft deferment, Lemansky applied to graduate schools. An *A* average in sociology, a Graduate Record Examination score in the 99th percentile, and selection as a Woodrow Wilson finalist, gained him acceptance into graduate programs of sociology at Harvard, Berkeley, Michigan and Chicago. Attracted by the pioneering work of sociologist Amos H. Hawley on human ecology and the promise of a full scholarship, Lemansky chose Michigan.[45] However, the drudgery of population studies and his desire to travel persuaded him to quit after only six weeks.[46]

When Lemansky returned to New York, he became Steve Martinot's roommate. Martinot had already joined the Progressive Labor Movement and introduced his new roommate to New York City's small circle of PLM activists, who were already busy painting the town red. For example, on 8 October 1962, a small group of PLMers that included Milt Rosen, the movement's chairman, unfurled their "Stop JFK—Hands Off Cuba" banner (measuring four feet by twelve feet) at the United Nations.[47] In the week following President John F. Kennedy's declaration, on 22 October 1962, of a U.S. quarantine of Cuba over the issue of Soviet missiles there, PLM distributed 40,000 pieces of literature and conducted several street meetings opposing the administration's Cuba policy. At a street meeting in front of Columbia University (at 116th Street and Broadway), Levi Laub, a PLM leader, declared, "We feel that the action of President Kennedy, and his statement that Cuba would be invaded if the quarantine is not successful, is a threat to the existence of mankind."[48] Lemansky found PLM's intelligent and energetic revolutionists attractive, but none more so than Milt Rosen, who impressed him as a "fuckin [sic] genius." Lemansky joined PLM.[49]

PLM'S MISSION TO MONROE AND SOUTHERN STRATEGY

The new PLMer would have liked nothing better than to have participated, along with Steve Martinot, in PLM's first student trip to Cuba,
which was being organized at the time, but the PLM leadership had
something else in mind for him. Progressive Labor Movement leaders
Fred Jerome and Jake Rosen had spent time in the South, where they
made contacts in Monroe, North Carolina. Monroe was the home of
Robert F. Williams, an advocate of armed self-defense for "Negroes."
When Williams fled to Cuba in 1961 to escape prosecution on a kidnapping charge, PLM resolved to send a group of PLMers to Monroe. As
open communists, they would advocate armed self-defense, teach Black
history and fight for jobs and welfare. Progressive Labor envisaged its
projected Monroe chapter as the centerpiece of a "southern strategy"
aimed at drawing PLM's contacts in the Student Non-Violent Coordinating Committee into PLM—hopefully placing it in the forefront of a radicalized civil rights movement.[50]

Fred Jerome used his considerable powers of persuasion to recruit
Lemansky for PLM's mission to Monroe.[51] Jerome "puffed up" Lemansky, convincing him that PLM's success in Monroe could spark revolution in the entire South, which could then move the entire country to
revolution—"all of the dominoes would fall." Lemansky was ready to
"go out and organize the Monroe Commune," and he expected to see the
dictatorship of the proletariat in "something under four years." Thus, Ed
Lemansky, and fellow PLMers Jake Rosen, Wendy Nakashima and Bob
Apter went to Monroe to sow the seeds of revolution. Excepting Rosen,
they reunited a few years later in order to organize industrial workers in
New York City's garment center. The close working relationships and organizing skills that they had developed in Monroe undoubtedly enhanced
their effectiveness in New York City's garment center, but their experience in Monroe also suggested some of the problems that would plague
PLM's garment organizing.[52]

ROBERT F. WILLIAMS AND "NEGROES" WITH GUNS

Monroe, North Carolina, the county seat of Union County, was a small
town of almost 11,000 inhabitants, nearly one third of whom were
Black.[53] Despite the image of racial cooperation that North Carolina projected, and Monroe's own self-image as a progressive town, native son
and civil rights leader Robert F. Williams maintained that Monroe, located only fourteen miles from the South Carolina border, was culturally

closer to South Carolina than to the more liberal environment associated with Chapel Hill, North Carolina.[54] Moreover, the southeastern regional headquarters of the Ku Klux Klan was located in Monroe.[55] In the mid-1950s, the already small NAACP chapter there, like others throughout the South, was dwindling under the threat of economic sanctions and violence by the Klan and White Citizens Council.[56]

However, Monroe's almost extinct NAACP chapter was revived by its vice-president, Dr. Albert E. Perry, Jr., a relative newcomer to Monroe, and by its president, Robert F. Williams, who had returned to Monroe after being an aircraft worker in New Jersey, an autoworker in Detroit and a U.S. Marine. Monroe's militant new NAACP, working class in composition and containing a strong contingent of veterans, aroused the wrath of the Klan, according to Williams, when it demanded that Blacks be given access—only one day a week—to a WPA-constructed swimming pool that was maintained by municipal taxes. According to the *Monroe Inquirer*, an estimated 7,500 Klansmen meeting in a field had described integrationists as "Communist-Inspired-National-Association-for-the-Advancement-of-Colored-association-People."[57] Williams embraced armed self-defense in reaction to the Klan violence that ensued. When an armed Klan motorcade attacked Dr. Perry's home in 1957, Black citizens shot back. Williams complained that "not a single white newspaper in America reported the incident," and that there was only very limited coverage in the Black press.[58]

However, when a White man charged with attempting to rape a Black woman was acquitted in 1959, and Williams responded by threatening that Blacks "would meet violence with violence," his statement was widely reported in the press. The NAACP's executive director, Roy Wilkins, suspended Williams for advocating violence, and the Fiftieth National Convention of the NAACP upheld the decision of the NAACP's Committee on Branches barring him from office for six months. Although disappointed, Williams was gratified that the publicity surrounding his stand on self-defense had forced a debate on the issue and pushed the NAACP to officially uphold "the right of Negroes to self-defense against racist violence."[59]

In July 1959 Williams began publishing *The Crusader*, a mimeographed newsletter that would, he claimed, "in accurate and no uncertain terms inform both Negroes and whites of Afro-American liberation struggles." However, his eyewitness accounts of racial equality in Cuba, which began appearing in late 1959, elicited a sharp rebuke from the NAACP's national headquarters. The NAACP leadership accused him of repeating the errors of Paul Robeson, world-renowned singer, actor and left-wing civil rights activist, whose passport was revoked by the U.S. State Department in the 1950s. Williams replied, "Paul Robeson is living proof that the Afro-American need not look upon the United States as 'Nigger heaven' and the last stop for us on this earth." Wilkins eventually expelled Williams from the NAACP; and in 1961, the U.S. State Department denied his request to travel to Cuba for the Twenty-sixth of July celebration. Ironically, just one month later, Williams fled to Cuba in order to escape criminal prosecution.[60]

The Union County NAACP's four-year-long struggle for public pool accommodations and the escalating racist violence it provoked—including attempts on Williams' life—came to a head in June-July 1961. According to Williams, the readiness of his followers to employ arms to defend themselves induced local authorities to protect them from a racist mob, averting a violent clash.[61] However, when the civil rights struggle in Monroe turned nonviolent, it was met (ironically enough) with "naked violence and brutality."[62] Seventeen Freedom Riders led by James Forman united with local youths who had been active in the swimming pool struggle to form the Monroe Non-Violent Action Committee. They picketed the Union County Courthouse to support ten demands—for desegregation and increased employment opportunities—that Williams had submitted to the Monroe Board of Aldermen. Forman wanted to show that nonviolence could further the demands of lower-class Blacks; it was his first personal involvement in the southern protest movement. Williams, although skeptical, sanctioned the nonviolent campaign. However, a week of increasingly violent attacks by racists on the nonviolent picketers ensued, culminating on 27 August in what Forman characterized as a "moment of death." A mob of several thousand Whites—some of whom were armed—attacked the picketers. Ironically, the injured and frightened picketers, who took refuge in the police station, were arrested for inciting to riot. (Forman was given a suspended sentence prohibiting him from demonstrating in North Carolina for the next two years.)[63]

Early that evening, according to Williams, cars full of armed Whites drove through his neighborhood and indiscriminately attacked people on the streets. In response, the Black community armed itself and prepared to fight back against the White mob that was massing in town. At about 6 P.M., a Black mob stopped a car at gunpoint less than a block away from Williams' house. They seized its occupants, Mr. and Mrs. G. Bruce Stegall of Marshville, North Carolina, a White couple whom they allegedly recognized as having driven through town the previous day with a racist banner declaring "Open Season On Coons." Mr. Stegall, allegedly a Klan member, and his wife were brought to Williams' house, where they were held captive for three hours and then released. While they were still in Williams' house, however, he received a telephone call from police chief A. A. Maury, who informed him that state troopers were on their way and that "In thirty minutes, you'll be hanging in the courthouse square."[64]

He fled to New York to focus attention on "racist oppression" in Monroe. According to Williams, he had rescued the Stegalls from almost certain death at the hands of the "raging" mob, but on the following day, a Union County grand jury indicted him, and four others, for kidnapping the White couple. When he learned of the kidnapping indictment, he went to Canada and then to Cuba in the belief that he "never would have gotten to a trial, not even to mention a fair trial."[65]

THE IMPROBABLE MISSION THAT WENT SOUTH

Williams had gone to Cuba, but his followers had not given up the struggle for "Freedom, Jobs and Justice." Two young men, twenty-year-old Richard Crowder and eighteen-year-old Harold Reape, former leaders of the Monroe Non-Violent Action Committee, now led the Monroe Youth Action Committee, whose thirty members were committed to carrying on the struggle that Williams had begun.[66] As Crowder put it, "We want to break up Jim Crow where it hurts, not only at the lunch counters." However, PLM believed that MYAC was facing a "rough battle" because three obstacles stood in its way. First, it lacked experienced leadership (Williams' broadcasts from Cuba notwithstanding) because most of the active local leadership was either under indictment for kidnapping (including Crowder and Reape) or serving a two-year suspended sentence (ending in August 1963) for inciting to riot. Second, as the result of a "total terror campaign" allegedly conducted by local police over the previous eighteen months, the Black community lived in fear. Third, "respectable" civil rights organizations such as NAACP and CORE were snubbing MYAC's appeals for help. Progressive Labor painted a bleak picture, but indicated that plans were under way to renew the struggle in the coming summer (1963) and hinted that "young people from around the country—and perhaps even some organizations" might get involved. Although PLM was not ready to announce its prospective mission to Monroe, it was preparing to fill the leadership vacuum created by Robert F. Williams' departure a year and a half earlier.[67]

Progressive Labor would not be able to operate successfully in

Monroe without local support. Fortunately for PLM's underfunded missionaries in Monroe, local Blacks provided them with money and chickens, but the Black community was not universally welcoming. At one point, PLMers—who were openly atheistic—had to, in Lemansky's words, "intimidate" Black ministers into letting MYAC meet in local churches.[68] However, religious Blacks such as James Barrett did not reject PLMers; although he had only a grade school education, he skillfully argued against the theory of evolution and promised to pray for Lemansky. Harold James White, PLM's youngest supporter, was only thirteen and lived with his very religious grandmother, who had worked for the railroads laying track. She also welcomed PLMers, whom she regarded as Jewish rather than White.[69]

They were even able to draw a small number of local Blacks into PLM's overtly leftist activities. One young woman, who was related to Robert Williams, joined PLM's first Cuba trip and had a baby in Havana; and Herbert Faulkner went to Cuba with PLM the following year. One of MYAC's young leaders, Harold Reape, accompanied PLMers on an organizing trip to the North. A handful of Monroe Blacks even joined PLM and lived with PLM's *outside agitators* in a rented home that was dubbed Freedom House, which became the center of a wider movement.[70]

According to Lemansky, Freedom House organizers did some "terrific things." After Freedom House boycotted local supermarkets for "a couple of months," Blacks were hired for the first time as cashiers at the Win Dixie and A & P. Freedom House won a wage increase for domestics, "the largest single group of Negro workers in the County," by merely threatening to organize them into its Women's League, which had chapters in both Union County, North Carolina and nearby Chesterfield County, South Carolina. Demanding an end to segregated education, a united front of MYAC, its Union County Women's League and the Union County NAACP organized a ninety-nine percent effective boycott of the Winchester School—the only school for Monroe's Black students—on its opening day. Attendance at White schools was sparse as well. With the help of Dorothy Salter, a PLM caseworker from Chapel Hill, Freedom House managed to get "fifty" families on welfare in "a couple of weeks," almost bankrupting Union County, according to Lemansky.[71]

Freedom House organizers did not achieve these modest successes without confronting the issue of racist violence, which Monroe's Blacks had experienced in previous freedom struggles and had come to expect. When the Monroe Youth Action Committee closed Black schools and picketed White schools in Monroe on the first day of school, local

Blacks—some of whom had seen military service—assumed the role of their protectors, riding around town with guns sticking out of their car windows to deter racist violence.[72] The Mayor's Better Citizenship Committee characterized the marches to local schools during August 1963 as "quiet demonstrations led by white boys."[73] Nevertheless, a march of about one hundred people—mostly Black teenagers—to Monroe's central business district encountered shoving and shouts of, "Kill the damn niggers!" Moreover, when the marchers returned to Newtown, Monroe's main Black section (where Freedom House was located), they were attacked by a car full of rock-throwing Whites, which fled when the marchers threw back the rocks, smashing its windows.[74]

The philosophy of armed self-defense seems to have been alive and well in Monroe's Black community. Lemansky was particularly impressed by Woodrow Wilson, a local Black leader who had built his house with rifle ports in the basement, where he kept an arsenal. Openly contemptuous of police authority, Wilson had once pointed a gun at police who were standing on his lawn. Lemansky regarded Wilson, who was illiterate, as "one of the most engaging minds I have ever encountered," and maintained that he was the "guy behind Robert Williams."[75]

In line with the self-defense philosophy of Wilson and Williams, Freedom House was guarded, and its organizers began carrying guns after an attempt was made on their lives. However, their attempts to protect themselves sometimes proved to be problematic. One night in the summer of 1963, Lemansky and two local Blacks, Richard Crowder and Frank Butler, were driving to Pageland, South Carolina, twenty miles from Monroe, to conduct a weekly class in "Negro History and Current Politics" when they were stopped by police for allegedly having a defective taillight. The police then "busted" the taillight, impounded the car and arrested Lemansky, the driver. They arrested all his passengers as well after a search of the car revealed the guns that PLMers had shoved under the seats. They were charged with carrying loaded and *concealed* weapons, and held for four days. Crowder and Butler were held in the Pageland jail, but Lemansky spent three of his four days in custody on the Chesterfield County chain gang. To avoid being sentenced to the chain gang for thirty days, Lemansky reluctantly pleaded guilty to a lesser charge. The Monroe Youth Action Committee paid its members' $270 fine, which had been reduced $5 in consideration of Lemansky's three days of hard labor. He quipped, "Considering that I was given a bed, three meals a day and some nice striped pants to wear, my pay was about average for this area."[76]

Not surprisingly, the Pageland Recorder's Court judge confiscated the PLMers' guns, which were difficult to replace and soon missed.[77] Five days later, while driving at night from Pageland to Monroe, Lemansky and his three passengers were ambushed by fifteen Whites in four cars. According to *Progressive Labor*, the MYAC car was "boxed in by the whites" for twelve miles and "shot at," and "bottles and bricks smashed against the car, shattering the front windshield and one of the side windows."[78] This incident was reminiscent of the violence that had persuaded Williams to advocate armed self-defense.[79] Isolated acts of violence produced momentary fear, but from Lemansky's point of view, there was not a "whole lot of physical menace" because Monroe's White population thought that gun-toting PLMers were "nuts" and, for the most part, stayed away from them.[80]

However, there were "lots of attacks" against PLMers in the local press, which called them "outside agitators," alleged that Monroe Blacks were happy, and defended Monroe on the grounds that it was "not Mississippi."[81] In fact, Monroe's city council and chamber of commerce adopted resolutions "endorsing the opening of accommodation establishments to Negroes"; and the "biracial" Mayor's Better Citizenship Committee, appointed by the mayor at the request of the city council, was involved in the "development of job opportunities for Negroes." North Carolina's governor, Terry Sanford, regarded such efforts as evidence that local government was "taking a lead in promoting justice for our Negro citizens." Even so, such gestures in Monroe produced few results by 1964; only the public outdoor playgrounds and some indoor facilities at the Main Street Recreation Center were desegregated. Even the ministerial association and chamber of commerce were still segregated.[82]

Nevertheless, the local press defended Monroe and attacked PLM. When a local newspaper publisher labeled MYAC organizers "Communists," PLM responded vigorously because red-baiting attacks threatened to undermine its support in the Black community. *Freedom*, PLM's biweekly newspaper in Monroe, reminded Blacks that the "small beginnings of progress we made this year [1963]—starting this summer— proved that when we stick together and are ready to fight hard for our rights, we can win."[83] *Freedom* admitted PLM's socialist orientation, accused its anticommunist detractors of being racists, and argued that only socialism could deliver the final blow to racism: "The Progressive Labor Movement—the group that the racists have attacked by calling it 'red'— has never denied that it stands for socialism and always said that without a socialist society the freedom fight will never be won."[84]

Progressive Labor, emphasizing the Black community's support for PLM, reported that "Mrs. Ruby Simpson, head of the Union County Women's League, told Mayor Fred Wilson, 'I don't care what their backgrounds are. I care about what they are doing for freedom.'"[85] Even if those who worked closely with PLM were not put off by red-baiting, others in the Black community probably were. Moreover, Mrs. Simpson, it seems, was willing to work with communists because they contributed to the civil rights struggle and not because she had revolutionary aspirations.

Robert F. Williams, who denied being a member of the Communist Party, had ridiculed anticommunist attacks leveled against him and the civil rights movement by observing that "Every freedom movement in the U.S.A. is labeled 'Communist'" even though "Most of our people have never even heard of Marx."[86] The members of PLM, who were open communists, understood that they were sowing the seeds of socialism in ground prepared by Williams. Attempting to assume leadership of his base, they emphasized both their own relationship with Williams and his association with communism. *Freedom* printed part of an interview with Williams in Havana and a letter from left-wing journalist Anna Louise Strong to PLM describing Williams' recent trip to Communist China. Like Williams, PLM supported Castro's Cuba, "Red" China, armed self-defense and progressive Black nationalism. However, in his Havana interview, Williams suggested that Blacks should cooperate with White allies but not allow them to dominate the movement—a policy that contained problematic implications for PLM's Monroe project.[87]

The PLM group that came to Monroe aspiring to lead the Freedom Movement in the South initially consisted of three Jewish men and Wendy Nakashima, a Japanese-American woman. Progressive Labor had tried to involve northern Blacks in their mission to Monroe. Ed Lemansky, Bob Apter and Harold Reape had approached members of the Harvard University SNCC support group, but to no avail, and Fred Jerome had as little success with Blacks in New York City. However, Blacks in Monroe were generally willing to work with PLM's "white guys" but many, possibly influenced by anti-Japanese feelings stemming from World War II, were resistant to working with Wendy Nakashima. This rejection must have been frustrating for Nakashima, whose antiracism undoubtedly grew out of her childhood experiences during the Second World War, when she and her family were interned by the U.S. Government for three years.[88]

In addition to differences with regard to race, religion, ethnicity and national origin, PLM's organizers were divided from Monroe's Black community by class differences. Unlike the vast majority of Monroe's Blacks, all of PLM's organizers from the North were college educated and had never done hard manual labor. Even though local Blacks liked Ed Lemansky, he never found a way to establish "relations of equality" with them. Because they perceived him as "so different" (and perhaps intimidating), they often were unwilling to challenge his views—assenting verbally but acting otherwise. Although he tended to dismiss the problem at the time, Lemansky subsequently concluded that PLMers' biggest obstacle in Monroe was the "social distance" that separated them from the vast majority of Monroe's Blacks.[89]

The members of PLM further distanced themselves from the Black community by professing their atheism, which offended the religious sensibilities of many, and by advocating communism, which, Lemansky acknowledged, "frightened some people."[90] Moreover, to avoid involvement in the broader, nonviolent civil rights movement, PLM made the significant mistake of declining to participate in the historic March on Washington in the summer of 1963. In addition, PLM continued to attack President John F. Kennedy in the pages of *Freedom* after Kennedy had further enhanced his standing in the Black community by taking a stronger position against racism. Following Kennedy's assassination in November 1963, Lemansky observed his portrait hanging "in everybody's house"—a measure of the significant political distance that separated local Blacks from PLM's leftist perspective.[91]

If these issues divided PLMers from Monroe's Black community, PLM made no attempt at all to approach Monroe's White majority. Given White Monroe's history of resistance to integration and hostility toward civil rights protesters, it is not surprising that PLMers were diffident toward local Whites, but it was a political mistake for Freedom House's integrated leadership to make no effort, beyond its own ranks, to bridge the racial divide, especially since the movement's immediate goal was desegregation.[92]

Regardless, PLMers had gone to Monroe in order to mobilize the Black community. However, after months of intense activity and some small successes, the pace of the civil rights revolution in Monroe slowed. Only a handful of PLMers had been assigned to Monroe, and they divided their time between Monroe and Atlanta, where they were attempting to proselytize SNCC organizers. There was a period during the winter of 1963–1964 when Ed Lemansky was the only experienced PLMer in Monroe; overstrained and fearful of making political mistakes, he delved into Nero Wolfe mysteries.[93]

Another mystery—one more consequential to the future of the freedom struggle in Monroe—was unraveling in the Union County Courthouse, where the trial of four civil rights activists accused of kidnapping
the Stegalls began on 18 February 1964. The kidnapping charge brought
against Robert F. Williams, Mae Mallory, Richard Crowder, Harold
Reape and John Lowery stemmed from the confrontation between
Blacks and Whites on 27 August 1961. Williams had escaped to Cuba.
The trial of the four remaining defendants was held up for two and a half
years while Mae Mallory attempted in vain to prevent her extradition
from Ohio to North Carolina.[94]

Writing, from his self-imposed exile in Cuba, about the upcoming
trial of his co-defendants, Williams judged that there was "no possible
chance of their obtaining justice." By challenging all of the six Blacks in
the jury pool—and only them—the prosecution obtained an all-White
jury, which convicted all the defendants after deliberating for only thirty-
five minutes. They were given sentences ranging from a minimum of
three years for John Lowery, a White college student from New York
City, to a maximum of twenty years for Mae Mallory, a Black New
Yorker.[95]

According to Lemansky, Monroe's Black community was outraged
at the verdict and the stiff sentences. However, he also acknowledged
that local Blacks, who made up a large majority of the spectators at the
trial, were "greatly troubled" at learning that Crowder, Reape and Lowery had admitted to the police and State Bureau of Investigation agents
that they were implicated in the kidnapping, and particularly disturbed
by the revelation that Crowder and Lowery had implicated others. Lowery had also given SBI agents the names of the Monroe Non-Violent Action Committee's leaders, and Crowder had named fellow members of
the rifle club organized by Williams to provide self-defense for the Black
community. Crowder had even directed police to some of the club's guns
and ammunition, which were hidden in his grandmother's attic.[96]

Even if the unsigned confessions were illegally obtained, as defense
attorney William Kunstler argued to the court, they were substantially
believable. Lemansky explained the kidnapping as the consequence of
the racist violence that preceded it, but he was obviously troubled—as
were local Blacks—by the revelation that the defendants had "weakened
earlier in the face of police terror." After a little more than a year in Monroe, Lemansky felt "boxed in" and returned to New York for a new PLM
assignment.[97]

Progressive Labor's overall southern strategy fared no better than its
improbable mission in Monroe. It had envisaged SNCC as a vehicle for

spreading its ideas in the South and, ultimately, as the basis for a Black-led communist movement in the South. With two hundred field secretaries committed to building real mass organizations of workers and farmers, SNCC was a prize worth winning. The militancy that SNCC displayed encouraged PLMers to believe that SNCC organizers could be won over to PLM's revolutionary communist outlook. Clearly, SNCC was overtly committed to nonviolent direct action, but its organizers in the deep South covertly carried guns and had been involved in a number of shootouts.[98] Furthermore, although SNCC was not an ideological organization, it dogmatically subscribed to, as one liberal journalist put it, "anti-anti-Communism," and had been influenced by leftists from early on.[99]

Jake Rosen, PLM's most important leader in the South, circulated *Freedom*, PLM's Monroe newspaper, among SNCC organizers in Atlanta, Georgia. Like other leftists, he probably exerted some influence on SNCC.[100] However, despite its concessions to progressive Black nationalism and relationship with SNCC organizers, PLM could not transform its SNCC contacts into a cadre for PLM's envisioned Black-led communist movement in the South. Like other Monroe PLMers, Lemansky visited SNCC organizers at their Atlanta headquarters and was keenly aware of their political differences with PLM. For example, Lemansky insisted that PLM acted correctly in proclaiming its communism, but PLM's contacts in SNCC argued that it would be wiser to *first* "do the right things" and then say "we are communists." On the other hand, SNCC organizers were committed to carrying out the voter registration campaign which Robert Kennedy had proposed to SNCC (in order to steer it away from confrontational politics), but Lemansky argued that registering Blacks to vote would only lead to having "Black elected officials who will fuck you."[101]

Moreover, although more and more of SNCC's Black activists became radicalized, they resisted being controlled by White radical groups (who were competing with them for Black recruits) and were increasingly attracted to Black separatism.[102] Ironically, PLM's literature and actions, according to Lemansky, pushed its closest friends in SNCC toward progressive Black nationalism, which—rather than being a step toward revolutionary socialism—further divided Black and White radicals. Ultimately, PLM was not able to use either its contacts in SNCC or MYAC to establish itself as a significant civil rights presence in the South.[103]

GO DIRECTLY TO CUBA

Ironically, the collapse of PLM's Southern strategy finally gave Lemansky a chance to see revolutionary Cuba. To carry out PLM's mission to Monroe, he had deferred going to Cuba with Steve Martinot in 1963. As soon as Lemansky returned to New York from Monroe, PLM leader Levi Laub asked him to lead PLM's second student trip to Castro's Cuba. A week later he arrived in Paris via El Al, traveling a secret and circuitous route to Havana.[104] Lemansky spent the next two months in Cuba.[105]

As leader of PLM's second group to visit Cuba in defiance of the U.S. State Department's travel ban, Ed Lemansky was invited to meet with Cuban government officials. In 1959 Lemansky had embraced the Cuban Revolution as an embodiment of his youthful ideals and the signal of a new revolutionary era. His admiration for the Cuban Revolution and its leaders influenced his decision to become a revolutionary. Now, after a yearlong delay in Monroe, he had the distinction of leading a group of American leftists to Cuba and an opportunity to meet the legendary leaders of the Cuban Revolution, including Ernesto "Che" Guevara, whose doctrine of guerilla warfare he had read in college.[106]

Progressive Labor and the Cuban government enjoyed fraternal relations and expressed their political differences privately—but not always politely. Members of PLM who visited Cuba in 1963, for example, brashly challenged Cuban officials, "cornering President Osvaldo Dorticos Torrado in his chambers, demanding to know why Cuba allowed Russia to take out the missiles against the will of the Cuban people?"[107] On the other hand, the Cuban officials whom Lemansky interviewed in 1964 challenged PLM's notion that it was politically necessary for communists to proclaim their communism. The victorious revolutionaries who rode into Havana in 1959 had not triumphed as communists and now strongly advised PLMers against being open about their own communism. But PLM saw itself as superior to "moribund" Old Left groups such as the Communist Party and the Socialist Workers Party, which it closely resembled, but which habitually concealed their political commitments. Members of PLM called before HUAC after PLM's 1963 trip to Cuba had not only defied their congressional interrogators but proudly proclaimed their communism.[108]

While Lemansky was in Cuba, the Harlem Rebellion (which a Manhattan grand jury and HUAC subsequently accused PLM of precipitating) erupted and made front-page news in the Cuban press.[109] Lemansky and a group of PLMers visiting Santiago, Cuba proposed demonstrating their support for the Harlem rebels near the U.S. Navy's base at Guantanamo Bay. The Cuban government, unwilling to allow hot-headed PLMers to provoke an international incident, told them "in no uncertain terms" that they would not be permitted to demonstrate.[110] Thus, although PLMers visiting Cuba publicly praised Cuba's impressive accomplishments, they sometimes had stormy exchanges with their Cuban hosts.[111] Five years later, PL publicly doubted that Cuba was socialist at all and sharply criticized Che.[112]

GET A JOB—IN GARMENT!

The day he returned from Cuba, in mid-August 1964, Ed Lemansky (along with three other "ban Busters") was handed a subpoena to appear before the House Un-American Activities Committee on 3 September 1964.[113] The day after he returned to New York from Cuba, Lemansky participated in a May Second Movement demonstration in Duffy Square against the Vietnam War. It was illegal to demonstrate in the Times Square area and forty PLMers, including Lemansky, were arrested. The following January, Lemansky began serving a two-month sentence for his militancy during the demonstration.[114]

When he was not fighting with police or in jail, Lemansky was busy either organizing street meetings and rent strikes on New York's Upper West Side, where PL had a clubhouse, or studying, reading, thinking about and discussing politics. He felt derelict in his duty if he did not attend meetings nightly, and if called to a party demonstration, he always appeared. In fact, he was prepared to do whatever PL needed done, and he was even ready to die for the revolution. To Lemansky, being a *professional revolutionary* and working for PL amounted to the same thing, but his communist career was about to take a new turn.[115]

In April 1965, soon after Lemansky was released from jail, the Progressive Labor Party held its founding convention. The vast majority of the participants were students who had never worked for a living; many did not attend classes regularly, and only a handful held jobs. However, on the day after the convention, Milt Rosen met with Lemansky to inform him that the party leadership had made a "major decision" to get its members to go to work. At first, he thought that Rosen simply wanted young PLers to become responsible adults and achieve financial stability, but he soon realized that PL's leadership viewed its campaign to convince young PLers to find employment as a necessary step toward transforming PL into a working-class party.[116]

In New York City, PL had been trying to recruit working-class people through its community organizing efforts on the Upper West Side, the Lower East Side and in Harlem. As a relatively inexperienced community organizer (in Monroe, North Carolina and on New York City's Upper West Side), Lemansky had relied on the power of his arguments to win friends for PL, but party leaders persuaded him that communist organizers could succeed only if they integrated themselves into the lives of working-class people. Since PL now considered it essential to lead workers at the point of production, Lemansky's first step was to get a job, but not just any job.[117]

In PL's view, the key force for revolution was the industrial proletariat. Following a strategy that the CP had employed, PL proposed a plan to colonize industry, that is, to send college-educated cadres into industrial jobs in order to lead workers at the point of production, and recruit them to the party. Progressive Labor's leaders, Milt Rosen and Mort Scheer had been CP industrial colonizers in Buffalo, New York. In their subsequent dispute with the CP's more moderate leadership (which eventually expelled them from the party), they suggested that their leftist views reflected a working-class perspective that they had gained as *industrial* cadres. They now proposed that a number of PL's rising young stars, including Ed Lemansky, also assume the lives of industrial workers.[118]

The leadership of PLP intended to send its handful of would-be industrial organizers in New York City into the garment center, whose large number of Blacks, Hispanics and women, laboring under miserable working conditions for the minimum wage, were among the most oppressed industrial workers in the city. The CP in New York had concentrated on the city's garment industry, and Milt Rosen, first as the CP's New York State labor secretary and then as PL's chairman, had organized communist street rallies in the garment center. However, PL's leaders understood that street rallies were not an adequate substitute for workplace organizers. Eventually, a number of young PLers, including Steve Martinot, Ed Lemansky and Dave Davis, did secure jobs in the garment trucking industry—not through any PL plan, however, but "by a fluke," because there were jobs available in garment trucking companies pushing racks and pulling hand trucks.[119]

THE REAL GUERILLA WARFARE OF WORK

Although he admittedly had no experience, Lemansky—whose age and demeanor may have made him look like a college student seeking summer employment—was able to get a job as a pusher at City-Wide Trucking on Thirty-eighth Street between Eighth and Ninth Avenues, in the heart of New York City's garment market. There were dozens of garment trucking companies. With six or seven truck drivers and about twenty helpers and rack pushers, City-Wide was a midsize firm. It picked up ladies' garments from manufacturers and delivered them to packing houses, railroads, over-the-road truckers and stores.[120]

As soon as he was hired, Lemansky was given a "big hand truck" and sent with a more experienced worker to pick up his first load. After showing him how to load the hand truck, his mentor taught him how to pace the work; they waited one-half hour before getting on the freight elevator to the street. His mentor also taught him to keep his heavily loaded hand truck down while pushing it, and how to get it off the curb low and fast to keep it from tipping over. Because his mentor was nice to him, Lemansky concluded that the workers were "wonderful."[121]

However, his first day on the job did not pass without incident. Despite his on-the-job training, Lemansky's hand truck tipped over while he was pushing it off a curb. Passers-by who helped him to reload it apparently also helped themselves; when he returned, he was two cartons short. Stealing was widespread in the garment center; there were, according to Lemansky, "millions of ways to do it." Stealing constituted grounds for immediate dismissal, but his employer correctly attributed the loss to Lemansky's inexperience, and did not fire him.[122] Lemansky was a physically imposing twenty-five-year-old and in reasonably good physical condition, but at the end of his first day, he was so stiff that he could hardly get home. That night, he dreamed of pulling hand trucks.[123]

The next day, he was assigned with another worker to push two racks of garments. By the end of the week, he knew how to manipulate a loaded hand truck or a rack full of garments and, perhaps more important, how much time to waste while doing the job. Ironically, City-Wide's bosses trusted him more than some of his co-workers, who thought that he was a management spy. This may have been because City-Wide's management was White and he was the only White working as a pusher. While Whites worked in the office, on the platform and as truck drivers at City-Wide, a White pusher was an oddity in any garment trucking firm. Lemansky was eventually promoted to the position of truck driver at City-Wide and in the next year led a number of rank-and-file work actions against both management and the ILGWU's Local 102. By that time, he was already a veteran of the unseen—but undying—daily struggle between workers and their bosses, the "real guerilla warfare of work." In some respects, he had become what he was pretending to be—a worker.[124]

Like many young intellectuals, Lemansky was stirred by the civil rights movement and the Cuban Revolution. His political awakening in college was part of the emerging new radicalism, and his background as a red diaper baby probably made Progressive Labor's new communism seem attractive. Joining PL gave him an opportunity to follow his family's tradition of communist politics, seek revenge for the damage done to his family by McCarthyism, and rebel against his parents' CP politics.

Lemansky was not one of PL's founders, but he and other red diaper babies who joined PL in the early 1960s were a bridge between PL's founding members and a new wave of PL recruits—mostly antiwar students—who joined the party in the latter half of the 1960s, and who were, for the most part, new to communist politics.

By the time Lemansky transformed himself into a garment trucker, he was already an experienced organizer. Over the next few years, while PL's student organizers were busy forming a pro-worker faction in SDS, Lemansky and his fellow intellectuals-turned-truck drivers put PL's theories about the industrial working class into practice at the point of production. This was PL's first attempt to transform itself into a party of industrial workers, and also the first test of the ideas PL was promoting on campus, that is, the party's confidence in industrial workers and its own organizing strategies.

CHAPTER 6

Communist Truckers Between a Rock and a Hard Place

Progressive Labor, Garment Trucking and Local 102, ILGWU, 1967–1970

The present chapter discusses the organizing efforts of three Progressive Labor colonizers in garment trucking—Steve Martinot, Ed Lemansky and Dave Davis—who were able to organize a surprising number of work actions in a fairly short period of time. These were among PL's first endeavors to organize industrial workers at the point of production, and illustrated both PL's possibilities and limitations in this field of action, which PL regarded as crucial to its transformation into a working-class party.

THE ILGWU'S PROBLEM CHILD, LOCAL 102

In their bid to lead a rebellion of garment truckers, PL's handful of organizers would have to run a gauntlet between the garment trucking companies and the ILGWU's Local 102, the Cloak & Dress Drivers' & Helpers' Union, which PL regarded as a "model of corruption."[1] The suggestion that Local 102 was corrupt antedated PL's involvement in garment trucking. The issue was raised in 1962 in hearings before Congressman Herbert Zelenko's subcommittee of the House Committee on Education and Labor, chaired by Congressman Adam Clayton Powell. The subcommittee investigated to what extent the ILGWU discriminated against Blacks and Puerto Ricans, and to what extent "racketeering and exploitation" prevailed in the union.[2]

The ILGWU's president, David Dubinsky, assumed the primary responsibility for defending his union against these allegations of discrimination and corruption. In testimony before Congressman Zelenko's subcommittee in August 1962, Dubinsky claimed that the ILGWU had a well-deserved reputation for character, militancy and determination "despite attempts made to besmirch and to undermine it." Dubinsky maintained, for example, that in 1940, when his union belonged to the Congress of Industrial Organizations, he made its reaffiliation with the American Federation of Labor contingent on the AFL assuming responsibility for getting rid of the racketeers who held office in its constituent unions; and he was physically attacked at the AFL's 1940 convention for introducing an antiracketeering resolution. The ILGWU president testified that in the twenty years since the ILGWU's reaffiliation with the AFL, he continued to oppose any corruption within the organization. Moreover, Dubinsky was proud of the ILGWU's efforts to rid itself of the "occasional betrayer of the trust." He estimated that in thirty years, the union had dismissed between forty and forty-five of its employees for "irregularity and personal conduct which drew a reflection on the organization with which they were affiliated."[3]

However, the ILGWU president admitted that Local 102 was "the problem child of the union." The ILGWU's problem with Local 102 was serious and long standing. Dubinsky revealed that numerous meetings of the ILGWU executive board had heard complaints against Local 102. There evidently was substance to these complaints, so much so that the ILGWU's joint boards for both the dress and the cloak industries refused to continue including Local 102 in their industrywide agreements. After that, Local 102 functioned without signing any contracts "for many years." The ILGWU's general executive board considered revoking Local 102's charter and expelling it from the international, but came to the conclusion that it was "better for our industry and better for them and for us to exert the measure of control we can." Dubinsky did not explain what measure of control the ILGWU leadership could reasonably expect to exert; and he fell short of promising to correct all that was wrong with Local 102. The same questionable Local 102 practices that Dubinsky had acknowledged in 1962 were reported by PL's garment truckers in the late 1960s. The testimony of Dubinsky and others before Congress in 1962 lends credence to PL's subsequent allegations of corruption on the part of Local 102 officials.[4]

The ILGWU president's acknowledgment of corruption in Local 102 was unavoidable. Several credible witnesses who testified before the subcommittee immediately prior to Dubinsky's appearance revealed egregious practices by Local 102 officials. In light of that testimony, Dubinsky—even if he had wanted to—would have found it difficult simply to deny any wrongdoing on the part of the ILGWU's problem local. For example, Fred Heinken, who had been employed as a freight handler at Fast Service Shipping Terminal—on Tenth Avenue between Thirty-second and Thirty-third Streets—for ten years, testified that he was not informed that Fast Service employees were represented by Local 102, ILGWU until Local 808 of the Teamsters Union attempted to organize the shop in early 1962. A few days after organizers for the Teamsters had approached Fast Service workers, Irving Abrams, who represented Local 102, appeared in the shop, informing Heinken that the union's new contract would raise his salary from $80 to $85 per week, which surprised Heinken because he was earning $60 for a 45-hour week. Despite the fact that Heinken had never encountered Local 102, Abrams informed him that the union had relations with his employer for twenty or twenty-five years. Furthermore, when Heinken hesitated joining Local 102—after both Abrams and the company manager, James Crombie, told him that he would have to do so—he was fired, and only rehired after he went to the union office and signed a membership card. Another Fast Service freight handler, Louis D'Amato, who had worked for the company close to thirteen years, also testified. He told substantially the same story, except for the fact that he reported working a 70-hour week for $60—less than the minimum wage.[5]

Jack Borofsky, president of Fast Service, confirmed the fact that his company had labor contracts with Local 102 for over twenty-five years. The contract covered the company's ten to twelve regular employees, but not most of the workforce, which Borofsky characterized as part-time. However, he admitted that four or five of the regular employees did not belong to the union and worked below union scale (receiving $60 rather than $80 per week), indicating that both the management and the union were ignoring the union shop clause in the contract. But Borofsky acknowledged that after the Teamsters tried to organize the shop, the Local 102 manager, Herbie Sherman, instructed the company's manager, Crombie, to fire Heinken for not joining the union. However, he denied that D'Amato, or any other Fast Service employee, had worked a 70-hour week for $60. But Borofsky could not document his denials because his copy of the Local 102 contract and his payroll records had been seized by Manhattan District Attorney Frank Hogan. One congressman observed that Local 102's agreement with Fast Service was a "sweetheart contract." Indeed, Borofsky admitted that his manager, James Crombie, also served as the Local 102 shop steward at Fast Service. Crombie acknowledged that he had simultaneously been shop steward and company manager for as many as fifteen years, and had ignored the union shop provision of the contract. Apparently, there was a seamless web of collusion between management and union—which for a considerable period were both embodied in the same person, Crombie. When asked who he would have represented in a grievance hearing, the unionized employee or the company, Crombie answered, "I think if you would ask any of the employees. I think I was fair in every way with them."[6]

Dubinsky, testifying on the following day, conceded that the Local 102 agreement was not enforced, and he thanked the committee for calling it to his attention. At this, Congressman Zelenko claimed to have almost fallen off his chair. But Dubinsky adamantly disassociated the ILGWU from Local 102's transgressions:

> You cannot condemn the ILGWU because a business agent or a manager neglected for one reason or another—and I don't think it is justified to make a reflection on the ILGWU that it has sweetheart contracts. It was not even mentioned that this is not the ordinary ILGWU local, it is Teamsters. When you say "Teamsters," something goes with it.[7]

But Local 102 was part of the ILGWU, and Dubinsky was ultimately responsible for rectifying it. Confronting the manager of Local 102, the angry ILGWU president asked, "Have I got to be embarrassed on account of you?" However, Dubinsky went no further than accusing the Local 102 manager of *negligence*: ". . . there is no evidence that he took money, you see," Dubinsky assured the congressmen. The ILGWU president chose not to remove the local manager from office, but was sure that he had put the fear of God in the manager's heart by teaching him that "there is a day of reckoning" when he has to account to "Papa." Dubinsky surmised that "maybe from now on it will be better."[8]

The testimony elicited by Congressman Zelenko's subcommittee in 1962 is consistent with the charges made by PL's garment organizers in the late 1960s. For example, although Local 102 had contracts with scores of shops that collectively employed between 10,000 and 20,000 truckers, PL claimed that there were only about 2,000 members of the union (Dubinsky had reported 1,776 members). The party went further than Dubinsky, charging that Local 102 went "out of its way to keep workers out of its ranks in exchange for payoffs from the bosses." This unholy arrangement, PL claimed, prevented thousands of mainly Black and Hispanic workers from getting the "already low union scale."

Whether Local 102 officials were racketeers, as PL alleged, or merely neglectful, as Dubinsky claimed, it can be inferred from the work actions that PLers were able to lead that there were more than a few dissatisfied garment truckers in shops represented by the union. These men were not union members, but sought union membership and the benefits that Local 102's contract promised. Progressive Labor's meager cadre of colonizers bravely set out to break Local 102's "stranglehold" on garment truckers. Their confrontation with both employers and union officials resulted in three years of hard-fought skirmishes that threatened to create havoc in the industry.[9]

MARTINOT AT SELMAN'S EXPRESS

These PL-led work stoppages began breaking out in the late fall of 1967. On Tuesday, 1 November 1967, a week after workers walked out at City-Wide Trucking, forty truckers at Selman's Express, including PLer Steve Martinot, went out on strike. The party, always heartened by any evidence of worker militancy, enthusiastically embraced this second garment workers' strike in an industry which "rarely" experienced strikes. The Selman's Express strike was more than justified, PL believed, because truckers at Selman's received no benefits, nothing more than "hard work, and starvation wages." The party considered the truckers' wage of $80 a week and the helpers' wage of $68 a week to be "rock bottom." These meager wages were hardly fair compensation, PL argued, for working 11-hour days in "dangerous" conditions. "The men work in congested streets," *Challenge* reported, "amidst hundreds of trucks, pushing heavy hand-trucks and bad racks. A man has to be on his toes at all times in order not to get hurt." In PL's estimate, "A man can stand these conditions just so long, and then must rebel." But this facile gloss of worker psychology did not explain the relative infrequence of garment strikes, which were only "a drop in the bucket," PL admitted, "considering the conditions that garment truckers work under."[10]

The immediate cause of the Selman's Express strike was Selman's broken promise to increase wages after relocating. The truckers' frustration had been mounting for four months while they waited for Selman's to finish moving part of its operation to New Jersey and grant the promised raise. With the move completed and no raise forthcoming, the truckers struck. One trucker interviewed by *Challenge* was concise: "On Tuesday morning, we shut the place down. Then, when it was shut down, we just left and went down to the union and signed up. All of us." Forty

Selman's truckers, in a dramatic gesture of defiance, marched through the garment center to the Local 102 hall that Tuesday and joined the union.[11]

Progressive Labor did not immediately reveal the central role of its members in the labor unrest at Selman's. *Challenge*'s initial report on the Selman's strike was uncritically pro-union, even though PL despised the union in question, the ILGWU's Local 102. But the honeymoon was brief. Although Local 102 claimed the right to appoint shop stewards, Selman's new union members insisted on choosing their shop steward, and elected two workers to the post, Steve Martinot, a veteran PLer, and Leroy Porter, a rank-and-file trucker. Martinot's importance in the strike and the union led to his election as shop steward. But *Challenge* only reported the shop steward election after Selman's new union members wildcatted in late November 1967, and did not mention Martinot's stewardship until after he was tried by the union, in January 1968, for leading that wildcat. Even then, *Challenge* only hinted at his role as a PL organizer. Progressive Labor had made a big point of proclaiming its communist politics at HUAC hearings, but the party, fearing that the workers would not defend Martinot because they lacked sympathy for communism, was reluctant in its reporting on the struggle at Selman's to let the communist cat out of the bag.[12]

However, striking truckers had proclaimed *their* goals. They wanted to be paid the union scale of $109 for drivers and $99 for helpers, much more than Selman's was then paying its workers. But three weeks after the strike, the newly formed Selman's Strike Committee, headed by shop stewards Martinot and Porter, complained that although forty-five of the fifty men had joined the union and were paid up, they were still not getting union scale. Posing manhood as the opposite of slavery, PL's rhetoric in garment trucking played on themes of both gender and race. Union wages, *Challenge* asserted, would make the garment district "a place a man can be a man and not a slave, . . . a place where 40 hours work will be enough to raise a family." But despite their brief strike and newly acquired union membership, they were still "working like dogs in a slave labor camp."[13]

The strike committee blamed Local 102 and called on workers to fight for both a "decent job" and a "decent union that takes care of its members, not one that keeps them down." The workers' struggle for union scale was slowed down by a dispute over the ownership of the company. At the beginning of November, Local 102 had promised to get the Selman's strikers union scale and benefits, but instead it had submitted the workers' demands to binding arbitration, the strike committee charged. Although Gilbert Carriers had purchased Selman's in April 1967, the Interstate Commerce Commission had not yet approved the transfer of the company's southern routes to Gilbert. So while Selman's claimed to have sold out to Gilbert, Gilbert denied ownership of Selman's pending ICC approval. *Challenge* was incredulous: "Can you imagine 50 guys, working under sweatshop conditions every day in the garment district, not knowing who their boss is?"[14]

Progressive Labor blamed both the bosses and the Local 102 leadership for trying to put one over on the workers, and condemned the notion of *impartial* arbitration. "For years the boss has been getting richer and richer, while these men have stayed poor," PL observed, and asked, "How can anyone be impartial about that?" The arbitrator, Herbert Pensig, ruled that, pending an ICC decision, at which time the workers' case would go back to arbitration, drivers would get a wage increase of $10 a week, and other workers would get $6 a week, provided that no one got less than $70 a week. The workers also won Blue Cross benefits and union recognition. These provisions represented significant gains for the Selman's workers, but PL believed that during the arbitration, the impartial arbitrator and the union leaders had shown that they were "all on the bosses' side." The proof for PL was in the pudding—the arbitration agreement did not give the workers union scale.[15]

Encouraged by their shop stewards, Martinot and Porter, the Selman's workers rejected the arbitration. Regarding the union's claim, that it could not identify the employer, as "a lot of crap," they went out on a wildcat strike the day before Thanksgiving. One determined worker commented:

> We get paid, don't we? Somebody signs our checks each week. We don't care if its Gilbert or Selman. Someone's making the profits. We want them to give us union scale. We're union men now.[16]

Ironically, however, the wildcat strike paired pride in union membership with derision of the union. On the picket line, some strikers sang, "Who are we working for? / We don't know. / Who is Local 102 working for? / Selman's Express and Gilbert Carriers." It would be difficult for workers to resolve the tension inherent in their position, demanding union scale and condemning the union for not getting it for them.[17]

The strike was almost one hundred percent effective at the beginning, but it only lasted for two and one-half days, and then "fell apart."

Progressive Labor attributed the strike's failure to management's scare tactics, which included threatening workers' jobs and claiming that the strike was weak because it lacked union backing. In PL's view, management was conning workers into believing that the "strike's real strength was its main weakness." The growing belief among wildcatters that the strike could not succeed without union support weakened the strike, PL thought. Martinot urged continuing the strike, but was outvoted. One frustrated worker lamented, "We had Selman over a barrel, and then we let him go."[18]

Local 102 and Selman's, however, did not let the strike leaders go. Retribution was swift. Two weeks after the wildcat, Local 102 removed Martinot and Porter as shop stewards. Local 102 then brought the two stewards up on charges for "calling meetings of the workers, leading a wildcat strike, and slandering the union." Selman's workers saw two main reasons for the union's attack on Martinot and Porter, namely, scaring workers into accepting the next arbitration ruling, and getting a shop steward who would represent the union in the shop and "keep the workers in line." The party characterized Local 102's hourlong trial as a "Kangaroo Court in which the defendant can't bring any witnesses for his defense and isn't shown any proof of his 'guilt.'" Martinot admitted calling the November meeting which voted to wildcat, but defended that meeting as representing the "best kind of democracy." According to *Challenge*, the Local 102 trial board, apparently indulging in a bit of redbaiting, "said that maybe that was communist democracy, but not their kind of democracy." Martinot and Porter were expelled from Local 102.[19]

These expulsions provoked PL to ask who is hurt by a strike, and answer, "The boss, that's who. And only the boss." PL concluded, "If the union leaders feel that the wildcat strike was against them, that is not the fault of the workers. It is the fault of these union bureaucrats for being on the wrong side." Under these circumstances, PL maintained, a shop steward must choose whether to "stick with the men" or "play ball with the bureaucrats and the boss, and go along with their rules and regulations." Martinot and Porter, PL believed, had been expelled for not playing ball, but the new steward, George Jackson, was cut from different cloth. "Mr. Jackson," *Challenge* observed, "seems to like hanging around with the union officials." Progressive Labor threatened that if the new shop steward would not organize the workers and lead them in struggle, "they will organize themselves without him, and put forward their own leaders."[20]

However, the rank-and-file leaders that PL optimistically expected to materialize would not include Steve Martinot, who was fired from his job at Selman's Express on 18 April 1968, nearly six months after the struggle at Selman's had begun. Martinot's boss followed him to Queens, waited for him to "take a coffee break at the end of his run, and then fired him for sleeping on the job." Martinot's dismissal on this "trumped-up charge" provoked a brief work stoppage at Selman's the following day. Selman's workers demanded Martinot's reinstatement and their long-sought-after goal of a contract and union scale. While the strike did not win back Martinot's job, it did get the workers' wage demands before the arbitrator, who brought them to within $6 of union scale. But Selman's delayed payment. "It is amazing," *Challenge* commented, "the lengths these people will go—bosses, arbitrators, or crooked union leaders—to keep men from making a half-way decent wage." With regard to Martinot, PL believed that Local 102 leaders were only "pretending" to defend him: ". . . all they're doing is taking the case to another arbitration, which will be rigged." Hoping to transform a tactical defeat at the hands of Local 102 leaders into a strategic victory for the insurgents, PL circulated a leaflet around the garment district calling on garment workers to form intershop committees "to fight for a democratic, fighting union."[21]

LEMANSKY AT CITY-WIDE

Selman's Express was not the only garment trucking company experiencing a PL-led union insurgency and labor unrest. On 23 October 1967, a week before Selman's Express truckers marched through the garment district, workers at City-Wide Trucking had struck for union membership and conditions. At 8 A.M., with trucks loaded to fill orders for the Christmas rush, City-Wide truckers told their employer, "We're on strike until we get into the union and get the union contract enforced."[22]

To justify the strike, PL recounted a long list of worker grievances at City-Wide: only four of the shop's forty workers were union members, even though the Local 102 contract called for all to join after thirty days; the contract was not enforced, even for the few who belonged to the union; drivers were compelled to work 50-hour weeks, "and then didn't get time-and-a-half"; helpers and rack pushers did not get union scale; no workers got paid sick leave, and many received no pay for holidays; most workers received only one week of vacation, not the minimum of two weeks called for in the contract; trucks, which were often defective and unsafe, were usually sent out without helpers, even if they were scheduled to make twenty-five stops; Black and Puerto Rican workers did not get equal pay for equal work; and every worker had "his own individual deal with the boss." However, the City-Wide strikers, *Challenge* was pleased to report, were putting the old motto "In union there is strength" into practice: "Black, white and Puerto Rican; drivers, helpers, and rack-pushers, they stood together against the boss."[23]

It only took three hours to settle the strike. By 9:30 A.M. the strikers were at the Local 102 hall, and all who had thirty days or more on the job signed up with the union. By 11 A.M., the company, fearing lawsuits from its customers if shipments were delayed, agreed to give the workers union scale and benefits as soon as they paid the $50 union initiation fee. Following their brief strike, City-Wide workers chose strike committee member Ed Lemansky, who had not yet publicly identified himself as a PLer, as their shop steward. The Local 102 business agent for City-Wide, Tommy Montanelli, acquiesced to this demand, which meant that Lemansky replaced Local 102 executive board member Louie Chanin as shop steward. *Challenge* claimed that Chanin's "main job" before the strike had been telling workers who wanted to join the union to seek permission from City-Wide's owner, Bernie Taylor. According to PL, the workers "knew" that Local 102 leaders were "completely on the bosses' side," but legally had to join Local 102 to get "any union at all" because 102 had a contract with City-Wide. Even if City-Wide workers were as critical of Local 102 leaders as PL claimed, PL's characterization of the workers' dilemma acknowledges that they primarily sought to gain benefits. The workers also understood that their fight had "only just begun," and that it would be a "long battle" to enforce and improve the contract. "Just as Rome wasn't built in a day," *Challenge* cautioned, "the working class won't change its conditions with a 3-hour strike."[24]

Progressive Labor was not entirely shocked to find that the first "roadblock" faced by City-Wide workers in their quest for union scale and conditions was erected by the union itself. Local 102 insisted that the $50 union initiation fee be paid in one lump sum, and simultaneously indicated that they would only fight for the "push-boy" scale of $70 for both rack pushers and truck helpers, even though the union scale for helpers was $99. *Challenge* noted that helpers making $70 a week found it difficult to pay the initiation fee all at once, and when City-Wide gave them a $5 raise, "few could see any point in paying to join a union that would get them no increase in wages and none of them joined." On the other hand, all the drivers joined, and began receiving the union scale of $109. Because the workers were divided, with all of the drivers and none of the helpers in the union, the employer was "able to play them off against each other." To cut the drivers' overtime, for example, City-Wide used lower-paid helpers to strip and load the trucks. Local 102 claimed that enforcing the union contract, which called for having helpers on all trucks and paying them the union scale of $99, would "put City-Wide out of business." For PL, this was simply a scheme "to protect the bosses' ability to make big profits." *Challenge* bitterly reproached the bosses and union leaders for having "engineered it so that the only honest way to make a living wage is working 50, 60 or more hours a week."[25]

In view of this need for overtime, it is no wonder that when City-Wide cut the hours of two union drivers by postponing their starting times, union drivers "forced" Local 102 to take this and other matters to arbitration. At the hearing, City-Wide and the Master Truckmen of America, the employers' association, accused union drivers of engaging in a rule-book slowdown by refusing to drive defective trucks. To substantiate their claim, the employers cited the shop steward's refusal to drive a truck at night that had no headlights, and his refusal to drive a truck with defective steering. (*Challenge* did not identify the shop steward as PLer Ed Lemansky until several months later.) After affirming the need to have a "happy ship" at City-Wide, the arbitrator, Herbert Pensig, announced that he would not enforce the contract if he felt that it would put the company out of business. He then adjourned the hearing for three weeks to "examine the situation."[26]

Progressive Labor examined the situation as well. In their struggle with City-Wide, the workers, PL believed, had won the first round "through a solidly organized strike." But they had lost the second round through "deals between the boss, the union and the arbitrator." However, this was "a fight to the finish" and there were "many more rounds to go." As one worker put it, "A lot of guys here are beginning to see that we've got to get ready for a long, hard fight if we want to improve our condition. And we've got to be ready to hang on to anything we win." Despite this observation, which expressed PL's optimistic view that workers were coming around to the party's way of thinking, City-Wide workers had already backed away from a "fight to the finish" against a union whose benefits they sought. *Challenge* thought that there were other important lessons to be learned as well: (1) when drivers and helpers are divided, they are weakened; (2) although workers need the union as a weapon, they must be strong enough to force the union to enforce the contract; and (3) workers must build relations with rank-and-file union members in other shops to "fight the sellouts of the union leadership."[27]

Prominent among the Local 102 "sellouts" targeted by PL was the business agent for City-Wide, Gaetano "Tommy" Montanelli. *Challenge* cited a long list of grievances at City-Wide: the boss did not divide the work equally during slow periods; he used different starting times to discriminate against union men; he gave militant drivers less overtime; he still sent out some trucks without helpers; and he paid truck helpers no more than $75, far below union scale. Montanelli's response to these grievances, PL's newspaper complained, had been "tough talk and no action," and it blamed him for creating the scenario that dissuaded helpers from joining the union. *Challenge* also accused him of refusing to raise any issue other than equal starting times at the arbitration. It was the shop steward, according to *Challenge*, who had insisted on grieving the company's failure to distribute overtime equally or provide helpers on all the trucks. When layoffs began soon after the arbitration was adjourned, Montanelli's response, *Challenge* charged, was slow and tepid. But PL's newspaper was more than generous in crediting Business Agent Montanelli with having the gift of gab. It paraphrased his diatribe against City-Wide's owner, Bernie "Mumbles" Taylor:

> Why that sonofabitch. We'll close him up. I know what kind of guy he is; I drove for Moledzsky for 32 years, and he's one of the worst stores in the garment center but this guy is even worse . . . we'll take that bastard to arbitration.[28]

Exasperated, *Challenge* commented, "And then he doesn't even do THAT."[29]

Progressive Labor was not surprised, however, that even when City-Wide workers succeeded in "forcing" Local 102 to take their grievances to arbitration, they lost. *Challenge* claimed that everyone at the two-hour arbitration hearing (employers, union officials and the arbitrator), except Lemansky, who was not allowed to bring his members into the hearing, agreed that contract enforcement would put City-Wide out of business. A three-week adjournment, called by the arbitrator Pensig to examine City-Wide's finances, became a three-month delay, during which the company "kept slicing down the improvements won through the October strike."[30]

Resisting the continued erosion of their working conditions, three nonunion helpers, accompanied by four union drivers, went to the union hall to join Local 102. Business Agent Montanelli promised that they would receive the new helper's scale of $105. But according to *Challenge*, the Local 102 manager, George Irvine, then began "ranting and raving about 'that %##*! Progressive Labor Party'" and "shouted" that if he kept reading articles in *Challenge* critical of the union leadership, he would remove Ed Lemansky from his position as shop steward. *Challenge* was publicly sold to garment workers, including Local 102 members. Local 102's leaders, who read with consternation *Challenge* articles critical of them, regarded PL's newspaper as a threat to their reputation and power. They threatened to take punitive action against Lemansky, showing that they blamed him for the *Challenge* articles they found so offensive.[31]

When City-Wide's union members barraged Irvine with their grievances, however, he yelled at Montanelli and promised to support them. But the next day, City-Wide fired Sammy Lugo, one of the three helpers who had joined the union, and took the two others, Leon Jones and Santos Garcia, off the trucks. Although Lugo's firing was rescinded when co-workers complained, all three were reduced to being pushboys at $75 a week (a $5 raise), but with no overtime. The ironic result, *Challenge* observed, was that "all three were going home with less than they had before joining the union."[32]

Local 102 leaders responded by taking all the outstanding grievances at City-Wide back to arbitration. After two sessions, the arbitrator ruled that the employer would retain discretion over the use of helpers on the trucks, pay all workers—union and nonunion alike—union scale, not discriminate with regard to overtime, rotate layoffs during slack seasons, and call on Jones and Garcia first when helpers were needed on the trucks. (Lugo had been lured by Montanelli into taking a "steady job as driver" at another garment trucking company, which fired him three days later.) In PL's estimate, the arbitrator had ruled in favor of the employer on "almost every important issue." As telling for PL, City-Wide did not implement the arbitrator's rulings that favored the employees. For example, instead of giving preference to Jones and Garcia, City-Wide kept three nonunion workers as helpers, and paid them only the pushboy wage, now $75.[33]

The workers' experience at City-Wide convinced PL that "... the garment truckmen have no real union to help their struggles to improve their conditions. At every turn they must not only fight the boss, but the union leaders and the arbitrator as well." Progressive Labor was emphatic in denouncing impartial arbitration: "... there is no such thing as being 'impartial' in the struggle between workers and their boss. You are on one side or the other—and every case of 'impartial arbitration' in the history of this country has been one of 'impartial' AGAINST THE WORKERS." Given PL's low opinion of arbitration, it is not surprising that *Challenge* castigated the ILGWU for making arbitration its "main" way of fighting employers. The party predicted that garment truckmen "had a long battle ahead of them—to build a rank-and-file movement to fight the bosses, the union leaders, and their phoney 'impartial arbitrators'."[34]

For Progressive Labor, the battle came to a head a year after it had begun. When City-Wide's owner refused to pay workers "what they were entitled to for Columbus Day," Lemansky and ten others went to the union hall. Montanelli, the business agent, refused to file a grievance, and removed Lemansky as steward, appointing the former steward, Chanin, in his place. When the workers asked why, Montanelli arrogantly replied, "No reason. I don't have to give you guys any reason for what I do. You don't run the union, I do." A week later, on 31 October, City-Wide fired Lemansky for allegedly having called the company's owner, Bernie Taylor, a "fat Bastard" a month earlier. Lemansky thought that Taylor's charge was merely a pretext: "He couldn't come up with anything better. . . ." The PLer also believed that his removal as shop steward by Montanelli had emboldened Taylor, who "didn't have the guts to start anything himself." Lemansky called for a work stoppage to force City-Wide to rehire him and abide by the contract: "ITS UP TO EACH MAN TO DECIDE FOR HIMSELF. BE A MAN OR BE A SLAVE."[35]

Local 102 filed for arbitration. But City-Wide workers agreed that arbitration was "the bosses' game," *Challenge* reported, and resolved to strike. Only three workers scabbed. When one of them, Louie Chanin, a Local 102 executive board member, tried to pull a truck out, "the picketers blocked it, shouting 'SCAB, SCAB, SCAB!'" But the strikers, apparently, did more than shout epithets. According to *Challenge*, it "took a couple of dozen cops to clear the way for the truck," although no one was arrested. The picket line was bolstered by rank and filers from other unions, and by members of the Students for a Democratic Society—Student Labor Action Project. It seems probable that PL organized all these strike supporters. By the middle of the day, only one truck was moving, freight was stacking up, customers were "howling" and threatening lawsuits, and City-Wide's owner was "seeing his profits slip away," *Challenge* was happy to report.[36]

At this juncture, Local 102 and City-Wide interceded to break the strike with what PL called the "old stick and carrot combination." Union leaders threatened that workers would be fired if they did not return to work. At the same time, the employer offered to pay everyone for the whole day if they did return to work immediately. Lemansky's case would be arbitrated the next day. According to PL, the "threats and offers began to take their toll." The attitude of workers shifted from defending Lemansky "as part of the fight to defend and improve their own conditions" to defending him "as an individual." Many workers, PL's newspaper believed, found the "complete unity of the boss and the union leaders" demoralizing. One cynical worker informed *Challenge*, "Most of us are convinced the union ordered the boss to fire Eddie."[37]

Whether or not that was true, Business Agent Montanelli and Organizer George Jackson (who had replaced Steve Martinot as shop steward at Selman's Express before getting a job with the union) undermined Lemansky by passing around his FBI record, which "detailed his life since he was old enough to walk." *Challenge* (which did not question how he had obtained it) claimed that there was "little of importance in it that was not known by most of the men," but admitted that it had shaken some of the strikers. Anticommunism and fear of being scrutinized by the FBI probably both played a role in dissuading workers from continuing to ally themselves with Lemansky, who had become an extremely controversial figure. One striker lamented, "It's bad enough to be fighting the Mafia—but when they're teamed up with the FBI—it's too much." Another worker was astounded:

> Just to break the strike we pulled to save Eddie's job, they used the union leaders, the guys from the Association, the cops, the FBI, and the Arbitrator. Maybe if there were a couple more communists in the garment center they'd call out the National Guard or start dropping napalm, or something.[38]

Challenge asserted that the employer and union leaders were determined to "get rid of" Lemansky because he was a member of PL. *Challenge* quoted some of the striking workers who apparently agreed. One commented, "They know they can't buy communists out, so they've got to get rid of them." Another reflected, "I never really understood why they hate communists so much, until today—it's because guys like Eddie are ready to fight right down the line with us—and not sell us out just to line his own pocket." At a meeting held by the strikers, Lemansky explained his communist viewpoint:

> The thing they are most afraid of is communists among the workers, because they know that we're fighting for all the marbles. We say the bosses are living off our labor—every cent of their profits is stolen

from us. The only way we'll ever have a decent life is when we take it all away from them—the shops, the schools, the government. As workers, we're the ones that make this country run, and we get nothing but abuse in return. The workers have the power to force the bosses to give in—if we're organized and determined to fight.[39]

Nevertheless, by early afternoon, *Challenge* complained, few of the strikers could appreciate their own power, how they were "hurting the boss," or the "real chance" of spreading the struggle to other companies. City-Wide workers had more reason to make a realistic assessment of the situation than PL, whose revolutionary optimism ignored the potential cost to them of staking their jobs on the possibility of spreading the strike. But PL regretted that "The power of the enemy was in their minds and it seemed unbeatable." Even when it may have been reasonable for workers to make a tactical retreat, PL was philosophically disinclined to sanction their decision to do so.[40]

Even so, the strikers voted to resume working pending the outcome of Lemansky's arbitration. They chose a committee to accompany him to the arbitration hearing and report back. The picket line was disbanded at 2:30 P.M. and the strikers returned to work. But *Challenge*, which remained convinced that City-Wide workers had "no intention of giving up their struggle," quoted a militant worker to support its point of view: "They may have held us down this time—but if they think they've got us licked forever, they're in for a big surprise."[41] Persistently optimistic about workers' commitment to the struggle, PL blamed their failure to persevere in the short run on the bosses. Committed to militancy, and full of blame for sellouts, PL seldom admitted the virtue of making tactical retreats or faulted itself or workers for the loss of a struggle.

Progressive Labor was not surprised by either the conduct or the outcome of the arbitration. As promised, three City-Wide workers accompanied Ed Lemansky to the arbitration hearing, which was held on the day after the strike. He was represented by Local 102's leaders, Irvine, Montanelli, Jackson and Chanin, the last of whom, *Challenge* noted, had scabbed during the wildcat. Irvine, Montanelli and City-Wide's owner, Taylor, met privately with arbitrator Pensig before the hearing began. At this very informal proceeding, Pensig insisted that the defense be presented first, even though Lemansky objected that he "still did not know when it was that he supposedly cursed Taylor." Pensig also declined to consider the testimony of City-Wide workers, who asserted that Taylor, rather than Lemansky, was abusive. Sam Berger, manager of the Master Truckmen of America, the employers' association, introduced into evidence a leaflet Lemansky had written after his firing. Lemansky sarcastically asked, "Was I fired for things I did after I was fired?" However, Berger explained that he had introduced the leaflet in order to prove that Lemansky was a "disruptive person out to destroy the industry." Arbitrator Pensig complained that City-Wide workers had failed to follow "correct procedures." Two weeks later, on 22 November, he ruled, without explanation, that Lemansky's firing was justified.[42]

However, the attack on Lemansky did not end with his firing from City-Wide. After the 6 November wildcat strike to defend his job, Local 102 brought him up on charges of "usurping the authority of the union, and slandering the union leaders." Progressive Labor's Garment Workers Action Committee published his reply to these charges on 13 November, the day of his trial. Lemansky, emulating Zola, took the offensive: "It is not I who should be on trial, but you. I accuse you of the following misuse of authority: . . . " Heading Lemansky's list of accusations against the Local 102 leadership was his charge that they had "prevented men from joining the union." Estimating that between 10,000 and 20,000 workers were employed by the trucking companies under contract to Local 102, he alleged that only 2,000 belonged to the union, and complained that "even those of us who are members are continually cheated and abused."[43] Lemansky was defiant:

> You may expel me from the union. You may prevent me from working in the garment center. BUT YOU CANNOT PREVENT THE RANK AND FILE WORKERS FROM ORGANIZING AND FIGHTING. ONE PART OF THAT FIGHT, I ASSURE YOU, IS TO KICK YOU AND YOUR KIND OUT, AND BUILD A STRONG, DEMOCRATIC UNION THAT ORGANIZES MEN, AND LEADS THEM IN REAL FIGHTS AGAINST THE BOSSES.[44]

Despite these angry words, Lemansky's firing from City-Wide and his expulsion from Local 102 were setbacks for the PL-led insurgency in Local 102. Lemansky, who had stung both employers and union leaders, admitted that they possessed the institutional power to prevent him from continuing to lead on-the-job struggles in garment, but he expressed confidence that the rank and file would rise again. However, he did not provide an analysis of the defeat at City-Wide to justify his confidence that the rank and file would eventually triumph.

DAVIS AT NEWMARK

If Progressive Labor was down, it was not out of garment trucking or Local 102. In January 1970 PL cited recent militant strikes by General Electric and telephone workers, and delineated four primary demands for Local 102's upcoming contract negotiations, namely, everybody in the union, job security, teamster money for teamster work, and at least enough of an increase to keep up with prices. The party urged garment truckers to start talking about these issues, and "figuring out how to fight in our shops." Progressive Labor did not have to wait long for an indication of militancy among garment truckers. Workers at Ideal Garment Trucking called a work stoppage, on 19 January 1970, to protest the company's refusal to pay them for Martin Luther King, Jr.'s birthday. *Challenge* reported that "the boss quickly came to his knees," and everyone was paid for the day that they had taken off. Progressive Labor drew a big lesson from this admittedly small fight: "In unity there is strength." The party called on garment truckers to apply this lesson to Local 102's contract negotiations in February.[45]

However, even unity among workers in a single shop could only be achieved by fighting both employers and union officials, PL thought. On 3 February garment truckers at Newmark-Hurwitz struck for union membership. Instead of punching-in at 8 A.M., workers gathered in front of the shop, displaying signs such as, "JOIN THE UNION—DON'T PUNCH IN, UNION MEN PLEASE HELP." The employer responded by offering to put everyone in the union except the "ring leader," PLer Dave Davis. The striking workers rejected this offer, many saying, according to *Challenge*, that "He is going to be the first one signed up, or nobody works."[46]

When the Local 102 business agent, Nat Newman, arrived, he asked strikers to return to work and sign up with the union the next day. But the strikers were adamant about joining the union immediately, and Newman, who PL described as "someone out of an old gangster movie," acquiesced, taking all forty workers to the union hall. Asked why the union had never attempted to organize Newmark's workers, Newman simply said, "We don't solicit. However, anyone who wants to join can do so." One "oldtimer" didn't agree: "That's a lot of baloney; I've been down here four times on my own, and every time I've been told to come back tomorrow." When the business agent asked who he had talked to at the union, the answer was, "You Mr. Newman, YOU."[47]

Challenge reported that union membership improved working con-

ditions at Newmark: "The men have a feeling of their own strength, confidence in each other, and know that the boss can't push them around so
easily as before." But the struggle for unity did not end with the acquisition of union membership. The new contract gave a $14 raise to drivers
and helpers, but only $5 to pushers, who the company had been paying
above union scale in order to retain a steady workforce. The new shop
steward, PLer Davis, informed both the management and the union business agent that the shop would walk out unless the pushers, who *Challenge* reported had been the "strongest fighters in the strike," received a
$14 raise. Nearly every worker signed a petition supporting this demand,
and the company "caved in!" Davis, PL's organizer at Newmark, urged
his co-workers to remain united behind the principle "AN INJURY TO
ONE IS AN INJURY TO ALL," and to help other garment workers to
overcome their fear of employers and union leaders, so that they could
emulate the struggle at Newmark. "We cannot," Davis argued, "remain a
union shop for too long in a sea of non-union shops."[48]

Progressive Labor did not have to wait long for another shop to consider striking for union membership. Following the Newmark-Hurwitz
strike, Major-Dependable Trucking, which was owned by Newmark, anticipating a strike for union membership by its workers, put them into the
union. Even more significant, from PL's point of view, workers at United
Marlboro Trucking Co. asked Newmark workers to help them organize a
strike. The Newmark workers responded favorably. *Challenge* reported
that "Meetings were held, plans discussed and agreed on." On Thursday,
12 March 1970, a little more than a month after the Newmark strike,
workers at United Marlboro, supported by Newmark workers, also
struck for union membership, but this time unity would be more difficult
to sustain. Even though some workers had been employed by United
Marlboro for five years or more, they were still not admitted into Local
102. "Hell, we all know 102 is run by the Mafia," one worker informed
Challenge, "but we want in so we can get union scale and the benefits for
everyone. Also it'll give us a chance to change the union around."[49]

From PL's point of view, the union needed a good deal of changing
around. When Business Agent George Jackson arrived, he refused to
consider demands in excess of 102's new contract, which brought union
scale to $132 for drivers, to $122 for helpers and to $90 for pushers. Pro-
gressive Labor maintained that the new contract had been forced on
union members without their consent; Local 102 members had rejected
the contract at a union meeting and had been "so mad that only the union
goons prevented the union leaders from being strangled." Subsequently,

the Local 102 leadership took a vote on the contract by mail. The "garment workers knew damn well that the leaders of 102 threw the mailed vote into the garbage and accepted the contract," PL charged. At United Marlboro, Local 102's new contract was especially problematic for striking pushers, who were already making between $85 and $90. Faced with Jackson's refusal to demand more for them than union scale, pushers asked, "What the hell did we strike for, if we aren't going to get a decent raise?" Many wanted to continue striking, and were supported by some drivers and helpers. But the shop was not united on the issue of continuing the strike to gain a significant wage increase for pushers. Nevertheless, although some left the union hall without joining, most of the striking workers signed up. Noting that the United Marlboro workers had won the first round, but then allowed themselves to be split, PL warned that disunity meant defeat. Two years before, the party recalled, City-Wide workers had staged a successful strike, but because only the drivers had won anything from striking, they could not defend their gains.[50]

The unity of United Marlboro workers was quickly tested again. On Friday, 13 March, the day after the strike, twenty workers were fired, and by Monday the picket line was back up. A leaflet issued by the workers claimed: "After we returned to work, some of us were transferred or fired with no reason. These transfers and firings are illegal. We are therefore obliged to strike." This leaflet also asserted that the workers had made a "big mistake" in going back to work before they had won their demand for a raise for pushers. Within three and a half hours the company agreed to rehire all the fired workers, but still refused to grant pushers the $14 wage increase that they were seeking. Even though the workers had achieved only a partial victory, once again PL argued that "the battle was important." Progressive Labor saw the firings at United Marlboro as an attempt by the employers and union leaders to "stem the rising tide of anger which is spreading throughout the garment industry." But instead of frightening workers, the firings had "made the guys madder, and more determined to fight even harder." This victory by United Marlboro workers had strategic importance because it was part of a growing movement of garment workers. *Challenge* believed that "this movement should spread," and that the key to spreading the movement was "fighting for the lowest paid workers."[51]

Apparently, the strike movement did spread, this time to Garment Carriers. *Challenge* allowed a leaflet written by one of the workers there to tell the story: "We the workers of Garment Carriers recently went on strike for unionization of the shop." The workers had gone to the Local

102 hall and signed up. But even though union officials had assured them that they were now represented by the union, and would begin receiving union scale, when they looked at their pay stubs that pay day, there was "no increase whatsoever." The leaflet's author castigated the union, the employer and his fellow workers:

> I accuse the union of dragging its feet. I also accuse the management of Garment Carriers of exploiting the Puerto Rican and Black workers in the Shop. . . . I also accuse them of treating us as if we were less than men and had no mentality whatsoever, but I don't blame them for it because I accuse us of accepting 2nd class pay and treatment.[52]

Echoing an important PL theme in garment trucking, the militant Garment Carriers worker insisted, "We have to stop letting this man divide us, for our strength lies in our unity." He called on his fellow workers to be cognizant of their power to improve their "conditions both monetarily and benefit-wise," but warned them to remember, "people only do what you let them do."[53]

Other shops were planning walkouts as well, and with the strike movement spreading, PL surmised that "the bosses had to act," and accused the "bosses and union leaders" of deciding to "smash the men's movement." The counterattack came at United Marlboro. The company had been chipping away at the gains won by United Marlboro strikers in early March. The company now reduced or entirely eliminated overtime for strike activists, and Mike Velasquez, one of the strike leaders, was "harassed continually." The United Marlboro workers responded by striking for a third time.[54]

With the police already on the scene, one of the company's foremen called the strike illegal and suggested that strikers could be subject to arrest if they did not return to work. But this threat, PL claimed, "increased the men's anger and made them stronger." When Business Agent George Jackson arrived, he told management, "If they don't go back to work, fire them all." He told strikers to "go back to work, you have no reason to be on strike." To emphasize his opposition to the strike, Jackson then pulled out a truck. While some strikers were enraged, others were demoralized by Jackson's action. Progressive Labor complained that they reacted this way because they had held the "illusion" that the union would "straighten things out," and that when Jackson "smashed" this "illusion," they were "jolted and temporarily confused." They began returning to work. Management fired strike leader Velasquez and, within a few days, "laid-off" eleven more workers. The party admitted that management had won round three of the fight at United Marlboro. A few days later, however, "guys from a number of shops were getting together and planning a new struggle," a hopeful *Challenge* reported, and "resolved to build a rank-and-file movement that would involve the mass of workers in many different shops who would fight harder and better the next time around—because everyone was convinced that there would be a next time."[55]

The next struggle was at Newmark, where grievances began to pile up over the summer. It appeared that new employees were not being admitted into the union. When one worker went to the Local 102 hall to join, George Jackson refused to accept his application, and on his return to the shop, he was fired. Even though Newmark workers were able to force his rehiring by threatening to strike, the union continued to deny him, and all other new employees, union membership.[56]

Local 102 then tried to rid itself of its principal antagonist at Newmark, PLer Dave Davis, whom the union attempted to expel in the fall of 1970. Davis brought ten workers from Newmark and five from United Marlboro to attend his trial. According to Davis, who wrote a letter to *Challenge* describing the situation, these workers "argued" with Local 102 officials for an hour. Davis noted that workers came to his defense despite the fact that George Jackson had deluged them with a "flood of threats and intimidation." Davis accused Jackson of warning Newmark's Dominican workers, many of whom were not citizens, that if they attended Davis' trial, they would, in addition to being expelled from the union, be reported to immigration, which would deport them for "supporting a known communist." To Davis, this "marked a new low in 102's long history of working for the bosses against the workers." The union leaders, he believed, were especially frightened of the unity between the Newmark and United Marlboro workers. These "leaders," Davis asserted, are "so scared of being swept away that they'll do anything to hang on." What frightened Local 102 leaders most, Davis thought, was communism, because "that's the program that will put them out of business for good."[57]

PLERS AND GARMENT TRUCKERS

In fact, the Local 102 leadership succeeded in putting the tenuous PL-led insurgency out of business. To be sure, PL organizers Martinot, Lemansky and Davis were successful for a time in leading wildcat strikes for union membership, and union scale and benefits. Determined to lead garment workers in struggle, these PL organizers often found garment truckers ready to militantly fight against their employers and, if necessary, their union leaders in order to have a better life. If garment truckers did not, for the most part, embrace revolutionary goals, they were, nevertheless, willing to elect PLers as their shop stewards in order to enhance their struggle for better conditions. Even if rank-and-file workers were not initially aware of their shop stewards' communist politics, they learned fairly quickly. Whether workers believed that PLers were useful to the struggle because they were communists or in spite of their being communists is difficult to determine. Party organizers, however, saw the small, hard-fought reform struggles that they led in a few garment shops as part of a historical process that would eventually make PL the vanguard of the working class. Garment truckers, with few exceptions, viewed their struggle in much less expansive terms. Because their respective outlooks differed, PLers and garment truckers sometimes made different cost-benefit analyses. Progressive Laborites, for example, were politically committed to promoting militant and unified struggle, while garment truckers sometimes retreated from high-risk militancy or sacrificed unity for immediate gains. The party rejected arbitration on principle, while garment truckers sometimes gave arbitrators the benefit of the doubt.[58]

However, despite these differences, garment truckers sometimes took significant risks to defend PLers. This may have reflected a combination of friendship, political principles, respect and personal loyalty forged through common work and common struggle, and an estimation that PLers had become an integral and, perhaps, necessary part of the struggle for better working conditions. But the willingness or ability of garment truckers to defend PLers was severely tested by both employers and Local 102 leaders, who seemed quite determined to use all the institutional power at their disposal to rid themselves of PL. They employed a variety of weapons against PL organizers, namely, removing PLers as shop stewards, expelling them from the union, and firing them. The employers and Local 102 officials may simply have been annoyed at the trouble that PL organizers seemed to be causing, or they may have acted out of an old aversion to communists, or they may have felt threatened by a potentially volatile combination of worker militancy and communist organizers and adopted an attitude of *better safe than sorry*. Local 102 only had 2,000 members. Another 15,000 workers were theoretically eligible for union membership and presumably frustrated that they were not receiving union scale and benefits. Had a significant number of these workers joined the union under PL's leadership, Local 102's leadership might have been defeated by a PL-led insurgency, placing PL in a strategic position within the garment industry.[59]

The stakes were high, but was there any real potential for such a development? There was some evidence that the strike movement for union membership and conditions might spread, but it is difficult to know how far PL might have gotten if unopposed by employers and union leaders, who—either separately or together—nipped the tiny PL-led insurgency in the bud. It is also hard to say whether a few more, or even many more, PL organizers in garment trucking would have made a difference. It does seem clear that the few PLers in garment trucking were simply no match for the forces arrayed against them. Ultimately, the garment truckers, despite the militancy that they sometimes displayed, were not bent on making a revolution. They only sought the limited benefits that attached, they hoped, to union membership. That was the heart of the problem for PL. It seems evident that garment workers trying to gain access to the union in order to reap the rewards that membership could bestow were often frustrated by the union itself. Progressive Labor's attempt to turn this frustration into insurgency was sometimes effective, but workers who became completely cynical about the union were likely to accept a modus vivendi with the employer and the union rather than incur significant risks in an uphill battle against both. The garment workers' problems were all too real, and their willingness to courageously fight for themselves is evident, but PL's colonists in the garment center, as a handful of outside agitators, could not shape the garment workers' struggle to suit their own revolutionary agenda.

After three years of fighting, the tiny PL landing party had not secured a beachhead in garment trucking companies; it had been wiped out by a pincers movement of garment trucking companies and Local 102 leaders. Progressive Labor's militancy appealed to some discontented truckers, some of whom defended PLers knowing they were communists. But garment truckers were not reckless, and anticommunism undermined support for PL organizers. Progressive Labor's rhetoric overestimated both the workers' militancy and their openness to communism. At first, PL advocated militancy and hesitated approaching the issue of communism, but it eventually insisted on pushing both of these themes as though the revolution were imminent. It ran counter to PL's ideology to advise compromise or soft-pedal the communist issue once it was on the table. If PL was overpowered by management and the union (with government assistance), it was also unwilling to admit that it had misestimated either the workers or the efficacy of its own tactics.

Despite PL's insistence on the long-range character of the struggle, PL's organizers in garment trucking were only sojourners in New York City's industrial heartland. Evidently, they were not able to recruit indigenous garment workers to carry on their campaign. But Progressive Labor did not give up on garment trucking. In February 1974 *Challenge* recalled the 1967 struggle to gain membership in Local 102, and called on garment workers to organize. Progressive Labor did not give up on New York City's garment industry, but it never regained even the tenuous foothold it had achieved in the garment trucking shops in the late 1960s and early 1970s.

CHAPTER 7

Anatomy of a Communist-Led Wildcat Strike

Progressive Labor, Figure Flattery
and Local 32, ILGWU, 1968

In August 1968 a wildcat strike broke out at Figure Flattery in the heart of Manhattan's West Side industrial district. According to the strike's leader, Felipe DeJesus, it was the "first" worker-led strike in New York City's garment industry in "forty years."[1] Even so, it was a relatively minor disturbance in a year marked by such major events as the Tet Offensive, the French general strike, the assassinations of Martin Luther King, Jr. and Robert Kennedy, and the student strike at New York City's Columbia University. Historian David Caute called 1968 "the most turbulent year since the end of World War II."[2] It was also the centenary of the Cry of Lares, the failed insurrection that proclaimed the Republic of Puerto Rico. The seminal Puerto Rican nationalist Ramon Emeterio Betances had urged his compatriots to rebel by declaring: "The great are only great because we are on our knees. Let us arise."[3] Strike leader DeJesus was a revolutionary Puerto Rican nationalist as well as a communist. Echoing Betances, who one hundred years before had urged his compatriots to arise, DeJesus told his co-workers at Figure Flattery that they could fight back and win, and they did—for a while. The wildcat strike at Figure Flattery was the most significant rebellion of industrial workers that Progressive Labor ever led in New York.[4]

A PRECOCIOUS REVOLUTIONARY
IN COLONIAL PUERTO RICO

Felipe DeJesus was born in 1943, and grew up in Arecibo, Puerto Rico during the 1940s and 1950s. His parents made a modest living from their small restaurant but did not earn enough to rise above their working-class status. Although he was only dimly aware of it, class differentiations bothered Felipe more than any other issue that he confronted as a youth. By the time he was thirteen years of age, he already considered himself a revolutionary.⁵

When DeJesus entered his teens in the 1950s, Puerto Rico was ruled by the repressive regime of Luis Munoz Marin, who had become the first Puerto Rican colonial governor in 1948, and the first head of the new Commonwealth of Puerto Rico in 1952. According to DeJesus, people could not converse freely in public, and the police might stop and search someone for any reason. Youths could not gather on a street corner or be out after 9 P.M. without risking arrest. From his point of view, Puerto Rico in the 1950s was a "classic police state."⁶

Commonwealth authorities had resorted to political repression in order to stifle the tradition of revolutionary nationalist insurrections begun by Betances and continued by Pedro Albizu Campos in the 1930s. In 1948, not long after Albizu Campos returned to Puerto Rico, university students struck. In response, Puerto Rico's Legislative Assembly passed the infamous Law 53, known as the *Law of the Muzzle*. Under this statute, which was a duplicate of the Smith Act, both communists and nationalists were imprisoned—including the Nationalist Party leader, Albizu Campos, who was sentenced to fifty-six years in prison.⁷

On 3 July 1950 the United States Congress passed Public Law 600, which paved the way for the creation of the Commonwealth. Nationalists emphatically rejected Law 600, the promised Commonwealth, and Munoz Marin, the Commonwealth's most prominent Puerto Rican proponent. On 30 October 1950 a few poorly armed nationalists attacked his residence, and there were subsequent outbreaks of violence in a number of Puerto Rican cities, including Arecibo, where the young DeJesus lived. On 1 November 1950, two nationalists attacked Blair House in Washington, D.C., but failed to assassinate President Truman. In Puerto Rico, Munoz Marin mobilized the National Guard and the state police to put down this futile insurrection, and he ordered the mass arrest of communists, nationalists and their sympathizers. Although Munoz Marin pardoned Albizu Campos, who was ill, in 1953, he revoked the pardon a year later, after four nationalists fired their weapons in the United States Congress, shouting "Long live free Puerto Rico!"⁸

The nationalist convulsions and consequent political repression that accompanied Puerto Rico's transition to Commonwealth status marked Felipe DeJesus' formative years, and help to explain his youthful com-

mitment to revolution. He secretly joined the *illegal* independence movement while still in his early teens. When he graduated from high school,
he was awarded a scholarship to the University of Puerto Rico at Rio
Piedras, but was required to improve his grades in order to retain it. On
campus he was active in the *Federacion de Universitarios Pro Independencia*, which had been founded in 1956. The atmosphere at the university had been repressive since the abortive student strike of 1948.
According to one observer who graduated from Rio Piedras and taught
there during the 1960s, *FUPI* was a "catalyst for the reforms desired by
the most progressive students." However, as a consequence of his political activity, DeJesus' grades went down, costing him his scholarship.
Like many other economically pressed Puerto Ricans at the time, he
came to New York seeking employment.[9]

NATIONALIST AND COMMUNIST IN NEW YORK

To earn a living in New York, DeJesus got a job in a print shop, but to fulfill his political aspirations, he joined the *Acion Patriotica Unitaria*,
which promoted the aims of the proscribed Nationalist party. Although
still quite young, DeJesus had been active in the Puerto Rican nationalist
movement throughout his teens, and *APU* trusted him sufficiently to appoint him as secretary of its New York branch.[10]

   However, *APU* was plagued by an ideological dispute between traditional nationalists and those who were oriented toward the working
class. The traditional nationalists were led by Ramon Medina Ramirez,
who had spent many years in jail for nationalist activities; he was a close
friend of Pedro Albizu Campos, and had led the Nationalist Party while
Albizu Campos was in prison. The pro-worker section of *APU* argued
that the national bourgeoisie and petty bourgeoisie in Puerto Rico had
failed to fulfill their historical mission of freeing Puerto Rico from imperialist domination. They further maintained that socialist ideology was
triumphant throughout the world, and that working people around the
world should lead the anti-imperialist struggle. The socialists were led
by another veteran Nationalist, Juan Antonio Corretjer, who also was a
close associate of Albizu Campos. However, Corretjer faulted Albizu
Campos for failing to focus on the needs of workers.[11]

   According to DeJesus, the majority of *APU*'s membership was oriented toward socialism. Even so, the organization was unable to resolve its ideological differences and disbanded early in 1963. Eighteen
months later, Corretjer founded *La Liga Socialista Puertorriqueña*,

which DeJesus helped to organize from its origins but could not join so long as he continued to live in New York. The Puerto Rican Socialist League had made a political decision that only Puerto Ricans residing on the island could be members (a rule which it later dropped). Like most Puerto Rican New Yorkers, DeJesus was planning to return to Puerto Rico, but his encounter with Progressive Labor provided him with new opportunities for political engagement in New York.[12]

The young Progressive Labor Movement, which had been founded by ex-CPers in July 1962, enjoyed fraternal relations with the newly formed Puerto Rican Socialist League. The League viewed protest movements in the United States as vital to the success of its own struggle in Puerto Rico. Corretjer wrote:

> So far as Puerto Rico is concerned the general protest movement, class oriented as well as nationalistic, is our Sierra Maestra. The Yankee protest movement, whether it involves workers, Negroes or be it against military service, is our Second Front.[13]

Corretjer's strategic outlook was echoed by Sandra Rodriguez, a Socialist League member who had recently come to New York from Puerto Rico. Speaking in Spanish at a PL garment rally in 1965, she urged Puerto Rican New Yorkers to protest their oppressive conditions. "By fighting for justice and equality here," she argued, "we fight for a better life in Puerto Rico as well." Progressive Labor welcomed her call for Puerto Ricans to support the revolutionary movement in the United States.[14] In view of their fraternal relations, it is not surprising that League supporters and PLers in New York frequently attended each other's meetings and demonstrations.[15]

DeJesus was favorably impressed by PL's community organizing efforts on New York's Lower East Side, where he lived. Progressive Labor had a "dingy storefront" headquarters on East Third Street, in the midst of a neighborhood that PL's local club leader, Alice Jerome, vividly described: "These 15 square blocks of ancient slums and bedraggled stores, interspersed with modest churches and shabby schools, contain about 100,000 people—of every nationality, religion and occupation in the world—but very few bankers." Progressive Labor's Lower East Side club had begun as the Integrated Workers in the summer of 1962; a nominally independent "social club of Puerto Rican and North American young people to fight against job discrimination," it officially affiliated with PLM in November 1962.[16]

According to DeJesus, PL's young organizers, most of whom were White North Americans, were not afraid to relate to people on the streets. "They did a beautiful job," he believed, tackling a variety of issues, but especially organizing against slumlords, and, consequently, they had a "good" base in the highly mixed neighborhood. But Alice Jerome, frustrated at her club's inability to recruit "active, stable" party members from its mostly Spanish-speaking circle of about one hundred supporters, warned her fellow community organizers, "If we cannot fit into the community, if we are not ready to live the life of the people, we had best get into other work and stop kidding ourselves."[17]

According to DeJesus, living "the life of the people" included participating in urban riots, which began breaking out in the mid-1960s. But although PL encouraged the Harlem Rebellion of 1964, it did not send White organizers into the riot-torn community. This decision, possibly motivated by pragmatic concerns, was consistent with PL's support of revolutionary nationalism (which it abandoned at the end of the 1960s). DeJesus disagreed, believing that ideology counted more than nationality or race. He was chagrined by the subsequent decline he observed in the effectiveness of PL's community organizing.[18]

When rioting broke out in Spanish Harlem, DeJesus wanted to participate, but PL's chairman, Milt Rosen, advised him to demur on the grounds that revolution was something else. DeJesus answered:

> My people are out on the streets. I've got to be with them. I cannot preach revolution and then say that's not the way its done.[19]

Ignoring Rosen's advice, he joined his rioting compatriots.[20] Disagreements might arise, but DeJesus believed that PL's struggle for socialism in the United States and support for national liberation struggles around the world, complimented the Socialist League's fight for Puerto Rican independence. Progressive Labor recruited him to become a reporter for *Desafio*, the Spanish-language version of its new newspaper, *Challenge*, which began publication in mid-1964. He became the editor of *Desafio* in 1966.[21]

FROM SOAPBOX ORATOR TO "ORDER PICKER"

In addition to DeJesus' work on *Desafio*, both as reporter and editor, he become a regular speaker at PL's weekly rallies in the garment center. Progressive Labor pinned its hopes for communist revolution on industrial workers, and in New York City that primarily meant garment workers—the city's largest group of industrial workers. Progressive Labor's preoccupation with garment workers predated the founding of PLM in July 1962. When he was the Communist Party's labor secretary in New York State in the late 1950s, PL's chairman, Milt Rosen, had organized communist street rallies in New York City's garment district, and the newly founded PL followed suit. These PL rallies were, according to DeJesus, open forums for anti-imperialist speakers of various ideological stripes.[22]

DeJesus evidently was an effective speaker at PL's garment center rallies. Speaking in Spanish, he usually drew an attentive, and sometimes an enthusiastic, audience. At one of these rallies, he pointed out "that while the government spends millions of the workers' tax dollars to build bases in Puerto Rico aimed at stifling people's revolutions in Latin America, it doesn't lift a finger to raise the minimum wage in New York above $1.25." He advocated fighting for higher wages in New York City as the reverse side of an anti-imperialist coin.[23]

According to DeJesus, his ability to address the concerns of working people in the garment center did not stem from personal charisma but from his own working-class background and experience of daily life in the barrio (New York's Lower East Side before its gentrification). However, he also praised PL for being well-organized, and—most important—for being effective from an "ideological and national point of view," that is, for espousing anti-imperialist politics, and for supporting national liberation struggles throughout the world, including the struggle for Puerto Rican independence, which was never far from his mind.[24]

From DeJesus' point of view, Puerto Rican workers, whether they lived in Puerto Rico or New York, were being exploited and oppressed by employers, the government and even such labor unions as the International Ladies' Garment Workers' Union. At another PL garment rally, he declared:

> Not satisfied with the sweatshops in New York, the ILGWU has moved its racketeering union to Puerto Rico. The 40,000 Puerto Rican garment workers are a tremendous potential force right here in New York to fight for their own organization and throw out the Dubinsky-type mis-leaders who sit on our backs."[25]

When he made this speech, DeJesus was editor of *Desafio*. His remarks echoed PL's strong disdain for the ILGWU, and reflected his own strong identification with the plight of Puerto Rican garment workers in New

York. By 1968, however, he had become one of the 40,000 "sweated" Puerto Rican workers in New York City's industrial heartland, and had an opportunity to tap—at the point of production—their "tremendous potential force."[26]

By the mid-1960s, the newly founded Progressive Labor Party wanted to shift the focus of its campaign to recruit working-class people from community organizing to organizing workers at the point of production. But PLP was almost entirely comprised of students and unemployed ex-students. To lead workers at the point of production, PL's young cadres would have to find jobs. From the PL leadership's point of view, getting some of its organizers to go work in the garment industry was the most important aspect of its campaign to turn PL in New York City into a party of the working class.[27]

The handful of PLers whom the PL leadership asked to find garment jobs were able to find work as rack pushers and truck helpers in the garment trucking industry, which became the main focus of PL's garment concentration. But despite the strategic importance of garment trucking, which linked thousands of small shops together into New York City's major industry, garment truckers, as we have seen, were atypical garment workers in at least one important respect—they were predominantly male in an overwhelmingly female industry.[28]

Moreover, PL's young, White, male garment organizers were quickly promoted from their starting slots as pushers and helpers (almost all of whom were Black and Hispanic) into positions as truck drivers. During the 1960s, according to Felipe DeJesus, garment workers considered garment truck drivers, whose salary and benefits far exceeded their own, to be a privileged group of workers—so privileged that from the point of view of low-paid garment workers, garment truck drivers were not garment workers at all. White drivers in particular, DeJesus alleged, "had it nice and easy" because, unlike Black and Hispanic drivers, they were typically sent out with a helper. To DeJesus, it was undeniable that Whites generally enjoyed a privileged position "at the production level."[29]

Nevertheless, one of PL's organizers in garment trucking, Ed Lemansky, used his new position as truck driver to get other PLers into garment shops. In the course of making deliveries and pickups, the affable Lemansky made friends with a supervisor at Figure Flattery, a ladies' undergarment factory on Manhattan's Lower West Side. Lemansky helped PLer Marcelino "Pancho" Lopez and Felipe DeJesus to get jobs at Figure Flattery.[30]

When DeJesus began working at Figure Flattery in early 1968, he was no longer editor of *Desafio*; he was technically a *friend* of PL rather than a party member. He did not resign from PL over political differences but because he was offended by PL's interference in his personal life. The party had criticized DeJesus, who was divorced, for having a number of sexual liaisons with women. However, since the women with whom he had relationships were educated professionals, he rejected PL's charge that he was exploiting them, and he left the party to escape its puritanical jurisdiction over his personal life.[31]

Nevertheless, Ed Lemansky was not disappointed in his expectation that DeJesus would organize on his new job as an order picker at Figure Flattery. Indeed, DeJesus started work with the intention of learning how to organize in the workplace; he looked upon Figure Flattery as a school for organizing, where he could learn from the workers. He worked closely with PL during the ensuing months, which turned out to be much more eventful than he could possibly have predicted.[32]

A SWEATSHOP ON TENTH AVENUE

The Figure Flattery Company occupied at least two floors of a building at Eighty-five Tenth Avenue, near Fifteenth Street, in the heart of Manhattan's West Side industrial district. It was a large factory that manufactured ladies' undergarments. The garment industry is seasonable, and the size of Figure Flattery's workforce fluctuated with the seasons, but estimating conservatively, the factory employed between four hundred and eight hundred workers. Like almost everything else about Figure Flattery, the size of its workforce became an issue in the debate between PL and the ILGWU. What seems less debatable is that the great majority of the workers were women, and either Black or Hispanic, with the Latin American workers, who came from a wide variety of countries, outnumbering the Black workers.[33]

The job of order picker required DeJesus to pick up various pieces of apparel (four brassieres, six pairs of panties, etc.) from bins located throughout the factory, and bring them to the shipping department. His job enabled him to speak daily with the Hispanic women who comprised a majority of the workforce. As an aspiring on-the-job organizer, he was in an ideal position to get to know a wide variety of his co-workers and to learn their problems. Apparently, there was a lot to learn.[34]

In February 1968, after working at Figure Flattery for only three weeks, PLer Marcelino Lopez wrote a piece for *Challenge* about conditions in the factory, but he withheld it from publication until much later because, he explained, "I considered it poor, and the information I had at hand was something from another world." According to PL's labor secretary, Wally Linder, Figure Flattery workers faced a host of "insufferable sweatshop conditions."[35]

The most apparent was low pay: the hourly rate of $1.55 for floor workers was $.30 above the federal minimum wage, and amounted to $62.00 for a 40-hour week. Part of the low-wage problem, according to DeJesus, was that many production workers worked on a piece-rate basis. The contract provided that piece rates be set to yield earnings "at least 20 percent higher than the minimum for the craft." But most of the piece-rate workers, DeJesus alleged, could not correctly calculate their wages, and consequently were "ripped-off" by the company. Moreover, discrimination and favoritism were evident in the distribution of overtime work, which these underpaid workers anxiously sought.[36]

According to PL, benefits were as problematic as wages. DeJesus claimed that management cheated workers out of benefits by making spelling and accounting errors. He alleged that in more than a few cases workers who had paid their union dues lost medical benefits or vacation pay simply because the company mistyped their names, or failed to record their payments. Some of these workers had between twelve and fifteen years of service. Another company practice that prevented workers from getting benefits involved employing them for sixty days, the time it took them to pay off their union books, laying them off for a few months, and then rehiring them, at which point they would have to pay off their union books all over again. Furthermore, the many workers who could not read English were unaware of the benefits described in their union contract, and even those who, like DeJesus, were literate in English found it very difficult to obtain a copy of the contract.[37]

Figure Flattery, according to Marcelino Lopez, "heaped insult on top of exploitation." In addition to cheating workers out of wages and benefits, the company accused them of stealing. DeJesus claimed that it was supervisors and administrators who actually stole from the company. Even so, management established a regime of constant spying. Worse still, they set up special fences inside the factory; gates barring all the emergency exits were locked fifteen minutes after work began. A sentry was posted at the only open door, and the company reserved the right to check wallets, pocketbooks and packages that workers brought in or out. DeJesus felt that the factory was run like a jail. This "lock-in" reminded Wally Linder of employer practices at the infamous Triangle

Shirtwaist Company, where 146 workers died in a fire on 25 March 1911 because management kept the exit doors locked. Even more inflammatory than evoking New York City's most infamous garment sweatshop, Linder likened Figure Flattery to a "concentration camp."[38]

Ironically, DeJesus felt that the most serious problem at Figure Flattery was sexual harassment, which he claimed was "rampant." He reported that in addition to being insulted and cursed at by their male foremen, female workers were obliged to tolerate sexual abuse in order to keep their desperately needed jobs. Marcelino Lopez cited the "despotism" of a Latin American foreman, who "picked on everybody around him, but was particularly disgusting with the women." This egregious exploitation of the women who worked at Figure Flattery was also reminiscent of the conditions that had prevailed in New York City's shirtwaist industry sixty years before. Just as women garment workers had done then, the women who worked at Figure Flattery rebelled. In 1909 it was the ILGWU that had, after a failed strike at Triangle Shirtwaist, led the victorious general strike of New York City garment workers; but at Figure Flattery in 1968, the strike was called in spite of the ILGWU.[39]

Not surprisingly, neither the Figure Flattery management nor the leadership of Local 32, ILGWU acknowledged the existence of sweatshop conditions at the factory, and vigorously denied PL's charges. DeJesus, who wanted to justify the wildcat, had reason to exaggerate the problems at the plant, just as both the management and the union were motivated to minimize the problems that may have existed in order to delegitimate the strike. However, it is highly unlikely that PL's charges were made up out of whole cloth. The fact that Figure Flattery workers struck suggests that there were serious problems at the plant; there simply was too much smoke for there to be no fire. The only alternative explanation is that DeJesus was able to motivate his co-workers to wildcat in the absence of any serious underlying problems involving wages and working conditions. That explanation stretches credulity; it ascribes too much power to DeJesus as a labor agitator.[40]

In any case, even if only half of PL's charges were true, conditions at Figure Flattery were very oppressive. Whether such conditions were typical of the industry is an important question. The Figure Flattery Company, like the infamous Triangle Shirtwaist Company, may have been worse than the average garment shop, but it is unlikely that conditions at Figure Flattery were absolutely atypical. The party was unable to spread the strike, but that does not rule out similar conditions in other shops. It may simply be that the presence of an effective labor agitator tipped the scales in favor of a wildcat at Figure Flattery. At least, both management and Local 32 treated DeJesus as though they believed that his leadership was an essential ingredient in the explosive mixture that ignited at Figure Flattery in August 1968.[41]

A CATALYST FOR REBELLION

DeJesus told his co-workers, individually and collectively, that "there was no need for them to be exploited or treated the way they were"; he let them know that they could fight the boss and win. That was a powerful message, but it was only a beginning. About four months after he started working at Figure Flattery, DeJesus, Lopez and other Local 32 members at the factory asserted their independence from the Local 32 leadership by forming a trade union caucus, which they called the Workers Action Committee. Subscribing to the theory that "the workers are the union," the committee undertook to educate Figure Flattery workers about the union's contract and constitution. Arguing that the workplace "is not a prison," it advised workers that they would have to learn about the labor laws as well. The committee, which held meetings weekly, was bold enough to demand time to meet in the shop during working hours.[42]

His co-workers on the ninth floor elected DeJesus as their Local 32 shop steward (but only after union officials had voided his two-to-one majority on the first ballot). The union leadership, according to PL's Wally Linder, *was* able to prevent the election of a "militant" woman on the tenth floor, but that did not stop the growing rebellion. Under DeJesus' leadership, the committee assembled a list of complaints and demands, which they presented to their union, Corset and Brassiere Workers Local 32, International Ladies' Garment Workers' Union.[43]

According to DeJesus, the Local 32 business agent whom they called treated their appeal as though it were a joke. DeJesus believed that the union had grown complacent because it had not struck for "forty" years. He was contemptuous of the Local 32 business agents; there were no Hispanics among them, he complained, only a Jew, an Italian and a Cuban, at least a "White guy" who claimed to be Cuban. In answer to the obvious objection, that the Cuban *was* Hispanic, he questioned whether a Cuban who worked for the bosses, or in their interest, could properly be called Hispanic. DeJesus may have been reacting to the fact that the union official in question was Cuban; in the 1960s New York was home to many White, middle-class, anticommunist refugees from the Castro regime. For DeJesus, ethnicity, at least with regard to Hispanics, implied

class loyalty and racial identity, that is, the term *Hispanic* carried class
and race connotations in addition to the linguistic and cultural character-
istics it denoted. He claimed that the workers had no one at the unionwide level to represent their interests; he believed that as shop steward he
was, for better or worse, their sole representative.[44]

On Friday, 9 August 1968, the Workers Action Committee challenged both the management and the union by publishing a leaflet that
made their complaints and demands public. The leaflet charged:

> The Afro-American and Latin workers who are employed by the Fig-
> ure Flattery Co. (on both the ninth and tenth floors) are forced to work
> under unbelievably bad conditions. Racial discrimination, personal hu-
> miliation, filthy expressions used by the bosses in front of women, hard
> work at starvation wages. Above all: An atmosphere which damages
> the mental, physical and moral health of the workers.[45]

The leaflet argued that the various forms of "coercion" used by management, including the prisonlike atmosphere and blocked exits, were "clear
proof of the contempt in which they hold the Latin American and Afro-
American workers." The workers' belief that they were being treated
contemptuously by management provoked them even more than the specific conditions they delineated. Their sense of frustration was magnified
by their feeling that the union had abandoned them. They charged that in
response to their complaints, the union had sided with the "bosses,"
which they interpreted as evidence of the union's corruption and complicity with management. The committee concluded by making the following demands: a wage increase big enough to meet the rising cost of
living; discussion and approval by all the workers of any new contract;
payment in cash on Wednesdays, as stipulated in the contract, or fifteen
minutes on Fridays to cash paychecks; a one-year contract; vacation pay
for all workers; and an equal division of overtime work.[46]

WOMEN WORKERS REBEL

On Wednesday, 14 August, after what WAC characterized as "long and
fruitless negotiations" with management, the "overwhelming majority"
of the workers decided to "suspend work" to gain their demands.[47] According to DeJesus, the committee, by letting workers know that they
could fight the bosses and win, was a catalyst for the strike. Nevertheless,
DeJesus claimed that he did not know precisely how the strike began.

Most of the women who were employed at Figure Flattery worked as sewing machine operators on the tenth floor. One of these women, Marina Garcia, who was very militant and had participated in PL activities, came down to the ninth floor to inform him that she had shut down the power, stopping all the machinery. She and her fellow operators refused to work or leave the factory; they had begun a sit-down strike.[48] According to the leaflet issued by the workers, the "final straw" that led them to stop work was the "complicity of the leadership of Local 32 in the bosses' injustices." Their strike was a protest against their union as much as against their employer.[49]

Although DeJesus did not initiate the strike, he felt obligated to give it direction. The operators, who had taken the first, bold step of shutting down the power and stopping work, had not considered what to do next. DeJesus told them that it was not enough to shut the power, that they would have to strike in an organized manner, which included setting up picket lines—something they had not considered doing and were not necessarily prepared to do. He explained that there was a big difference between arguing with the boss and spitting in his face, especially while fighting the union at the same time. He assured them that they were in for a big struggle. DeJesus immediately proposed setting up a strike committee. The strike leadership was primarily drawn from the Workers Action Committee, which sent workers to spread news of the strike to other shops, and met with the management and the union to resolve the workers' grievances.[50]

With production stopped, union officials, according to DeJesus, were "forced" to come down to the factory to sort things out. Understandably, the management expected Local 32, whose contract contained a no-strike clause, to get its members at Figure Flattery back to work. The union had every reason to end a rebellion that raised questions about conditions in ILGWU shops and doubts about the union's ability to control its members, a rebellion which might spread. However, the "hours and hours" of negotiations that ensued, which involved the Figure Flattery management, Local 32 officials and representatives of the striking workers, proved to be difficult. The company denied the existence of the egregious conditions described by its workers, and blamed "rabble rousers" for the strike. The exasperated managers were bewildered. They claimed that they treated their workers in various parts of Latin America, including Puerto Rico, the Dominican Republic and Chile, in the same way as they treated Figure Flattery workers, without encountering similar complaints. Why then, they wondered, were they facing a strike at

Figure Flattery? Spokesmen for the Figure Flattery workers readily responded that they refused to be treated like their counterparts in Latin America. The managers and workers had diametrically opposed perspectives. Not surprisingly, there was no meeting of minds and no agreement; the work stoppage continued.[51]

DeJesus proposed picketing the union headquarters. He argued that if the workers did not put the union leadership on the defensive, it would be able to bust the workers' wildcat strike. Because the committee wanted to "expose" the "union bosses," the strike would be a two-front war, directed against both union officials and company managers. Consequently, DeJesus led an orderly march of about two hundred workers to Local 32 headquarters on Seventh Avenue and Twenty-fifth Street. Leaving the bulk of the workers to picket on the sidewalk, over a dozen representatives went up to meet with the Local 32 leadership. When the meeting began, these officials did not know that the union hall was being picketed, but they were informed of the picketing by police officers who had arrived on the scene. The police asked DeJesus to disband the pickets, but he answered that he had already done his job by bringing them there, and insisted that he had only done what the workers asked him to do. He told Local 32 business agents, who also wanted him to end the picketing, to go down there themselves and tell the workers to go back to work. But he added that, in his opinion, they would not listen. After this fruitless meeting, DeJesus told his picketing co-workers that Local 32 officials did not want to listen to them and thought that they were kidding. The struggle would have to continue.[52]

On Thursday morning, 15 August, the striking workers began mass picketing outside the factory. According to DeJesus, the strike was "pretty solid as strikes go." Very few workers crossed the picket line, although not all the striking workers participated in the picketing. When the strike began, for example, a woman who worked at Figure Flattery introduced herself to DeJesus as the aunt of a young PL leader. She did not cross the picket line, but neither did she picket. However, the workers who picketed were militant, and the strike continued all day.[53]

The workers sent a committee to seek help from the ILGWU. The strike was solid enough to arouse the concern of Louis Stulberg, who in 1966 had succeeded David Dubinsky as the ILGWU's president. He invited the strike committee to his office in order to find a way to end the dispute. Stulberg promised to appoint a committee of his own to investigate the workers' grievances on condition that they first return to work. He assured them that unless they returned to work he could "do nothing."

The strike committee, headed by DeJesus, told Stulberg that they would not back down on their demands, but the workers were not prepared to dismiss his offer of help.[54]

On Friday morning, 16 August, the workers tested the value of Stulberg's good offices by temporarily returning to work. But *fifty* workers participated in a two-hour negotiating session in the manager's office, an inner sanctum that they had never been permitted to enter. However, the lengthy meeting, which involved a sufficiently large number of workers to be considered a partial work stoppage, failed to resolve the dispute. That afternoon, Sabby Nahama, whom PL's Wally Linder accused of participating in AFL-CIO expeditions to organize anticommunist unions in Latin America, addressed a shopwide meeting at Figure Flattery. Nahama worked for Local 22, but he was fluent in Spanish, a skill that Local 32 officials lacked, but sorely needed at this point. According to Linder, he disparaged the workers' charges as a "pack of lies." However, DeJesus and other militants received an ovation, Linder reported, when they "denounced the union mis-leaders as sell-outs." According to DeJesus, the workers maintained their determination to continue fighting, but Local 32's active opposition to their struggle may have caused many workers to doubt the efficacy of persevering.[55]

By this time, the Figure Flattery workers had struggled against both their employer and their union for three arduous days. However, after stopping work and sitting-in, picketing the union and meeting with Local 32 officials, picketing the factory and virtually shutting it down, meeting with the head of the ILGWU and negotiating en masse with management, they were back at work and had not achieved their demands. The next move was made by management.

AN INJURY TO ONE IS AN INJURY TO ALL

On Monday, 19 August, the Figure Flattery management fired both Marina Garcia, who had started the strike by turning off the power on the tenth floor, and the newly-elected shop steward and strike leader, Felipe DeJesus. Apparently, company managers were increasingly frustrated with the lingering disruption of the normal flow of production, and may have felt emboldened by the union's active opposition to the militants and intervention on behalf of labor peace. The management, probably with the advice and consent of the union, estimated that the strike leaders' support had weakened, and that absent its leaders, the workers' struggle would collapse.[56]

The firing of Garcia and DeJesus occurred after the workday had begun. Moreover, according to PL, "fifty to sixty" additional workers (potential strikebreakers) had been brought into the factory to "push out the work," and workers were being intimidated by both company foremen and union "goons." But if management expected their well-calculated stroke to bring a quick return to normalcy, they were disappointed. A core of "one hundred and fifty" militants walked out in protest, vowing to shut down production at Figure Flattery until the fired strike leaders were reinstated. At that point, all one hundred and fifty were also fired or laid off.[57]

The fired workers immediately reestablished picket lines in front of the factory; the second phase of the strike had begun. Bernard Korman, the company president, denounced the walkout as a wildcat strike. According to the *Daily News*, about seventy-five workers had walked out, supporting "a temporary worker fired for what the company called a one-man sit-down strike." The company, apparently abetted by the union, hardened its position and counterattacked. At this point, the workers on the street had little to lose by putting up a fight. This second phase of the strike promised to be harder fought than the first, and it was.[58]

Picketers carried handmade picket signs such as: "Local 32, ILGWU: Sell-Out Local"; "Sell-Out Union. Out With Them!"; and "Local 32, ILGWU, Sellouts to the Bosses!!!"[59] When Figure Flattery attempted to bring food in for the strikebreakers, a number of women picketers charged the food wagons. The police, who had been called in to maintain order, arrested three of these militant women, and charged them with disorderly conduct. (Although they were released the same day, they were required to appear in court on 28 August.) Following this confrontation, union officials came out of the factory to present a new management offer to their striking members, who were picketing the factory. The workers would receive a two percent wage increase and the one hundred and fifty workers who had been fired or laid off would be reinstated, but Felipe DeJesus' firing would be submitted to impartial arbitration. The striking workers unhesitatingly rejected this offer, committing themselves to remaining on strike until their shop steward was also reinstated.[60]

By Tuesday, 20 August, there were indications that the strikers' solidarity and militancy might bring victory. They were able to set up militant picket lines on three sides of the building, preventing all but forty workers from entering the factory. Perhaps as important, truckers were respecting the picket lines. That meant that there would be few pickups or deliveries, making continued production both pointless and impossible.[61]

Progressive Labor believed the strike's effectiveness had been enhanced to some degree by the appearance on the picket line at 7 A.M.
that morning of strike supporters which it had organized. The party decided to make the Figure Flattery strike a focus of its activities in New
York City. According to Linder, the picket lines were bolstered by rank-
and-file workers from other garment locals and other unions outside the
garment industry. He suggested that this welcome display of strike solidarity had resulted from word of the strike having spread. However,
these strike supporters were, for the most part, PLers and their close
friends. The party considered strike solidarity to be an essential ingredient of labor militancy, and brought twenty-five to fifty of its members
and friends to the picket line, which was as many as it could muster so
early in the morning.[62]

There were only a handful of PLers in garment locals, and because
most of PL's members and supporters were college-educated, there was a
preponderance of welfare workers and teachers among the trade unionists whom PL brought to the Figure Flattery picket line. This was an opportunity for them to support the industrial workers whom PL believed
would be the backbone of the coming revolution, and it was an important
opportunity to help the party establish itsef in New York City's industrial
heartland.[63]

STUDENTS FOR A DEMOCRATIC SOCIETY
ENTERS THE FRAY

The students who supported the strike were part of SDS's Work-In,
which originated in an SDS National Council resolution, and involved
350 students across the nation getting summer jobs in "factories, warehouses, loading docks and offices in order to talk with working people
about the Vietnam War, racism, the student movement and topical political questions."[64] Work-In leader Dennis Kamensky, a PLer who belonged
to the City University of New York chapter of SDS, claimed that fifty
to sixty students a day bolstered the picket lines at Figure Flattery. If
even half that number actually showed up, their presence on the picket
line would have made an impression. It seems that the Figure Flattery
management did notice. Bernard Korman, the company's president,
complained that the picket signs "apparently" came from the radical
Students for a Democratic Society. According to Kamensky, the company attempted to "student bait," blaming DeJesus for bringing in "outside agitators." But the company's tactic failed inasmuch as striking

workers continued to welcome students who showed up to picket with them.[65]

The company's consternation at the intrusion of radical students into the strike was echoed by conservative, nationally syndicated labor columnist Victor Riesel, who wrote an article entitled "SDS Spreads Revolt from Campus to Labor," in which he warned that SDS's "self-appointed revolutionaries" had begun to "rough up the labor front as though it were an Ivy League Campus." He noted with alarm that there "did not seem to be anything reformist about the invasion of a brassiere factory on New York's Lower West Side." With regard to the Work-In, he suggested that "The objective is to catch the spirit of Paris in the Spring," and warned, "No one thought that it could happen there either."[66]

In addition to picketing Figure Flattery, the student strike supporters engaged in several leaflet distributions in the garment center; Kamensky claimed that they handed out over "forty thousand" strike leaflets that garment workers looked forward to receiving. Most of the leaflets were written by workers, and were distributed by workers and students, but the students also wrote and distributed their own Work-In leaflets, in which they praised workers for fighting the bosses, cops and corrupt union leaders.[67]

However, the Work-In students felt duty bound to politicize the workers by casting the strike in an anti-imperialist mold, a theme which PL later amplified. Figure Flattery was a small link in a worldwide chain of enterprise. Kayser-Roth, the world's leading manufacturer and distributor of apparel, owned Fruit-of-the-Loom, which in turn controlled Figure Flattery. Kayser-Roth's extensive manufacturing operations in the United States were augmented by Kayser-Roth South America and Kayser-Roth International, with plants in Europe, the Middle East and Asia, making Kayser-Roth a worldwide enterprise of mammoth proportions. It directly employed over 26,000 workers, but only seventeen of its 117 plants in the United States, thirty-four of which were in the South, were unionized. Progressive Labor accused Kayser-Roth of employing ruthless anti-union tactics in Dayton, Tennessee, where the Textile Workers of America was currently on strike against the company's "arrogant" refusal to bargain. However, PL alleged that in New York City, Kayser-Roth had a "nice, cozy" relationship with the ILGWU, and contributed money to New York State's Liberal Party. Millionaire philanthropist Chester H. Roth, president of the Kayser-Roth Corporation, had been New York general chairman of B'nai B'rith's Anti-Defamation League. Progressive Labor noted that when B'nai B'rith had recently given Kayser-Roth an award, the Dayton strikers picketed B'nai B'rith's New

York City offices. Progressive Labor concluded that "the fight of the Figure Flattery workers—who are overwhelmingly Latin American and Black—is the same fight being waged by their white and Black brothers and sisters in the South, and their fellow working people throughout the world." The Work-In students emphasized that "The same bosses that own businesses like Kayser-Roth run our universities."[68]

However, PL's main purpose in the Work-In was not to influence workers, which could only be done in a limited way over the summer, but to win students in SDS to PL's pro-worker perspective. In 1968, SDS was primarily divided over the issue of which social group should be relied on to radically change America. Advocates of the "new working class" (college-educated workers) contested with PL's Worker-Student Alliance. Progressive Labor's national student organizer, Jeff Gordon, wrote that the SDS National Convention in June 1968, attended by eight hundred delegates, was "marked by sharp class struggle." The question that deeply divided SDS, according to Gordon, was whether SDS would "lead the student movement into an alliance with the Black and white working class, or embark on a 'student power-new working class' course?" The "debate was intense," he reported, "occasionally bordering on violence." Gordon alleged that SDS's National Office caucus, which was oriented toward the new working class, had attempted to expel Progressive Labor's members and supporters from the convention to consolidate power in its own hands.[69]

The Figure Flattery strike played a role in the debate that was raging in SDS. From PL's point of view, the students who participated in the strike had an opportunity to learn first hand that workers were ready, willing and able to fight back. The party regarded the strike as yet another proof of the revolutionary character of industrial workers, and used it, among other things, to batter down their opponents, who proposed relying on the new working class. Herbert Marcuse was the theoretical mentor of PL's despised opponents in SDS, and PL was anxious to attack his views. Two prominent advocates of the new working class, Carol Neiman and Greg Calvert, had written in the *Guardian* that Marcuse's *One Dimensional Man* "is the most sophisticated analysis of oppression in advanced capitalism thus far produced."[70] Dennis Kamensky, a PLer and SDS leader at CCNY, argued that the rebellion of low-paid workers at Figure Flattery refuted Marcuse's argument in *One Dimensional Man* that "Our society distinguishes itself by conquering the centrifugal social forces with Technology rather than Terror, on the dual basis of an overwhelming efficiency and increasing standard of living."[71]

COMMUNIST IN NAME AND DEED

Progressive Labor students were able to use the Figure Flattery strike as ammunition in the civil war that raged in SDS. Figure Flattery workers may have felt less isolated as a result of the support they received from PL students, but the workers would have to continue to do most of the fighting to win the strike, and they did. Their display of strength and determination on Tuesday morning persuaded management to make a new offer that afternoon, namely, a four percent wage increase and reinstatement of every fired worker, except DeJesus. The striking workers again rejected the company's attempt to rid itself of the thorn in its side. Apparently, both the management and the workers agreed that DeJesus was the central figure in the strike. During the course of the Figure Flattery struggle, "goons" beat him up in front of the factory six times, telephone callers threatened to kill him and his children, and the police ransacked his apartment (on South Third Street in the Williamsburg section of Brooklyn, New York) and confiscated his papers. The workers not only defended DeJesus' right to return to work, but protected him from being arrested by the police. Moreover, his fellow workers came to understand that in supporting DeJesus, whom they primarily knew as a militant Puerto Rican worker who defended their rights, they were siding with a communist.[72]

When the strike began, DeJesus started meeting on a daily basis with PL leaders Milt Rosen, Wally Linder and Ed Lemansky, who gave him both tactical and political advice. They wanted DeJesus to win the strike, but to push the party line too. They urged DeJesus, against his better judgment, to reveal his communist politics. He had been selling PL's newspaper, *Challenge*, in the factory (as many as "thirty to forty" a month were being sold by PLers and their supporters at Figure Flattery). Early in the strike, some of his fellow workers knew "on a personal level" that he was a communist, but in general most workers in the shop did not regard him as a communist.[73]

Nor did he believe that it was the right time to tell them that he was. In his view, he had not been in the shop long enough. His relationships were mainly personal, rather than political. For example, if a fellow worker missed a week of work due to an illness, DeJesus collected money in the shop to help him out. It was, in his eyes, a human thing to do, rather than a political act, but it helped him to get close to the other workers. In other words, his fellow workers trusted him because he would help them if they were in trouble, and not because he was pushing PL's line.[74]

Nevertheless, PL wanted DeJesus to act as an open communist. In response, he argued that PL should change the masthead of *Challenge* to read "Revolutionary *Communist* Newspaper" (a change which PL soon made). He thought that the paper should say the *c* word, not him. Moreover, he argued that it is not what you say you are that counts, but what you do, that is, how you relate to people in your everyday life. From his point of view, he was trying to live as a communist, dealing with people's problems, from the personal to the political, but he did not think that he should shove his politics in people's faces.[75]

In the end, however, he did what PL wanted. The party rented a hall on Union Square so that DeJesus could address the Figure Flattery strikers. He told them that the "system" teaches people that communism is bad, and that communists are monsters, but he reminded his fellow strikers that he worked with them and suffered under the same conditions as they did. He also reminded them that they knew the sort of person he was. Then, he announced that he was a communist. (He could not say that he was in PL, because at the time he was not.)[76] Moreover, he told them that being a communist made him different from (and, presumably, better than) the "bosses" and "union mis-leaders."[77]

Challenge drew what it considered to be an important lesson from DeJesus' speech: "The workers stood by DeJesus knowing him to be a communist who would never give up the struggle for the interests of the working class against the bosses, and knowing that the boss fired him because he was a communist." To what extent DeJesus lost support because he declared his communist politics, and to what extent his declaration blunted the effect of red-baiting by the company and the union is difficult to judge. DeJesus claimed that the workers continued to support him despite his dramatic public pronouncement of his political faith.[78]

VICTORY AT LAST

It would, however, take more than defending DeJesus to win the strike. Once again, militant women went on the offensive, throwing eggs at "scabs" leaving the factory at closing time on Tuesday afternoon. The police then "waded in," according to Wally Linder, and arrested one of the strike leaders, "brutally" dragging him by the neck into a waiting police car. Then, the son-in-law of one of the women picketers, who had come to take her home, was beaten by police; and when his mother-in-law came to his aid, she was beaten as well. Both were arrested, the man for assaulting a police officer. Members of PL in other unions raised money to bail him out of night court.[79] The strikers were undeterred. Asserting that their grievances had been "ignored" by Local 32 officials, and that they had been "fooled" by Stulberg and other ILGWU representatives, they vowed to continue their struggle "for better salaries and working conditions."[80]

On Wednesday morning, 21 August, the strike remained solid, and an incident occurred which revealed how the attitude of female strikers toward gender roles may have shaped their support for DeJesus. A union official went among the picketers, telling them that they should not stay out "for one man," DeJesus, and advised them not to get "hurt" or sacrifice themselves for his sake. One of the militant women on the picket line responded by telling him that if he were a "man," he should not speak "behind Felipe's back" but should "tell him to his face." Undaunted, the official said, "bring him to me," but the picketer answered, "No, you go to Felipe." *Challenge* reported, with obvious delight, that the official then absented himself from the scene, crawling away like a worm. To this militant woman, Felipe was more manly than his detractors in the male-dominated Local 32 hierarchy. For some of the women who actively participated in the strike, then, the perceived manliness of male strike leaders, in this predominantly female workforce, may have counterbalanced the authority of Local 32's male officials.[81]

In any case, preparing for a protracted struggle, strikers met during the day in a nearby church, where a PL welfare worker explained how they could apply for welfare benefits. When the picketers reassembled at 4 P.M., toward closing time, for another round of mass picketing, they were greeted by one hundred and fifty helmeted police officers. Two police wagons and additional officers were waiting in reserve on a side street. Evidently, the police were prepared to prevent a replay of the previous day's assault on the "scabs" who were leaving work. The police told the picketers that they would have to picket from across the street (well out of egg-throwing range). The picketers balked at this restriction. After considerable arguing, the police agreed to allow twenty-five strikers to picket in front of the building, but threatened that if more than that number attempted to join the line, they would arrest everyone. The strikers discussed this compromise offered by the police, but rejected it. Instead, the strikers resolved to form a mass picket line in front of the building, and to resist any attempt by the police to arrest them. The strikers converged in front of the building that housed their factory, but the police, failing to follow through on their threat, made no attempt to arrest them, only chasing PL photographers across the street.[82]

In addition to sending support pickets in the mornings and evenings, Progressive Labor was attempting to spread the strike by handing out tens of thousands of leaflets in the garment center, especially at shops organized by Local 32, where Linder claimed that "workers were reacting enthusiastically to the inspiring fight" at Figure Flattery. Even if that were true, it was unlikely that the strike would spread as a result of these leaflets, or even as a result of the rallies that PL planned to hold in the garment center to spread news of the strike. The party also was forming a Trade Union Solidarity Committee to Aid the Figure Flattery Workers, and planning to set up boycott picket lines in front of midtown stores, such as Macy's, that sold Fruit-of-the-Loom products.[83]

Before all these plans could be set in motion, the company acquiesced to the workers' "most immediate" demands: reinstatement of all terminated workers, including the two main strike leaders, Garcia and DeJesus; a four percent raise, retroactive to 1 July; an elected price committee to negotiate piece rates; unblocking the fire exits; elected shop stewards in all five departments; and ending such punitive practices as docking workers fifteen minutes for being only a few minutes late. According to PL's Wally Linder, "united, militant, rank-and-file struggle" had won the day.[84] It had, but PL saw this struggle as a sign of revolution, not mearly a militant work action. Subsequent events, however, would cast doubt on the revolutionary significance of the Figure Flattery strike and PL's long term prospects in the garment industry.

CHAPTER 8

Anatomy of an Anticommunist Purge
Progressive Labor, Figure Flattery and Local 32, ILGWU, 1968–1969

The workers' victory celebration at Figure Flattery was short-lived. As soon as the strike ended, the company and Local 32 launched a counteroffensive against the Workers Action Committee and Progressive Labor. This chapter discusses the six-month period that followed the strike, during which both the management and the union waged an anticommunist campaign to dislodge the PL-led insurgents and regain control of the Figure Flattery workforce.

THE LESSON: GROW OR BE CRUSHED

Progressive Labor wanted to turn unions into schools for communism. According to PL's Wally Linder, the lessons that the workers learned from the Figure Flattery strike were even more important than the substantial demands that they had won. He was enthusiastic and hopeful:

> With little money and no official labor support to sustain them, their solidarity and unbreakable unity, around demands to change the most oppressive conditions, had triumphed over all that had been thrown against them. They refused to be split from their rank-and-file leadership and accepted no bribes tossed to them by the bosses and their ILGWU henchmen. They were learning how to fight U.S. imperialism in its own back yard and teaching a vital lesson to hundreds of thousands of fellow workers suffering under the same yoke.[1]

For communists such as Linder, the Figure Flattery workers' willingness to go out on a limb to defend DeJesus as an open communist was a vital issue, not merely from the point of view of winning the strike, but from the point of view of sustaining a fighting communist presence in the shop, which was the only way communist ideology could be spread and communist leadership secured. The party believed that it would not be able to win industrial workers to its brand of communism unless they were willing to defend the PL cadres who were leading them in on-the-job struggles. Linder's reference to the anti-imperialist aspect of the struggle undoubtedly resonated with DeJesus and some other Latin American workers at Figure Flattery, but getting other garment workers to emulate the Figure Flattery strike would prove more difficult than Linder expected.

However, Linder's prediction that the struggle was far from over turned out to be right on the mark. The workers, he warned, had only won a "partial" victory, and the few concessions made by the company were only promises that would have to be enforced by a vigilant shop committee. Moreover, the management would attempt to undermine the workers' unity by dividing Black from Hispanic workers, buying off militants with selective wage increases and promotions, and getting rid of rank-and-file leaders who could not be bought. If such management tactics succeeded, Linder warned, the workers' hard-won gains would be slowly and quietly eroded. However, he was confident that a "united and militant" shop committee, linked to garment workers across the industry, could defeat management's splitting tactics and enforce the promised alleviation of "intolerable working conditions." The workers' partial victory, in other words, signaled a new, more difficult stage in their ongoing struggle with management, and achieving victory would now require building an industrywide movement.[2]

A month after the strike ended, the Workers Action Committee leafleted Figure Flattery. The committee complained that the company, rather than living up to their promises, had "tried to spread confusion and disunity among the workers." The committee's principal complaint, however, was that the workers had not won all their original demands. Declaring that they would not be satisfied with the "few crumbs" that had been thrown their way—as if they were "dogs"—by Local 32's leaders, committee members vowed to achieve complete victory in the new Local 32 contract, due in December. They demanded: a minimum salary of $100 a week for all (which had just been won by Hospital and Nursing Home Workers Union, Local 1199); ten days paid sick leave per year; the Fourth of July and Good Friday as paid holidays; increased medical benefits; no denial by the union of maternity benefits to pregnant women who were not "legally" married; union books as soon as the initiation fee was paid; a membership assembly to discuss and vote on the new contract; and a one-year contract. Moreover, paraphrasing Malcolm X, they warned, "We will not give up our right to use any methods we think necessary to win justice," and concluded by threatening, "If necessary—we will strike again!"[3] Recognizing that one shop could not shape the upcoming unionwide contract, the Workers Action Committee urged its brothers and sisters in Local 32's other shops to organize similar rank-and-file committees to "fight the bosses and their flunkies who run the union."[4]

THE GOLDENBERG-DEJESUS DEBATE

The wildcat had been an embarrassment to Local 32 leaders; rejection of a new contract and another unsanctioned strike would be humiliating. According to DeJesus, Max Goldenberg, manager-secretary of Local 32, had tried to buy him off during the wildcat. Complimenting the shop steward on his extraordinary writing ability, the union leader had offered to pay for his education and give him anything else he wanted, but to no avail. Now Local 32's leader used his column, "As I View It," in the September *Corset and Brassiere Workers Bulletin* to discredit his left-wing critics in the Workers Action Committee. As Goldenberg viewed it, the "outlaw strike" at Figure Flattery was the work of a few left-wingers bent on distorting the truth, smearing the union, and disrupting labor peace.[5]

To begin with, he accused the strike of being both precipitous and unlawful. It was precipitous because all the alternative means of resolving grievances had not been exhausted. Goldenberg reminded his readers that his door had been open to "anyone with a question, a complaint or a grievance of any kind." Although the union had "acted promptly" to address complaints and settle grievances, no one from Figure Flattery ever came to his office for help. He alleged that the wildcat's few leaders had avoided using "orderly processes" because they wanted to precipitate a strike "for their own reasons." In doing so they had "victimized" Local 32 members in the shop, making promises which could not possibly be fulfilled. The strike was unlawful inasmuch as it violated the no-strike clause in the contract.[6]

The strike leaders, Goldenberg thought, had circumvented peaceful processes for settling grievances in the service of their leftist agenda. He was struck by the "immediate" support that the wildcat received from "extreme left-wing groups," which "brought pickets up from Greenwich Village." Some of the leaflets supporting the strike were issued by SDS, which he identified as the "left-wing student group that caused so much trouble at Columbia last Spring."[7]

What he found obnoxious about these leaflets, other than their source, was their "misstatements, misinformation and plain lies" about the union. For example, he disputed WAC's claim that only twenty-five of the eight hundred Figure Flattery workers had received vacation pay. Goldenberg countered that there were only four hundred and forty-three union members at the factory, and of these, four hundred and thirteen had received their checks, which they cashed in the union office. With twelve checks uncollected, there were only eighteen workers unaccounted for, who may have been relatively new workers. The union leader concluded that his leftist detractors had no regard for the truth because they believed that lies made better propaganda. He took some comfort in the observation that similar leaflets had attacked other ILGWU affiliates. Although he upheld the right of leftists to express unpopular opinions, no one, he argued, had the right to "misrepresent the facts."[8]

Felipe DeJesus assumed responsibility for responding to Goldenberg's "ill-intentioned twisting of the facts" and "malicious mud-throwing." DeJesus focused on Goldenberg's failures and addressed other issues raised by WAC. DeJesus denounced the contract's no-strike clause (Article 27), which deprived workers of their "main weapon." By agreeing to a contract clause prohibiting strikes, the union leadership had in a "vile and barefaced manner" reduced the workers to slavery. By asking the workers to conduct their struggle in an "orderly way," Goldenberg was telling them to submit to their enemy's order.[9]

Moreover, the shop steward maintained that numerous delegations of Figure Flattery workers had "appeared personally before the business agent to present their demands." Why was the union head unaware of their complaints? DeJesus speculated that Goldenberg may have been preoccupied by his organizing trips to Puerto Rico, but the shop steward was distinctly unimpressed. Goldenberg, he thought, would do no more for workers in Puerto Rico than he had done for Puerto Rican and Black workers in New York. By blaming the workers for failing to bring their complaints directly to him, Goldenberg was treating the workers like "expiatory goats."[10]

DeJesus rejected the union leader's impugning of his and other strike leaders' motives. The workers had decided to strike for reasons that they outlined in their leaflet, but Goldenberg, DeJesus alleged, could not conceive of the workers having "sufficient intelligence and capacity to declare a strike themselves and fight for their own interests."[11]

On the vacation pay dispute, DeJesus did not attempt to reassert

WAC's original claim that only twenty-five workers had received the benefit. Instead, he replied that in a majority of cases these checks were "ridiculously small" because the union had deducted as much as a year's worth of back dues, which it had not forced the company to collect in a timely fashion. Moreover, DeJesus cited *El Diario-La Prensa* to the effect that the company claimed to have eight hundred workers. If only a little more than half that number were in the union, then approximately one-half of the Figure Flattery workers were not unionized. To DeJesus, this meant that strikes were not prohibited. However, Local 32 was still the certified bargaining agent for Figure Flattery workers, and DeJesus' debating point did not nullify the union contract's legally binding no-strike clause.[12]

DeJesus called attention to a recent unsanctioned strike at the Naomi, Atlanta and Ramona Bra Co. in Puerto Rico, which was organized by Local 32. He speculated that Goldenberg might be falling into disgrace within ILGWU leadership circles for not carrying out his "worker-suppressing task with any effectiveness lately." DeJesus concluded: "All his crying and lying may fool his friends. It will fool no workers at Figure Flattery." However, the union and the management employed a variety of means to regain control of the workforce at Figure Flattery.[13]

THE NEWSPAPER WAR:
CHALLENGE-DESAFIO V. *EL TIEMPO*

As the slow season approached during the fall, the company laid off hundreds of workers, and "made it so rough" on some others that they quit, *Challenge* reported. By mid-December the workforce had been reduced from eight hundred to four hundred, only two hundred of whom had been employed at Figure Flattery at the time of the strike in August. The Workers Action Committee not only was unable to palpably influence the terms of Local 32's new three-year contract, or persuade Local 32's membership to reject it, but found itself increasingly under attack.[14]

According to Figure Flattery worker and PLer Pancho Lopez, during the week before Christmas, two celebrities, the Puerto Rican boxer Jose "Chegui" Torres, an ex-light-heavyweight champion, and his manager, Johnny Manzanette, toured Figure Flattery almost daily. Although Torres spoke against DeJesus and the Workers Action Committee, he assured DeJesus privately, "I'm a left winger too." But as PL viewed it, anyone who disagreed with the party could not be considered a leftist.

Challenge characterized Torres as a friend of such "fake radicals" as the writer Norman Mailer and the democratic socialist Michael Harrington, and alleged that he was closely tied to the "revisionist" Communist Party, which controlled the "'left-wing'" faction in the Bronx Reform Democrats. *Challenge* derided Torres as a "phoney 'left-winger'" and alleged, without naming its source, that Manzanette had been identified as a member of the Police Department's undercover Bureau of Special Services, sometimes called the "red squad." To *Challenge*, Torres and Manzanette were nothing but a sinister "odd couple."[15]

Still, the unprecedented appearance on the factory floor of a Hispanic celebrity such as Torres alerted Figure Flattery workers that "something was up." Lopez now alleged that Torres and Manzanette were "agents" of Stanley Ross, editor-in-chief of New York's *El Tiempo*, a Spanish-language daily newspaper. Lopez sarcastically reported that following Torres' appearances at the factory every worker received an unusual Christmas bonus from their "good and charitable" employer—the 26 December issue of *El Tiempo*, which contained a scathing attack on Felipe DeJesus and communism.[16] *El Tiempo*'s editor, focusing on DeJesus' role in the Figure Flattery strike, alleged:

A few month's ago a professional communist agitator managed to organize a wildcat strike at Figure Flattery, one of the largest factories covered by the Local 32 contract. This strike only brought the workers a lot of headaches.[17]

Pancho Lopez, using the pages of *Challenge* to answer *El Tiempo*'s anticommunist editorial, argued that the strike had won important gains, including a four percent cost-of-living increase, which "the bosses had refused to concede and which the union had refused to fight for." The strike also put an end to the company's "intolerable anti-worker practices," such as stationing guards to monitor the number and length of workers' trips to the bathroom, and locking the doors and fire exits, which made workers feel as though they were in prison. Lopez further argued that the role of the "agitators," who belonged to the Workers Action Committee, was not to make promises but to force Local 32 to represent its members' interests and fight for their demands. If "left-wing extremists" had produced nothing, Lopez rhetorically asked, why was *El Tiempo* bothering to editorialize against them? The answer, he thought, was that the newspaper, rather than caring about the plight of workers, was in the company's pay. Furthermore, it was the company, not communists, that had created the long-standing grievances that had provoked the strike: "starvation wages, dictatorial rules, oppressive conditions, and daily insults to the dignity of the workers."[18]

Lopez struck out at *El Tiempo*'s editor, Stanley Ross, with malice. He faulted Ross for acting in bad faith, that is, for staying in the manager's office to "savor his expensive liquors," rather than verifying the facts by interviewing Figure Flattery workers individually. Neither Ross nor any of his "agents," Lopez complained, had visited the factory before the strike to investigate working conditions. Concluding that Ross was no friend of the workers, Lopez convicted him of guilt by association for finding his friends among the "Trujillos, the Batistas, Somozas and other dictators, racketeers and Mafia gangsters."[19]

Even so, *El Tiempo* reported that "Max Goldenberg, business agent of the Local, called a membership meeting to ratify the new contract, and the communist agitator was booed and thrown off the stage."[20] The ILGWU newspaper, *Justice,* similarly reported that "An attempt by an individual identified with an obscure pro-Chinese Communist element to inject irrelevancies into the discussion was decisively hooted down by members, who enthusiastically acclaimed the contract gains." Moreover, Goldenberg's announcement of his retirement "evoked cries of No! No!" In contrast to DeJesus, Goldenberg received a standing ovation.[21]

Lopez denied that the new Local 32 contract was a "great victory" for the workers, or that it had been ratified by a majority of Local 32's members, as Ross and the union implied. Most workers, Lopez contended, did not attend the ratification meeting, which took place at the Statler Hilton Hotel on 19 December 1968. Moreover, he charged that the meeting was run in the "usual gangster-like fashion," that is, the leadership only revealed parts of the contract, and denied the membership any opportunity for discussion or questions. Many of the workers who did attend the meeting, he alleged, soon walked out "in disgust." Lopez acknowledged that DeJesus had been booed, but suggested that this was done by "very elegantly dressed" union agents, not by the workers.[22]

According to DeJesus, many workers at the meeting were willing to listen to him, and even applauded him at some points. However, a majority of those at the meeting—which, he believed, included members of Cutters Local 10 (who were covered by the contract)—were White, and these workers told him that if he did not like the United States, he should go back to Puerto Rico. DeJesus acknowledged that he was finally shouted down from the floor. The credibility that DeJesus had gained

among Figure Flattery workers was based on personal relationships and
a shared experience that did not extend to the Local 32 membership in
general. The Workers Action Committee had not been able to involve
Local 32 members outside of Figure Flattery. Furthermore, because there
was no unionwide opposition caucus, the supporters of Local 32's leadership were more likely to attend the meeting than disaffected union
members. Under the circumstances, it would have been surprising if De-
Jesus had been able to sway the union membership at a contract ratification meeting chaired by the Local 32 leadership.[23]

El Tiempo concluded that communism was justifiably unpopular in
the Hispanic community. The editorial claimed:

> Communist agitators have not been warmly received by the Spanish
> community. The majority of Spanish workers, like those in Local 32,
> understand that their best hopes for the future lie in the orderly
> progress which they can make through unions led by intelligent and re-
> sponsible men.[24]

In response, PLer Pancho Lopez claimed that Figure Flattery workers had learned that *El Tiempo* was not their friend, but the ally of the
"bosses and union misleaders." He optimistically suggested that an increasing number of Hispanic workers were learning the same lesson, and
asserted that all workers should learn that "the bosses run the big newspapers and will always lie about workers' struggles." Whether they were
lying or not, the "big" newspapers, such as *El Tiempo*, had a much wider
circulation than *Challenge* and, therefore, far more influence. Though
Lopez did not deny *El Tiempo*'s assertion that most Hispanic workers
were anticommunist, or at least noncommunist, he remained convinced
that communists could extend their influence beyond Figure Flattery. Ultimately, it was a matter of growing or being crushed.[25]

THE FINAL BLOW

On 27 December the professional boxing trainer Johnny Manzanette
paid another visit to Figure Flattery, this time accompanied by the
renowned Puerto Rican artist Bobby Capo. George Alamo, a member of
the Workers Action Committee, distinguished by his militancy and bold-
ness during the strike, greeted this new celebrity visitation with sardonic
humor: "For a while, we workers at Figure Flattery thought that we were
going to have a visit from the Peace Corp, the OEO, and the United Na-

tions too." But he also accused Figure Flattery's famous Puerto Rican visitors of helping to initiate a plot against his shop steward, DeJesus.[26]

On 29 December an incident occurred that profoundly affected the course of the struggle at Figure Flattery. In order to seek someone out, possibly in connection with a grievance, DeJesus went to drink some water. As DeJesus recollected it, when one of the department supervisors, Al Wyloge, spoke to him in a "nasty" way, DeJesus "smacked him in the face." The foreman was taken to the hospital, where he was diagnosed as having a "linear fracture of the skull." According to George Alamo, the foreman had made DeJesus "the object of constant persecution." Nevertheless, DeJesus understood that hitting a supervisor was a fireable offense. Striking out in anger at the foreman, an act which DeJesus later attributed to youthful ignorance, was self-destructive, and handed his enemies an opportunity to intensify their offensive against the Workers Action Committee. Not surprisingly, DeJesus was immediately fired and arrested for felonious assault, which carried a maximum sentence of five years in prison. According to *Challenge*, "The ILGWU hack 'leaders' were overjoyed."[27]

Despite the circumstances, DeJesus' supporters at Figure Flattery decided to defend him. They adopted a two-pronged strategy. The committee announced that an undisclosed number of workers on the ninth floor, which DeJesus represented as shop steward, had met and voted "unanimously" to hold a work slowdown in order to pressure management into reinstating DeJesus and dropping all charges against him. They also resolved to seek aid from other rank-and-file workers and students, who would picket in solidarity with the workers' slowdown. A Workers Action Committee leaflet declared:

> Today we must demonstrate that we are men and women with dignity. We must fight to defend the rights of those who have fought to defend us. DeJesus has fought—defending our rights as workers. EVERYONE MUST SUPPORT THE SLOWDOWN AS A METHOD OF WINNING BACK FELIPE'S JOB AND GETTING THE CHARGES DROPPED. TO DEFEND DeJESUS IS TO DEFEND OURSELVES.[28]

The workers on the ninth floor who were determined to defend their chosen leader, DeJesus, began their work slowdown on 2 January 1969. *Challenge* did not estimate the strength of the slowdown, which would have been difficult to accurately assess. But the decision to slow down rather than strike suggests that the Workers Action Committee was weaker than it had been the previous August.[29]

GOONS, GINKS AND COMPANY FINKS

Nevertheless, the slowdown was strong enough to arouse the ire of the company and the union. Any slowdown raised the price of production, and also raised the specter of a strike. At an apparently heated meeting in the company manager's office that same day, *Challenge* charged, "five ILGWU-hired hoodlums threatened to 'blow up' DeJesus and other rank-and-file leaders." These threats were not surprising to *Challenge*, which alleged that every "crooked" union leadership stayed in power by "using a handful of killers and hoods to threaten, beat or murder any militant workers who stand in their way." However, the workers participating in the slowdown apparently were not intimidated, and the slowdown, its main strength on the ninth floor, continued. The atmosphere in the factory was evidently charged; a group mainly made up of women workers walked off the job when the company posted on its bulletin board an *El Tiempo* article attacking DeJesus. However, this spontaneous, and probably short-lived, gesture of support for DeJesus did not turn into a strike.[30]

Union and company agents, whom *Challenge* universally characterized as "goons," were called in to break the back of the protest. According to *Challenge*, the company president, Bernard Korman, allowed "goons" to "parade around the factory spreading lies," and even turned over his office to them. They called the workers in, two or three at a time, alternately proffering the carrot and applying the stick. They promised that DeJesus' firing would be submitted to impartial arbitration, and they established a grievance committee, but they also tried to turn the workers against DeJesus, or simply threatened them. While the workers were being subjected to these techniques of persuasion, the company refrained from firing any more workers. *Challenge* surmised that the company acted with restraint to avoid provoking another full-fledged strike.[31]

The core of the labor unrest at Figure Flattery was the Workers Action Committee, whose base of support was predominantly Hispanic. Before DeJesus was fired, these workers had been visited by Puerto Rican celebrities, the boxer Jose Torres and the artist Bobby Capo, and each worker had been given a copy of *El Tiempo* containing an editorial attacking DeJesus. Shortly after the slowdown began, they were approached in the factory by various "leaders" of the Hispanic community, who allegedly had heard about their grievances and wanted to help them. One of the first to arrive was John Oliva, who identified himself as both an official of the Puerto Rican Federation of Civil Liberties and a representative of the Mayor's office, but produced no credentials to substantiate these claims. Oliva became the liaison officer at Figure Flattery, a newly created post which involved resolving workers' grievances. Undoubtedly, he intended handling workers' complaints very differently than had DeJesus, the former shop steward. According to *Challenge*, Oliva had been the director of a District 65 training program, which was funded by the government as a "poverty program." The minutes of the 29 April 1968 meeting of District 65's general council indicated that Oliva's "resignation was accepted because he had accepted loans from certain employers." *Challenge* was blunt: "In other words, he was fired for taking bribes."[32]

Oliva accused Korman, the company's president, of exploiting the working class, and he castigated Local 32 as a racketeer union. Alamo agreed with both of these charges, but characterized Oliva as a hypocrite who was trying to infiltrate the workers' ranks. Korman, according to Alamo, spent $3,000 to construct an office for Oliva, who Alamo derisively labelled "our Robin Hood." Apparently, the company believed that it needed an in-house Hispanic, who was not identifiable as an agent of management, to provide an alternative to WAC's leadership of Hispanic workers at Figure Flattery, something Local 32 had not been able to supply. The workers finally saw through Oliva's offers to help them, according to Alamo, but the company president also hired the services of about a dozen "mobsters" to "tour the factory and terrorize the workers."[33]

However, sharper confrontations were occurring on the street below, where workers and students (PLers and their immediate base) who were picketing in solidarity with the slowdown inside were allegedly attacked by agents of the company. According to *Challenge*, "Over two hundred trade unionists and students were physically attacked with clubs, iron bars, [and] broken bottles while the Lindsay cops stood by and watched or joined in the attack whenever the pickets, in fighting back, seemed to be getting the advantage of the goons."[34] George Alamo accused Korman of hiring "gangsters" to attack and break up the picket line; they assaulted women, he claimed, and "dragged them through the streets."[35] *Challenge* reported no instance of a picketer being seriously injured, and only one case of a picketer being arrested, but PL protested what it considered to be the bellicose tactics of the company's special security force.[36]

Student picketers chanted: "Workers, yes! Bosses, no! Rehire Felipe, Goons must go!" According to PLer Ira Perelson, a member of the Students for a Democratic Society Labor Project, the "hundreds" of high school, university and college students from New York City and New Jersey who picketed four or five times during their week of final examinations (6–10 January 1968) "got some real-life education about ruling class violence." The student activists had experienced the use of force by the police, who were sometimes called in by college administrators to break up their antiwar sit-ins and demonstrations, but they had never encountered company "goons." Perelson was proud that students had "stood firm and fought back against the goons when attacked," and he praised women students in particular for being exemplary in their "spirited defiance of the goons." He claimed that an increasing number of students showed up to picket despite the use of violence by "organized goons," and interpreted this as a sign of the developing alliance between workers and students.[37]

Perelson maintained that the "goons" and the police operated in the interest of the ruling class. He argued, for example, that at San Francisco State College, whose students were then striking, "the 600 police that have been called out to suppress students also work to suppress the strikes of working people." Perelson claimed, without substantiation, that "many eyes were opened" when students made a chance discovery that one of the "head goons" at Figure Flattery was an undercover policeman.[38]

Even so, why did the company hire a special security force? Figure Flattery strikers had attacked *scabs* the previous August, but there was no strike in January. Progressive Labor's informational picket line presumably posed no threat to Figure Flattery workers, whether they were cooperating with the slowdown or not. But DeJesus had struck and injured a supervisor, and the company may have regarded the picketers as a threat to its management staff and property. Moreover, picket lines, informational or otherwise, also threatened to turn away truckers, and presumably embarrassed and angered the company. Finally, the company may have been afraid that the presence of pickets would embolden its workers, and turn the slowdown into another strike. Thus, for a variety of possible reasons, the company hired a security force, which apparently adopted an aggressive stance toward PL's picket line.

Who were the so-called "goons" who attacked the picket line? *Challenge* alleged, without indicating its source, that many of the attackers were right-wing Cuban exiles, some of whom were veterans of the CIA-trained Brigade 2506 that invaded Cuba at the Bay of Pigs in April 1961.

Others belonged to the Black and Latin American League, an organization composed of antipoverty workers. *Challenge* alleged that one of the aims of this group was to "get the Jew commies," a conjunction of ethnicity and ideology that *Challenge* denounced as an "old ruling class lie." People paid by antipoverty programs had "broken heads to prevent riots" after the assassination of Martin Luther King, Jr. in April 1968, *Challenge* charged, but this was the first time that they had been involved in a labor dispute. *Challenge* reported that one of these "goons," Skip Ballinger (also known as Balaguer), who allegedly worked for Head Start, wound up "getting his head split open during one of the street battles." By contrast, the picketers sustained no serious injuries, and only one arrest. Progressive Labor believed that its readiness to engage in street battles with those whom it identified as scabs, goons and right-wingers, and even the police, was justifiable, and an expression, in a non-revolutionary period, of its commitment to the politics of violent revolution.[39]

Challenge's unsubstantiated assertions—especially about Manzanette, shadowy individuals and groups in the pay of antipoverty programs, and right-wing Cuban exiles—were mainly based on hearsay (*Challenge-Desafío* "has received information that" or so-and-so "has been identified as"), and are difficult, for that reason, to accurately assess. But even if *Challenge*'s account is not entirely creditable, WAC and PL faced a motley assortment of opponents, which included the following: Torres, allegedly a CP-oriented Reform Democrat; Manzanette, allegedly a member of the red squad; *El Tiempo*, a popular Spanish-language daily; Oliva and Ballinger, allegedly antipoverty workers; a goon squad, allegedly involving both right-wing Cuban exiles and members of the Black and Latin American League; the police; and the ILGWU—all of whom, *Challenge* argued, were working in the interest of Figure Flattery. Certainly, the company and the ILGWU shared a common interest in suppressing the Workers Action Committee and ending PL's influence in the shop.[40]

STRIKE OR STRIKE OUT

Progressive Labor would have to act soon and decisively to win the struggle at Figure Flattery or risk being expelled from the shop. At closing time on Friday, 10 January, after a weeklong slowdown supported by solidarity picketing, DeJesus attempted to lead a march of Figure Flattery workers to a nearby meeting hall, where he intended to propose that the slowdown be transformed into a strike, but the "goons," protected by the police, broke up the march, and the meeting did not occur until the following Monday. DeJesus told his fellow workers that the combination of a slowdown and solidarity picketing did not "hurt the bosses enough," and concluded that only a strike had "sufficient force to do that."[41]

DeJesus outlined the continuing problems that he believed demanded strike action: miserable wages of less than $70 a week for many workers; continual verbal and physical abuse; a union leadership that had sold out to the bosses; job insecurity; racism, which kept Black and Hispanic workers at the lowest level jobs; insufficient medical care; no sick leave; and being cheated out of vacation pay and other benefits. These were compelling issues, but he warned that a strike, although winnable, would be difficult. DeJesus told Figure Flattery workers:

> We all know what a strike will mean. The bosses are rich and powerful and will not give in quickly or easily. But if we are determined to fight, we can win.[42]

However, the Workers Action Committee could not mobilize sufficient support for a strike. *Challenge* suggested that while the workers were angry about the firing of DeJesus, the terms of the new "sellout" contract, and the worsening conditions in the plant, they were not prepared to strike because they began to rely on the solidarity picket line to win the struggle for them. It seems evident, however, that from the outset they wanted to avoid striking.[43]

With the threat of a strike diminishing, the company stepped up its offensive. On Tuesday, 21 January, management called a meeting for the packers, and proposed that they begin working on a piece-rate system. According to Francisco Rosario, an active member of WAC, the packers were unanimous in rejecting this proposal because they viewed it as a way to exploit them even more. Management responded by firing the workers' spokesman.[44]

On the following day, Wednesday, 22 January, management called another meeting, after working hours. This time the workers were addressed by John Oliva, designated by the company to handle their grievances, and the company president, Korman, who declared, "The company had a cancer, which we have gotten rid of, but now we have to root out the remains of that cancer." He singled out the packing department, indicating that there was a group of "troublemakers" who would have to be eliminated in order to achieve "peace" in the company. This was a declaration of war against the Workers Action Committee, whose members continued to argue with him. When Korman, for example, complained that the workforce had been reduced from eight hundred to five hundred due to labor unrest, Pancho Lopez blamed the company's decision to begin manufacturing in Mexico. But management blamed the packers' slowdown for its decision to lay off some cutters "for the first time since the factory opened." Rosario saw this as an attempt to turn the cutters against the packers.[45]

After the meeting, Rosario was called into the company president's office; Korman informed him that he was being laid off because it was the slow season, an explanation that Rosario considered "a lie—pure and simple." Rosario pointed out that while he had been with the company for almost *two* years, and a union member almost as long, there were ten new workers who were not yet union members. Management told him that he was right, and that he should come to work the next day but not discuss what had happened with anyone. However, when he tried to punch in the next morning, his card was missing. He was sent to Oliva, who told him that he was being laid off because his decision to talk about what had happened created problems for the company—which planned to lay off a large number of workers on the ninth floor, especially the packers, who had refused to work on a piece-rate basis. In other words, the company intended to lay off the members and strongest supporters of the Workers Action Committee.[46]

Rosario, the father of a family, went to Local 32, and spoke to its manager, Max Goldenberg, who sent him back to the factory to see Mr. Birch, the union's business agent for Figure Flattery. But Birch told Rosario that he could only handle his problem at the union office after 4 P.M. In answer to Rosario's demand that his seniority be respected, Birch answered, "Don't worry, after you, lots of others will go." Moreover, Birch told Rosario that the company had the right to lay off whomever they pleased because the contract said nothing about seniority with regard to layoffs. Rosario was left without a rejoinder: "I had to accept what he said," Rosario explained, "because in the two years I was in the union, I never once saw this famous 'contract,' and therefore I don't know my rights under the union even though its written on paper." He added, "None of my fellow workers have seen it either."[47]

Rosario concluded that the Local 32 leadership had not defended the workers' jobs because it was in league with management, and like management, also regarded them as a "cancer." Rosario reminded his fellow workers that they had defended themselves the previous August, and suggested that they would have to do it once again if they were "going to change the miserable working conditions and low salaries which exist at Figure Flattery, at all shops under Local 32, and throughout the garment industry."[48] The workers had won the first round, but the company had won the second. *Challenge* anticipated a third round, in which new leaders would emerge and work with those who had been ousted, but that turned out to be wishful thinking. The company had succeeded in defeating the insurgents, and PL was unable to renew the struggle at Figure Flattery or foment another such uprising of factory workers in New York City's garment industry.[49]

On 22 January, the day that Rosario was laid off, DeJesus appeared in court to answer the assault charge against him. The Manhattan District Attorney's office had reduced the charge of felonious assault against DeJesus to simple assault, a misdemeanor that carried a maximum sentence of a year in jail. *Challenge* reported that during the hearing, three of the "goons" who had attacked the picket line were in court; one of them, allegedly an undercover police officer, held numerous conferences with the prosecuting attorney and the supervisor whom DeJesus had struck. The judge, who denied a defense motion to dismiss the case for lack of evidence, commented that he was an old friend of Local 32's manager, Max Goldenberg, and a number of the union's business agents. A trial date was set for 11 February.[50] DeJesus received a one-year suspended sentence, but was required to stay out of trouble for three years, which he succeeded in doing.[51]

DeJesus looked back on the Figure Flattery struggle as a wonderful experience, not least because he learned a lot from his fellow workers. To begin with, he was surprised that they had enough solidarity and consciousness to fight as hard as they did. The workers' fighting spirit confirmed his ideology, that workers at the production level could change society, solidifying his trust in the working class. He learned that workers do have class consciousness, but they also have needs: "If they see a need to fight, and you are honest," he observed, "they will listen to you." Somehow, he had been able to formulate what people wanted, and still has friends in New York City and in Puerto Rico whom he knew from the strike. His belief that an individual could change society had been verified, but he concluded, "You can not be a Messiah, but people want to know how far you are willing to go," and added, "I don't look at myself as a leader."[52]

PROGRESSIVE LABOR AND FIGURE FLATTERY WORKERS

Figure Flattery was a large manufacturing operation by New York City garment industry standards, and one of Local 32's biggest units. But from the point of view of its low salaries and oppressive working conditions, it was not a particularly unique shop, although it may have been worse than others in some respects—the locking of emergency exits, for example. What made the situation at Figure Flattery unique, other than the relatively large concentration of workers, was the presence of a group of communists, led by DeJesus, intent upon heating up the class struggle.

Moreover, these PL organizers at Figure Flattery were atypical PLers. The great majority of PL's members, although not all, were college-educated Whites. In that respect, garment truckers Martinot, Lemansky and Davis were typical PLers. But PL viewed Black and Hispanic industrial workers as the social group with the greatest revolutionary potential, and PL had a dearth of organizers who belonged to that social group. The PLers at Figure Flattery were an exception. They were much closer to their fellow workers ethnically and socially than were PL's cadres in Local 102, for example; and they were, therefore, able to more thoroughly integrate themselves into the workforce.

The strike in August was the consequence of serious grievances, union complacency, and effective leadership by communists, especially DeJesus, who were an integral part of the workforce. Both the company and the union were caught off guard; neither had as much influence among the Hispanic workers at Figure Flattery as PL's Workers Action Committee. The strike succeeded because there was a conjunction between the workers' frustration with the union leadership and eagerness to fight for better wages and working conditions, and PL's determination to build an insurgent movement in the ILGWU and lead workers in struggle at the point of production. It should be noted, however, that the workers essentially wanted to force the union to give them better representation, while PL wanted to turn the ILGWU into a school for communism, a difference that could lead to a parting of the ways.

In the aftermath of the strike, both the company and the union moved aggressively to discredit PLers and eventually dislodge them from the factory. To accomplish their goal, the company and the union launched an anticommunist attack on PL, and attempted to bring in a noncommunist Hispanic alternative to the leadership of the Workers Action Committee. By assaulting a supervisor, which gave the company the opportunity it sought to fire him, DeJesus allowed the company to intensify its campaign against WAC. The slowdown and solidarity picket line could not effectively thwart the company's attack. Undoubtedly, some workers who defended DeJesus when he was their strike leader in August, were unwilling to strike in order to uphold his right to hit a foreman. Moreover, PL's attempt to politicize the workers dovetailed with the company's and union's red-baiting to make communism the main issue. No matter how much the workers respected the communists in WAC and PL, they were not communists, and unwilling to strike for communism. Whereas in August, PL had supported the workers' struggle, which was quite militant, in January the fight between PL and the company's security forces tended to eclipse the slowdown, which was only partially supported and, like slowdowns generally, could not be easily enforced or sustained. In the end, PL was marching to the sound of its own drummer, but the workers were not following its red flag. Progressive Labor saw potential revolutionaries on every shop floor, but this inflated sense of the possible and its own importance was not justified by the outcome at Figure Flattery.

Although PL made friends among the workers at Figure Flattery, it could not, with few exceptions, recruit them. Many of the Figure Flattery workers were fiercely militant in their quest for a decent life and dignity. However, they were either not motivated by the revolutionary ideas that SDS activists found increasingly appealing in 1968–1969, or if they were, not the singular strategy that PL insisted was the only possible road to revolution. They were not ready to imitate PL's solidarity picketers, who were professional revolutionaries in the sense that they placed the revolution above all things. Ultimately, PL could not parlay its initial successes at Figure Flattery into an expanding base of revolutionary garment workers.

Conclusion

Progressive Labor's organizing in New York City's garment industry, as well as everything else PL did, was a function of the party's antirevisionist politics. Progressive Labor's leaders were politically trained in the Foster-led Communist Party USA of the late 1940s and early 1950s. Their political temper was forged in the darkest days of the Cold War between the hammer of Stalinist imperative and the anvil of anticommunist crusade. Committed Marxist-Leninists, qua Stalin, they blamed revisionism for both the CPUSA's defeat by McCarthyism and Stalin's posthumous defeat at the hands of Khrushchev. Expelled from the CPUSA for factionalism, they resolved to build a new vanguard party faithful to the political certainties that guided them. The new party resembled the CPUSA in almost every respect, but to PL's leaders, what separated PL from the CPUSA was crucial. They were inspired by the notion that they had rescued communism from the jaws of revisionism, and they were imbued with a sense of mission that pervaded PL as it attempted to push the new radicalism of the 1960s and 1970s toward its brand of new communism.

Contrary to the theory of American exceptionalism that the Browder-led CPUSA had endorsed, PL was confident that the American working class was unexceptional in being, potentially at least, as revolutionary as workers were elsewhere. As far as PL was concerned, this was a fundamental and unshakable article of its communist faith. Progressive Labor believed that CPUSA revisionism had prevented a revolution from occurring during the Great Depression of the 1930s. If the role of party intellectuals was indispensable to the revolutionary process, as PL's

Marxist-Leninists believed, then the communist movement's failure to win workers to revolution was cause for introspection, self-flagellation, and innovation.

However, Progressive Labor's capacity for pragmatism was circumscribed by its political inheritance, that is, the revolutionary potential of the working class, the preeminence of industrial workers, the imminence of revolution, the need for a disciplined party, et cetera. Committed to an antirevisionist paradigm, which attributed the CPUSA's defeat to lack of militancy, and defensiveness in the face of red-baiting, PL attempted to revolutionize the American working class by being super-militant and brashly proclaiming its communist politics. Progressive Labor argued that the American working class was ready, willing and able to see the virtue of communism if communists only showed some militancy and explained communism to them.

Progressive Labor attempted to break out of its political isolation by supporting Kentucky miners, sending students to Cuba, demonstrating against the Vietnam War, and supporting the Harlem Rebellion. Progressive Labor's revolutionary optimism, energy, willingness to defy authority, and aggressiveness were evident. But although PL attracted a small following of young, radical intellectuals, it was unable to recruit the militant workers it supported. Nevertheless, PL was undeterred by its inability to recruit workers or by its New Left critics, who doubted that workers were revolutionary. But it had yet to demonstrate in practice that its class analysis was correct and that it possessed a workable strategy for winning workers to revolution.

Nevertheless, the 1960s were marked by a sharp rise in radicalism in the United States and internationally. The outbreak of Mao's Cultural Revolution suggested to PL that communism could be realized through direct appeals to the masses—doing away with the need for concessions to bourgeois power. The Cultural Revolution, which elevated the utopian element in communism, resonated deeply with PL's idealistic leaders and their young followers. So much so that when Mao reversed course, PL broke with the Communist Party of China, and criticized all the concessions that leading communists had made to capitalism, from Lenin's New Economic Policy and Stalin's United Front Against Fascism to Mao's New Democracy. Putting all its faith in the ability of the masses to grasp the compelling need for communism, PL elevated the call for revolution over the fight for reforms. By the early 1980s, the party rejected socialism, calling instead for the establishment of egalitarian communism immediately after the revolution. Combining Maoist populism with

Leninist party-mindedness, and believing that property, rather than power, corrupted, PL imagined a postrevolutionary society that was economically egalitarian, international in scope, and run by a party of millions along democratic-centralist lines into the far distant future.

Progressive Labor's vision had become increasingly utopian as America and the world became increasingly conservative from the mid-1970s onward, and the prospects for revolution receded. Rather than making a tactical retreat, PL followed the logic implicit in its conception of antirevisionism, becoming even more strident in its advocacy of communism, and less willing to devote its meager resources to reform struggles. In the end, some PLers rejected fighting for reforms at all—because reform struggles, they thought, inevitably built illusions about the viability of capitalism. This was the kind of sectarianism that Milt Rosen had warned young PLers against at PL's founding convention in 1965. But Rosen and PL had come a long way from their CP roots. Progressive Labor's utopianism won out over its quest for power.

The tension between reform and revolution that PL wrestled with, however, was inherent in communism. From its inception, PL viewed reform struggles as a means to garner support for communism and win party recruits. There was nothing new in this; the CP had done the same. But PL was always fearful that reform would eclipse revolution. Despite PL's optimism about the openness of American workers to communism, PL was afraid that the American working class would pull the party toward reformism, rather than the party pushing the workers toward revolution. Despite PL's communist faith in the revolutionary potential of the working class, and a flood of optimistic reports in the party press, few revolutionary workers were discernible in America during the 1960s and 1970s. All of PL's communist rhetoric and militant participation in reform struggles produced very little in the way of working-class recruits for the party. Nothing in PL's practice on the labor front justified PL's claim that American workers could be won to revolutionary politics or that PL possessed a workable strategy.

However, hundreds of students, intellectuals and professionals did respond to PL's pro-worker rhetoric. Radical students frustrated at their inability to reshape America in their own radical image avoided despair by adopting PL's theory of a revolutionary working class. Progressive Labor's Worker-Student Alliance became a major player in the internal strife that finally fractured Students for a Democratic Society in 1969. Promoting the idea of a revolutionary working class gave PL a prominent place in the history of 1960s student radicalism.

It also gave PL a few hundred potential organizers, whom PL counted on to turn its notion of working-class revolution into reality. Progressive Labor asked its college-educated recruits to save the theory of working-class revolution that they found persuasive by organizing workers for communism. As PL's college-educated cadres matured in the 1970s and became active in a variety of unions in the public and service sectors, PL struggled with them to proselytize the high school students or welfare clients whom they served, or their less educated co-workers, especially Blacks and Hispanics. Faced with dismal results, PL argued that to become effective organizers in the labor field its college-educated recruits would have to shed their middle-class values and integrate themselves into the working class. This criticism, which became the leitmotif of PL's inner-party struggles, underscored the party's dilemma. Although it claimed to represent the interests of the working class, it was a party of students, intellectuals, professionals and college-educated workers.

Moreover, the party argued that it would be doomed to failure unless it could recruit a sizeable number of industrial workers. In New York City, PL tried to build a base among industrial workers in garment, the city's biggest industry, where the majority of the workforce was comprised of low-paid Black and Hispanic women, whom PL regarded as potentially the most revolutionary section of the American working class. In addition to garment manufacturers, PL challenged the imperious ILGWU, which was widely respected for being progressive and was a powerhouse in local and national politics. But the garment workforce had become increasingly stratified along racial and ethnic lines, and the Jewish men who led the ILGWU had come under increasing attack for failing to adequately represent the union's newest members, Black and Hispanic women. Progressive Labor despised the anticommunist ILGWU leadership, and, believing that the union had allowed the wages and conditions of its disempowered Black and Hispanic members to deteriorate, it saw an opportunity to build an insurgent movement among garment workers.

At first, PL could do no more than hold rallies in the garment center, but by the mid-1960s, PL sent a handful of colonizers into garment jobs, where they tested PL's theories. Some of PL's college-educated organizers secured employment in garment trucking, the cheap and fast transportation system that tied the thousands of small garment shops together into an industry. Progressive Labor's garment organizers were radical intellectuals who, although still in their mid-twenties, had already amassed a surprising amount of political experience. Ed Lemansky, for example, a red diaper baby from Brooklyn, New York, developed his radical ideas at Antioch College and at Oxford University's Ruskin College. He gained organizing experience by fighting for civil rights in Monroe, North Carolina (after Negro self-defense advocate Robert F. Williams had gone into exile), and by leading a student trip to Cuba in defiance of a U.S. State Department ban. Lemansky and other early PL recruits, many of whom were red diaper babies, became the bridge between PL's leaders and a wave of PL recruits in the late-1960s who were new to Marxist-Leninist politics. Although Lemansky's garment organizing did not lead to PL's having a base among garment workers, it gave him credibility as a labor organizer among PL's younger cadres.

Lemansky and two other PL organizers, Steve Martinot and Dave Davis, were able to lead garment truckers in a surprising number of wildcat work stoppages aimed at gaining union membership, and increased wages and benefits, for workers who had been illegally prevented from joining Local 102, ILGWU. In 1962 a congressional investigation of Local 102 had uncovered evidence of union-management collusion, and the union probably had not improved very much since then.

However, these insurgent work actions, which began to spread at one point, were eventually defeated by concerted efforts on the part of both the union and management. Acting on their political principles, PL's organizers urged their fellow workers to be ever more united and more militant in confronting their bosses and union leaders. These PL truck drivers, who were White, urged fellow truck drivers, many of whom were White as well, to fight for the interests of low-paid helpers and pushers, almost all of whom were Black and Hispanic. But garment truckers, who generally did not have revolutionary aspirations and who needed their jobs, were usually more willing to accept compromises than was PL.

Progressive Laborites answered red-baiting attacks by explaining the virtues of communism. But although their fellow workers respected PLers for being militant leaders, the workers were not prepared to defend communism in an all out fight with the company, which provided them with a job, and the union, whose benefits they sought. While PLers were able to lead their co-workers in militant reform fights, they could not persuade them to pursue the struggle along revolutionary communist lines. Militant tactics got them fired long before they had a chance to convert their co-workers to communist politics. Even if that could have been done, it would have taken considerable time. In the case of garment trucking, militant tactics—which PL used to distinguish itself from "fake radicals" and "union sell-outs"—and communist agitation did not prove to be the high road to communist conversions.

At Figure Flattery, PL's Hispanic organizers were socially and ethnically similar to the workers whom PL believed had the greatest revolutionary potential. Essentially a male group, they were nonetheless able to form an alliance with women production workers. Felipe DeJesus, the most effective organizer for PL at Figure Flattery, had developed his political ideas in the socialist wing of the Puerto Rican nationalist movement. Although he respected PL and became a party member, he also followed his own political ideas. He was sometimes more militant than PL, but he was less insistent on pushing communist politics, believing that raising the political consciousness of workers was usually a protracted process.

Figure Flattery, part of a worldwide garment manufacturing enterprise, seems to have been a sweatshop. The workers, most of whom were Hispanic women, had serious grievances, which Local 32, ILGWU had not adequately addressed. DeJesus, leading an insurgent caucus, was the catalyst for a wildcat strike, which won a number of important demands. The company and the union, recognizing that they had lost control of the Hispanic workers, mounted a counteroffensive to reassert their authority. They launched a two-pronged attack that (1) used prominent Hispanics to red-bait DeJesus and supplant his leadership, and (2) employed pressure tactics—including violence. When DeJesus struck a supervisor and was fired, his followers organized a work slowdown, which was supported by PL pickets. But the workers were unwilling to strike, and the insurgents were soon ousted from the plant. In the end, the struggle revolved around the issue of communism, and it devolved into a series of street battles between PLers and company security forces. Even if PL had been more successful in recruiting Figure Flattery workers—who belonged to a nonrevolutionary workforce and community—it seems unlikely that they would have been willing to pursue PL's confrontational and openly communist style of organizing.

In many respects, New York City's garment industry was the acid test of PL's class analysis and organizing methods. Progressive Labor tried to establish a communist beachhead among very oppressed industrial workers, who were low-paid Blacks, Hispanics and women. There is enough evidence to suggest that these workers were not adequately represented by the ILGWU: many of the garment truckers were prevented from joining the union and receiving union scale and benefits, and in the case of Figure Flattery, sweatshop conditions prevailed. Moreover, PL's organizers were experienced, capable and dedicated. It is difficult to imagine PL having on-the-job organizers who could have done much better than Lemansky, Martinot, Davis and DeJesus. In the case of Figure Flattery, PL even had the advantage of Hispanic organizers who were confronting an ILGWU local that had to bring in Spanish speakers to represent its point of view. This was an atypical situation for PL, most of whose organizers were White North Americans. Local 32's inability to control Hispanic workers at Figure Flattery pointed out the union's problematic relationship with its newest members, just as Figure Flattery's eventual closing was indicative of the garment industry's flight to low-wage areas outside of New York City—a runaway shop syndrome that the ILGWU's low-wage strategy was designed to stop.

Progressive Labor organizers in the garment industry were able to initiate a surprising number of struggles. One might conclude that never have so few stirred things up so much. By any definition, the workers were militant, but they fought in pursuit of very limited goals. In both garment trucking and Figure Flattery, the workers wanted access to union benefits. But PL's organizers, whose militancy garnered worker support, had a communist agenda which went far beyond winning the workers' immediate demands. Militancy gave PL an opportunity to distinguish itself from accommodationist union leaders, and sharp struggles lent credibility, PL believed, to its revolutionary rhetoric. But the workers' willingness to engage in militant struggle was necessarily limited by cost-benefit analyses that were grounded in the practical concerns of working-class life. However, PL's commitment to militancy knew few bounds. As a consequence, PL sometimes found itself trying to lead workers where they did not want to go.

Inevitably, PL or its detractors raised the issue of communism. Workers showed considerable willingness to defend popular shop stewards, who happened to be communists. In both garment trucking and Figure Flattery, however, the issue of communism wound up becoming the main issue, and the workers, who were not committed to communism, refused to fight as hard to defend their communist stewards as PL urged. In neither case did the heat generated by the public controversy over the communist issue seem to enhance PL's ability to recruit workers.

Ultimately, PL did not discover a revolutionary section of garment workers. To be sure, the workers were militant (that a few PL organizers could lead so many work actions in a short period of time suggests as much), but PL's garment organizing did not show that the most oppressed industrial workers were inclined to become revolutionaries. The workers were willing to ally with communists, but not because they were communists. Progressive Labor's confidence that it could win industrial workers to the party by exposing them to communist ideas and leadership proved baseless, that is, PL's experience in New York City's garment center did not confirm PL's theory that oppressed industrial workers would join PL if party organizers led their shop struggles and raised communist ideas in the process. Progressive Labor's experience in New York City's garment center did not demonstrate that building a revolutionary communist movement among industrial workers in the United States was feasible, or that PL's approach to organizing such a movement was realistic.

Ironically, PL organizers went into garment—and fought so militantly and with such determination there—because they were committed to communism, but their attempt to build a *communist* base in the garment industry reduced their effectiveness in the reform struggle that interested workers. They mobilized enough workers to elicit sharp attacks from employers and union leaders, but they were not able to gain enough support from workers to defend themselves. Their employers rejected them because they were communist labor agitators, but the workers did not embrace them as communist prophets.

In the end, PL's flurry of militant activity in New York City's garment center in the late 1960s and early 1970s did not contribute to transforming PL into a party of the industrial working class. Ironically, PL's garment organizing probably had more of an impact on PL's student following than on the political ideas of garment workers. Despite PL's militancy in the garment industry, to which workers initially responded, and which resulted in gains for them, PL could not force garment workers into its revolutionary communist mold. Progressive Labor's opponents were powerful, and garment workers, as opposed to PLers, were not prepared to sacrifice their jobs for the sake of militancy, especially in a fight where they were burdened with having to defend communism as well. Skillful and committed organizers, such as Lemansky and DeJesus, could foment rebellions against union-management collusion and sweatshop conditions, but they could not win over their fellow workers to sustaining a frontal, revolutionary assault on the whole garment establishment. Progressive Labor remained a party of the college-educated, whose revolutionary faith was invested in an industrial working class that showed few signs of being revolutionary itself.

Progressive Labor had faced the 1960s determined to prove the validity of its pro-worker politics. The party counted on unbridled militancy and unflinching proclamations of communist politics to awaken revolutionary impulses in the American working class. These tactics did not work. Garment workers were both more militant and more willing to accept communist leadership than antiworker student radicals might have predicted, but they were less militant and revolutionary than PL had anticipated, or if they were, they were not persuaded that PL possessed a winning strategy. Although PL won a sizeable number of SDSers to its pro-worker point of view, its labor organizing failed to show that American workers were revolutionary, as PL claimed they were.

Progressive Labor remained a party that was predominantly composed of the college educated. It continually revised its approach to organizing in order to make inroads into the working class, but its antirevisionist assumptions drove the party in a sectarian direction; PL elevated revolution over reform despite overwhelming empirical evidence that the American working class was reformist and growing more conservative. Progressive Labor had theorized that if it did not transform itself into a party that was primarily composed of, and led by, industrial workers, it would go astray politically. Yet PL's persistent inability to industrialize itself did not induce the party to doubt its own importance or question its increasingly utopian formulas. Quite the contrary, the more sectarian it became, the more the party saw itself as indispensable.

Ultimately, PL was more effective in SDS than in the garment center. Although garment workers proved more willing to follow communist leadership in shop struggles than many political activists at the time supposed, the history of PL's garment organizing in New York City in the late 1960s and early 1970s does not refute the prevailing view in the literature on the radicalism of the period that PL's confidence in working-class revolution was unrealistic, and that PL's labor strategies were unworkable. However, PL-led struggles in the garment industry suggest that PL was more than a campus-oriented organization. A balanced evaluation of PL requires examining its labor organizing, which was extensive relative to PL's small numbers. Radical labor insurgencies, such as the ones that PL led in the garment industry, constituted an important aspect of the new radicalism, and should be studied. Leftist labor agitation was an especially important aspect of the new radicalism in New York City, which was becoming increasingly divided along racial and ethnic lines during the 1960s and 1970s. Progressive Labor's venture in garment was only one episode in this New York story, and only one facet of PL's attempt to revolutionize the labor front in New York City and elsewhere. For the most part, the story of the new labor radicalism, and the role Progressive Labor played in it, remains to be told.

Notes

In citing works in the notes, short titles have generally been used. Periodicals, authors and works frequently cited have been identified by the following abbreviations:

CD	*Challenge-Desafio*
EL	Edward Lemansky
FD	Felipe DeJesus
HUAC	House Un-American Activities Committee
InCar	International Committee Against Racism
JU	*Justice*
LSW	*Lenin: Selected Works*
NP	*New Politics*
PL	*Progressive Labor Magazine*
RT	*Revolution Today*
RR I	*Road to Revolution*
RRII	*Road to Revolution II*
RR III	*Road to Revoluution III*
RR IV	*Road to Revolution IV*
SDS	Students for a Democratic Society
SWM	*Selected Works of Mao Tse-tung*
TW	*The Worker*

INTRODUCTION

[1] New radicals saw the new radicalism of the 1960s as a heterogeneous, student-based movement, but the socialist Hal Draper was critical of those who

"with straight face" discussed the "unreconstructed Stalinists of the Progressive Labor group as if they were new radicals too." "Political humor," he thought, "can go no further." Although it was difficult to define "new radicalism" with precision, Draper was certain that PL did not fit the definition. Hal Draper, "In Defense of the 'New Radicals,'" *New Politics* 4, no. 3, 5–12. PL originated in the CPUSA, but also reflected the new radicalism. Because PL both continued and broke with CP traditions, I find *new communist* the least confusing label for PL.

² Ibid., 16–19.

³ Ibid. The sociologist C. Wright Mills, in "Labor Leaders and the Power Elite" (1954), concluded that organized labor was part of the corporate system, and the philosopher Herbert Marcuse, in *One Dimensional Man* (Boston: Beacon Press, 1964), suggested that poor Blacks could become the new agents of revolutionary change. See Stanley Aronowitz, "New Working Class, Old Labor Movement," *NP* 10, no. 2, 62–63. According to Hal Draper, many new radicals "were imbued with the image, fostered by the academy and Madison Avenue, of the labor movement as one, monolithic, undifferentiated Fat-Cat Establishment, of no interest to radicals." He argued that the socialist idea of grassroots organizing, which involved "entering the factories, organized or unorganized, as rank-and-file workers, and organizing and educating inside and outside of the union on a shop basis," was "entirely unknown to the new radicals." Draper, "In Defense of the 'New Radicals,'" *NP* 4, no. 3, 17–19. David Nolan, an activist in the Southern Student Organizing Committee, explained, "We adopted, or were given a series of gurus—from Paul Goodman to Timothy Leary to Herbert Marcuse—who told us that there were other, more up to date, agencies of social change." Nolan lamented, "The working class became the baby thrown out with the bath water." David Nolan, "Toward a Student Worker Alliance," *NP* 10, no. 4, 25.

⁴ SDS sent students into "factories, warehouses, loading docks and offices in order to talk with working people about the Vietnam War, racism, the student movement and topical political questions." Steering Committee, Chicago Work-In, "Work-In 1968: SDS Goes to the Factories," in *SDS Work-In 1968: Toward a Worker-Student Alliance* (SDS pamphlet, n.d.), 2.

⁵ For example, the former SDS leaders Greg Calvert and Carol Neiman, in *A Disrupted History: The New Left and The New Capitalism* (New York: Random House, 1971), argued that the millions of baby-boomers who were becoming college students during the 1960s constituted a new working class that was becoming the new social basis for radical change; and they derided the attempt by PL and other revolutionary SDS factions to use Leninist and Maoist strategies in an advanced capitalist society such as the United States. The former SDS leader Todd Gitlin, in *The Sixties: Years of Hope, Days of Rage* (Toronto, Can.: Bantam Books, 1987), observed that the student movement oscillated between believing

itself to be the historical instrument of radical social change and searching for the "real" instrument of change. The principal contenders for that honor were PL's working class, the Revolutionary Youth Movement's working-class youth, and the Weathermen's Third World. Gitlin criticized the strident Marxism-Leninism and violent revolutionism that, he believed, led to the implosion of SDS.

⁶ Ibid., 383.

⁷ The point of departure for much of the criticism of the labor movement during this dismal decade and a half was C. Wright Mills, *The New Men of Power: America's Labor Leaders* (1948; repr., New York: August M. Kelly, 1971). Even though Mills, a sociologist, noted the development of an industrial labor aristocracy, he hoped for an alliance between labor intellectuals and labor leaders in opposition to the rapidly consolidating corporate order. By 1960, however, Mills no longer looked to labor as a potential agency of radical social change. He advised the British New Left to abandon its confidence in workers, a view that he characterized as a vestige of Victorian Marxism. The political scientist Daniel Bell, in *The End of Ideology: On the Exhaustion of Political Ideas in the Fifties* (New York: Collier Books, 1961), the historian William A. Williams, in *Contours of American History* (Cleveland, Ohio: The World Publishing Company, 1961), and other leading intellectuals expressed similar doubts about the potential for radicalism of affluent American workers. Mills, in particular, influenced many new leftists to discount workers as a potential agent of radical social change. See Peter B. Levy, *The New Left and Labor in the 1960s*, (Urbana, Ill.: University of Illinois Press, 1994), 111–113, and C. Wright Mills, "The New Left," *New Left Review* (Sept.-Oct. 1960).

⁸ For example, in the winter of 1961, the Chicago trade unionist and labor commentator Sidney Lens called for new leaders to reawaken the "insurgent impulse," which he argued had been missing in the labor movement for at least a decade and a half. Sidney Lens, "American Labor at Dead-End, *NP* (fall 1961–winter 1961): 60. In the *New Federationist* (Nov. 1963), Gus Tyler, assistant president of the International Ladies' Garment Workers' Union, labeled the views of the such liberal intellectuals as Lens, Paul Jacobs, Jack Widick, Al Nash and Herman Benson—who believed that the labor movement was losing momentum—as "new leftism," which he viewed as an "enemy within" the house of labor, a phrase that smacked of Cold War anticommunism. See Sidney Lens, "Labor's New Conservatives," *NP* 3, no. 2, 54. Although Tyler called labor's critics "reactionary radicals," their criticism of the labor movement reflected the contemporary resurgence of radicalism and labor militancy. The hostile response of Tyler and other labor leaders to labor's leftist critics may have hastened their departure from the labor movement. Economist Sumner M. Rosen noted "a growing attitude of discontent, disillusion, and despair among liberal and radical

intellectuals," who were leaving the labor movement at an increasing rate. Sumner M. Rosen, "Labor's Critics and Labor's Crisis," *NP* 3, no. 3, 54.

[9] For example, in "Rebellion in American Labor's Rank and File," the labor commentator Stan Weir noted the upsurge in rank-and-file militancy, as well as the unionization of teachers, social workers and various kinds of professionals, and argued that these intellectuals would be able to establish an independent base within organized labor. See Gerry Hunnius, G. David Garson and John Case, eds., *Workers' Control: A Reader on Labor and Social Change* (New York: Vintage Books, 1973). The labor commentator Stanley Aronowitz, in *False Promises: The Shaping of American Working Class Consciousness* (New York: McGraw-Hill, 1973), based his confidence in an upsurge of labor radicalism less on the activities of an ideological Left than on the development of new conditions and the spontaneous struggle of workers.

[10] For example, in *Working Class Hero: A New Strategy For Labor* (New York: The Pilgrim Press, 1983), Stanley Aronowitz, primarily addressing the progressive wing of the trade union movement, argued for the necessity of a new anticorporate electoral coalition based on class struggle and a militant wave of union organizing carried out in conjunction with movements of Blacks, women and professionals. Mike Davis, in *Prisoners of the American Dream: Politics and the Economy in the History of the U.S. Working Class* (London: Verso, 1986), rejected the use of the Democratic Party as an instrument to achieve labor's demands, but saw the possibility of future rainbow coalitions as the basis of independent socialist politics. The labor commentator Kimberly Moody, in *An Injury to All: The Decline of American Unionism* (London: Verso, 1988), attributed the decline of the American labor movement to the victory of business unionism over the social unionism that, he believed, the Congress of Industrial Organizations had practiced in the 1930s. Moody surveyed the rank-and-file insurgencies of the 1960s and 1970s, which he viewed as attempts to overcome the constraints imposed by business unionism. Although Moody profiled various labor insurgencies, and indicated the importance of cooperation between socialists and working-class activists in these movements, he did not describe in detail the radical forces that were involved, and he wrote little about the activities of labor radicals in New York City.

[11] Initially, discussions that encompassed both radicalism and labor viewed them as distinct movements and examined their relationship. For example, the Old Left historian Philip S. Foner, in *American Labor and the Indo-China War: The Growth of Union Opposition* (New York: International Publishers, 1971), described the cooperation between antiwar students and like-minded unionists. The historian Paul Buhle, in *Marxism in the United States: Remapping the History of the American Left* (London: Verso, 1987), did briefly describe the insurgent new

leftists in the labor movement of the 1970s. The historian Peter B. Levy's *The New Left and Labor in the 1960s* (1994) delineated a complex and changing relationship between the New Left and the labor movement that included both confrontation and cooperation. Levy's informative study has helped to bridge the gap between accounts of radicalism and labor in the 1960s. Levy examined student involvement in union organizing and strike support. However, aside from discussing several radical Black labor insurgencies in the automobile industry, he did not examine the insurgent activities of new labor radicals. Some studies of individual unions have discussed the role of the Movement or labor radicals in trade union struggles. For example, the sociologist J. Craig Jenkins, in *The Politics of Insurgency: The Farm Worker Movement in the 1960s* (New York: Columbia University Press, 1985), argued that the United Farm Workers exemplified the goals and strategies of the 1960s social movements; and the journalist Kenneth C. Crowe, in *Collision: How the Rank and File Took Back the Teamsters* (New York: Charles Scribner's Sons, 1993), mentioned the involvement of members of the International Socialists in Teamsters for a Democratic Union. However, I found few detailed studies of the new labor radicalism, and only one discussion of a PL-led labor union insurgency, an account of PL's role, through its Workers Action Movement, in the sit-down strike at Chrysler's Mack Avenue Plant in 1973. See Heather Ann Thompson, "Auto Workers, Dissent and the UAW: Detroit and Lordstown," in *Autowork*, eds. Robert Asher and Ronald Edsforth (Albany: State University of New York Press, 1995), 200.

[12] Some important examples are: District Council 37, American Federation of State, County and Municipal Employees; Hospital and Nursing Home Workers Local 1199, Retail, Wholesale Department Store Workers Union; the United Federation of Teachers, American Federation of Teachers; and the independent Committee of Interns and Residents.

[13] For example, the race, class and gender biases of White, college-educated caseworkers in the independent Social Service Employees Union, members of the "new working class," hindered them from allying with less empowered Black and Hispanic, working-class women clerical workers and welfare clients. See Leigh David Benin, "Radicals in the Real World: The Social Service Employees Union and the Limits of the New Radicalism of the 1960s" (Ph.D. seminar paper, Department of History, Graduate School of Arts and Science, New York University, 1987).

[14] New York City's labor radicals fought for a redivision of social wealth and power within a complex and changing environment. The historian Daniel J. Walkowitz argued that New York, as it became a "global city," became sharply divided between "an affluent, technocratic, professional white-collar group managing the financial and commercial life of an international city and an unemployed

and underemployed service sector which is substantially black and Hispanic." He argued that because its labor market is divided between white-collar work and worklessness, New York resembles a Third World city. Daniel J. Walkowitz, "A Tale of Two Cities," in *Snowbelt Cities: Metropolitan Politics in the Northeast and Midwest Since World War II*, ed. Richard M. Bernard (Bloomington: Indiana University Press, 1990).

CHAPTER 1. ANTIREVISIONISM IN ACTION

[1] First, "Progressive Labor" is a convenient, but possibly confusing, name for a coherent communist group that developed organizationally in three distinct stages: *Progressive Labor* began publication in January 1962; *PL*'s editors formed the Progressive Labor Movement in July 1962; and the Progressive Labor Party was founded in April 1965. When it seems necessary to avoid confusion, I will stipulate the specific organizational form of PL to which I am referring. Second, the period discussed in this chapter begins with Khrushchev's speech to the Twentieth Congress of the Communist Party of the Soviet Union in 1956, which created the turmoil within the Communist Party USA that led to the creation of *Progressive Labor* by ex-CPers six years later, and it ends in 1965, when Progressive Labor Party was formed from the Progressive Labor Movement. Third, Chapters 1–3 consider some major themes in the history of PL; they do not attempt to provide a systematic history of PL in its first twenty years.

[2] First, *Progressive Labor* began publication in January 1962. The Progressive Labor Movement was formed in July 1962. The PLM was transformed into the Progressive Labor Party in April 1965. Second, I will refer to the Communist Party USA simply as the "CP" unless "CPUSA" is needed to avoid confusion with another communist party, such as the Communist Party of the Soviet Union (CPSU).

[3] House Committee on Un-American Activities, *Hearings on Subversive Influences in Riots, Looting, and Burning: Part I*, 90th Cong., 1st Sess., October 25, 26, 31 and November 28, 1967 (Washington, D.C.: U.S. Government Printing Office, 1968), 894. "CP Statement on Unity and the Fight Against Disrupters," *The Worker*, 28 Jan. 1962, 5, 8. For a discussion of Lenin's conception of the party, see Richard T. De George, *Patterns of Soviet Thought: The Origin and Development of Dialectical and Historical Materialism* (Ann Arbor, Mich.: The University of Michigan Press, 1966), 128–145. Lenin was convinced that a disciplined party was an essential ingredient of working-class revolution. "I assert: (1) that no revolutionary movement can endure without a stable organization of leaders maintaining continuity." V. I. Lenin, *What Is To Be Done: Burning Questions of Our Movement (1902)*, repr. in *V. I. Lenin: Selected Works*, 3 vols. (Moscow: Progress Publishers, 1975), 1: 187. (hereafter cited as *LSW*) "In its

struggle for power the proletariat has no other weapon but organization." V. I. Lenin, *One Step Forward, Two Steps Back (1904)*, repr. in *LS W*, 1: 413.

⁴ "The History of the Progressive Labor Party, Part One," *PL* (Aug.-Sept. 1975): 56–57. PL outlined three concepts necessary to make democratic centralism work: "the ability to engage in full frank discussions from top to bottom"; "ties to the people"; and the "willingness to subordinate your individual desires and thoughts to the will of the majority." "On the Party," *PL* (Jan. 1965), repr. in Progressive Labor Party *Revolution Today: U.S.A.: A Look at the Progressive Labor Movement and the Progressive Labor Party* (New York: Exposition Press, 1970), 86.

⁵ "CP Statement," *TW*, 28 Jan. 1962, 5, 8. According to Lenin, "It is not only Right doctrinairism that is erroneous; Left doctrinairism is erroneous too." He chastised the German and British Left Communists who, in his judgement, were causing "very grave prejudice to communism" because they recognized "only one road, only the direct road" and would not "permit tacking, conciliatory manoeuvres, or compromising." V. I. Lenin, *Left-Wing Communism: An Infantile Disorder* (1920), repr. in *LSW*, 3: 358.

⁶ "The History," *PL* (Aug.-Sept. 1975): 57. Eduard Bernstein (1850–1932), an influential German Social Democrat, "claimed that communism was a utopian ideal, unattainable for a long time to come." Consequently, he emphasized working for the "present improvement of the lot of the working class." Bernstein's doctrine, which came to be known as "Revisionism," was condemned by orthodox Marxists and has become a "term of abuse." De George, *Patterns of Soviet Thought*, 108–111. For the context of Bernstein's thought, see James Joll, *The Second International: 1889–1914* (New York: Harper & Row, 1966). In his formal declaration of war against revisionism, Lenin declared, "The ideological struggle waged by revolutionary Marxism against revisionism at the end of the nineteenth century is but the prelude to the great revolutionary battles of the proletariat, which is marching forward to the complete victory of its cause despite all the waverings and weaknesses of the petty bourgeoisie." V. I. Lenin, *Marxism and Revisionism*, (1908), repr. in *LSW*, 1: 56. "Some of the main premises of the classic revisionism of Bernstein and the Second International are presently reappearing in transparent disguises, namely: that the state in a bourgeois society is above classes and mediates the class struggle, and that revolution is no longer desirable or necessary, especially in the advanced countries where parliamentary democracy provides the vehicle for an evolutionary and gradual transfer of power to the working class." "Road to Revolution I," *PL* (Mar. 1963), repr. in *RT*, 90–91 (hereafter cited as "RR I").

⁷ The correct political path was narrow and periodically shifted. At such times, it was often difficult for communists to avoid the accusation that they had strayed from it. "Today the party is attempting to steer a middle course between

the Scylla of 'right revisionism' and the Charybdis of 'left sectarianism' . . . The new line is a hard one to follow and the editorial writers of the Daily Worker . . . constantly find themselves in hot water for veering too far to the right or left." A. H. Raskin, "Report on the Communist Party (U.S.A.)," *New York Times Magazine*, 20 Mar. 1947, repr. in *American Society Since 1945*, ed. William L. O'Neill (Chicago, Ill.: Quadrangle Books, 1969), 172. CPer George Charney reported that ". . . we found to our dismay that we could be as guilty anticipating a new line as deviating from it after it was adopted. But we were neither prophets nor dissidents." George Charney, *A Long Journey* (Chicago, Ill.: Quadrangle Books, 1972), cited in Theodore Draper, *A Present of Things Past: Selected Essays* (New York: Hill & Wang, 1990), 127.

[8] Unlike Russia during Lenin's lifetime, the United States in the twentieth century has not been a revolutionary society. However, the anticommunist crusade reinforced American communists' conviction that their political decisions were more consequential than they actually were. It was the fate of American communists that America's rulers took the threat of communism more seriously than American workers took the promise of communism.

[9] "The History," *PL* (Aug.-Sept. 1975): 55. For a discussion of the Twentieth Congress of the CPSU, see Edward Crankshaw, *Khrushchev: A Career* (New York: Viking Press, 1966), 227–244; and William J. Tompson, *Khrushchev: A Political Life* (New York: St. Martin's Griffin, 1997), 143–173. For an interesting contemporary discussion, see I. F. Stone, "The Meaning of Khrushchev's Revisions," *I. F. Stone's Weekly* (29 Feb. 1956), repr. in id., *The Haunted Fifties: 1953–1963* (Boston, Mass.: Little, Brown & Company, 1989), 123–126. PL also took a longer view of its origins: ". . . in a fundamental sense, the history of PLP begins with the earliest strivings of the world's workers to get rid of capitalist exploitation." "The History," *PL* (Aug.-Sept. 1975): 55.

[10] "Having vanquished two former general secretaries of the Communist Party, Jay Lovestone in the 1920's and Earl Browder in the 1940's, Foster was not about to surrender to John Gates in the 1950's." Maurice Isserman, *If I Had a Hammer: The Death of the Old Left and the Birth of the New Left* (Urbana, Ill.: University of Illinois Press, 1987), 25–26. The shifting fortunes of the Left and the Right within the CPUSA reflected, to a great extent, changes in the line of the CPSU. "A rhythmic rotation from Communist sectarianism to Americanized opportunism was set in motion at the outset and has been going on ever since." Theodore Draper, *The Roots of American Communism* (New York: Viking Press, 1957), cited in id., *American Communism and Soviet Russia: The Formative Period* (New York: Vintage Books, 1986), 448, and in id., *A Present of Things Past*, 121.

[11] "The History," *PL* (Aug.-Sept. 1975): 55. Despite its attack on CP "revisionism," PL recognized that, "the communist movement in our country in its

militant days created a legacy of dedicated and courageous struggle." Moreover, PL recommended, "Young radicals can learn from and emulate the devotion to the working class and socialism of such outstanding figures as William Z. Foster." "RR I," repr. in *RT*, 143. Although Foster did not break with Khrushchev's CPSU, he later characterized Stalin as "one of the greatest fighters ever produced by the world's working class" and maintained that his "death was a tremendous loss to the Soviet people and the international movement for peace and freedom." William Z. Foster, *History of the Three Internationals: The World Socialist and Communist Movements from 1848 to the Present* (New York: Greenwood Press, 1968), 524–525.

[12] Isserman, *If I Had a Hammer*, 6.

[13] For example, when the Cold War was at its peak prior to 1956, Foster argued that war between the U.S. and the Soviet Union was inevitable. Ibid., 6. More than twenty-five years later, an apocalyptic article in *Progressive Labor* on the anti-nuclear movement began, "A third World War, with both conventional and nuclear weapons, is inevitable. The struggle between U.S. and Soviet bosses for global economic supremacy has become the central fact of life everywhere in the past decade." "The Anti-Nuclear Movement: Cover for Bosses' War Plans," *PL* (May 1982): 1. PL retained the idea of an inevitable American-Soviet war, but no longer as a clash between capitalism and socialism. PL believed that socialism had been reversed in the Soviet Union, and that the coming war would be an inter-imperialist struggle, similar in this respect to Wold War I. For Lenin's views on imperialism, see *Imperialism, The Highest Stage of Capitalism* (1917), repr. in *LSW*, 1: 634–731. In addition, the CP during the 1950s and PL during the 1960s sent some party members underground. See Isserman, *If I Had a Hammer*, 7–8; and Phillip Abbott Luce, *The New Left* (New York: David McKay Company, Inc. 1966), 42.

[14] "The History," *PL* (Aug.-Sept. 1975): 55–56.

[15] "As the self-proclaimed vanguard of the working class, the communist party placed great stress on the proletarian background of its cadres." Harvey Klehr, *Communist Cadre: The Social Background of the American Communist Party Elite* (Stanford, Calif.: Hoover Institution Press, 1978), 42. William Z. Foster "liked to depict his own forces as the real workers in the Party; interestingly enough, however, he could also count on the support of many Communist doctors, dentists, and lawyers who looked on him as their proletarian conscience." Isserman, *If I Had a Hammer*, 24–25. Milt Rosen probably played this role for many professionals in PL. According to John Williamson, who was then organizational secretary of the CPUSA, "71% of the Party in New York City consists of white collar workers, professionals and housewives." *Political Affairs* (Feb. 1946), cited in Subcommittee to Investigate the Adminstration of the Internal

Security Act and Other Internal Security Laws of the Committee on the Judiciary, United States Senate, *The Communist Party of the United States of America: What It Is, How It Works, A Handbook for Americans* (21 Dec. 1955), 45.

[16] "CP Statement," *TW*, 28 Jan. 1962, 8.

[17] "The History," *PL* (Aug.-Sept. 1975): 56. Harvey Klehr, in his study of the CPUSA of the 1930s, estimated that between 1930 and 1935 one third of all CPers lived in New York. Harvey Klehr, *The Heyday of American Communism: The Depression Decade* (New York: Basic Books, 1984), 164. The Federal Bureau of Investigation's Figures, drawn up in 1951, indicate that of 31,608 members of the CP, 15,458 lived in New York. United States Senate, *A Handbook for Americans*, 34. For a full discussion of the CP's concentration in Buffalo's steel industry and the HUAC investigation, see Joseph Cantor, "Steelworkers in Buffalo: A Personal Perspective," in *The Cold War Against Labor,* 2 vols. eds. Ann Fagan Ginger and David Christiano (Berkeley, Calif.: Meiklejohn Civil Liberties Institute, 1987), 2: 681–706. Cantor (pseud.), a member of the United Steelworkers of America, was one of five steelworkers fired from the Lakawanna Plant of the Bethlehem Steel Company for being an "uncooperative witness" before HUAC. According to Cantor, "The local union leadership was aligned with the Company throughout our ordeal. And the Western New York Director's office not only did not come to our support, but participated in attacks on us for not cooperating with HUAC." Ibid., 693. For PL's response to subsequent HUAC hearings in Buffalo, see "Buffalo PL Hits McCarran Act and Nazi," *PL* (Nov. 1962): 5; "PL Faces Fire in Buffalo," *PL* (Apr. 1964): 19; "Buffalo Smashes HUAC," *PL* (May 1964): 14–15; and Milt Rosen, "HUAC On the Rocks," *PL* (June 1964): 13, 18–19.

[18] "The History," *PL* (Aug.-Sept. 1975): 56.

[19] "CP Statement," *TW* , 28 Jan. 1962, 8.

[20] "RR I," in *RT*, 100.

[21] "CP Statement," *TW*, 28 Jan. 1962, 8. "Thus, Yugoslavia became the Chinese *bete noir*, and Albania served the same purpose for the Russians . . . Albania—already long experienced in the struggle against Yugoslav revisionism—had embarked upon the defense of Stalin and Stalinism." Dan N. Jacobs and Hans H. Baerwald, eds., *Chinese Communism: Selected Documents* (New York: Harper & Row, 1963), 199.

[22] "Milt Rosen Expelled," *TW*, 7 Jan. 1962, 10.

[23] "The History," *PL* (Aug.-Sept. 1975): 57.

[24] "Milt Rosen Expelled," *TW*, 7 Jan. 1962, 10.

[25] Ibid.; "CP Statement," *TW*, 28 Jan. 1962, 5.

[26] "The History," *PL* (Aug.-Sept. 1975): 57.

[27] Isserman, *If I Had a Hammer*, 32.

[28] The CP leadership was apprehensive about the decision of the United States Supreme Court on 5 June 1961 upholding the "monstrous McCarran Act." "CP Statement," *TW*, 28 Jan. 1962, 5.

[29] Isserman, *If I Had a Hammer*, 31.

[30] "The History," *PL* (Aug.-Sept. 1975): 55.

[31] Ibid., 57. However, there were other reasons as well. When PL did criticize the CP in 1964, some leading PLers defected. Ibid., 67–69.

[32] "For An Alternative Labor Policy: A Statement of Policy by the Editors," *PL* (Jan. 1962): 1–3.

[33] Ibid.

[34] "CP Statement." *TW*, 28 Jan. 1962, 5. For a discussion of the relationship of trade unions to communist revolution, see John Kelly, *Trade Unions and Socialist Politics* (London: Verso, 1988); A. Lozovsky (pseud. for Dridzo Solomon Abromovich), *Marx and the Trade Unions* (Westport, Conn.: Greenwood Press, 1976); and V. I. Lenin, *On Trade Unions: A Collection of Articles and Speeches* (Moscow: Progress Publishers, 1970).

[35] Milt Rosen's political report to the December 1961 meeting of one dozen communists projected building a new communist party, and at the July 1962 meeting which founded the Progressive Labor Movement, ". . . it was agreed that our objective must be to establish a disciplined party that would function according to the principle of democratic centralism. . . ." "The History," *PL* (Aug.-Sept. 1975): 57–58. "Only in a party apparatus, where people are serious and disciplined, can we begin the necessary cadre development—the winning of people at various political levels to a total revolutionary perspective." "On the Party," *PL* (Jan. 1965), repr. in *RT*, 82. "It is the job of a communist party to bring this revolutionary consciousness into the working class, while immersed in workers' struggles, so that the party can become the working class' general staff in the class war." "U.S. Workers: Key to Revolution," *PL* (Aug. 1969), repr. in *RT*, 310.

[36] "The History," *PL* (Aug.-Sept.): 56.

[37] "For An Alternative," *PL* (Jan. 1962): 1–3. *TW*, wary of its new competitor, warned its readers not to be deceived by *PL*, an organ which it believed would "divert from a real development of a left-progressive movement in the trade unions," and whose policies it thought could only "isolate left forces from the broad masses." "CP Statement," *TW*, 28 Jan. 1962, 5.

[38] "For An Alternative," *PL* (Jan. 1962): 1–3. For a discussion of the anti-communist crusade in the labor movement, see: David Caute, *The Great Fear: The Anti-Communist Purge Under Truman and Eisenhower* (New York: Simon & Schuster, 1978), 349–400; Bert Cochran, *Labor and Communism: The Conflict that Shaped American Unions* (Princeton, N.J.: Princeton University Press, 1977), 248–331; Robert H. Zieger, *The CIO, 1935–1955* (Chapel Hill, N.C.:

University of North Carolina Press, 1995); and Herbert L. Marx, Jr., ed., *American Labor Unions: Organization, Aims, and Power* (New York: H. W. Wilson, 1950), 163–192.

[39] "CP Statement," *TW*, 28 Jan. 1962, 5.

[40] "For An Alternative," *PL* (Jan. 1962): 1–3. In 1946, C. Wright Mills called attention to the "threat of increased labor-business cooperation within the system of private enterprise." Mills warned, "This is the blind alley into which the liberal is led by the rhetoric of cooperation." C. Wright Mills, *The New Men of Power*, 233. For the newly merged AFL-CIO's sense of its mission, see George Meany, "On Labor's Future," *New York Times Magazine*, 4 Dec. 1955, repr. in *American Labor Since the New Deal*, ed. Melvyn Dubofsky (Chicago, Ill.: Quadrangle Books, 1971), 164–171. For a contemporary discussion of the "crisis" in organized labor, see: Sidney Lens, *The Crisis of American Labor* (New York: A. S. Barnes, 1961); Solomon Barkin, *The Decline of the American Labor Movement* (Santa Barbara, Calif.: Center For the Study of Democratic Institutions, 1961); Solomon Barkin and Albert A. Blum, eds., "The Crisis in the American Trade-Union Movement," *The Annals of the American Academy of Political and Social Science* (Nov. 1963); and Paul Jacobs, *The State of the Unions* (New York: Atheneum, 1963). For a more recent account of organized labor's decline, see Moody, *An Injury to All*.

[41] "For An Alternative," *PL* (Jan. 1962): 1–3.

[42] "The heart of any alternative program to be fought for by communists, is based on the fact that the problems of the workers will never be solved under capitalism." "RRI," in *RT*, 101.

[43] "We have said that there could not have been Social-Democratic consciousness among the workers. It would have to be brought from without. The history of all countries shows that the working class, exclusively by its own effort, is able to develop only trade union consciousness, i.e., the conviction that it is necessary to combine in unions, to fight the employers, and strive to compel the government to pass necessary labor legislation, etc." Lenin, *What Is To Be Done?* in *LSW* 1: 114. "This dual character of U.S. trade unions—tremendous class struggle alongside an inability to move beyond the capitalist system—has marked the last 100 years." "U.S. Workers: Key to Revolution," *PL* (Aug. 1969), repr. in *RT*, 307.

[44] ". . . the overwhelming majority of workers can be won to active battle against the ruling class, and for socialism, and are destined to consign that class to the scrap heap of history." "U.S. Workers: Key to Revolution," *PL* (Aug. 1969), repr. in *RT*, 301. ". . . throw out the bosses' servants in the trade union movement and fight to establish the unions as class instruments in the workers' interests. The latter strategy will become a major tactic in attaining the still

longer-range strategic goal of smashing the system." Ibid., 313. "We said—and still say—that the working class, especially its industrial segment, is the key force for revolution in the U.S." "Improve Our Base Building," Summary of PLP National Committee Meeting, January 1969, repr. in *RT*, 72. Max Danish, writing from an anticommunist perspective, recognized the importance of organized labor to communists. "But the labor unions have been their targets, for without control of the trade unions, their advance would amount to a crawl. . . . The labor organizations, the commissars knew, are the largest and most vital nongovernmental bodies in America's big industrial communities. The influence of organized labor, they were well aware, reaches far beyond its millions of members and their families." Max D. Danish, *The World of David Dubinsky* (Cleveland, Ohio: The World Publishing Company, 1957), 241.

[45] "Just as the Center cannot move forward without the Left; the Left cannot operate at all without the Center." "U.S. Workers: Key to Revolution," *PL* (Aug. 1969), repr. in *RT*, 318.

[46] At the Progressive Labor Movement's founding in July 1962, some of the participants opposed taking steps toward building a vanguard party, and advocated instead forming a communist educational association. This "rightist" opposition argued that "The workers struggle daily without us." But PL's "trade union (T.U.) comrades" maintained that ". . . it is only through active participation by communists in day-to-day battles that workers can really grasp the ideas of communism and the necessity for a communist party to lead the workers' revolution for socialism." "The History," *PL* (Aug.-Sept. 1975): 58. Thus, PL's leaders conjoined the need for a party and the necessity of fighting for leadership in the labor movement. Subsequently, when the Communist Party of Australia (Marxist-Leninist) argued against strengthening trade unions on the grounds that they were "thoroughgoing instruments for the administration of capitalism," Walter Linder, who functioned as PL's labor secretary, argued that despite the old communist movement's history of right opportunism, communists working within reformist trade unions would not necessarily succumb to economism. Walter Linder, "Trade Unions Are Schools For Communism," *PL* (Nov. 1969): 29–32.

[47] "Eventually we hope to involve tens of millions in sharp struggle. Where are they to come from? They are not about to fall from the sky. They are going to be those who at the moment don't seem interested in changing society. But we say that sooner or later objective processes will sharpen the contradictions between most working people and the system. Then whom will the people trust? Those whom they know and have confidence in." Milt Rosen, "Build a Base in the Working Class," *PL* (June 1969), repr. in *RT*, 24.

[48] "The History," *PL* (Aug.-Sept. 1975): 58. By the spring of 1963, *PL*'s rhetoric was more assertive: "This May Day must bring an increased sense of

dedication to American revolutionary Socialists to raise to higher and higher levels the fight for Socialism." "May Day—Symbol of Workers' Power," *PL* (May 1963): 1–2.

[49] "The History," *PL* (Aug.-Sept. 1975): 58. Milt Rosen was elected chairman of a 14–member national coordinating committee, and Mort Scheer was elected vice-chairman. Rosen called for organizing: ". . . even as we walk on one leg of a program—even as we begin now to draft the program for our new party—we must step off on the leg of organization." Rosen urged the organization of "Progressive Labor Clubs, Marxist study circles, and class-conscious single-issue organizations, as the most important levels of organization in the coming period." "PL Conference: A Step to Secure the Future," *PL* (July-Aug. 1962): 5.

[50] "The History," *PL* (Aug.-Sept. 1975): 58–60; Camilo de Chispa, "Class War Rages in Kentucky Coal Fields," *PL* (Jan. 1963): 1–8. De Chispa sent the following telegram from Hazard, Ky. to New York City: "RELIEF NEEDED DESPERATELY . . . HUNGRY BABIES CRYING, COLD IS EVERYWHERE STOP STRIKERS PREPARED TO CONTINUE AS LONG AS THEY CAN EAT STOP CONDITIONS UNBELIEVABLE REPEAT RELIEF NEEDED IMMEDIATELY. SEND CANNED GOODS, BLANKETS, ALL SIZE CLOTHES AND MONEY AT ONCE REPEAT AT ONCE. Camilo." Ibid., 8. De Chispa wrote, "UMWA [United Mine Workers of America] officials are doing everything in their power to help break the strike." Ibid., 1. According to de Chispa, "Gibson predicted that the strike would win despite pressures from the government, terror from the bosses, and sell-outs by the leadership of the United Mine Workers of America (UMWA)," "Government in Cahoots with Coal Bosses," *PL* (Feb. 1963): 1. *PL* concluded, "Berman Gibson and the new miners' rank and file leaders shatter the idea that American workers are hopeless, corrupt, and won't fight back. THE HAZARD MINERS ARE HEROES!" "PL Statement on Hazard," ibid., 3. On 7 February 1963, *The Miner's Voice* responded to red-baiting in the *Hazard Herald*: "We know the *Hazard Herald* is trying to use this 'red' fear to stop our strike. . . . Name calling can't scare us and it won't stop us. . . . If helping the strikers makes you a communist, then you just keep on helping us buddy, because we're not going to stop fighting." *The Miner's Voice*, 7 Feb. 1963, repr. in *PL* (Mar. 1963): 8. Milt Rosen wrote a letter, 12 Feb. 1963, to the editor of the *Hazard Herald* in response to its article entitled "Communism Comes to the Mountains of East Kentucky," ibid., 9. According to de Chispa, the UMWA, "once the most militant force in these mountains, doesn't seem to have it any more." Camilo de Chispa, "Kentucky Strike Puts UMW on Spot," ibid., 7. In March 1964, Stanley Aronowitz, addressing the Hazard Conference on Jobs and Poverty, explained that the UMWA was pulling out of eastern Kentucky because the miners there became a "financial liability" to the union. Ed Clark, "Kentucky

Miners Move to Political Action," *PL* (May 1964): 12–13. According to Phillip Luce, who defected from PL, in 1963 several PL members "took a truckload of guns and clothing to the miners in Hazard Kentucky." Luce, *The New Left*, 110.

⁵¹ See John W. Hevener, *Which Side Are You On?: The Harlan County Coal Miners, 1931–39* (Urbana, Ill.: University of Illinois Press, 1978); and Michael Harrington, *The Other America: Poverty in the United States* (New York: The Macmillan Company, 1962).

⁵² "The History," *PL* (Aug.-Sept. 1975): 58–60. For a discussion of the New Left's involvement in Hazard, see Levy, *The New Left and Labor*, 34–37.

⁵³ "The History," *PL* (Aug.-Sept. 1975): 60–61. "At the General Assembly despite massive police forces which made the Assembly galleries resemble a stockade, PL members were able to unfurl a banner saying "Stop JFK—Hands Off Cuba"; "PL Organizes Against U.S. Aggression," *PL* (Nov. 1962): 3. Also see: "State Department Pulls Strings to Keep U.S. Students From Cuba," *PL* (Jan. 1963): 11; Milt Rosen, "Washington's Would-Be War on Cuba," *PL* (Mar. 1963): 13; "Students Crash 'Kennedy Curtain,'" *PL* (July-Aug. 1963): 16; and Luce, *The New Left*, 61–81. A press release by the ban-breakers stated, "We intend to break through the Cane-Curtain imposed by our State Department to limit travel to Cuba." Ibid., 69. Also see Phillip Abbott Luce, *The New Left Today: America's Trojan Horse* (Wash., D.C.: The Capital Hill Press, 1971): 51–58; and Van Gosse, *Where the Boys Are: Cuba, Cold War America and the Making of a New Left* (London: Verso, 1993): 234. For background on Cuba, see: Theodore Draper, *Castro's Revolution: Myth and Reality* (New York: Frederick A. Praeger, 1962); Graham T. Allison, *Essence of Decision: Explaining the Cuban Missile Crisis* (Boston, Mass.: Little, Brown & Company, 1971); and Hugh Thomas, *The Cuban Revolution* (London: Weidenfeld & Nicolson, 1986).

⁵⁴ "Students See Cuba, State Dept. Sees Red, Washington Launches Attack Against PL," *PL* (Sept. 1963): 1.

⁵⁵ "U.S. Grand Jury Calls PL Leaders—Milton Rosen Blasts Kennedy 'Fear,'" ibid.

⁵⁶ "Students See Cuba, State Dept. Sees Red," ibid., 3.

⁵⁷ Fred Jerome, "Washington Won't Touch Birmingham Killers, Steps Up Attacks on Students, PLM," *PL* (Oct.-Nov. 1963): 1.

⁵⁸ *New York Times*, 14 Sept. 1963, repr. in *PL* (Oct.-Nov. 1963): 3.

⁵⁹ Ibid.

⁶⁰ Luce, *The New Left*, 76.

⁶¹ Fred Jerome, "Washington Won't Touch Birmingham Killers, Steps Up Attack On Students, PLM," *PL* (Oct.-Nov. 1963): 5.

⁶² Letter, Bertrand Russell to the Committee to Uphold the Right to Travel, repr. in *PL* (Oct.-Nov. 1963): 3.

[63] Caute, *The Great Fear*, 103.

[64] Editorial, *PL* (Oct.-Nov. 1963): 3. PL's aggressive tactics at HUAC hearings probably hastened the committee's demise.

[65] "The History," *PL* (Aug.-Sept. 1975): 61.

[66] Ibid., 60–61; Phillip Luce, "Students to Cuba—Bury Travel Ban," *PL* (June 1964): 14, 16–17 [Luce had travelled to Cuba in 1963, was a member of the executive committee of the Student Committee for Travel to Cuba, and was one of three students under federal indictment for the 1963 trip.]; "Declaration of Student Committee for Travel to Cuba," ibid., 14; Judy Warden, "Cuba Ban-Busters Back, Face HUAC Quiz," *Challenge-Desafio*, 29 Aug. 1964, 2; "With the 84 Americans in Cuba," *PL* (July-Aug. 1964): 16–17; Judy Warden, "Cuba Ban-Busters Indicted," *CD*, 26 Sept. 1964, 3; Michael Brown for the Executive Board of S.C.T.C., "SCTC Comments," *PL* (Dec. 1964): 8–11. "After thirteen of the travellers were indicted, some on multiple counts that might result in possible jail terms of up to 20 years, the leadership of PL decided against further trips. They dropped the public relations campaign against the travel ban and their support for those indicted." Luce, *The New Left*, 80. Luce left PL in February 1965. Ibid., 41–42. PL believed that Luce was motivated by a "mortal fear of imprisonment," and accused him of being a "heroin user, a thief, and a police agent." "Warning: A Statement from the National Steering Committee of the PLM, Issued March 30, 1965." *PL* (Apr. 1965): inside front cover; Felipe DeJesus, "Cuba Trip Stoolie Would Rather Switch Than Fight," *CD*, 2 Nov. 1965, 2. Luce testified against three PLers on trial in federal court for traveling to Cuba in violation of the U.S. State Department's ban. Perhaps, Luce defected from PL and later testified against PLers because he was chastened by the prospect of punishment.

[67] "The History," *PL* (Aug.-Sept. 1975): 61. "The path that leads from the cult of 'the rebel' (whether the book by Camus or Nick Adams in his Confederate Army cap on the TV Western of the same name) to the beginnings of the cult of Fidel begins with 'desire' in its rawest form, and both its politics and lack of politics." Gosse, *Where the Boys Are*, 53.

[68] "The History," *PL* (Aug.-Sept. 1975): 61–63; Fred Jerome, "May 2 Protests Hit U.S. War in Viet Nam: Nationwide Demonstrations Biggest Yet," *PL* (May 1964): 2–3; The Editors, "Johnson's War in Vietnam," *PL* (July-Aug. 1964): 1. For background on the Vietnam War, see: Hugh Higgins, *Vietnam* (London: Heinemann, 1975); Michael Charlton and Anthony Moncrieff, *Many Reasons Why: The American Involvement in Vietnam* (New York: Hill & Wang, 1978); George C. Herring, *America's Longest War: The United States and Vietnam, 1950–1975* (New York: Alfred A. Knopf, 1979); and Stanley Karnow, *Vietnam: A History* (New York: Viking Press, 1983).

[69] Jerry Weinberg, "Freedom in Times Square," *PL* (Sept.-Oct. 1964): 17–20; Sheryl Clark, "The March East," ibid., 20; *Vietnam: Defeat U.S. Imperi-*

alism, (PL pamphlet, n.d.); Luce, *The New Left,* 110–118; id., *America's Trojan Horse,* 93–96. HUAC later investigated PL's antiwar activites; a joint statement by PLP witnesses on 19 August 1966 declared, "The House Un-American Activities Committee (HUAC) hearings of August 16–19th, 1966, were a victory for the American people's movement against the genocidal war on Vietnam and a defeat for the U.S. ruling class which is conducting that war. . . . A victory because the intent of the Johnson administration was to muster support for the reactionary repression of the peace movement (the Pool Bill). The grossness and clumsiness of HUAC's response to our movement's aggressiveness resulted in their alienating even many people who might have given support to the cesspool bill . . . due to our actions, the mass media were forced to report who we are and what our ideas are—a very unusual twist." For the Progressive Labor Party: George Ewart, Rick Rhoads, Steven Hamilton, Steven Cherkoss, and Jeff Gordon, "On HUAC's Cesspool Bill," *PL* (Oct.-Nov. 1966): 3. The purpose of the hearings was in part to support the Pool Bill, H.R. 12047 and to amend the Internal Security Act, Title 4, Sections 401–3. "A Statement by the Progressive Labor Party (PLP), August 19, 1966," ibid., 2.

[70] "The History," *PL* (Aug.-Sept. 1975): 61–63. First, PL complained that PLM never won the war against drugs inside M2M. However, drug use was also extensive in SDS, which did grow into the main center of radical student politics following its massive antiwar rally in Washington D.C. in April 1965. Second, to preserve the integrity of their radicalism, many M2M and PLM members opposed dissolving M2M and joining SDS. But sectarianism probably inhibited M2M's growth from its inception, impelling PLM's leaders to advocate joining SDS, and PL's critics in SDS cited PL for being sectarian. Third, PLM did not make fighting racism a central issue in M2M, which consequently did not attract Black youth or build alliances with militant Black organizations such as the Student Non-Violent Coordinating Committee. However, even when PL did make fighting racism the main focus of its student organizing, it did not develop a significant base among Black students. "Other politicos, including myself, were edgy. We'd been smoking grass regularly . . . ," Todd Gitlin, *The Sixties,* 212. According to Luce, eleven of the thirteen members of the national coordinating committee of the May Second Movement were members of Progressive Labor. Luce, *The New Left,* 112. "Fervent activists of the Progressive Labor Party, the rigid sectarian group bent on taking over SDS, pushed their doctrine of a 'student-worker alliance' as opposed to 'student power.' " Tom Hayden, *Reunion: A Memoir* (New York: Random House, 1988), 278. " 'In principle,' Steve Max told me, 'an agent for the FBI and an agent for PL are the same thing. Both have our welfare at heart and both are dispatched by the same manipulative mentality.' " Gitlin, *The Sixties,* 191. PL formed the International Committee Against Racism in the early 1970s. Academics at the University of Connecticut called a meeting

in February 1973 to organize against the "reemergence of racist ideas and practices." In October 1973, a "Resolution Against Racism," signed by 1400 academics, appeared as an ad in the *New York Times*. In November 1973, 1200 people attended a national conference in New York City. *InCAR and the Struggle Against Racism*, (InCAR pamphlet, 1977). Despite a significant number of antiracist activities by InCAR throughout the 1970s, PL did not recruit a significant number of Blacks. See *What is InCAR* (InCAR pamphlet, 1983).

[71] Powell, a fifteen-year-old schoolboy, was shot three times and killed by Lt. Thomas Gilligan, an off-duty policeman. *We Accuse: Bill Epton Speaks to the Court*. (PL pamphlet, 2 Feb. 1966); "The History," *PL* (Aug.-Sept. 1975): 63–65; HUAC, *Subversive Influences in Riots*, 923–928. "Let no one doubt it—there are communists in Harlem—black communists. . . . The rebellions have receded for the moment but the witch hunt is now on in full force. . . . The attempt by the police and the mayor to keep Bill Epton, PLM and the Harlem Defense Council from 'assembling, gathering together, convening, parading, marching, demonstrating or acting in concert in the public streets, squares, sidewalks and other public areas' of Harlem is scurrilous and shows their fear of socialist ideas and their fear of the people." Bill Epton, Fred Jerome and Milton Rosen, "Armed Police Terror," *PL* (July-Aug. 1964): 4.

[72] Editorial, *CD*, 25 July 1964, 1, 5, cited in HUAC, *Subversive Influences in Riots*, 898; Fred Jerome, "What They Can Never Restrain," *CD*, 1 Aug. 1964, 1, 4, repr. as "Romerstein Exhibit No. 4" ibid., 986–987.

[73] *We Accuse* (PL pamphlet, 2 Feb. 1966); "The History," *PL* (Aug.-Sept. 1975): 63–65; Keesings Research Report 4, *Race Relations in the USA, 1954–1968* (New York: Charles Scribner's Sons, 1970), 166–170. In response to Epton's indictment for criminal anarchy, PL commented, "Mayor Wagner, Chief Murphy and Nelson Rockefeller are fearful, as they should be, over the growth of the PLM." "Criminal Anarchy?" *PL* (Sept.-Oct. 1964): 24. For a detailed account of the grand jury proceedings, and the indictment, conviction and imprisonment of PLers, see "It is Happening Here," *PL* (Mar. 1965): 25–26; "The New McCarthyism. . . . History of Grand Jury Persecution," ibid., 30–36; "Ellie Goldstein has been sentenced to 30 days in this House of Horrors [the Women's House of Detention] because she refused to 'cooperate' with the Grand Jury Inquisition." James A. Wechsler, "Free Elinor Goldstein!" *New York Post*, 8 Mar. 1965, repr. ibid., 29; Robert Leighton, "Epton Denied Lawyer," *CD*, 2 Nov. 1965, 2.

[74] *We Accuse* (PL pamphlet, 2 Feb. 1966). The *Manchester Guardian* printed a letter from 110 members of Oxford University (including David Caute) to John Lindsay, the Mayor of New York City, protesting the "unjust conviction" of Epton. This letter and others from around the world were reprinted in "In Defense of Freedom," *CD*, 15 Feb. 1968, 4. Also see S. Davidowicz, "400 Protest

Epton Conviction," ibid. "Were I in New York, I should certainly be guilty of trying to overthrow the Government of the State of New York." Bertrand Russell, *PL*
(Apr. 1965): 16. The one offer of support rejected by PL came from the CPUSA,
which wrote, "To convict Bill Epton is a travesty of Justice. . . ." The CP had criticized PL's actions in Harlem: "They [PL] exist only as parasites on the body of
the Negro freedom movement working to sap its strength and divert its energies."
"CP Condemns Adventurers of 'Progressive' Labor," *TW*; "The conscientious
community leaders . . . will certainly give such adventurers as the PLM's top
brass a wide berth. . . ." James Jackson, "The PLM in Harlem Are Salesmen of
Shoddy Wares," *TW*; and "During the recent activities of residents of Harlem,
Progressive Labor Movement resorted to adventuristic and provocative acts. . . ."
Elizabeth Gurley Flynn [Chairman of the CPUSA], *Pravda*, 1 Sept. 1964, all
cited at length in an editorial, " 'They're Crawling Out of the Wall Again,' " *PL*
(Mar.-Apr. 1966): 9.

[75] *We Accuse* (PL pamphlet, 2 Feb. 1966).

[76] Ibid. See Truman Nelson, *The Right of Revolution* (Boston, Mass.: Beacon Press, 1968), 51–76.

[77] HUAC, *Subversive Influences in Riots*, passim. "From July 18, 1964 to
July 23, 1966, there have been no less than 20 uprisings in ghettos across Amer-
ica." Black Liberation Commission of the Progressive Labor Party, *Black Libera-
tion—Now!* (PL pamphlet, n.d.), 1, cited ibid., 897. Also see Black Liberation
Commission of the Progressive Labor Party, *The Plot Against Black America*,
(PL pamphlet, n.d.), 5–6. For background on Black rebellions in the 1960s, see:
Report of the National Advisory Commission on Civil Disorders (New York:
Bantam Books, 1968); Keesing's Research Report 4, *Race Relations in the USA,
1954–1968* (New York: Charles Scribner's Sons, 1970); Claude M. Lightfoot,
Ghetto Rebellion to Black Liberation (New York: International Publishers,
1968); Manning Marable, *Race, Reform and Rebellion: The Second Reconstruc-
tion in Black America, 1945–1982* (Jackson, Miss.: University Press of Mississippi, 1984); and Harvard Sitkoff, *The Struggle for Black Equality, 1954–1980*
(New York: Hill & Wang, 1981).

[78] HUAC, *Subversive Influences in Riots*, 928, 1093. Two important issues
were debated: the causes of the Harlem Rebellion and whether or not it was a
"race riot." "Radical Negro Militants are turning to Mao Tse-Tung for support in
overthrowing the U.S. Government. The words you read below are not those of
little old ladies in tennis sneakers. These are the facts of the most frightening
news story of 1964." William Worthy, "The Red Chinese American Negro," *Es-
quire Magazine*, 1964, cited in *The Plot Against Black America* (PL pamphlet,
n.d.), 3. PL responded, "They are saying in effect: 'Our niggers were happy until
the Chinese stirred them up!' " Ibid. "Extremism is a very generalized senti-

ment—the death wish for Whitey—is quite easily discernible among people in the ghetto . . . ," *Life Magazine*, 10 June 1966, cited ibid. "They were not riots of Negroes against whites or whites against Negroes." F.B.I., Report, 26 September 1964, summarized in Keesings Report No. 4, *Race Relations in the USA*, 169.

[79] "The History," *PL* (Aug.-Sept. 1965): 65.

[80] "Program for Black Liberation," *PL* (Feb. 1969), repr. in *RT*, 263–264; *A Plan for Black Liberation: Articles by the Progressive Labor Party*, (PL pamphlet, n.d.).

[81] "I don't propose that there be a white Marxist party and a black Marxist party. What I suggested was that there develop a black nationalist type of organization to pull together this latent feeling in the black community and give it its own direction." Bill Epton, "The Black Liberation Struggle and the Right to Revolution, Minutes of the October, 1964 meeting of the National Co-ordinating Committee of the Progressive Labor Movement," *Pre-Convention Discussion Bulletin # 2*, repr. in HUAC, *Subversive Influences in Riots*, 1104. "We failed to point out that the 'political and economic basis of all nationalism is capitalism' and that it is 'bourgeois ideology.' " National Committee of the Progressive Labor Party, "Progressive Labor Party (PLP) and Black Struggle," (19 Apr. 1969), in *A Plan for Black Liberation* (PL pamphlet, n.d.), 2. Epton did not accept PL's total rejection of nationalism and left the party. "Bill Epton and Geri Steiner have been expelled from the Progressive Labor Party on charges of organizing for the purpose of destroying the PLP . . . Bill Epton was removed from the National Committee of the Progressive Labor Party many months ago. . . his removal from leadership proved too much for his own sense of self-importance." "Notice from the National Committee of the Progressive Labor Party," *PL* (Sept. 1970): 18.

[82] "Historically socialist revolutions have been successful only when intellectuals and students have cast their lot with the working class. In the final analysis a decisive determining factor in whether an intellectual is revolutionary or not will be his attitude and especially actions toward going out to the workers. Those who oppose it (in essence) will be against the revolution; those who support it, for it." John Levin, "Power in the University," *PL* (Nov.-Dec. 1967): 41.

[83] "There is a large turnover in membership in Progressive Labor, and there are probably only about 1,000 actual 'card-carrying' members in the country." Luce, *The New Left*, 94; "PL numbered a few hundred, if that." Gitlin, *The Sixties*, 191. ". . . whom have we been recruiting? It is mainly teachers, welfare workers and students, independent radicals and professionals." "Improve Our Base Building" repr. in *RT*, 72. "The central problem of our party has been the struggle to make it a working-class party in ideology and composition. And that problem arose from the fact that our party grew primarily from the student movement." "The Future Is Bright," *PL* (June 1970), repr. in *RT*, 347.

[84] "The History," *PL* (Aug.-Sept. 1975): 66.

[85] Ibid. For a discussion of the Sino-Soviet split, see John Gittings, *The World and China, 1922–1972* (New York: Harper & Row, 1974).

[86] See: David Schub, *Lenin: A Biography* (Baltimore, Md.: Penguin Books, 1966); E. H. Carr, *The Bolshevik Revolution, 1917–1923*, vol. 1 (Hammondsworth, Middlesex, Eng.: 1966); Adam B. Ulam, *The Bolsheviks: The Intellectual, Personal, and Political History of the Triumph of Communism in Russia* (New York: Collier Books, 1968); Alexander Rabinowitch, *The Bolsheviks Come to Power: The Revolution of 1917 in Petrograd* (New York: W. W. Norton, 1978); and Sheila Fitzpatrick, *The Russian Revolution, 1917–1932* (Oxford, Eng.: Oxford University Press, 1984).

[87] See: George F. Kennan, *Russia and the West Under Lenin and Stalin* (Boston, Mass.: Little, Brown & Company, 1961), 278–330; E. H. Carr, *Twilight of the Comintern, 1930–1935* (New York: Pantheon Books, 1982); and R. Palme Dutt, *Fascism and Social Revolution: A Study of the Economics and Politics of the Extreme Stages of Capitalism in Decay* (1934; repr., San Francisco, Calif.: Proletarian Publishers, 1974). While Stalin had considered German social-democrats to be enemies in the early 1930s, Hitler's destruction of the German Left convinced him to seek alliances with the "bourgeois" democracies in 1935, and when that failed, to sign a non-aggression pact with Nazi Germany in 1939.

[88] "From the start, SDS had known in its bones that it was a tiny minority among students who were themselves a minority." Gitlin, *The Sixties*, 192.

[89] "Consequently, ideology is a matter of life or death." Milt Rosen, "Main Report," to PL Convention in April 1965, *PL* (May-June 1965): 18. "The sixties are best described as the years in which a communist movement emerged in the United States." "The Future is Bright," *PL* (June 1970), in *RT*, 346.

[90] "The History," *PL* (Aug.-Sept. 1975): 67.

[91] "RR I," in *RT*, 89.

[92] See: Leningrad Institute of Philosophy Under the Direction of M. Shirokov, *Textbook of Marxist Philosophy* (Leningrad Institute of Philosophy, 1937; repr., Chicago, Ill.: Proletarian Publishers, 1978); David Guest, *A Textbook of Dialectical Materialism* (New York: International Publishers, 1939); Howard Selsam, *What is Philosophy? A Marxist Introduction* (New York: International Publishers, 1939); id., *Philosophy in Revolution* (New York: International Publishers, 1957); Gustav A. Wetter, *Dialectical Materialism: A Historical and Systematic Survey of Philosophy in the Soviet Union* (New York: Frederick A. Praeger, 1958); and Ira Gollobin, *Dialectical Materialism: Its Laws, Categories, and Practice* (New York: Petras Press, 1986). PL attempted to popularize Dialectical and Historical Materialism. See *What the Progressive Labor Party Stands For: The Basic Ideas of Marxism-Leninism*, (PL pamphlet, n.d.).

[93] "Revisionism, like imperialism, runs counter to the tide of history." "Road to Revolution II," *PL* (December 1966), repr. in *RT*, 199 (hereafter cited as "RR II"). "Once a revolutionary has contracted the infantile disorder of leftism, he cannot stop, for if whipping up the old world is the ultimate goal, the meaning of life, then importance lies not in the result but rather in the process of changing things, of rejecting all that was in the past." Alexander S. Tsipko, *Is Stalinism Really Dead?: The Future of Perestroika as a Moral Revolution* (San Francisco, Calif.: Harper San Francisco, 1990), 133.

[94] PL outlined what it considered to be past and present revisionist fallacies: the bourgeois state is above classes; revolution is neither necessary or desirable in democratic societies; "U.S. Imperialism" will not wage wars because it fears a nuclear holocaust; all wars should be avoided because any war might escalate into nuclear war; the success of the USSR will draw underdeveloped countries into the socialist camp; and the U.S. welfare state can mitigate the class struggle. "RR I," in *RT*, 90–91.

[95] "The History," *PL* (Aug.-Sept. 1975), 67.

[96] "RR I," in *RT*, 92–93. Glancing backward, Gus Hall expressed contempt for all the CP's "sectarian" rivals: "The rise and fall of 'Left' and 'radical' sects has continued apace. Many of these groups attach themselves to such words as 'Communist' and 'Marxist-Leninist.' But such groups come and go because they do not meet the test of history or reality." Gus Hall, "The Communist Party: A Product of History," *Political Affairs* (Sept. 1978), repr. in Gus Hall, *Working Class USA: The Power and the Movement* (New York: International Publishers, 1987), 235.

[97] "RR I," in *RT*, 103–104.

[98] The CPUSA declined from a high of nearly 100,000 members in 1938 to a low of 5,000 in 1958. Klehr, *The Heyday*, 367 and Isserman, *If I Had a Hammer*, 32, respectively. The CPUSA's membership may have risen to 13,000 by the late 1960s. U. S. News & World Report, *Communism and the New Left* (Washington, D.C.: Books by U.S. News & World Report, 1970), 16. PL had between 200 and 1,500 members. HUAC, *Subversive Influences in Riots*, 894.

[99] "RR I," in *RT*, 91–92.

[100] Ibid., 119–130. For a discussion of the Soviet Union under Stalin, see: Central Committee of the C.P.S.U. (B.), *History of the Communist Party of the Soviet Union (Bolsheviks): Short Course, 1939 Edition* (1939; repr., San Francisco, Calif.: Proletarian Publishers, n.d.); Stephen Graham, *Stalin: An Impartial Study of the Life and Work of Joseph Stalin* (1931; repr., Port Washington, N.Y.: Kennikat Press, 1971); Hewlett Johnson (Dean of Canterbury), *The Soviet Power: The Socialist Sixth of the World* (New York: International Publishers, 1940); Bertram D. Wolfe, *Three Who Made a Revolution: A Biographical His-*

tory (New York: Dell Publishing Company, 1964); Robert Payne, *The Rise and Fall of Stalin* (New York: Avon Books, 1966); Ian Grey, *Stalin: Man of History* (Garden City, N.Y.: Doubleday & Company, 1979); Tsipko, *Is Stalinism Really Dead?;* and Valentin M. Berezhkov, *At Stalin's Side: His Interpreter's Memoirs From the October Revolution to the Fall of the Dictator's Empire* (New York: Birch Lane Press, 1994).

[101] "RR I," in *RT*, 137–142. "Progressive Labor is now generally known as 'Mao's Marauders.'" Luce, *The New Left*, 86. For a discussion of the Chinese Communist line, see: C. P. FitzGerald, *Mao Tse-Tung and China* (New York: Penguin Books, 1977), 111–130; Proposal from the Central Committee of the CCP to the Central Committee of the CPSU, repr. in *Major Doctrines of Communist China*, ed. John Wilson Lewis (New York: W. W. Norton, 1964), 234–280; The Editorial Department of Hongqi [Red Flag], *More on the Differences Between Comrade Togliatti and Us* (Peking: Foreign Languages Press, 1963); and Gittings, *The World and China*, 236–260. Some PLers, including the party's San Francisco leadership, argued that engaging in open polemics with the CPUSA was sectarian. Ironically, PL argued that those PLers who opposed publication of "Road to Revolution," because of their lingering ties to the CPUSA, were treading a "sectarian path." According to PL, they did not understand that this pamphlet was a "vital document in the fight to win new young fighters to communism because that was not their main focus." "The History," *PL* (Aug.-Sept. 1975): 67.

[102] At the April 1965 convention, the proposal to change PL's name to "American Revolutionary Movement" (ARM) and to call its youth section "American Revolutionary Movement Youth (ARMY) was "defeated with straight faces." Luce, *The New Left*, 86.

[103] "PL Constitution," *PL* (May-June 1965): 4.

[104] Ibid.; "The tendency to destroy is the inevitable price paid for a romantic (i.e., unrealistic) attitude toward the future, the price of the right to live, even if only for a moment, in a visionary's world where life is having a feast." Tsipko, *Is Stalinism Really Dead?*, 130.

[105] Ibid. See V. I. Lenin, *Lenin on the Revolutionary Proletarian Party of a New Type* (Peking: Foreign Languages Press, 1960). This is a collection of Lenin's statements, taken from a variety of his works, explaining his concept of a communist party.

[106] "As early as 1924, Kamenov insisted on the need to liquidate the leaders of the Trotskyist opposition, a move that was quite in keeping with the prevailing spirit of the time." Tsipko, *Is Stalinism Really Dead?*, 41; "The unnumbered and anonymous masses who were killed were not asked to abase themselves, for their self-abasement would have served no purpose. The leaders had to abase themselves

because their self-abasement served to augment the safety of Stalin." Payne, *The Rise and Fall of Stalin*, 475.

[107] PL Constitution, *PL* (May-June 1965): 5.

[108] Ibid.: 5–8; Mort Scheer, "Summation Speech," delivered at PLP's founding convention in April 1965, Ibid., 39. The "top" leadership also included: Walter Linder, Fred Jerome, Jake Rosen, Levi Laub and Sue Warren. Luce, *The New Left*, 86–93.

[109] Milt Rosen, "Main Report," delivered at PLP's founding convention in April 1965, *PL* (May-June 1965): 18.

[110] "One could sum it up by saying that there is a lot of right opportunism in the work and in the thinking, and on the other side of the coin, there's a great deal of sectarianism which we have been attacking by paying attention to developing our individual relationships with other people. And in our opinion these are two sides of the same revisionist's coin." Milt Rosen, Speech Opening the Second PLP Convention, May 1968, in "Build a Base," repr. in *RT*, 60.

[111] Mort Scheer, "Summation Speech," *PL* (May-June 1965), 39–40.

[112] "The Future Is Bright," *PL* (June 1970), repr. in *RT*, 354.

CHAPTER 2. PURIFYING THE COMMUNIST MOVEMENT AND SEARCHING FOR UTOPIA

[1] "Road to Revolution" (RR I), March 1964; "RR II," December 1966; "RR III," November 1971; "RR IV," Spring 1982.

[2] Tony Smith, *Thinking Like a Communist: State and Legitimacy in the Soviet Union, China, and Cuba* (New York: W. W. Norton, 1987), 13. "Without the development of a serious approach to theory and its application, we would be reduced to hopeless pragmatists." Milt Rosen, "Main Report," *PL* (May-June 1965): 18.

[3] "RR II," in *RT*, 168–177. See: "Classes and Class Struggle in the USSR," *PL* (spring 1981): 48–69; "The Concept of State Capitalism," ibid., 8–19; and related articles on "Soviet Capitalism.," ibid. "Socialist ownership of the means of production had developed to the full and become the unshakable foundation of the life of the Soviet people. The socialist economy had now [1958] established itself as totally dominant." M. P. Kim, et al., *The History of the USSR: The Era of Socialism* (Moscow: Progress Publishers, 1974), 462–463. "The enterprise had a stake in its own development, not only through the use of these profits for bonuses and expansion, but also on the payment of interest on capital invested in it. . . . In 1966, hundreds of enterprises were absorbed into the new system of managerial incentive. . . ." William L. Blackwell, *The Industrialization of Russia: An Historical Perspective* (Arlington Heights, Ill.: Harlan Davidson, 1982), 165. Also see: Alec Nove, *An Economic History of the U.S.S.R.* (New York: Pen-

guin Books, 1982); Carl A. Linden, *Khrushchev and the Soviet Leadership, 1957–1964* (Baltimore, Md.: The Johns Hopkins University Press, 1966), 202–221; and Kenneth Murphy, *Retreat From the Finland Station: Moral Odysseys in the Breakdown of Communism* (New York: The Free Press, 1992), 203–221.

4 "RR II," in *RT*, 192. See "A Brief Look at Soviet History," *PL* (spring 1981): 28–30; and related articles, ibid. Also see "The Retreat from Revolution," *PL* (summer 1979): 10–31; and John Ericson, "Origins of Revisionism in the USSR," *PL* (Oct.-Nov. 1966). "In 1931, Stalin told a conference of Soviet managers: 'The backward are beaten. . . . The history of the old Russia . . . consisted of the fact that she was always being beaten because of her backwardness.' " Bertram D. Wolfe, *An Ideology in Power: Reflections on the Russian Revolution* (New York: Stein & Day, 1969), 53. During the celebration of the fortieth anniversary of the October 1917 Revolution in Russia, representatives of political parties allied to the U.S.S.R. attended a meeting in Moscow, which issued a Declaration defining the "laws governing the struggle for socialism." One of the "laws" called for "the carrying out of a socialist revolution in the sphere of ideology and culture and the creation of an intelligentsia devoted to the cause of socialism." Kim, *The History of the USSR*, 460. "Furthermore, Engels explains in detail the meaning of the expression 'ideology.' 'Ideology is a process accomplished by the so-called thinker consciously, indeed, but with a false consciousness.' " I. P. Razumovskii, "The Nature of Ideology," in *Problems of the Marxist Theory of Law, 1917–1961* (Moscow, 1925), 24–35, repr. in *Soviet Political Thought: An Anthology*, ed. Michael Jaworskyj (Baltimore, Md.: The Johns Hopkins University Press, 1967), 219.

5 "RR II," in *RT*, 191–199. For Mao's views on political education, see John Bryan Starr, *Continuing the Revolution: The Political Thought of Mao* (Princeton, N.J.: Princeton University Press, 1979), 223–247. In 1982 PL paraphrased Mao's dictum that power flows from the barrel of a gun, to emphasize the primacy of ideas, which Mao's Cultural Revolution had stressed: PL declared, "Political power grows less from the barrel of a gun than from the ideology of the worker holding the gun." R. T. L., "Communist Parties Are the Custodians of the Future," *PL* (spring 1982): 46. As early as 1966, PL implied that putting forward genuinely revolutionary ideas would obviate the need to ever compromise communist principles—that the road to revolution could be made straight. "The Chinese communists are making a thorough-going effort to transform the thinking and develop the ideology of hundreds of millions of people. Under the leadership of the Communist Party of China, led by Mao Tse-tung, the Chinese people are demonstrating that people determine the course of history." "RR II," in *RT*, 192. "When we ask the river to yield the way, it must yield! Is such a hypothesis groundless? No, we are not insane, we are pragmatists; we are Marxists, seeking

truth from facts." Mao Tse-tung [1958], quoted in Starr, *Continuing the Revolution*, 71.

⁶ Luce, *The New Left*, 86.

⁷ U.S. News & World Report, *Communism and the New Left*, 26.

⁸ "Consequently, it is a very logical development that the Mao Tse-tung leadership moves for accommodation with U.S. imperialism. Ping-pong diplomacy is a consistent development of right-wing policies." *Road to Revolution III* (PL pamphlet, 1974): 12 (hereafter cited as *RR III*). This was first published as "Statement of the National Committee of the Progressive Labor Party, Road to Revolution III: The Continuing Struggle Against Revisionism," *PL* (Nov. 1971). "I would begin a dialogue with Communist China. In a subtle triangle of relations with Washington, Peking, and Moscow, we improve the possibilities of accommodations with each as we increase our options toward both." Nelson Rockefeller, quoted in Stephen R. Graubard, *Kissinger: Portrait of a Mind* (New York: W. W. Norton, 1974), 252. For a discussion of Nixon's opening to Communist China, see Robert S. Parmet, *Richard Nixon and His America* (Boston, Mass.: Little, Brown & Company, 1990).

⁹ "Road to Revolution III," *PL* (Nov. 1971): 8–24.

¹⁰ "The Great Proletarian Cultural Revolution and the Reversal of Workers' Power in China," in *RR III*, 18–19; "Whither China," *PL* (Aug. 1972): 68–87. This article was reprinted from the *Canton Printing System Red Flag, No. 5* (Mar. 1968): 3–6. "Although the specific attack of the Cultural Revolution was on the malfeasance of individual party members and the overgrown and rigidified party structure, there seemed to be in the initial stages of the movement an implicit attack on the party as an institution, in the call for new organizational forms to take the place of the party." Starr, *Continuing the Revolution*, 90. For a discussion of the Cultural Revolution, see: David Milton and Nancy Dall Milton, *The Wind Will Not Subside: Years in Revolutionary China, 1964–1969* (New York: Pantheon Books, 1976); David Milton, Nancy Milton and Franz Schurmann, eds., *People's China: Social Experimentation, Politics, Entry Onto the World Scene, 1966 through 1972* (New York: Vintage Books, 1974); Jack Gray and Patrick Cavendish, *Chinese Communism in Crisis: Maoism and the Cultural Revolution* (New York: Praeger, 1968); and Molly Joel Coye and John Livingston, eds., *China Yesterday and Today* (Toronto, Can.: Bantam Books, 1979), 390–432.

¹¹ "The Great Proletarian Cultural Revolution," in *RR III*, 24. Mao's ". . . political thought challenges the validity of a dichotomous classification of pragmatists and visionaries by attempting to achieve a new synthesis of the respective approaches of the two." Starr, *Continuing the Revolution*, 71.

¹² "The Great Proletarian Cultural Revolution," in *RR III*, 27–31. "The free supply system, after a struggle in the Central Committee, was virtually abolished

by the end of 1958 on the grounds that it would prejudice incentives to labour."
Gray, *Chinese Communism in Crisis*, 34–35. "Economic rationalization was accompanied by an attempt at ideological adjustment, in which a balance was
sought between the mass-line techniques of 1958 and the need for responsible
management and technical advice." Ibid., 37. "In Mao's view, however, pragmatism alone is not enough. What is needed, he said later in the same year [1958], is
to 'walk on both legs, with Russia's revolutionary fervor and America's practical
spirit.' It is the revolutionary fervor—'revolutionary romanticism' as he referred
to it on other occasions during that year—which informs the objectives toward
which *praxis* is directed." Starr, *Continuing the Revolution*, 71.

   [13] "When the great production advances failed to materialize, the CCP (just
like the Russians and western commentators) blamed the excessive 'Leftism' of
the communes and took steps to retreat from those measures. In fact, the production difficulties of 1959–1961 resulted from a combination of severe natural
calamities, unrealistic output targets, and especially the incorrect over-emphasis
on heavy industry which the CCP had taken over from the Soviet experience."
"The Great Proletarian Cultural Revolution," in *RR III*, 30. "By 1960 severe economic crisis had begun to grip the economy. In this context of economic crisis,
evaluations of the Great Leap Forward became the central issues of debate."
Stephen Andors, *China's Industrial Revolution: Politics, Planning, and Management, 1949 to the Present* (New York: Pantheon Books, 1977), 97. "China was
hungry; of this there was no doubt." Anna Louise Strong, *The Rise of the Chinese
People's Communes* (Peking: New World Press, 1959), repr. in part in *China:
Yesterday and Today*, ed. Coye, 383. For a discussion of the Great Leap Forward,
see Gray, *Chinese Communism in Crisis*, 29–36.

   [14] "It was the Right forces within the party which seized control after the
Great Leap." "The Great Proletarian Cultural Revolution," in *RR III*, 35.

   [15] "RR I," in *RT*, 89–147; "RR II," ibid., 148–205; "The Great Proletarian
Cultural Revolution," in *RR III*, 35–36.

   [16] *RR III*, 2–9. For a more detailed discussion of New Democracy by PL, see
"New Democracy," *PL* (Apr.-May 1978): 53–56. "Who are the people? At the
present stage in China, they are the working class, the peasantry, the urban petty
bourgeoisie and the national bourgeoisie. These classes, led by the working class
and the Communist party, unite to form their own state and elect their own government; they enforce their dictatorship over the running dogs of imperialism—
the landlord class and the bureaucratic-bourgeoisie, as well as the representatives
of those classes, the Kuomintang reactionaries and their accomplices—suppress
them, allow them only to behave themselves and not to be unruly in word or
deed." Mao Tse-tung, "On the People's Democratic Dictatorship, In Commemo-
ration of the Twenty-eighth Anniversary of the Communist Party of China," (30
June 1949), repr. in Mao Tse-tung, *Selected Works of Mao Tse-tung,* 4 vols.

(Peking: Foreign Languages Press, 1967), IV: 417–418 (herafter cited as *SWM*). Also see Mao Tse-tung, "On New Democracy" (January 1940), repr. in *SWM* (1965), II: 339–384. "By 1939, he was referring to this new stage as that of the New Democracy—a stage that was a bourgeois-democratic revolution of a new type, the unique character of which was determined by the fact that it was taking place in the wake of the October Revolution in Russia. Its novelty lay in the fact that, although led by the proletariat and aiming at the overthrow of imperialism and feudalism, it sought the active participation of a range of 'revolutionary' classes and groups, and it did not aim at the overthrow of capitalism in China, since capitalism was 'capable of contributing to the anti-imperialist, anti-feudal struggle.'" Starr, *Continuing the Revolution*, 263. Also see Chester C. Tan, *Chinese Political Thought in the 20th Century* (Newton Abbot, Devon, Eng.: David & Charles, 1972), 352–355. "The New Economic Policy was proclaimed as being intended 'seriously and for a long time.' Within a few months, in October 1921, the Nep was presented as a 'temporary retreat.' A few more months and Lenin had another formula: we have stopped our retreat." Ulam, *The Bolsheviks*, 521. For the Soviet Communist view of the New Economic Policy, see V. I. Lenin, "The Tax in Kind (The Significance of the New Policy and Its Condition)" (Moscow: State Publishing House, May 1921), repr. in *LSW*, 3: 526–556; and Central Committee of the C.P.S.U. (B.), *History of the Communist Party of the Soviet Union*, 248–279. For a further discussion of NEP, see: Nove, *An Economic History of the U.S.S.R.*; Blackwell, *The Industrialization of Russia*; and Carr, *The Bolshevik Revolution*. For a discussion of the United Front Against Fascism, see Carr, *The Twilight of the Comintern*, 403–427. PL called the Bolsheviks' belief that peasants could not be won to socialism a "tragic error." "The Bolsheviks and the Peasants," *PL* (fall 1979): 68–79. "Workers and oppressed people on the march all over the world will prove too much for U.S. imperialism." Editorial, "Defeat U.S. Imperialism," *PL* (Sept. 1970): 5.

[17] *RR III*, 9–13. "Individual leadership is thus appropriate and legitimate, in Mao's view. 'If we did not have Stalin,' he put it succinctly in 1939, 'who would give the orders?' It is blind obedience to individual leaders that is illegitimate. Nonetheless, in a widely cited remark to Edgar Snow in 1965, he took what appeared to be a different position regarding the cult of the individual. He noted that Khrushchev had probably been overthrown because he lacked a cult of personality. Moreover, immediately after this conversation, there began the encouragement of a cult of personality around Mao that culminated during the Cultural Revolution, and that appeared to rival Stalin's excesses in this regard." Starr, *Continuing the Revolution*, 92–93. "Long live the great proletarian cultural revolution. Long live the red sun in our hearts, the greatest leader Chairman Mao and long life, long, long life to him!" The Shanghai Workers' Revolutionary Rebel

General Headquarters and ten other revolutionary mass organizations, "Take Firm Hold of the Revolution, Promote Production and Utterly Smash the New Counterattack Launched by the Bourgeois Reactionary Line," repr. in *The Great Proletarian Cultural Revolution in China, No. 10* (Peking: Foreign Languages Press, 1967): 5–10, repr. in *People's China*, ed. Milton, 293–298. For a discussion of the Paris Commune, see: Karl Marx, *The Civil War in France. Address of the General Council of the International Working Men's Association* (1871), repr. in Karl Marx and Frederick Engels, *Selected Works* (New York: International Publishers, 1968), 274–313; Alistair Horne, *The Fall of Paris: The Siege and the Commune, 1870–71* (New York: St. Martin's Press, 1965); Stewart Edwards, *The Paris Commune, 1871* (Chicago, Ill.: Quadrangle Books, 1971); John Hicks and Robert Tucker, eds., *Revolution & Reaction: The Paris Commune, 1871* (Boston, Mass.: University of Massachussetts Press, 1973); and Eugene Schulkind, ed., *The Paris Commune of 1871: The View From the Left* (New York: Grove Press, 1974).

[18] *RR III*, 13. For a discussion of Khrushchev's criticism of Stalin, see G. F. Hudson, *Fifty Years of Communism: Theory and Practice, 1917–1967* (New York: Basic Books, 1968), 166–174. It can be argued that PL never escaped the influence of the Stalin cult.

[19] *RR III*, 13. "Mao characterized the process of reeducation with two slogans, both of which are intended to emphasize what he saw as the dialectical framework within which the process is to take place. The first of these slogans is 'struggle-criticism-transformation,' the second, 'unity-criticism-unity.' Struggle and criticism are the two crucial elements of the process of reeducation." Starr, *Continuing the Revolution*, 245. "In modern democracy it is held that no one may disobey the orders of the oligarchs, for in so doing the people sin against themselves, defying their own will spontaneously transferred by them to their representatives, and thus infringing democratic principle." Robert Michels, *Political Parties: A Sociological Study of the Emergence of Leadership, the Psychology of Power, and the Oligarchic Tendencies of Organization* (1915; repr., New York: Dover Publications, 1959), 221.

[20] "Wipe out all vestiges of cultism. They have held us back in the past. Intensify the struggle against individualism in ourselves. As a start, the NC [National Committee] has approved the idea of suppressing the glorification of individual images that may arise in the party. Every member of the party must be able to present the party line. We do not believe in relying on the verbal or political dexterity of a few 'experts.'" *RR III*, 17.

[21] Ibid., 9. "Perhaps we haven't come up with all the answers or even the right ones; but we have tried to go beyond the shibboleths dished out by various forces in the movement." Ibid., 15. "The objection is invalid that the incorrupt-

ibility and efficiency of our party officials, and their love for the great cause, would suffice to raise a barrier against the development of autocracy within the party. The very opposite is true. Officials of high technical efficiency who unselfishly aim at the general good . . . are more than all others inclined, being well aware of the importance of their own services, to regard as unalterable laws whatever seems to them right and proper, to suppress conflicting tendencies on the ground of the general interest. . . ." Wolfgang Heine, cited in Michels, *Political Parties*, 229. "The moral priorities are drawn up intermittently by the Wisest Man in the world and reflect mainly the thought of the Wisest Man in the world. He makes his decisions in his capacity as chairman of a Committee of the Next Wisest Men." Barrington Moore, Jr., *Injustice: The Social Basis of Obedience and Revolt* (White Plains, N.Y.: M. E. Sharpe, 1978), 504.

[22] *RR III*, 13.

[23] "Mao's contribution to the Chinese Revolution was an enormous one, but the theoretical legacy he left behind poses substantial problems for his successors, if they were to attempt to implement it. The problems are suggested in the most recent of his comments cited above: 'first we disorder it, then rule it.' In the absence of a towering revolutionary figure such as Mao became over the course of his career, who will be able with equal confidence to disorder and then rule the vast and diverse political system that unites a quarter of the world's population?" Starr, *Continuing the Revolution*, 307. "How can one question someone who controls the army?" *RR III*, 11. "But Marxist-Leninists, including the left of the GPCR, know that there is no such thing as a non-violent revolution. The class struggle for state power has never been peaceful; it was not peaceful during the GPCR, and it will never be peaceful." Ibid. In 1989, the student-led democracy movement in China was condemned and suppressed fairly quickly by the CPC. Chen Yun, chairman of the Central Advisory Commission, speaking at an emergency Standing Committee meeting, had warned, "If the turmoil created by this small handful of people is not resolutely put down, then there will be no peace in the Party or the country." Orville Schell, *Mandate of Heaven: A New Generation of Entrepreneurs, Dissidents, Bohemians, and Technocrats Lays Claim to China's Future* (New York: Simon & Schuster , 1994), 133. In 1917, Lenin, who invented "party-mindedness," went over the heads of overcautious Bolshevik leaders, who were reluctant to call for insurrection, by making direct appeals to the masses. Shub, *Lenin*, 270–272.

[24] "The importance of the Party in Lenin's theory can scarcely be overemphasized. The Party is the vanguard of the proletariat and the proletariat is the most progressive element of the masses. The Party is thus in the forefront of all of humanity and the leader of progressive elements. . . . But if one believes that the Party is indeed the most progressive element of mankind, then it does make sense

to invest it with great power to bring about man's ultimate dreams. . . . Moreover, the Party, in its function as the most advanced element of society, is in a position to determine, without class bias, what is true or false, right or wrong, better or worse for society." De George, *Patterns of Soviet Thought*, 137. Also see V. I. Lenin, *What is to be Done?* (1902), repr. in *LSW*, I: 177–190; V. I. Lenin, *One Step Forward, Two Steps Back (The Crisis in Our Party)* (1904), repr. in *LSW*, I: 242–421; V. I. Lenin, *Two Tactics of Social-Democracy in the Democratic Revolution* (1905), repr. in *LSW*, I: 425–527; and Stuart Kahan, *The Wolf of the Kremlin* (New York: William Morrow & Company, 1987).

[25] "The organizational theory of the party is democratic-centralism. The scientific method of evaluating and learning from all experiences, good and bad, is criticism and self-criticism." "On the Party," *PL* (Jan. 1965), repr. in *RT*, 78. "We want to absorb the lessons of previous experiences in order to advance beyond them. We seek to draw upon what is positive in these experiences and to learn from the negative." *RR III*, 1. "Communists have always been in the forefront of workers battles . . . led the fight against fascism and imperialist wars. . . . In the course of this great progressive struggle, numerous errors were made which caused serious harm to revolutionary advance. . . . The PLP does not repudiate the history of the communist movement. We are part of it. We study it and defend it in order to develop it further. Naturally we cast aside all that is negative while we cultivate all that is positive." "The History," *PL* (Aug.-Sept. 1975): 55. "There is little difference, as far as practical results are concerned, between individual dictatorship and the dictatorship of a group of oligarchs." Michels, *Political Parties*, 385.

[26] *RR III*, 12. Also see Jake Rosen, "Is Cuba Socialist?" *PL* (Nov. 1969): 52–63; and *Vietnam: Defeat U.S. Imperialism*, (PL pamphlet, 1970–1971).

[27] *RR III*, 15.

[28] "So long as there is a class struggle in this country there will be a revolutionary force. Because of the developing contradictions of U.S. imperialism a new revolutionary party will arise in this country stronger than ever." "RR I," in *RT*, 104.

[29] "So, in fact, if the international movement is smaller in numbers than before, its development is higher than ever. Newly emerging revolutionary forces all over the world can benefit enormously from the Thought of Mao Tse-Tung. They can avoid the mistakes of Indonesia, the Algerians, and the Arab world, to mention a few." Rosen, "Build a Base," *PL* (June 1969), repr. in *RT*, 19. Rosen's view was plausible. "We must thus reckon with the prospect that further totalitarian revolutions of a more or less 'Chinese' type may be victorious in various parts of the underdeveloped world, and we can be sure that Mao's China will give them any aid and encouragement of which it is capable." Richard Lowenthal, "Prospects For Pluralistic Communism," in *Marxism in the Modern World*, ed.

Milorad M. Drachkovitch (Stanford, Calif.: Stanford University Press, 1965), 245. However, Rosen recognized the importance of China to world revolution. "The revisionist defeat of China would be a terrible set-back to us and to all revolutionaries." Rosen "Build a Base," *PL* (June 1969), repr. in *RT*, 18. According to PL, revisionism had triumphed in China; but PL was convinced that the GPCR's defeat was temporary. PL was mistaken. However, *RR III* argued that the GPCR had advanced communism, and PL acknowledged *RRIII*'s debt to the Chinese Left. "This profound revolution enriched Marxism-Leninism and enabled the international communist movement to advance. We would never have been able to discuss many of the ideas in this report without the forward thrust of the left forces during the GPCR." *RR III*, 13. Also see Draper, *American Communism and Soviet Russia*.

[30] *RR III*. "We have a world to learn—and a world to win." Ibid., 17.

[31] "Road to Revolution IV," *PL* (spring 1982): 3 (hereafter cited as "RR IV").

[32] Ibid. "Equality of condition among their subjects has been one of the foremost concerns of depotisms and tyrannies since ancient times, yet such equality is not sufficient for totalitarian rule because it leaves more or less intact certain communal bonds between the subjects, such as family ties and common cultural interests. If totalitarianism takes its own claim seriously, it must come to the point where it has 'to finish once and for all with the neutrality of chess,' that is with the autonomous existence of any activity whatsoever." Hannah Arendt, *The Origins of Totalitarianism* (San Diego, Calif.: Harcourt Brace Jovanovich, 1979), 322.

[33] "For An Alternative," *PL* (Jan. 1962): 1.

[34] See: Frantz Fanon, *The Wretched of the Earth* (New York: Grove Press, 1963); id. *A Dying Colonialism* (New York: Grove Press, 1965); Richard Lowenthal, "The Prospects For Pluralistic Communism," in *Marxism in the Modern World*, ed. Drachkovitch, 225–271; Hudson, *Fifty Years of Communism;* John Gerassi, ed., *The Coming of the New International: A Revolutionary Anthology* (New York: The World Publishing Company, 1971); Massimo Teodori, ed., *The New Left: A Documentary History* (Indianapolis, Ind.: Bobbs-Merrill, 1969) and Isserman, *If I Had a Hammer*.

[35] For a discussion of the retreat of communism, see: Hedrick Smith, *The New Russians* (New York: Random House, 1990); Murphy, *Retreat From the Finland Station* (Indianapolis, Ind.: Bobbs-Merrill, 1996). and "New China Bosses Consolidate Power," *PL* (Apr. 1977): 19–29.

[36] For a discussion of the contrast between socialism and communism, see Emile Durkheim, *Socialism* (New York: Collier Books, 1962), 64–79. This book is based on lectures delivered by Durkheim in the mid-1890s.

[37] Every triumph of "revisionism" led PL to reexamine the roots of revisionism, and to further rid communism of the compromises that it believed had nurtured revisionism.

[38] *RR III*, 2–9; "RR IV," *PL* (spring 1982): 9.

[39] "RR IV," *PL* (spring 1982): 9.

[40] See Karl Marx, *Critique of the Gotha Program* (1875), repr. in Marx and Engels, *Selected Works,* and V. I. Lenin, *The State and Revolution,* repr. in *LSW,* II: 238–327.

[41] "Marx and Lenin described socialism as the early stage of communism. These great revolutionaries doubted that the working class could move immediately from socialism to communism. They and others believed that important concessions to capitalism and capitalist ideas were necessary to win enough people to socialist revolution. They thought that socialism would eventually lead to communism." "RR IV," *PL* (spring 1982): 6.

[42] Ibid., 6, 15. See Milovan Djilas, *The New Class: An Analysis of the Communist System* (New York: Frederick A. Praeger, 1957). "In the second place, and most important of all, emotional revolution is followed by traditionalist routine. The hero of faith, and, even more, faith itself fades away or becomes (which is even more effective) part of the conventional jargon of political philistines and technicians." Max Weber, "Politics as a Vocation" (1919), repr. in *Weber: Selections in Translation,* ed. W. G. Runciman (Cambridge, Eng.: Cambridge University Press, 1978), 222.

[43] "RR IV," *PL* (spring 1982): 7. "Within the Soviet administration during the 1930's, all attempts to keep officials from becoming privileged and authoritarian were abandoned." Theda Skocpol, *States and Social Revolutions: A Comparative Analysis of France, Russia, and China* (Cambridge, Eng.: Cambridge University Press, 1979), 229.

[44] Ibid., 6–7. "As everyone who has read *The New Class* knows, the proposition proceeds as follows: the society that has arisen as the result of Communist revolution, or as a result of military actions of the Soviet Union, is torn by the same sort of contradictions as are other societies. The result is that Communist society has not only failed to develop toward human brotherhood and equality, but also out of its party bureaucracy there arises a privileged social stratum, which, in accord with Marxist thinking, I named 'the new class.' " Milovan Djilas, *The Unperfect Society: Beyond the New Class* (New York: Harcourt, Brace & World, 1969), 8. "The consciousness of power always produces vanity, an undue belief in personal greatness. The desire to dominate, for good or for evil, is universal." Michels, *Political Parties,* 206. "Engels, who was endowed with an extremely keen sense of the essence of democracy, regarded it as deplorable that the leaders of the German socialist party could not accustom themselves to the idea that the mere fact of being installed in office did not give them the right to be treated with more respect than any other comrade." ibid., 222.

[45] R. T. L., "Communist Parties are the Custodians of the Future," *PL* (spring 1982): 51.

[46] "RR IV," *PL* (spring 1982): 9.

[47] Ibid.

[48] Progressive Labor's membership certainly never exceeded two thousand.

[49] "RR IV," *PL* (spring 1982): 9.

[50] See: McGeorge Bundy, George F. Kennan, Robert S. McNamara, Gerard Smith, "The President's Choice: Star Wars or Arms Control," in *The Reagan Foreign Policy*, ed. William G. Hyland (New York: Meridian, 1987), 165–179; Casper W. Weinberger, "U.S. Defense Strategy," ibid., 180–202; Theodore Draper, *Present History: On Nuclear War, Detente, and Other Controversies* (New York: Random House, 1983); Robert Jay Lifton, *The Future of Immortality: and Other Essays for a Nuclear Age* (New York: Basic Books 1987); and Carl Sagan and Richard Turco, *A Path Where No Man Thought: Nuclear Winter and the End of the Arms Race* (New York: Random House, 1990).

[51] Sidney Hook, *From Hegel to Marx: Studies in the Intellectual Development of Karl Marx* (Ann Arbor, Mich.: University of Michigan Press, 1962).

[52] "For Communist Economics and Communist Power," *PL* (spring 1982): 16.

[53] "RR IV," *PL* (spring 1982): 5–6.

[54] Ibid., 9. See: Mortimer Scheer, "Nationalism Divides Workers," *PL* (Nov. 1969): 6–18; "Revolutionaries Must Fight Nationalism," *PL* (Aug. 1969): 3–13; and William Pfaff, *The Wrath of Nations: Civilization and the Furies of Nationalism* (New York: Simon & Schuster, 1993). The demand of totalitarian movements "for total, unrestricted, unconditional, and unalterable loyalty of the individual member . . . is made by the leaders of totalitarian movements even before they seize power . . . it follows from the claim of their ideologies that their organization will encompass, in due course, the entire human race." Arendt, *The Origins of Totalitarianism*, 323.

[55] See: Helmut Gruber, ed., *International Communism in the Era of Lenin* (Garden City, N.Y.: Doubleday & Company, 1972); Carr, *Twilight of the Comintern*; Daniel Mason and Jessica Smith, eds., *Lenin's Impact On the United States* (New York: NWR Publications, 1970); and Stephen Koch, *Double Lives: Spies and Writers in the Secret Soviet War Against the West* (New York: The Free Press, 1994).

[56] On October 30, 1982, PLP held communist conferences in New York City, Chicago, Houston, Minneapolis and Oakland. The combined attendance at these conferences amounted to about one thousand people. "Communist Conferences: Another Nail in the Bosses' Coffin," *CD*, 10 Nov. 1982, 2–3. An article about the New York City conference indicated PL's international aspirations: "Over three hundred black, Latin, Asian and white workers and students attended the conference from Boston, Washington, D.C., and cities in-between. Immigrant workers attended, living proof of the internationalism we are fighting for. Among the countries represented were Haiti, Trinidad, Jamaica, the Dominican Republic, Cuba, El Salvador, Nicaragua, Argentina, Ecuador, Spain,

France, Britain, Iran, Puerto Rico, etc." "International Unity in PLP Conference," ibid., 2.

[57] "For Communist Economics," *PL* (Jan. 1982): 18.

[58] "RR IV," *PL* (spring 1982): 6. "The party needs a core of tested, devoted, competent leaders. Leaders who can earn the hatred of the enemy, the respect and devotion of the party's members and the masses." "On the Party," *PL* (Jan. 1965), repr. in *RT*, 86. "One of our main perspectives, one of our key tasks, has been to develop a core of people who would be considered professional revolutionaries in the traditional sense. That is, to serve the revolution and the party and the people comes first, that is the primary thing in their life. Because no serious revolutionary party can exist, and be successful, without serious revolutionaries, without a cadre, without a leadership." "Fight Individualism," [Speech Opening Second PLP Convention, May 1968], repr. ibid., 47–48.

[59] "RR IV," *PL* (spring 1982): 6.

[60] "Nevertheless, by declaring that the primary vehicle of revolutionary consciousness would henceforth be the party and not the working class, Lenin was establishing the framework for a subsequent revision of the character of the postrevolutionary dictatorship of the proletariat. Now, instead of the self-government of the working class that Marx had anticipated, Lenin had prepared the ground for the party to monopolize political power." Tony Smith, *Thinking Like a Communist: State and Legitimacy in the Soviet Union, China, and Cuba* (New York: W. W. Norton, 1987), 73–74. "Lenin ridiculed those Marxists who were always waiting for the development of the elemental impulses of society. He asserted the dictatorship not of an empirical proletariat which was very weak in Russia, but of the idea of the proletariat with which an insignificant minority could be permeated." Nicolas Berdyaev, *The Origins of Russian Communism* (1937; repr., Ann Arbor, Mich.: University of Michigan Press, 1987), 121.

[61] "RR IV," *PL* (spring 1982): 6.

[62] "In a party, it is far from obvious that the interests of the masses which have combined to form the party will coincide with the interests of the bureaucracy in which the party becomes personified." Michels, *Political Parties*, 389. "In a word, Marxism denies that totalitarianism is a historical possibility. How then could Marxists have anticipated the crimes of Stalin or mobilized to protest them once they had occurred? It was to be the ironic fate of Marxism itself to demonstrate most dramatically the potency of ideas, leaders, and political organization on human destiny." Smith, *Thinking Like a Communist*, 93.

[63] "All communist theories formulated later derive from Platonic communism, of which they are hardly more than variations." Durkheim, *Socialism*, 68; Plato, *Republic*, in *Plato: The Collected Dialogues*, eds. Edith Hamilton and Huntington Cairns (New York: Pantheon Books, 1961), 575–844. "Another notion that has troubled the minds of people who have pondered political problems

since the day when Plato wrote his dialogues is that 'the best people' ought to be the ones to govern a country. The consequence of that aspiration has been, and perhaps still is, that good souls go looking for a political system that will make the concept a reality, or at least point the way to doing so." Gaetano Mosca, *The Ruling Class* (1939; repr., New York: McGraw-Hill, 1939), 448. A. E. Taylor denied that socialism or communism was to be found in the Republic. "In Book VIII, it is carefully indicated that one of the first signs of the degeneration of the ideal state into a 'timocracy' is the acquisition of real and personal property by the two superior classes [guardians] . . . but nothing is said of the first introduction of private property among the [civilian population] . . . , who thus must be presumed to have enjoyed it all along." A. E. Taylor, *Plato: The Man and His Work* (Cleveland, Ohio: Meridian Books, 1956), 276–277. "By taking over a city, the philosophers make sure that their subjects will not be savages; by expelling everyone older than ten, they make sure that their subjects will not be enslaved by traditional civility." Leo Strauss, "Plato," in *History of Political Philosophy*, eds. Leo Strauss and Joseph Cropsey (Chicago, Ill.: Rand McNally, 1963), 32. "The young people are the most active and vital force in society. They are the most eager to learn and the least conservative in their thinking." Mao Tse-tung, introductory note to "A Youth Shock Brigade of the No. 9 Agricultural Producers' - Cooperative in Hsinping Township, Chungshan County" (1955), "The Socialist Upsurge in China's Countryside," Chinese ed., Vol. III., in Mao Tse-tung, *Quotations From Chairman Mao Tse-tung* (Peking: Foreign Languages Press, 1972), 290.

[64] "For Communist Economics," *PL* (spring 1982): 17.

[65] Ibid.

[66] Presumably, there would be no legitimate role for independent trade unions in a PLP-led society.

[67] "The Party must be, first of all, the vanguard of the working class. . . . If it desires really to direct the struggle of the class it must at the same time be the organized detachment of its class. . . . The Party is the highest form of class organization of the proletariat. . . . The Party is an instrument of the dictatorship of the proletariat. . . . The Party represents unity of will, which precludes all factionalism and division of authority in the Party." Joseph Stalin, *Foundations of Leninism* (1939; repr., New York: International Publishers, 1970), 109–121.

[68] "Organizing for revolution means educating masses of workers, soldiers and students with communist ideas. To agitate successfully, to fight and win battles, to educate people politically, we must know workers very well. We must build long-term relations that can lead to the total transformation of most individuals, including ourselves, as we become convinced that we can no longer live in the same old way, that we can no longer tolerate capitalism." "RR IV." *PL* (spring

1982): 9. PL presented no evidence that it could, through an educational campaign so conceived, totally transform most people. "The indifference which in normal times the mass is accustomed to display in ordinary political life becomes, in certain cases of peculiar importance, an obstacle to the extension of the party influence." Michels, *Political Parties*, 55. "If the party does not assert power, and control power for the purpose of building a society based on 'from each according to his ability, to each according to his need,' communism, an end to oppression, war, and privilege, which will result in the most freedom (and the most 'things') for virtually everyone, then some other group will assert power for some other purpose, namely special privilege, capitalist oppression, etc." "For Communist Economics," *PL* (spring 1982): 17.

[69] "Centralism is the expression of the most freedom for the most people, if you believe that communism is the hope of the future, and freedom is defined by the quality and quantity of social relations. Using that definition of democracy, centralism is the best, the only, expression of democracy. Opposing communist centralism will simply lead to capitalist centralism—it is communist centralism or capitalist centralism." "For Communist Economics," *PL* (spring 1982): 19. "The incompetence of the masses, which is in the last analysis always recognized by the leaders, serves to provide a theoretical justification for the dominion over these." Michels, *Political Parties*, 88.

[70] It was even difficult for party members to be thoroughly communist in their outlook. "Our Party's main obstacle is the influence and ideology of bourgeois society within our ranks." "Criticism and Self-Criticism," *PL* (June 1966), repr. in *RT*, 209. "Even after 22 years of trying to help build a revolutionary movement, I believe that one of my main motives still is self-serving. That is, I do my work more to satisfy something within me than to serve the people." Rosen, "Build a Base," *PL* (June 1969), repr. ibid., 13.

[71] Lenin, *The State and Revolution*, repr. in *LSW*, II: 308.

[72] "For Communist Economics," *PL* (spring 1982): 20.

[73] "As far as mixing people up because of the other definition of 'communism' as being the society after the need for violence, jails, laws, etc. is over, I [Milton Rosen] believe that those who read 'RR IV' will understand pretty clearly that we are not making the idealist-anarchist mistake of believing that such a society could be set up immediately. The role of the dictatorship of the proletariat and the party in maintaining the system is unmistakable in our Manifesto." "For Communist Economics," *PL* (spring 1982): 21. "For thousands of years, the appetite for power being dispersed in countless tyrannies, great and small, which have raged here and there, the moment seems at hand when that appetite must finally collect and concentrate in order to culminate in a single power, expression of that thirst which has devoured, which still devours the globe, last

word of all our dreams of mastery, the consummation of our hopes and our aberrations." E. M. Cioran, *History and Utopia* (New York: Seaver Books, 1987), 41. For the resonance of Puritanism with PL's utopian vision, see the discussion of Christian egalitarianism in R. T. L., "Communist Parties Are the Custodians of the Future," *PL* (spring 1982): 44–45. "When mankind began to buy and sell, then he did fall from innocency: for then he began to oppress and cozen one another of their creation birthright." Gerard Winstanley, quoted in Eduard Bernstein, *Cromwell and Communism: Socialism and Democracy in the Great English Revolution* (1895, 1930; repr., New York: Schocken Books, 1963), 119. "God reveals his mind to his ministers." Gouge, "God's Three Arrows," quoted in Gerald R. Cragg, *Freedom and Authority: A Study of English Thought in the Early Seventeenth Century* (Philadelphia, Pa.: The Westminster Press, 1975), 139. "The Puritan ministers provide, perhaps, the first example of 'advanced' intellectuals in a traditional society." Michael Walzer, *The Revolution of the Saints: A Study of the Origins of Radical Politics* (New York: Atheneum, 1974), 121. Also see T. Wilson Hayes, *Winstanley the Digger: A Literary Analysis of Radical Ideas in the English Revolution* (Cambridge, Mass.: Harvard University Press, 1979). "Looking back on it [Massachussetts Bay Colony under John Winthrop], I am bound to say that it also bears some striking resemblances to a communist or other totalitarian government." Alistair Cooke, *Alistair Cooke's America* (New York: Alfred A. Knopf, 1973), 86.

[74] "But the 'Left Communists' must be argued with because it is Marxists who are making a mistake, and an analysis of their mistake will help the working class to find the true road." V. I. Lenin, *'Left-Wing' Childishness and the Petty-Bourgeois Mentality* (1918), repr. in *LSW*, II: 634.

[75] "The bosses use the examples of capitalist countries like Russia, China, and Poland to discredit communism. They cynically pretend that these fascist returns to the profit system are communist societies." "RR IV," *PL* (spring 1982): 9.

[76] For an interesting discussion of the role of ideological rigidity in the failure of American socialism, see Daniel Bell, *The End of Ideology: On the Exhaustion of Political Ideas in the Fifties,* (Glencoe: Free Press, 1960), ch. 12, repr. as "The Problem of Ideological Rigidity," in *Failure of a Dream? Essays in the History of American Socialism*, eds. John H. M. Laslett and Seymour Martin Lipset (Berkeley, Calif.: University of California Press, 1974), 3–29; also see Laslett, "Comment," ibid., 30–45, and Bell, "Reply," ibid., 46–51. Bell uses Weber's distinction between the "ethic of responsibility" and the "ethic of conscience" to construct his critique of ideological rigidity. "It is perfectly true, and confirmed by all historical experience, that the possible cannot be achieved without continually reaching out towards that which is impossible in this world." Max Weber, "Politics As a Vocation," (1919), repr. in part in Weber, *Weber: Selections in Translation*, 225.

[77] See "RR I," in *RT*, 89.

[78] "Radicals saw it as a moment when the system broke down. Like Bolsheviks contemplating the first World War, they found the sixties horrible in themselves but desirable for bringing the revolution closer. . . . It was partly because the radicals overreached themselves that the decade ended so badly. And they would find, like the Wobblies and communists before them, that repression works as often as not." William L. O'Neill, *Coming Apart: An Informal History of America in the 1960's* (Chicago, Ill.: Quadrangle Books, 1971), 426. "By the end of 1968, it seemed clear that the old order was intact, exhibiting remarkable endurance." William H. Chafe, *The Unfinished Journey: America Since World War II* (New York: Oxford University Press, 1986), 380.

[79] For examples, see "Bosses Plan War For Oil," *PL* (winter 1979–80): 10–13; and "Liberals Pave the Way for Fascism," ibid., 18–33.

[80] For a discussion of American exceptionalism, see Werner Sombart, *Warum gibt es in den Vereinigten Staaten Keinen Sozializmus?* (Tubingen, 1906), 112–142., repr. in *Failure of a Dream*, ed. Laslett, 452–467; also see Adolf Sturmthal, "Comment 1," ibid., 468–476; and Iring Fetscher, "Comment 2," ibid., 477–483. "During the Popular Front era, the Party for a short time did appreciate the idea of 'American exceptionalism' and consequently experienced expansion." Guenter Lewy, *The Cause That Failed: Communism in American Political Life* (New York: Oxford University Press, 1990), 294. Also see Earl Browder, *The People's Front* (New York: International Publishers, 1938).

[81] For a discussion of American society and culture, see: Max Lerner, *America As A Civilization: Life and Thought in the United States Today* (New York: Simon & Schuster, 1957); Larry T. Reynolds and James M. Henslin, eds. *American Society: A Critical Analysis* (New York: David McKay, 1973); Edmund Fawcett and Tony Thomas, *The American Condition* (New York: Harper & Row, 1982); and Oxford Analytica, *America in Perspective* (Boston, Mass.: Houghton Mifflin, 1986).

[82] "The first to try fail. Revolution is a long process. Before every success lie scores of failures. Somtimes so many fail that the generation's spirit dies altogether." Gerassi, ed., *The Coming of the New International*, 3. "Modern revolutionaries are believers no less than the Christians or Muslims of an earlier era. What is new is the belief that a perfect secular order will emerge from the forcible overthrow of traditional authority. This inherently implausible idea gave dynamism to Europe in the nineteenth century, and has become the most successful ideological export of the West to the world in the twentieth." James H. Billington, *Fire in the Minds of Men: Origins of the Revolutionary Faith* (New York: Basic Books, 1980), 3. "The problem of revolutionary politics might well be illuminated by a brief reference to the injunction repeatedly put upon the solid

middle-class Puritans who came to American shores in the seventeenth century, not merely to found their own 'City on a Hill' but to undertake the even more breathtaking task of reforming the Reformation itself—and thus the whole world. . . . They must remain, they were constantly reminded, *in* the world but they must never become *of* the world." Warren I. Susman, *Culture As History: The Transformation of American Society in the Twentieth Century* (New York: Pantheon Books, 1984), 75. "To achieve communism, we need to turn the coming imperialist WW III into a war of workers against bosses." "War: Bosses' 'Answer' to Depression-Level Unemployment Rate," *CD*, 20 Oct. 1982, 2. "Yet what began to unfold was an epoch of unprecedented political and social turbulence against a backdrop of anxiety, malaise and lack of confidence related to triple images of apocalypse: nuclear Armageddon, natural disaster, and the continuing belief of radicals in an impending terminal capitalist crisis. This epoch culminated not simply in a utopian upsurge but also in the emergence of many new cults and the rebirth of religious Fundamentalism in the Fourth Great Awakening." Brian J. L. Berry, *America's Utopian Experiments: Communal Havens from Long-Wave Crises* (Hanover, N.H.: University Press of New England, 1992), 237. Also see William G. McLoughlin, *Revivals, Awakenings, and Reform: Essays on Religion and Social Change in America, 1607–1977* (Chicago, Ill.: University of Chicago Press, 1978).

CHAPTER 3. REFORM, REVOLUTION, AND THE SEARCH FOR THE WORKING CLASS

[1] "We can only win the confidence of genuine revolutionaries and workers by the actual development of deeds and the advancing of Marxist-Leninist concepts." "RR I," repr. in *RT*, 147. The reform era that is commonly referred to as "the 1960s" began most clearly with two changes in the struggle for civil rights, which had started in the South during the mid-1950s. Local 1199's successful strike of low-paid Black and Hispanic hospital workers in New York City in 1959 and the sit-in by Black college students in Greensboro, North Carolina in 1960 signaled a qualitative change in the scope and character of the civil rights movement. The decline of the reform spirit that animated significant segments of the American people during the long decade of the 1960s was signaled by two major events that occurred in 1973, namely, the withdrawal of U.S. combat troops from Vietnam, which removed a major cause of disaffection in American life, and the Arab Oil Boycott, which signified the end of the revolution of rising expectations and social optimism generally. The denouement of the 1960s occurred in 1974, when Watergate undid the Nixon Presidency, and in 1975, when a fiscal crisis hit New York City and the last Americans withdrew from Saigon. For a discussion of

how and when the 1960s began and ended, see Godfrey Hodgson, *America in Our Time* (New York: Vintage Books, 1976); and Chafe, *The Unfinished Journey.*

[2] "The Future is Bright," *PL* (June 1970), repr. in *RT*, 350. For a discussion of the mass movements of the 1960s, see: O'Neill, *Coming Apart*; Milton Viorst, *Fire in the Streets: America in the 1960's* (New York: Simon & Schuster, 1979); Chafe, *The Unfinished Journey*; Terry H. Anderson, *The Movement and the Sixties* (New York: Oxford University Press, 1995); Sitkoff, *The Struggle for Black Equality*; Marable, *Race, Reform and Rebellion*; Teodori, ed., *The New Left*; Gitlin, *The Sixties*; Foner, *American Labor and the Indo-China War*; Kate Millett, *Sexual Politics* (Garden City, N.Y.: Doubleday & Company, 1970); Anne Koedt, Ellen Levine and Anita Rapone, eds., *Radical Feminism* (New York: Quadrangle, 1973); Marcia Cohen, *The Sisterhood: The True Story of the Women Who Changed the World* (New York: Simon & Schuster, 1988); Sheila Rowbotham, *The Past is Before Us: Feminism in Action Since the 1960s* (Boston, Mass.: Beacon Press, 1989); and Sara M. Evans, *Born for Liberty: A History of Women in America* (New York: The Free Press, 1989).

[3] Phillip Luce put PL's membership at 1,000 in 1965. Luce, *The New Left*, 94.

[4] See Chapter 1 of the present study for a detailed discussion of PLM's four national campaigns.

[5] "The Future Is Bright," *PL* (June 1970), repr. in *RT*, 348. Perhaps PL's frequent use of the word "struggle" derived from "Dare to struggle and dare to win," the title of Chapter 7 of Mao's so-called "Little Red Book." See *Quotations From Chairman Mao Tse-tung*, 82. "We must build on this inherent strength of the working class—its unfailing capacity to wage the class struggle—and take up the eternal challenge to the exploited down through history: Dare to fight! Dare to Win!" "U.S. Workers: Key to Revolution," *PL* (Aug. 1969), repr. in *RT*, 345. "However, workers will fight back and will continue to respond as long as we dare to win the working class." "The Future Is Bright," *PL* (June 1970), repr. in *RT*, 355.

[6] "Build a Base," *PL* (June 1969), repr. in *RT*, 24–25.

[7] "What had been the movement was increasingly the Left, period—the current incarnation of a historical perennial; or that alluring next step, The Revolution. . . . So the no-longer-new Left trapped itself in a seamless loop: growing militancy, growing isolation, growing commitment to The Revolution. . . ." Gitlin, *The Sixties*, 380. "The three R's for SDS began with reform, led to resistance, and have unofficially ended at revolution." Adelson, *SDS*, 203.

[8] "This unprecedented expansion gave the U.S. ruling class the maneuverability to buy off sections of the working class. And this, despite some resort to violence, was the policy followed even in the most severe times of depression. . . . On balance, despite thousands of devoted revolutionary-minded

members, the CP was a party of reform not revolution." "RR I," repr. in *RT*, 93. Cf., Irving Bernstein, *A Caring Society: The New Deal, the Worker, and the Great Depression* (Boston, Mass.: Houghton Mifflin, 1985). Also see Chapter 1 of the present study for a discussion of PL's critique of CP "revisionism."

[9] "From the earliest days of the communist movement in the United States to the present, revisionism and its political manifestation, class collaboration, has been the chronic weakness." "RR I," repr. in *RT*, 92.

[10] "Build a Base," *PL* (June 1969), repr. in *RT*, 25.

[11] Ibid.

[12] Gitlin, *The Sixties*, 377–408. Cf., Adelson, *SDS*, 225–248.

[13] "... young professionals are recently off the campuses, 'hot-beds of radicalism,' and are more open immediately to radical ideas. Industrial workers are more removed from the radical, anti-war movement and therefore not as prone to listen to our advanced ideology." "Improve Our Base Building," repr. in *RT*, 72.

[14] "Build a Base," *PL* (June 1969), repr. in *RT*, 25.

[15] "Therefore these years of patient, slow winning and training people and developing ties among the masses, no matter how protracted they may seem, are vital." "Build a Base," *PL* (June 1969), repr. in *RT*, 50. "As one young SDS activist put it recently, after a certain amount of frustration you decide that at least you can turn yourself into a brick and hurl yourself." Staughton Lynd, summer 1969, quoted in Gitlin, *The Sixties*, 377.

[16] "Build a Base," *PL* (June 1969), repr. in *RT*, 25–26. See Chapter 1 of the present study for Rosen's experience as a CP steelworker in Buffalo.

[17] Ibid., 27..

[18] "It is the job of a communist party to bring this revolutionary consciousness into the working class, while immersed in the workers' struggles, so that the party can become the working class' general staff in the class war." "U.S. Workers: Key to Revolution," *PL* (Aug. 1969), repr. in *RT*, 310. "... communists must be in the thick of working-class struggles if workers are to realize fully how necessary they are at all levels of the fight against the bosses. Only when the working class understands this will it be ready to defend communists and their ideas." Ibid., 327. "... the Meany-Reuther misleadership and their flunkies ... collaborate with the bosses ... although frequently assuming a militant-sounding front." Ibid., 314. "Such [labor] 'leaders' came on the scene riding the wave of the ruling class' anti-communist crusade. One of the factors making it possible for them to consolidate their power was the C.P.'s failure to lead a militant fight against the monopolies onslaught." "RR I," repr. in *RT*, 100.

[19] *RR III*, 16–17.

[20] Walter Linder, "Don't Abandon the Workers," *PL* (Nov. 1969): 31.

[21] "In other words, the idea is to raise the Party's line *from the very begin-*

ning on every issue that arises, every struggle we participate in. We're always afraid who we're going to 'turn off' by the Party's line, rarely concerned about who we might 'turn on.'" PLP National Committee, "Some Notes on T.U. Work and Party Building," *Internal Bulletin on Party Building* (PL, 1975), 37.

[22] "Two general types of deviation exist within the work of the whole party. In a minority of cases, some cadre are virtually isolated from the mass movement and individuals within it. This reflects lack of confidence in the line and the working class. . . . The second, larger and, hence, more significant deviation, is that when comrades do get into the mass movement (a development which is generally taking place), they tend to abandon the party line. . . . We shy away from political base-building because we are afraid of entering into sharp, protracted political struggle. . . . Consequently, right opportunism within our midst is a failure a) either to be in a position to raise the line of the party or b) a failure to do so when we are in such a position. The main reason for this is fear of anti-communism or fear of the working class." "National Committee Report," *Internal Bulletin: N.C. Reports & Supporting Documents* (PL, 20 Dec. 1974), 1–5.

[23] "Build a Base," *PL* (June 1969), repr. in *RT*, 75.

[24] "PLP's Communist Leadership Helps Spark Sit-Down Strike in Auto," *CD*, 6 Sept. 1973, 1. The wildcat strike at Chrysler's Mack Avenue plant in Detroit was led by members of PL and the Workers Action Movement (WAM), which PL organized. ". . . the 700 workers at the '74 Chicago [WAM] convention and the 300 at the L.A. [WAM] convention were of a size to give the participants a real feeling of a *MASS* of workers acting together around their demands." "Notes on a 1975 WAM Convention," *Internal Bulletin on Party Building* (PL, 1975), 32.

[25] "By May Day the party membership must ask 1,000 friends of the party to join the PLP. . . . By May Day we must recruit 300 people to the party." "National Committee Report," *Internal Bulletin* (PL, 20 Dec. 1974), 5–6. "It is about seven months since we started our current intensified recruitment campaign . . . we recruited over 400 members in the U.S. and into the CPL [Canadian Party of Labour] in Canada." "Build a Large Communist Party—Make the Party a Vital Factor in the Class Struggle," *National Committee Report from Aug. 1–3 Meeting* (PL, 1975), 1. The CPL and PL were closely allied at this time.

[26] "Our group has become a formal caucus, with a militant veteran worker elected president. The group saw to it that I got elected steward (with one dissenting vote—the outgoing hack)." "From a Craft Worker in Basic Industry," in "Notes on Base Building," *PL* (Mar.-Apr. 1968): 15. "During the teachers strike, I was able, as chairman of the shop, to put forward openly in the meetings that Rizzo [Mayor of Philadelphia] was using racism to break the PFT [Philadelphia Federation of Teachers]. . . ." "Importance of Shop Stewards," *PL Convention*

Bulletin #7 (PL, 1973), 15. "In fact, Party members have been elected to local-wide office [AFSCME Local 1006 in Chicago], one member is Chief Shop Steward (and can now set up a Council of Stewards of about 50 which he would lead), and we and WAM [Workers Action Movement] control a majority of the Executive Board, etc." PLP National Committee, "Some Notes on T.U. Work and Party Building," *Internal Bulletin on Party Building* (PL, 1975), 35. It was fairly common for PLers in unions to hold positions as shop stewards.

[27] "Over a period of a couple of years I made known my left-wing opinions to my fellow workers, who respected me for my fight in the shop against the boss but didn't necessarily agree with my long-range views. After I joined the Progressive Labor Party I made this fact known to them. By then we had been in joint struggle for many years, and I had made a number of personal friends among them. When shop stewards were to be chosen in my shop I was nominated in my department and elected overwhelmingly. At that point all the workers involved in the election knew I was a PLP member, as well as workers and stewards throughout the entire shop. Several of them bought PLP literature from me regularly." "From a Worker in an Unskilled Industry," in PLP National Committee, "Some Notes on T.U. Work and Party Building," *Internal Bulletin on Party Building* (PL, 1975), 16.

[28] "In shops and schools we shy away from putting forward the Party and relating the momentary struggle to the need for revolution." "National Committee Report, Oct. 18–19 Meeting," *Internal Bulletin* (PL, 3 Nov. 1975), 1.

[29] "They [CPUSA] attempted to establish a coalition of forces—a united front—between themselves (the Left) and the vast majority of workers (the Center) who wanted to engage in militant struggle against the bosses but didn't necessarily agree with the ultimate goal of socialism. The aim was correct. . . ." "U.S. Workers: Key to Revolution," *PL* (Aug. 1969), repr. in *RT*, 311. However, PL criticized the CP for uniting with "'good' capitalists" and for refusing to criticize "reformist CIO [Congress of Industrial Organizations] misleaders." Ibid.

[30] "New York City, Oct.—Members of PLP took over for an hour a branch of Citibank at 94th St. and Columbus Ave., protesting against the eight branches that this bank has in South Africa, and relating the support Citibank gives to apartheid in South Africa to the racist layoffs and cutbacks forced on the working class due to the $2 billion the City of New York has to pay in interest every year to banks like this." "Smash U.S. and S. African Racism!" *CD*, 28 Oct. 1976, 1.

[31] "In summing up this strategy it can be seen that the Left-Center coalition and its basic organizational form, the caucus, is a major stepping stone to the long-range goal of the working class—defeating the old state power and creating one to serve its interests. This intermediate strategy towards ultimate revolution can help bridge the gap between the present level of the workers and a revolu-

tionary society." "U.S. Working Class: Key to Revolution," *PL* (Aug. 1969), repr. in *RT*, 325. "We can fight for and win power only if we work with others. Therefore the party strategy of *united front from below* becomes primary. The development of left-center caucuses is the chief tactic for conquering power in the unions. . . . Therefore WAM cannot be viewed as a dual union. We bring workers into WAM to heighten their class outlook and to guarantee that the left has an organized presence and program within the labor movement. We build WAM to build the unions. We work in the unions to build WAM." "National Committee Report," *Internal Bulletin* (PL, 20 Dec. 1974), 1. "The decade of the 70's will see an ever-increasing fight for the shorter work week. . . . WAM is circulating a petition to the union leaders demanding that they make 30 for 40 the main negotiating demand in coming contracts. Thousands have already signed—millions will." "Join the Workers Action Movement," *Workers Action* [WAM newspaper], June 1972, 2. "The International Committee Against Racism seeks to effectively articulate the growing outrage of faculty, students and community people against the exponents of neo-racism. More than that, it seeks to alert the campus and community to the immense dangers and consequences of resurgent racism and to mobilize a broad coalition of forces to struggle against its revival." "What is InCAR?" *InCar and the Struggle Against Racism* (InCAR pamphlet, 1977).

[32] "There was unanimous agreement that WAM activity has been a decisive factor in recruiting workers to the Party, in helping to create and strengthen caucuses and in sparking fights for immediate demands." "Report from March 1st N.C. on WAM," *Internal Bulletin On Party Building* (PL, 1975), 22.

[33] "If the effect of 350 or 700 workers at the '74 convention was able to produce all of the results everyone cited, especially recruits, what would 2000 workers in one hall produce? A mass Party? A real Left force in the trade union movement? Etc.?" "Notes on a 1975 WAM Convention," *Internal Bulletin on Party Building* (PL, 1975), 33.

[34] "The new InCAR members wrote and circulated a 'Resolution Against Racism,' which was eventually signed by more than 1400 academics representing more than 200 colleges and universities across the country, and which appeared as an ad in the *New York Times* in October 1973." *InCAR and the Struggle Against Racism* (InCAR pamphlet, 1977), 2. "Chicago—In a magnificent display of solidarity and rank-and-file democracy, more than 700 workers from 29 cities across the U.S. and Canada assembled here on the week-end of Oct. 12–13 at the 4th (and largest ever) convention of the Workers Action Movement, to organize a massive offensive against the bosses' attempt to shift the burden of a threatening depression onto the backs of the working class." "700 Attend Fourth WAM Convention," *CD*, 7 Nov. 1974, 3. "After all, over 4,000 people marched under the Party's banner on May Day [1975] around the continent. A 'WAM' auto meeting

was held in Detroit in January. Ten people came, 9 in the Party." "Report on Trade Union Work," *Report from National Committee Meeting of May 16–18* (PL, 1975), 20.

[35] "They [CP] did not fight the bad ideas of the reformists who operated within the system and whose goal was to preserve it, not defeat it. They feared such a struggle would 'split' the united front. Instead, the Left became submerged within it and gradually assumed a reformist position." "U.S. Workers: Key Revolutionary Force," *PL* (Aug. 1969), repr. in *RT*, 311. "Therefore, the Left must lead the Center into greater confrontation with the 'ground rules' of the capitalist system in order to avoid the path the ruling class chooses and the consequent movement to the Right." Ibid., 316. "Therefore, it is vital for the Center and the Left to fight red-baiting all the way. Here the Left leads by making the Center aware of the existence of the Left, although not necessarily all of its members, from the earliest moment possible." Ibid., 316–317.

[36] "The failure to follow a real Marxist-Leninist line, to politicize the working class and to expose the fakers in the CIO leadership and the Democratic Party, all took its toll. The right-wing leadership that had controlled the AFL for so many years was now firmly in the saddle in the CIO, too—all the more decisive because the CIO had unionized the basic industries." Ibid., 313.

[37] "In those cases where workers were brought to the Party through WAM, it was a case of WAM's 'line' nearly being the Party's line, except for Socialism." "Report on Trade Union Work," *Report from the National Committee Meeting of May 16–18* (PL, 1975), 25.

[38] "May Day, the holiday commemorating the historic fight for the shorter work week was celebrated in Wash., D.C., Buffalo, Houston, Los Angeles, Toronto and Seattle by members of WAM, PLP, SDS, CPL and other organizations." *Workers Action!* [WAM newspaper] June 1972, 2.

[39] "City-wide WAM meetings in most cases are the Party and its base, something like an expanded Party meeting. Many good trade union discussions and plans for action took place at these meetings, but they could just as well have been called directly in the Party's name. Certainly most workers who attended these meetings knew the Party was, more or less, running WAM." "Report on Trade Union Work," *Report from National Committee Meeting of May 16–18* (PL, 1975), 25.

[40] "That is, it allowed us to function in the trade unions as WAM members, maybe even saying a lot of things PL'ers would say, but avoiding functioning as *communists* in the unions, and certainly holding back from recruiting workers to the Party. . . . With whatever base we have in the unions, WAM very easily became an obstacle to putting forward the Party directly." "Report on Trade Union Work," Ibid., 26.

[41] "In fact, for many months in city after city, WAM *DIDN'T* function at all, and sometimes was only resurrected because some Party leader called from New York or the National Committee to discuss WAM's not functioning. If that wasn't done are there 50 non-Party workers around the country who would miss WAM, who would protest that it's 'going out of business,' who would fight to keep it? The very fact that we can realistically pose that question serves to answer it." Ibid.

[42] "The most glaring weakness in our trade union work is the lack of consistent on-the-job struggle led by the Party and its ideas 52 weeks a year." Ibid., 9.

[43] According to the 28 November 1974 issue of *Challenge*, PLP could be contacted in the following cities: Little Rock, Los Angeles, San Diego, San Francisco, Chicago, Gary, Baltimore, Boston, Minneapolis, Detroit, St. Louis, Kansas City, Buffalo, New York City, Durham, Columbus, Philadelphia, Pittsburgh, Houston, Seattle and Madison. PL's membership in these cities ranged from a handful in the smaller chapters to several hundred in New York City, the Party's headquarters. Over the years, some chapters folded and others were organized.

[44] The following headlines, chosen more or less at random from several issues of PL's newspaper *Challenge*, are indicative of the range of locales, issues and activities that were typical of PL during the 1960s and 1970s: "Texas Boycotters Back Workers," "Boston Students in Welfare, Transit Fights: Wide Struggle Marked by Confrontation, Arrests," Dec. 1968, 17, 22; "Chicago PLP Rallies Support for Coming Auto Strike," "L.A. Auto Workers Back PLP Program: UAW, Bosses Call Cops," "Rochester Cops Frame-up Attempt Fails to Stop Challenge Sales," 24 Aug. 1970, 6, 7, 9; "Phila.: 1st Black Union Official Elected, Fighting Communist-Led Slate Wins," "St. Louis: Petition Against Firings," "San Francisco: Student Nurses, Fight Racist Harassment," 29 May 1975, 3, 5, 7; "Tennis' Davis Cup: Racist Apartheid Is No Game—PLP Attacks U.S.-South Africa Love-Match," "Detroit Welfare: Fight Goes On for Rehiring of PL'er," "Rio Grande Valley, Texas, 1st Communist Event in Valley," "University of Arkansas: A Communist Campaign," 28 Apr. 1977, 1, 3, 4, 5; "Detroit: Workers, Clients Fight Cuts," "Oakland: March Against Hospital Layoffs," 29 Sept. 1982, 4.

[45] "For the first time in our history, nearly 600 workers and trade unionists came together at one gathering in which the party played the leading role in organizing as well as ideologically." "Report on the NYC WAM Convention," *PLP Convention Bulletin #8* (PL, May 1973), 1. "With fists raised, chanting '30 hours work for 40 hours pay!' workers from 19 cities in 22 industries closed out an enthusiastic, stirring and hard-working 2nd annual convention of the Workers Action Movement (WAM) here [NYC] on the week-end of April 28–29." "WAM

Convention a Milestone On Road to 30/40 Victory," *CD*, 17 May 1973, 3. "The Sacramento March for Jobs was a tremendous success and a significant victory for the working class and the Party. . . . Over 2,000 people, 90% workers, participated in this great event." PLP National Committee, "Evaluation of the Sacramento March for Jobs and Future Plans for the March for Jobs Coalition," *Internal Bulletin on Party Building* (PL, 1975), 50. "On May Day, 4,500 people marched with the Party throughout the continent." "Build a Large Communist Party—Make the Party a vital factor in the class struggle," *National Committee Report from Aug. 1–3 Meeting* (PL, 1975), 4.

[46] ". . . because it is a party unlike other political parties—a party of the U.S. working class built on the theoretical foundations of Marxism-Leninism—it has the sacred responsibility of wholeheartedly serving the U.S. working class." "On the Party," *PL* (Jan. 1965), repr. in *RT*, 78.

[47] PL sometimes gave the impression of being larger than it really was. For example, PLers sometimes attended several demonstrations in a single week. This constant, collective activity also had the effect of keeping Party members from becoming overly preoccupied with their private lives, which would have detracted from their commitment to PL.

[48] *Desafío*, the Spanish edition of *Challenge* was printed back to back with *Challenge*, which the party often referred to as *Challenge-Desafío*. The subtitle of *Challenge* was changed from "The Revolutionary Newspaper" to "The Revolutionary Communist Newspaper" at the end of the 1960s.

[49] *CD*, 16 Oct. 1972, 2. This was the conclusion of a regularly appearing insert that described the goals of PLP and its newspaper.

[50] Lenin, *What Is to be Done?* repr. in *LSW*, I: 211–231.

[51] "Sales of the monthly C-D [*Challenge-Desafío*] reached 100,000 in the summer of 1970." "Reform and Revolution: Which Way for Socialism?" *CD*, 14 Oct. 1976, 7. This was the high point of *Challenge*'s circulation. "About six months ago the NC discussed C-D sales, with the question arising as to whether or not we should remain a bi-weekly or go back to once every three weeks. Since then (when sales were a little over 30,000), sales went up at one point to nearly 37,000 and then dropped back down to the latest figure (end-of-Aug. to early Sept.) of about 30,000. Thus, in overall sales, we are just about holding our own." "National Committee Report on *Challenge-Desafío*," *National Committee Reports (meeting of Sept. 23–24)* (PL, 1972), 8. *Challenge* sales between January 1981 and March 1981 ranged from a low of 3,414 to a high of 5,740, discounting subscriptions, military mailing and bulk sales. "Report on C-D Sales," *Internal Bulletin* (PL, Apr. 1981), 50–52.

[52] For a discussion by PLers about selling *Challenge*, see *PLP Convention Bulletin #6: Special Bulletin on Challenge-Desafío* (PL, 1973). On Sept. 21,

1974, there were 6,120 *Challenge-Desafío* subscriptions. "National Committee Report on *Challenge-Desafío*," *National Committee Reports (meeting of Sep. 23–24)* (PL, 1974), 8. This report emphasized the higher quality of sales. "That is, concentration sales—at factory gates, in industries in which we want to have an impact, among certain basic groups of workers in auto, steel, etc.—are increasing." Ibid., 6. "I found out on May Day that I could bring 84 workers to the PLP led demonstration in Washington. The 14 key workers, here, who brought all the rest of the people had been reading Challenge-Desafío, consistently, for over a year. . . . Everyone should sell 100 papers an issue, without sweating. It is a question of selling on the job, selling on the streets, and giving workers on the job and worker friends off the job 3, 4, 5 papers that they will sell. And we've only got to do these three tasks each issue for the influence of the Party to expand geometrically . . . 84 times 600 or so party members could logically mean 50,000 workers at our May Day of 1975, instead of the 3,000 that there were on May 4th, 1974." "Selling Lots of Challenges Creates Immediate Party Forces," *Internal Bulletin #9* (PL, 1975), 31. Also see "Report from Chicago on Challenge/Desafío, follow-up of NC Meeting," *National Committee Report from Aug. 1–3 Meeting* (PL, 1975), 8.

[53] *CD*, 16 Oct. 1971, passim.

[54] "Our goal as communists is not to put forth the most surprising, shocking statements, which after long argument we can ultimately win people to, even when the statements are consistent with a communist position." "Further Discussion on Criticisms of Challenge," *PLP Convention Bulletin #9* (PL, 1973), 42.

[55] An article in a 1974 internal bulletin addressing "certain objections to the style and content of *C-D* that are often raised by intellectuals and teachers" pointed out that "Disagreements over 'style' are largely really over content." Against the objection that "Challenge makes it sound like the revolution is going to happen tomorrow," the article answered that "*C-D* has a militant style because it *reflects* struggles of workers, students, etc., and *encourages* them." The article also charged that the "pseudo-'objective' style" of mainstream journalism "is a fraud. . . . The bourgeois press doesn't speak of bosses any more than it does of American imperialism—for obvious reasons. But without understanding that these words describe reality in a way that 'employers' doesn't, people are really weakened in their ability to fight for more jobs, oppose racism, etc. It is the language used by the New York Times that is 'jargon,' that doesn't correspond to reality." "Win Our Base to *Challenge-Desafío*," *Internal Bulletin: N.C. Report & Supporting Articles* (PL, 20 Dec. 1974), 43–52.

[56] "The *reality* is that class struggle is advancing. The militant, partisan style and tone of *C-D* reflect that [the] fact that workers are they [the] key force in society; that they have immense potential power; that the reality of their existence

leads workers to struggle and take forceful action against the bosses; and that these struggles hold valuable lessons from which, armed with communist ideas, workers can learn and advance to revolution." Ibid., 48.

[57] PL's chairman sometimes used this rhetoric in speeches.

[58] "A few issues ago *C-D* carried a story about a factory in which PL'ers and WAM members helped organize a meeting of several dozen workers to go beyond their union misleaders and plan strategy to win a strike. According to the ruling class view of the world, this fact (besides being undesirable) is insignificant. But *C-D* recognizes that such a meeting is far *more* significant than a Democratic Party meeting of thousands. It is workers organizing and struggling which will determine all progressive movements in this country. This is the communist view; it is borne out by history, and it is correct." "Win Our Base to *Challenge-Deasafio*," *Internal Bulletin: N.C. Report & Supporting Articles* (PL, 20 Dec. 1974), 43.

[59] "The press started writing SDS's obituary. The *New York Times* was almost ecstatic in an editorial which wistfully boded 'the decline of the SDS.' Least of all would [the decline] . . . 'be a loss to the campuses of the nation,' the *Times* noted. 'On the contrary, it would clear the way for legitimate dissenters on campuses from Cambridge to California who share many of the SDS ideals but reject its arrogant and coercive ways'." Adelson, *SDS*, 243. Adelson's account is the only one written by a non-PLer that is sympathetic to PL's role in SDS. "Very rarely does a book appear which deals rationally and almost accurately with the 'New Left movement,' or any aspect of it. SDS by Alan Adelson, though limited in its scope, fits both of the above mentioned categories." "SDS—A Profile," *PL* (Mar. 1972): 37.

[60] "Chrysler Mack Plant After Rebels Launch Sit-In," *Detroit Free Press*, 15 Aug. 1973, 1; Jack Crellin, Jack Burdock, Ronald L. Russell and Anne Getz, "UAW men help police open plant," ibid.; "PLP's Communist Leadership Helps Spark Sit-Down Strike in Auto," *CD*, 6 Sept. 1973, 1. Bill Bonds of WXYZ-TV in Detroit observed that it was the first time in UAW history that the union mobilized to keep a plant open. Thompson, "Auto Workers, Dissent and the UAW," in *Autowork*, ed. Asher, 200. Also see Moody, *An Injury to All*, 91–94.

[61] "John Brown lives within us as we go marching on to socialist revolution and the final destruction of racism, to the building of communist society, where the workers of the world shall be the human race." R. A., "John Brown's Raid—Guns Against Slavery," *PL* (fall 1979): 52. "We are at war with the system: the class struggle is not some abstract concept. It is a struggle of life and death. It is a struggle of one class to defeat and destroy the other one. That is what it is. And that is the struggle we're in." "Fight Individualism," Speech Opening, Second PLP Convention, May 1968, repr. in *RT*, 49. "These actions and others show the

emergence of new militant leaders in the working class, and it creates ever broader possibilities for our party's growth . . . if a communist party exists, militants can see an alternative to rotten conditions." "The Future is Bright," *PL* (June 1970), repr. in *RT*, 352.

[62] "On the second front of the anti-racist campaign, 15 members and friends of SDS marched into the office of the Director of Financial Aid to demand that a black student from Nigeria be given a loan denied him because he was a foreign student." "SDS Puts Lid On White Supremacist Trash," *CD*, 22 Mar. 1973, 15. "New York City . . . Flinging two doors open members of the Workers Action Movement and the Progressive Labor Party poured into a regular meeting of the Central Labor Council and turned it into an irregular meeting." "WAM Busts into Council Meeting," *CD*, 30 Jan. 1975, 5. "Chicago, Nov. 2—Chanting 'Racist ACLU Protects Nazis,' and 'No Free Speech for Fascists,' 50 members of Committee Against Racism and PLP stormed angrily into the lobby of the Francis Parker School where ACLU was conducting a meeting about 'police surveillance' to demand they stop giving legal aid to the American Nazi Party." "PLP Confronts Chicago ACLU," *CD*, 20 Nov. 1975, 4. "Chicago, April 9—In the finest tradition of the international communist movement which smashed Hitlerite fascism world-wide, a multi-racial group of Chicago-area workers—including members of the Progressive Labor Party—gave Hitler's modern-day descendants a taste of the future last Friday night, April 7, when they invaded the Nazi office here and left their headquarters and the Nazis themselves in a shambles." "Communists Smash Nazis," *CD*, 19 Apr. 1978, 1. "On September 13, 1980, the largest, most violent branch of the Ku Klux Klan attempted to rally its forces in the small farming town of Scotland, Conn. Hundreds of anti-racists, led by InCAR and the Progressive Labor Party, staged a counter-demonstration whose main slogan was 'Death to the Klan—Power to the Workers' . . . The Klan fully understands who its friends are. It quotes Shockley about 'genetic enslavement.' It cites Jensen's 1969 *Harvard Educational Review* article as 'proof' of 'racial inequality.' It glowingly mentions Herrnstein's 1971 piece in the *Atlantic Monthly* and quotes Herrnstein as saying that when unemployed black workers fight for jobs, they are 'rebelling against their genes.'" "Bury the Jensen-Shockley-Herrnstein-Wilson Racists: Smash the KKKollege Konnection!" (InCAR leaflet, n.d.), repr. in *CD*, 15 Oct. 1980, 2. "Evanston, ILL., Oct.19—Fifteen hundred anti-fascist demonstrators pelted ten Chicago Nazis with bricks, eggs and flashlight batteries for five minutes today stopping their rally." "1,500 Pelt Nazis, InCAR Leads," *Arrow* [InCAR newspaper], Nov. 1980, 1.

[63] "In San Francisco, on the night of August 7, 1967, Mission District Police broke into a party. . . . Although the cops claimed that they were there on a noise complaint, it is evident that their intrusion was part of a planned political attack

on the Progressive Labor Party and the Mission Tenants Union. . . . PLP had held a demonstration at the Mission district police station to protest the beatings of several neighborhood youths. . . . John Ross, PLP candidate for Supervisor and active in Mission District struggles, was badly beaten, and 10 people were arrested, seven on charges of felonious assault. . . . Eric Johnson, PLP's west coast trade union organizer, was found guilty . . . sentenced to one year in jail and is presently serving that sentence. . . ." " 'Those who are guilty are going to pay. . . .' " (PL pamphlet, n.d.). "On June 18, the Los Angeles Police Dept. attacked a demonstration and march through the L.A. garment center, organized by the Committee Against Racism (CAR) in which members of PLP participated. The marchers defended themselves. . . . As a result of this attack, ten cops are suing PLP, its leaders and others for $2 million. They claim 'injury to their bodies and shock to their nervous system.' " "L.A. Cops Sue PLP," *CD*, 21 July 1977, 1. Also see: "It IS Happening Here! Police Trial Against Communist PLP Means Fascism," (PL pamphlet, n.d.); "LAPD vs. PL Trial: An Attack on All Workers," *CD*, 4 Aug. 1982, 3; and Randy Heard, "Not Naming Names," *L.A. Weekly*, 6–12 Aug. 1982, 3. "Tupelo, Miss., July 7—Sixty-five anti-racist marchers, organized by the International Committee Against Racism and the Progressive Labor Party, were marching through the streets here chanting 'Death to the Klan' when shots rang through the air." "In Struggle," *PL* (fall 1979): 83. "The attempt by the administration of the University of Arkansas in Little Rock, in addition to scores of politicians throughout the state, to fire Dr. Grant Cooper from his post at the university is running into stiff opposition by students, faculty members, and workers." "Progressive Labor Party Rocks Arkansas," (PL pamphlet, n.d.); this pamphlet reprinted a number of articles from the *Arkansas Democrat* and the *Arkansas Gazette* concerning Cooper's firing.

[64] "Winning people to the party must always be central to our planning and organizing in the mass movement." "N.C. Report," *Internal Bulletin: N.C. Reports & Supporting Articles* (PL, 20 Dec. 1974), 1.

[65] "If we unite on broadening out the work, these initial efforts could lead to a serious groundswell. BUT THE BIG JOKER IS THAT, IN DOING THIS WORK, WILL WE BUILD THE LEFT AND WILL WE BE ABLE TO RESIST THE DEMANDS OF OUR BROADENED BASE AND CONTACTS TO UNITE WITH THE ENEMY?" "Some Problems in the Work," ibid., 32.

[66] "Fascism and Busing in Boston: The New U.S. Nazis and Their Liberal Masters," (PLP pamphlet, 1975), 5; "Boston Summer," *PL* (Dec. 1975): 27–42; "Fascists Routed in Boston," *CD*, 15 May 1975, 2–3. To steel its forces for an anticipated fight against fascism, PL published two historical articles on the antifascist struggle: "Fascism: Past . . . and Future? (Part One)," *PL* (Apr. 1976): 12–38; and "Stopping Fascism: Allies vs. Comrades," *PL* (Sept. 1976): 13–55. For PL's

prediction of war, see W. Blakelee, "War or Revolution," *PL* (July-Aug. 1978): 7–22; and "Turn the Guns Around!" (PL pamphlet, 1981).

[67] "Reform and Revolution," *CD*, 14 Oct. 1976, repr. in *PL* (Apr.-May 1978): 37–52.

[68] Ibid., 37.

[69] Ibid., 45–47.

[70] Ibid.

[71] Ibid., 37.

[72] Ibid., 41.

[73] For PL, the May Day turnout turned into the equivalent of an annual earnings report. From its earliest days, PL began making its following conscious of the importance it attached to May Day. See "May Day—Symbol of Workers' Power," *PL* (May 1963): 1.

[74] This was really an admission that it was very difficult to convince reformist workers to commit themselves to communist revolution; but absent a revolutionary mass, less involvement in the tactical leadership of reform struggles and more intensive preaching of communism was hardly a prescription for mass recruitment.

[75] "Reform and Revolution," *CD*, 14 Oct. 1976, repr. in *PL* (Apr.-May 1978): 52.

[76] PL's most ambitious May Day celebration involved a national motorcade that converged on Washington, D.C. "May Day Motorcade for Socialism—1974," *PL* (Oct.-Nov. 1974): 43–50.

[77] ". . . our practice has tended to trail somewhat behind that line. As our practice and experience moves forward, there will be more changes. This is not something to be afraid of . . . Comrades and friends: a future of revolution was never brighter. The objective situation is worsening. . . . Against all this the working class can take the offensive, if led by a communist party that follows a line of putting revolution first, that bursts the chains of capitalist reformist ideology. This is our historic task; let's get to it." "Reform and Revolution: Which Way for Socialism?" *CD*, 14 Oct. 1976, 9.

[78] "Other than the briefly notorious student delegations to 'break the travel ban,' organized by the Progressive Labor Party, in 1963–64, these radical peaceworkers carried out the only serious efforts to bridge the gap with Cuba between the Missile Crisis in late 1962 and the rise of the antiwar movement in the late 1960s." Gosse, *Where the Boys Are*, 234. Also see "The History," *PL* (Aug.-Sept. 1975): 60–63.

[79] Chapter 5 of the present study will discuss the political background of PL's young garment organizers.

[80] "Build a Base," repr. in *RT*, 45.

[81] "RR I," repr. ibid., 146.

[82] "Build a Base," repr. ibid., 44.

[83] "Criticism and Self-Criticism," *PL* (June 1966), repr. ibid., 209.

[84] In addition to being concerned about its class composition, PL was uneasy about its racial make-up, which was overwhelmingly White. While PL, which was led predominantly by men, addressed the issue of women's oppression from its inception as a party, and increasingly as the women's liberation movement developed, gender issues were never treated as seriously by PL as class and race matters. Furthermore, PL saw the women's movement as threatening its ability to recruit women to a class outlook, to see the solution to women's oppression in revolutionary socialism. "The women's liberation movement has already made great headway with its 'man-blaming' ideology. The Party must move *swiftly* and *seriously* to defeat this devisive tendency. . . . If our struggle is to succeed, feminists and potential feminists must be won to fighting the ruling class and *not* men." "Winning Women to the Struggle," *PLP Convention Bulletin #8* (PL, 1973), 26. See Chapter 4 of the present study for further discussion of this issue.

[85] For a discussion of PL's origin in the CPUSA, see Chapter 1 of the present study.

[86] Rosen and Scheer were about forty years old in the mid-1960s.

[87] C. Wright Mills, "The New Left," *New Left Review* (Sept.-Oct. 1960), repr. in C. Wright Mills, *Power, Politics and People: The Collected Essays of C. Wright Mills*, ed. Irving Louis Horowitz (New York: Ballantine Books, 1963), 256.

[88] Jeff Gordon, "SDS: An Analysis," *PL* (Oct. 1968): 99–116; Bob Leonhardt, "Campus Worker-Student Alliance: Students Reject Elitist Habits," *PL* (Feb. 1970): 66–76.

[89] "The History," *PL* (Aug.-Sept. 1975): 58–60.

[90] Ibid., 69; U.S. News & World Report, *Communism and the New Left*, 19, 26.

[91] Leonhardt, "Campus Worker-Student Alliance," *PL* (Feb. 1970): 66–76; Gordon, "SDS: An Analysis," *PL* (Oct. 1968): 99–116; Irwin Unger, *The Movement: A History of the American New Left, 1959–1972* (New York: Harper & Row, 1974), 55.

[92] "The Future Is Bright," *PL* (June 1970), repr. in *RT*, 347. For a discussion of the French rebellion, see "France: May 1968, Workers Rebel!" *PL* (Feb.-Mar. 1978): 7–23; and David Caute, *The Year of the Barricades: A Journey Through 1968* (New York: Harper & Row, 1988), 211–255.

[93] *SDS Work-In 1968: Toward a Worker-Student Alliance*, (SDS pamphlet, n.d.). "The politics expressed in this pamphlet represent one significant tendency within sds."

[94] Levy, *The New Left and Labor*, 147–151.

[95] There is a voluminous literature on SDS, which discusses the split. For examples, see Adelson, *SDS*; Kirkpatrick Sale, *SDS* (New York: Random House, 1973); and Gitlin, *The Sixties*. "At the June, 1969 convention of Students for a Democratic Society (SDS), forces opposed to a worker-student alliance attempted to destroy the organization by splitting off from it." Leonhardt, "Campus Worker-Student Alliance," *PL* (Feb. 1970): 66.

[96] "Improve Our Base Building," repr. in *RT*, 72.

[97] Ibid., 72–73.

[98] Ibid., 73.

[99] "The ability, social consciousness and conscience, political sensitivity and honest realism of today's students are a prime cause of student disturbances. . . . That they seemingly can do so little to correct the wrongs through conventional political discourse tends to produce in the most idealistic and energetic students a strong sense of frustration. . . . Many of these idealists have developed with considerable sophistication the thesis that these flaws are endemic in the workings of American democracy." *Crisis at Columbia*, Report of the Fact-Finding Commission Appointed to Investigate the Disturbances at Columbia University in April and May 1968 (New York: Vintage Books, 1968), 4–5.

[100] "Improve Our Base Building," repr. in *RT*, 72.

[101] "Black Workers: Key Revolutionary Force," *PL* (Feb. 1969), repr. ibid., 269.

[102] Ibid., 271.

[103] Ibid., 268; "Program for Black Liberation," *PL* (Feb. 1969), repr. ibid., 244.

[104] "Black Workers: Key Revolutionary Force," *PL* (Feb. 1969), repr. ibid., 268.

[105] Ibid., 276–278.

[106] "While racism is the greatest source of profit for the ruling class, it is also its Achilles Heel." "Program for Black Liberation," *PL* (Feb. 1969), repr. ibid., 267.

[107] "For An Alternative," *PL* (Jan. 1963): 1–3.

[108] "Program for Black Liberation," *PL* (Feb. 1969), repr. in *RT*, 244.

[109] Ibid., 246, 250–255.

[110] "Black Workers: Key Revolutionary Force," *PL* (Feb. 1969), repr. ibid., 269.

[111] See "Revolutionaries Must Fight Nationalism," *PL* (Aug. 1969), repr. ibid., 279–297.

[112] "Black Workers: Key Revolutionary Force," *PL* (Feb. 1969), repr. ibid., 277.

[113] "Program for Black Liberation," *PL* (Feb. 1969), repr. ibid., 266. "To unite men and women workers against their common enemy requires a real fight by the working class—and especially the Left—against the bosses' ideology of male supremacy and for special demands such as equal pay for equal work, women in leadership of unions of which they are members, special provisions for maintenance of seniority while women workers are on maternity leave, two years maternity pay from the boss, [and] special recognition of the demands of Black

and other minority group women." "U.S. Workers: Key to Revolution," *PL* (Aug. 1969), repr. ibid., 339–340. Also see "Fight Against Women's Oppression Parallels Struggle Against Racism," *PL* (Nov. 1973): 24–29; and *Smash Sexism! With Socialist Revolution!* (PL pamphlet, 1980). This pamphlet was produced to facilitate PL's organizing among garment workers in L.A.

[114] "Program for Black Liberation," *PL* (Feb. 1969), repr. in *RT*, 266–267.

[115] Ibid., 267.

[116] "Perhaps the most glaring example of sexism in the party is the fact that we really don't have a line on it at all—except that we're against it." "Fighting Sexism," *PLP Convention Bulletin #3* (PL, 1973), 29. Also see "On Male Chauvinism," *PLP Internal Bulletin #9* (PL, 1973), 58; and "Comments on Fighting Sexism in Bulletin III," ibid., 66. The convention [PLP's third convention, held 13–15 July 1973 in NYC] resolutions admitted the undeveloped character of PL's line on sexism. "I have been in the Challenge office and heard women described as 'chicks' or 'broads'—as a joke? I have heard party members laugh when told women are harassed sexually while selling the paper, and refuse to discuss ways to handle this. I have repeatedly heard party members repeat uncritically vicious ruling-class slander against women's liberation groups, without trying to distinguish friends from enemies. And men in the party are often not criticized for chauvinist relationships with women as long as they are 'serious,' i.e. monogamous, rather than promiscuous. In general my impression is that one's attitudes toward the oppression of women, except as it is related to the trade union movement, is seen as a personal, not a political thing. Like rooting for the Mets." "On Male Chauvinism," *Internal Bulletin #1* (PL, 23 July 1973), 73. "In the face of racist genocidal war in Vietnam and genocidal policies of the US government at home, problems of women pale in significance. Yet this article will argue that 1) the fight against sexism, far from being a diversion, must be an integral part of the fight against racism. Capitalist ideologies bolster each other. 2) Sexist exploitation is crucially important to the capitalists and a direct fight against it as part of the trade union movement is a winning strategy. 3) Although women will fight for a revolution (in fact, after minority workers, be most militant) and state power could be seized without an explicit fight against sexism, socialism could never be achieved if we don't fight sexism from the beginning. Anything which oppresses more than half the population must be fought. The only chance to end sexism is to overthrow capitalism, but revolution doesn't guarantee an end to sexism." "Women's Oppression Under Capitalism." Ibid., 78–96. "Women have often dropped out of the party when they have children for lack of a plan of what they can do politically as mothers (especially if they choose to stay home with the children for a length of time) and subjectively see having children as a contradiction to effectively carrying out political work, i.e.

neglecting the children vs. neglecting political work." "Women Taking Leadership in the Party," *Internal Bulletin #2* (PL, Sept. 1973), 8. "In the late 1960's in campus work and in the anti-war movement, the party members in SDS were vigilant against MC [male chauvinism]. The party devoted space in C-D and PL to the issue. Today we seem to be approaching the issue in a muddled way. Just what is our alternative to the bourgeois feminist movement? . . . Many women who were in the party have dropped out after having children. Many wives of party leaders have dropped out of the party after having children. . . ." A San Francisco comrade, "On Male Chauvinism," *Internal Bulletin* (PL, 8 Mar. 1977), 21. "In the last NPW [non-public work] mid-west Cadre School the group I was in got into a discussion on Sexism, that was not a written part of the agenda, however, we were discussing basebuilding and the obstacles to it. The response of some comrades when the issue was raised was that 'racism was more important' and 'we should organize a discussion at another time.' This type of response is one that many party members and party leaders feel comfortable with. This *must* change." A Black woman comrade from Detroit, "On Sexism," *Internal Bulletin* (PL, 5 Apr. 1977), 98. Also see "Fighting Sexism," *Internal Bulletin* (23 Nov. 1977), 38.

[117] "But whom have we NOT been recruiting? Industrial workers (except in rare instances)." "Improve Our Base Building," repr. in *RT*, 72. PL claimed to be for the industrial working class, but it was not made up "of" them or created "by" them, despite the fact that PL's leaders had functioned as CP industrial cadres. In the final analysis, there really was not much of a radical working-class movement for PL to capture. Moreover, because PL opposed Black nationalism and feminism, it was not equipped to win leadership of the radical wings of those movements.

[118] "On the Party," *PL* (Jan. 1965), repr. in *RT*, 81.

[119] Ibid., 85.

[120] Ibid.

[121] "Prior to the edicts regarding dress, haircutting, and beard shaving, the comrades from China would have been quite dismayed with the average member of Progressive Labor." Luce, *The New Left*, 95. "With his long hair, Fu Manchu beard and his personal life-style, Tom Jenkins hardly seems the stereo-typed blue-collar factory worker. Yet Jenkins, who works in a Detroit auto factory, is typical of other young workers interviewed across the country." Haynes Johnson and Nick Kotz, *The Unions* (New York: Pocket Books, 1972), 40. "The young radical soon learns to be ashamed of his intellectual bias, and after an ineffectual effort to squeeze himself into the mind of the workingman drifts away disillusioned from his timid collegiate radicals. His energy evaporates, because intellectual radicalism was afraid to be itself." Randolph S. Bourne, *The New Re-*

public, VI (11 Mar. 1916): 161; A review of Seymour Deming, *The Pillar of Fire* (Boston, Mass.: Small, Maynard & Co., 1915), repr. in *War and the Intellectuals*, ed., Carl Resek (New York: Harper & Row, 1964), 141.

[122] "Criticism and Self-Criticism," *PL* (June 1966), repr. in *RT*, 211–213.

[123] "Two sub-species [of intellectuals], the idealists and the apostates, place themselves by preference at the head of revolutions." Robert Michels, *Roberto Michaels' First Lectures in Political Sociology* (*Corso di Sociologogia*, 1927; repr., New York: Harper & Row, 1965), 111.

[124] "Can we fail? Yes, its quite possible for us to fail, although the working class eventually must succeed." "Criticism and Self-Criticism," *PL* (June 1966), repr. in *RT*, 242.

[125] In 1961, there were twice as many workers as students in the little group led by Milt Rosen that decided to form a new communist party. It is unlikely that PL's future leaders could foresee the problematic that would soon preoccupy them and their student base. See Chapter 1 of the present study.

CHAPTER 4. NEW COMMUNISTS CHALLENGE OLD SOCIALISTS

[1] The terms used in the title require some consideration because they are either controversial or confusing. First, I have chosen to call Progressive Laborites (PLers) "new communists" because I believe that it is the best descriptive term available and avoids the unproductive controversy over whom should be regarded as part of the "New Left." Phillip Abbott Luce, a notorious early defector from Progressive Labor, used the terms "new communist Left" and "Communist New Left" to distinguish PL from radical organizations that he found less objectionable. These included civil rights groups such as the Student Non-Violent Coordinating Committee and the Congress of Racial Equality, and pacifist groups such as the Committee for a Sane Nuclear Policy and the Committee for Non-Violent Action. He did not consider these groups part of the New Left because, unlike PL, they were not "devoted to armed revolts, riots, 'underground' networks, and attempts at the revolutionary overthrow of the United States government." Luce, *The New Left*, 3–5. But the term "New Left" has been variously understood. Massimo Teodori, for example, distinguished between a non-ideological "New Left," based on participatory democracy, and "fringe groups of the traditional left," which together comprised the "new radicalism" that encompassed everyone from the social-democratic Irving Howe to the Maoist Progressive Labor Party. Massimo Teodori, ed., *The New Left*, 4–5, 36–37. In the same vein, Paul Buhle distinguished between the "New Left," which stressed "human rights and visions of cultural change," and the communist and socialist Left, characterized by the

"struggles of labor and the promise of egalitarian industrial progress." Paul Buhle, "New Left" in *Encyclopedia of the American Left*, eds. Mari Jo Buhle, Paul Buhle and Dan Georgakas (Urbana, Ill.: University of Illinois Press, 1992), 517. David Caute, on the other hand, regarded the willingness of PLers to proclaim their communism before the House Committee on Un-American Activities as indicative of the differences between the "new generation of young radicals" who "scorned to conceal their commitments" and Old Leftists, "who remained reticent before their inquisitors." Caute, *The Great Fear*, 103. So while I favor a definition of "New Left" broad enough to include PL, the term "new communism" is less likely to cause confusion. Second, the International Ladies' Garment Workers Union, which was founded in 1900, can reasonably be called an "old" union. Third, the ILGWU was famous for its anticommunism since the late 1920s. In 1957, Max Danish credited long-time ILGWU president, David Dubinsky with more than thirty years of "unrelenting resistance to communism throughout the needle trades' domain." Danish, *The World of David Dubinsky*, 240. Fourth, PL referred to New York City's garment district as "Dubinsky's plantation" in order to accuse the ILGWU leadership of complicity in the garment employers' racist "super-exploitation" of their Black and Hispanic workers. Fifth, the period discussed in this chapter begins with the creation of *Progressive Labor* in 1962, and it ends with David Dubinsky's retirement as ILGWU president in 1966, at which point PL was on the verge of being able to lead shop struggles in NYC's garment center.

[2] Progressive Labor sent a handful of its best young organizers into the NYC garment center to bring garment workers into PL's orbit; this was PL's first "industrial concentration." Their political development and organizing for PL in the garment industry is discussed in the following chapters of the present study.

[3] "The History," *PL* (Aug.-Sept., 1975): 56. Articles about NYC's garment industry and PL's efforts to organize there appear in PL's newspaper *Challenge* throughout the period from 1962 to 1982.

[4] Robert Laurentz, "Racial/Ethnic Conflict in the New York City Garment Industry, 1933–1980" (Ph.D. dissertation, State University of New York at Binghamton, 1980), 6.

[5] "The heart of the low-wage situation in New York City is to be found in its huge clothing industry. This industry which employs some 300,000 workers is the largest industry in New York." Milton Rosen, "I.L.G.W.U.: Jim Crow and Dubinsky Rule," *PL* (Oct. 1962): 10. "The garment bosses and the ILGWU bosses get fat today off the backs of the Negro and Puerto Rican workers." Milton Rosen, "Dubinsky 'Strikes' Out Again," *PL* (Mar. 1964): 19.

[6] "Thus, in the struggle for the emancipation of man, philosophy finds its material weapon in the proletariat just as the proletariat finds its intellectual weapon in philosophy." De George, *Patterns of Soviet Thought*, 40. But accord-

ing to Lenin, ". . . the spontaneous struggle of the proletariat will not become a genuine 'class struggle' until it is led by a strong organization of revolutionists." Lenin, *What is to be Done?*, quoted ibid., 139.

[7] "The shops that mass-produce the dresses, coats, pants and undergarments that women wear gross billions of dollars each year. But there is no General Motors among them, no United States Steel, no single tycoon who dominates. There are in the garment center many moguls whose success depends, season after season, on their interpretations of style . . . competition is savage. . . ." David Dubinsky and A. H. Raskin, *David Dubinsky: A Life with Labor* (New York: Simon & Schuster, 1977), 7. "The margin of profit in our industry is 1 percent. The competition is keen and the chiseling is great. The profits are not great but the chiseling is great." House Committee of Education and Labor, Congressman Herbert Zelenko's subcommittee, Hearings on the Garment Industry, Federal Court House, Manhattan, New York, 24 Aug. 1962, David Dubinsky, testimony, repr. in "ILGWU President Testifies," *JU*, 1 Sept. 1962, 8.

[8] "New York City, the financial, commercial and cultural center for the U.S. ruling class is broke . . . the ultimate cause . . . is the decline of U.S. imperialism." "The Decline and Fall of Fun City," *PL* (Dec. 1975): 43. PL often used the phrase "U.S. imperialism." "The hypothesis of American imperialism attained its immense popularity in part because it seemed so well to describe Vietnam. In defense of its reactionary client regime in Saigon, the U.S. had mobilized half a million men and unprecedented fire power to crush an indigenous movement of revolutionary peasants." Allen J. Matusow, *The Unraveling of America: A History of Liberalism in the 1960's* (New York: Harper Torchbooks, 1986), 327.

[9] See: Jack Newfield and Paul Du Brul, *Permanent Government: Who Really Runs New York?* (New York: Pilgrim Press, 1981), 63–99; Ken Auletta, *The Streets Were Paved With Gold* (New York: Vintage Books, 1980), xii; and Martin Shefter, *Political Crisis/Fiscal Crisis: The Collapse and Revival of New York City* (New York: Basic Books, 1985), 107–109.

[10] See Auletta, *The Streets Were Paved With Gold*, xii-xiii; Alexander Bloom, *Prodigal Sons: The New York Intellectuals and Their World* (New York: Oxford University Press, 1986), 11; Terry A. Coony, *The Rise of the New York Intellectuals: Partisan Review and Its Circle, 1934–1945* (Madison, Wis.: University of Wisconsin Press, 1986), 10–37; and William Phillips, ed., *Partisan Review: The 50th Anniversary Edition* (New York: Stein & Day, 1984).

[11] "The History," *PL* (Aug.-Sept. 1975): 55–57.

[12] Dubinsky, *David Dubinsky*, 8.

[13] Ibid., 9–10.

[14] Ibid., 12.

[15] Ibid., 9.

[16] Herbert Hill, "The ILGWU—Fact and Fiction," *NP,* 2, no. 2, 25.

[17] John Dewey, *David Dubinsky: A Pictorial Biography* (New York: Inter-Allied Publications, 1951), 18–19, 21.

[18] Dubinsky, *David Dubinsky,* 9.

[19] Ibid., 9.

[20] Letter, President Harry S. Truman to John Dewey, 14 Apr. 1949, repr. in Dewey, *David Dubinsky: A Pictorial Biography,* 29.

[21] Letter, The League for Industrial Democracy to David Dubinsky, Apr. 1949, repr., ibid., 18.

[22] Ibid., 12.

[23] "'Labor History' Issue Depicts Dubinsky Role," *JU,* 1 Apr. 1968, 11.

[24] J. B. S. Hardman, "David Dubinsky, Labor Leader and Man," *Labor History, Special Supplement* (spring 1968): 43, 54.

[25] Philip Taft, "Dubinsky and the Labor Movement," ibid., 26.

[26] Joel Seidman, "The I.L.G.W.U. in the Dubinsky Period," ibid., 67.

[27] Ibid., 67–68.

[28] Jack Barbash, "The I.L.G.W.U. as an Organization in the Age of Dubinsky," ibid., 114. "We have passed out of that phase of our history in which our best energies were used to fight primitive battles on the picket lines to lift ourselves a notch higher above the subsistence level of living. In those battles we fought bitterly and savagely to rip from the hands of a hostile industry and a hostile society another dollar for our pay envelopes, another hour of daylight out of the shop for ourselves. . . . We lifted ourselves and dragged a reluctant society upward. Today, for the most part, we have won those elementary battles and unions have achieved prestige, status, power and responsibility. . . . Now we can lift ourselves only by broad social and political pressures exerted within national concepts of welfare and security." "The More We Change," *JU,* 1–15 June 1962, 20.

[29] "This union—which for more than six decades has been the portal through which masses of immigrants have integrated into American life—is charged with discrimination." "The Attack on Our Union," *JU,* 1 Sept. 1962, 2. For a discussion of the relationship of immigration to the development of "business unionism" in the United States, see Gerald Rosenblum, *Immigrant Workers: Their Impact on American Labor Radicalism* (New York: Basic Books, 1973).

[30] "In sum, what has happened in American labor politics since the mid-1930s is that unions have spoken less about a third party and have acted more as a 'third force' in American politics. The International [ILGWU] has been part of that current flowing into the mainstream." Gus Tyler, *Look for the Union Label: A History of the International Ladies' Garment Workers' Union* (Armonk, N.Y.: M. E. Sharpe, 1995), 225. It should be noted that the economic and political establishment's understandable fear of working-class radicalism abetted

Dubinsky's opposition to labor radicalism and smoothed the path to progressive reform. For a discussion of the emergence of the American welfare state, see Bernstein, *A Caring Society.*

[31] Dubinsky, *David Dubinsky,* 8.

[32] ". . . the idea of labor's common interest with business, not only as management, but also in the global role of imperial agent and anti-communist crusader. With this viewpoint it was natural that David Dubinsky and his union should have played such a key role in the process that has made so much of American organized labor an active partner in U.S. foreign policy in recent years. . . . Dubinsky and Woll formed the core of anti-communist militancy in the AFL (and later the AFL-CIO)." Michael Myerson, "ILGWU: Fighting for Lower Wages," *Ramparts* (Oct. 1969): 55. Also see Dubinsky, *David Dubinsky,* 11–12. The ILGWU newspaper *Justice* contained innumerable articles attacking communism and supporting U.S. foreign policy in the Cold War. For examples, see Averell Harriman, "The Hope for Survival," *JU,* 1 Feb. 1961, 12; Willy Brandt, "The Communists Are No 'Supermen,'" *JU,* 1 Apr. 1961, 12; Dean Rusk, "Vietnam," *JU,* 1 May 1965, 13; "ILG Chief Supports LBJ on Vietnam, Domingo," *JU,* 1 June 1965, 17; "No Dealings With Communist Company-Unions!" *JU,* 15 Nov. 1967, 12; and "Fifty Years Later: Experts at a Hoover Institution on War Symposium" [Sidney Hook, Bertram D. Wolfe and Henry M. Jackson], *JU,* 1 Dec. 1967, 6.

[33] Danish, *The World of David Dubinsky,* 240; "Mourn Max Danish: First Editor of 'Justice,' Dean of Labor Journalists," *JU,* 15 Jan. 1964, 9.

[34] Danish, *The World of David Dubinsky,* 45.

[35] Ibid., 240.

[36] David Dubinsky, "A Warning Against Communists in Unions," *New York Times Magazine* (11 May 1947), cited ibid., 241.

[37] Dubinsky, *David Dubinsky,* 9; Walter Linder, "Labor Statesman," *CD,* 24 Aug. 1965, 8. "In early February 1953, the CIO executive board named a committee of officials headed by Reuther to meet with an AFL committee headed by Meany, to discuss unity. Reuther said: 'The CIO wants a united labor movement with all the Communists and racketeers kicked out,' and recalled that the CIO had 'rid itself of nine Communist unions some years ago.'" Ginger, ed., *The Cold War Against Labor,* II: 667–668.

[38] Danish, *The World of David Dubinsky,* 240.

[39] Milton Rosen, "Low Wages in New York City, First of Two Articles," *PL* (Jan. 1962): 11. In pointing the finger of blame at the ILGWU, Rosen was not original. Three years before Rosen's article appeared in the new *PL* magazine, Roy Helfgot published *Made in New York,* a study of the garment industry which, by implication, criticized the ILGWU. Helfgot observed that despite the shortage of skilled operators, few economically disadvantaged Black and Puerto Rican women, who had become a significant portion of the garment labor force, were

advancing, as an earlier generation of Jewish and Italian men had done, from low-paying jobs involving standardized work to high-paid jobs as tailors. Roy B. Helfgot, *Made in New York: Case Studies in Metropolitan Manufacturing* (Cambridge, Mass.: Harvard University Press, 1959), cited in Laurentz, *Racial/Ethnic Conflict*, 300–301.

[40] Laurentz, *Racial/Ethnic Conflict*, 301.

[41] Ibid., 302.

[42] Rosen, "Low Wages in New York City, First," *PL* (Jan. 1962): 11.

[43] Milton Rosen, "Low Wages in New York City, Second of Two Articles," *PL* (March 1962): 10. "Union membership has not kept pace with the labor force or the potentially organizable population and has remained about stationary since World War II." Labor Research Association, *Labor Fact Book 16* (New York: International Publishers, 1963), 74. "The dispute over organizing goes deeper than a mere numbers game. At its heart, the disagreement involves how much effort, money and trouble should be invested to bring union benefits to those workers furthest down the economic ladder—the poor and minority workers." Johnson, *The Unions*, 177.

[44] "Indeed, quite a few Party joiners, both Negro and white, were primarily motivated in the beginning by a desire to 'do something' about segregation and discrimination per se; and they believed that they could accomplish this aim by identification with the Party, which patterned much of its program around the question of Negro rights." Wilson Record, *The Negro and the Communist Party* (New York: Atheneum, 1971), 293. Milton Rosen was a member of the CPUSA from the late 1940s to the end of 1961. For PL's early recognition of the importance of the civil rights movement, see "For An Alternative," *PL* (Jan. 1962): 1–3.

[45] Leon Fink and Brian Greenberg, *Upheaval in the Quiet Zone: A History of Hospital Workers' Union, Local 1199* (Urbana, Ill.: University of Illinois Press, 1989), ix–xvii, 1–27.

[46] Ibid., 19; Laurentz, *Racial/Ethnic Conflict*, 284; Luce, *The New Left*, 86–93. Of the eight PLP leaders whom Luce mentioned as comprising the new party's national steering committee—Milt Rosen, Mort Scheer, Bill Epton, Jake Rosen, Fred Jerome, Levi Laub, Sue Warren, and Walter Linder—almost all were Jewish and all but one male. Luce identified Milt Rosen, Mort Scheer, Jake Rosen and Fred Jerome as PLP's elite leaders, and "people such as Epton and Laub" as "near-elites." In that case, PL's "elite" leaders were all Jewish men.

[47] Rowbotham, *The Past is Before Us*, 218–219. All of PL's principal leaders, discussed by Luce in *The New Left*, 86–93, were men.

[48] In 1960, there were 154,246 women and 100,148 men working in the apparel industry in NYC. Laurentz, *Racial/Ethnic Conflict*, 278. The ILGWU estimated that by 1980, 80% of the garment workforce in NYC was comprised of women. Ibid., 411. ". . . the predominance of women in the hospital labor

force. . . ." Norman Metzger and Dennis D. Pointer, *Labor-Management Relations in the Health Services Industry: Theory and Practice* (Washington, D.C.: Science & Health Publications, Inc., 1972), 12. For the militancy shown by women garment and hospital workers, see Tyler, *Look for the Union Label*, 46–62; and Fink, *Upheaval in the Quiet Zone*, passim. For the male domination of the ILGWU and Local 1199, see Laurentz, *Racial/Ethnic Conflict*, 148–153; and Fink, *Upheaval in the Quiet Zone*, 241.

    [49] Rosen, "Low Wages in New York City, Second," *PL* (Mar. 1962): 10. ". . . an industry that had come out of World War II with wage rates among the highest in any manufacturing field and now ranked well down on the list." Dubinsky, *David Dubinsky*, 16.

    [50] Laurentz, *Racial/Ethnic Conflict*, 301. The ILGWU received some support for its opposition to raising the minimum wage in New York. Ralph Gross, Executive Vice President of the Commerce and Industry Association of New York, believed that wages were tied to productivity and should not be set by law. Roy Helfgot, who represented the Industrial Relations Counselors, Inc., thought that raising the minimum wage was "a quack doctor's prescription that would kill the patient by driving industry from the city." Ibid., 333.

    [51] Ibid., 467–472.

    [52] Ibid., 236–267.

    [53] Ibid., 188–200. "The Puerto Rican migration of the 1940's and 1950's became a forerunner of other movements from Caribbean nations. Puerto Ricans, as American citizens, were not technically immigrants; they had the right of unrestricted migration to the mainland. Among the factors contributing to this large migration after World War II was cheap air fare between New York and San Juan." David M. Reimers, *Still the Golden Door: The Third World Comes to America* (New York: Columbia University Press, 1985), 128.

    [54] Laurentz, *Racial/Ethnic Conflict*, 239–244. Laurentz concluded that the "forces of the industry that degraded the labor of garment workers in general had not significantly manifested themselves during the time that Jews and Italians participated in the New York garment industry in large numbers." However, the situation was quite different for Puerto Rican and Black garment workers, especially women, who were "locked into what were, for the most part, dead-end, low-wage jobs with little opportunity to escape." Even those jobs were beginning to disappear. Ibid., 283. "We would like to see that the Puerto Ricans and Negroes go to higher brackets, where the earnings are better, but we are not the masters of it. What you can do with employers, frankly, I don't know." House Committee on Education and Labor, Congressman Herbert Zelenko's Subcommittee, Hearings on the Garment Industry, Federal Court House, Manhattan, New York City, 24 Aug. 1962, David Dubinsky, testimony, repr. in "ILGWU President Testifies," *JU*, 1 Sept. 1962, 10.

[55] Laurentz, *Racial/Ethnic Conflict*, 289–291.

[56] Herbert Hill, "The ILGWU Today—The Decay of a Labor Union," *NP* 1, no. 4, 16. The ILGWU had helped Jewish and Italian immigrants to assimilate into American society; but the ILGWU apparently found it more difficult to integrate Blacks and Puerto Ricans into the union's craft locals and leadership ranks.

[57] In the mid-1940s, the New York State Commission Against Discrimination upheld the complaint of a Black member of Dressmakers' Local 22 who had been barred from the higher-paying jobs controlled by Italian Dressmakers' Local 89. The Commission elicited an agreement from the ILGWU that Blacks and Hispanics would no longer be excluded from membership in the ILGWU's two Italian locals, Dressmakers' Local 89 and Cloakmakers Local 48. However, twenty years later, there was still "not a single Negro or Spanish speaking person" holding membership in these locals. Laurentz, *Racial/Ethnic Conflict*, 295. "It then would have known why no Negro, no Jew, no Tasmanian, no Hindu, not anyone but an Italian-American can hold membership in Local 89 which through its great manager, Luigi Antonini, was a lone anti-Fascist voice at a time when others were oblivious to the danger. It would have applauded the origin of this local in the desire of Italian immigrants to participate in the affairs of the union at a time when they were conducted in Yiddish, the language of another immigrant group." "The Attack on Our Union," *JU*, 1 Sept. 1962, 2. In 1957, four hundred Black and Puerto Rican garment workers in the Bronx picketed the ILGWU's offices to "secure a measure of democratic rights within the union and to stop collusive practices with the employer." They even petitioned the National Labor Relations Board to decertify the ILGWU as their bargaining agent. Laurentz, *Racial/Ethnic Conflict*, 296. In 1958, Puerto Rican workers in Brooklyn who belonged to Underwear Workers' Local 62 organized a wildcat strike against their company and, as a *New York Herald Tribune* reporter noted, "against the workers' own union." In 1958 as well, two hundred members of Novelty Workers' Local 132 picketed the ILGWU headquarters demanding that union meetings be conducted in Spanish and rejecting their ILGWU-negotiated contract. Ibid., 297.

[58] Laurentz, *Racial/Ethnic Conflict*, 297–299; "State Unit Stalls Cutter Hearing on 'Bias' Slur," *JU*, 15 Aug. 1961, 4.

[59] Laurentz, *Racial/Ethnic Conflict*, 300.

[60] Ibid., 308; "Dubinsky Rebuffs 'Bias' Charge At Congressional Unit's Hearing," *JU*, 1 Sept. 1962, 1.

[61] Rosen, "I.L.G.W.U.: Jim Crow and Dubinsky Rule," *PL* (Oct. 1962): 1.

[62] Letter, Gus Tyler to the editors of *Harpers*, repr. in Jacobs, *The State of the Unions*, 132.

[63] Rosen, "I.L.G.W.U.: Jim Crow and Dubinsky Rule," *PL* (Oct. 1962): 1.

[64] Stanley Levey, "Dubinsky Scores House Inquiry; Denies Bias in Garment Union," *New York Times*, 25 Aug. 1962, 1, repr. in "Dubinsky Rebuffs 'Bias' Charge At Congressional Unit's Hearing," *JU*, 1 Sept. 1962, 1; "ILGWU President Testifies: Service Based on Merit, not Race; No 'Class' membership in ILGWU," Ibid.

[65] Barrett McCurn, "Dubinsky: Who's on Trial?" *New York Herald Tribune*, 25 Aug. 1962, 1, repr. in *JU*, 1 Sept. 1962, 9.

[66] John D. Pomfret, *New York Times*, 12 Sept. 1962, repr. in "No Sept. 12 Session Held of House Probe," *JU*, 15 Sept. 1962, 4, and cited in Rosen, "I.L.G.W.U.: Jim Crow and Dubinsky Rule," *PL* (Oct. 1962): 1.

[67] *New York Daily Mirror*, 22 Sept. 1962, cited in Rosen, "I.L.G.W.U.: Jim Crow and Dubinsky Rule," *PL* (Oct. 1962): 2.

[68] Emmanuel Perlmutter, *New York Times*, 18 Sept. 1962, cited ibid., 1.

[69] Ibid. According to A. H. Raskin: "While sycophants were still shaking Dubinsky's hand and applauding him for humiliating his detractors, he was telling me: 'Here is our union, a pioneer in pensions, welfare, paid vacations. We led everybody else in factory wages only a few years ago; now we are criticized because our wages are too low. And it is true, many of them are low. That has affected me deeply. Where did we go wrong?' " Dubinsky, *David Dubinsky*, 16.

[70] Laurentz, *Racial/Ethnic Conflict*, 309–310; Hill, "The ILGWU Today," *NP* 1, no. 4, 7–8; Hill, "The ILGWU—Fact and Fiction," *NP* 2, no. 2, 15–21. New York Dress Shipping Clerks Union, Local 60–60A rejected the "false and malicious charges of discrimination" levelled against it. "60–60A Members Assail Allegations of 'Discrimination,'" *JU*, 15 Sept. 1962, 4. David Dubinsky also addressed the issue of Local 60–60A in his appearance before Congressman Zelenko's subcommittee on 24 August, 1962. See "ILGWU President Testifies," *JU*, 1 Sept. 1962, 2.

[71] *New York Daily Mirror*, 22 Sept. 1962, cited in Rosen, "I.L.G.W.U.: Jim Crow and Dubinsky Rule," *PL* (Oct. 1962): 2.

[72] Laurentz, *Racial/Ethnic Conflict*, 312; Levey, "Dubinsky Scores House Inquiry," *New York Times*, 25 Aug. 1962, 1, repr. in "Dubinsky Rebuffs 'Bias' Charge at Congressional Unit's Hearing," *JU*, 1 Sep. 1962, 1; "ILGWU President Testifies," ibid.

[73] Laurentz, *Racial/Ethnic Conflict*, 312–314. Another important issue raised at the hearings concerned an alleged "sweetheart contract" involving Local 102, the Cloak & Dress Drivers & Helpers Union. PL sent a small group of communist organizers into Local 102 in the latter part of the 1960s. Local 102 and PL's attempt to build an insurgent movement within it are discussed in Chapters 5 and 6 of the present study.

[74] Gus Tyler, "The Truth About the ILGWU," *NP* 2, no. 1, 6–7; "Zimmerman Hurls Accusal Of Anti-ILGWU Frame-Up," *JU*, 1 Sept. 1962, 3.

[75] Emmanuel Perlmutter, *New York Times*, 18 Sept. 1962, cited in Rosen, "I.L.G.W.U.: Jim Crow and Dubinsky Rule," *PL* (Oct. 1962): 1–2.

[76] Ibid., 1.

[77] Hill, "The ILGWU Today," *NP* 1, no. 4, 6–8. To bolster his claim that the ILGWU did make efforts to develop Puerto Rican leadership, Dubinsky made a section of the general executive board's report to the 1959 ILGWU convention part of his testimony before Congressman Zelenko's subcommittee on 24 August 1962. Part of the section he read stated, ". . . Pres. Dubinsky, in the presence of Fernando Sierra Berdecia, Puerto Rican Secretary of Labor, stressed the need for the development of such leadership." "Developing Puerto Rican Leadership," *JU*, 1 Sept. 1962, 8. To combat the charge of racial discrimination made against the ILGWU, Dubinsky also read into the 24 August, 1962 hearing record a passage from the 1934 ILGWU convention proceedings, which described how the union relocated the meeting place of its convention in Chicago when it discovered that the Medinah Club failed to live up to its promise of "no discrimination." ". . . the General Executive Board decided that although it might involve additional expense, our organization which is committed to equality, justice and resistance to oppression, should actively resist this discrimination and we decided to move our convention out of that hotel. (Applause.)," "ILGWU Action Against Discrimination," *JU*, 1 Sept. 1962, 9.

[78] "ILGWU Action Against Discrimination," *JU*, 1 Sept. 1962, 8–17.

[79] Lester Granger, "Manhattan and Beyond," *Amsterdam News*, 1 Dec. 1962, repr. in *JU*, 1 Dec. 1962, 5.

[80] Gus Tyler, "The Truth About the ILGWU," *NP* 2, no. 6, 6–7.

[81] Ibid., 8–9, 17. Hill replied quite effectively. Hill, "The ILGWU—Fact and Fiction," *NP* 2, no. 2, 7–27.

[82] Hill, "The ILGWU—Fact and Fiction," *NP* 2, no 2, 26–27.

[83] Ibid. In responding to Tyler, Hill clarified his position that "At no time did I charge the ILGWU with discriminatory practices emanating from a conscious racist ideology." Hill explained that the "social fact of discrimination" was rooted in "the interaction of the old union leadership with the changing social composition of the membership and the nature of the industry." The ILGWU's "all-white top leadership" saw the increasing numbers of "Negroes and Puerto Ricans," who made up more than half of the union's membership in the New York area, as a "growing threat to its monopoly of control." The ILGWU leadership, Hill further alleged, was "contemptuous of the younger, less educated, the less sophisticated—the altogether different—newer members who are overwhelmingly Negro and Puerto Rican." Most important, the ILGWU was committed to main-

taining "a cheap labor market for the garment industry in New York City." Hill opposed this "fundamental decision to keep the industry in New York City on the basis of maintaining low wages and minimum standards for tens of thousands of unskilled workers, i.e., Negroes and Puerto Ricans." Ibid., 2, 8.

[84] Paul Jacobs, "David Dubinsky: Why His Throne is Wobbling," in id., *The State of the Unions*, 112–128. "The warning of our GEB that recognition of the union within the union could only mean the establishment of a permanent internal faction, with all its evils, has been verified by events." "The ILGWU Since 1959: Excerpts from Report of the General Executive Board to 31st ILGWU Convention," *JU*, 16 May 1962, 10. The FOUR controversy was made much of in the pages of *Justice*. For examples, see: "GEB Acts on Union Within a Union," *JU*, 15 Feb. 1961, 3; "Four Questions," *JU*, 1 May 1961, 5; "A Union Within a Union?" ibid., 12; "Union Within a Union: The Decisive Issues," *JU*, 15 May 1961, 4; "A Union Within a Union," *JU*, 1 June 1961, 4; "Union of Employees—Yes! Faction of Officers—No!" *JU*, 1 Aug. 1962, 12; and "Union Within a Union," *JU*, 1 May 1965, 8.

[85] Jacobs, "David Dubinsky: Why His Throne is Wobbling," in id., *The State of the Unions*, 118–119, 126–127.

[86] Paul Jacobs, "Postscript," in id., *The State of the Unions*, 129–136; Hill, "The ILGWU—Fact and Fiction," *NP*, 2, no. 2, 26–27; J. Fogel, *Jewish Daily Forward*, 10 Dec. 1962, cited ibid., 26; Burton Hall, "Gingold's Law; Or Why Does the ILGWU Continue to Decay?" *NP*, 11, no. 3, 69; Charles Zimmerman, "Why I resigned from the NAACP," *JU*, 16 Oct. 1962, 12; "Randolph Flays Attack on ILG," *JU*, 1 Sept. 1962, 2; "Norman Thomas Hits Attacks Against ILG," ibid., 10; "New York City AFL-CIO Rallies to ILG," ibid., 2. In a letter to Roy Wilkins, executive secretary of the NAACP, AFL-CIO Pres. George Meany wrote, "I am sure that by now you have had a chance to familiarize yourself with the facts, so that you know the extent to which these attacks smear a union [ILGWU] whose civil rights record is unsurpassed." "Meany Tells NAACP: Anti-Union Falsehoods Harming Fight for Civil Rights," *JU*, 1 Dec. 1962, 5. "Two years later, Dubinsky introduced to the union's national convention 'the most constructive, sane, able, intelligent leader' in the civil rights movement of the day: Roy Wilkins of the NAACP. Wilkins responded by praising Dubinsky for his long fight against communism, and by sloughing off the Hill matter. But the clincher was his ringing affirmation that an examination of official [ILG] policy "does not reveal any—not even the slightest—deliberate policy of racial restriction, even where the effect might be construed as racial in character.'" Michael Myerson, "ILGWU: Fighting for Lower Wages," *Ramparts* (Oct. 1969): 53–54.

[87] When such a split did occur over school decentralization in 1968, it was not primarily Jews who charged the "Jewish" United Federation of Teachers with

racism and who were charged with anti-Semitism. Instead, Blacks and Jews confronted each other directly with charges of racism and anti-Semitism. For a discussion of the racial and ethnic conflict between Jews and Blacks in NYC during
the late 1960s, see: Diane Ravitch, *The Great School Wars: New York City,
1805–1973: A History of Public Schools as Battlefield of Social Change* (New
York: Basic Books, 1974), 251–378; Marjorie Murphy, *Blackboard Unions: The
AFT and the NEA, 1900–1980* (Ithaca, N. Y.: Cornell University Press, 1990),
232–251; and Jonathan Kaufman, *Broken Alliance: The Turbulent Times Between Blacks and Jews in America* (New York: Charles Scribner's Sons, 1988).

[88] "Recently, Dubinsky was asked how he managed to stay so young. 'I do
two things,' replied D. D. 'I take care of myself and I take care of my enemies.' "
Letter, Gus Tyler to the editors of *Harper's Magazine*, repr. in Paul Jacobs, "Postscript," in id., *The State of the Unions*, 131. "A poll was taken which I keep as the
best souvenir of my career. The poll was taken before and after the hearing, and
predicted he [Rep. Zelenko] would pay with his political life for this action."
Keynote address, 32nd ILGWU convention, Miami Beach, Florida, 12 May
1965, David Dubinsky, repr. in *JU*, 1 June 1965, 2.

[89] Jacobs, "Postscript," in id., *The State of the Unions*, 133–136.

[90] "The imperialists use racist ideas to justify their brutal exploitation of national minorities at home and workers and oppressed people abroad. They do this
to set one group of people against another and so cover up the fact that the basic
and common enemy of all workers is the class of big businessmen and the imperialist system of private ownership . . . imperialism can only be replaced by socialism." "Program for Black Liberation," *PL* (Feb. 1969), repr. in *RT*, 245. "To
unite men and women workers against their common enemy requires a real fight
by the working class—and especially the Left—against the bosses' ideology of
male supremacy and for special demands such as equal pay for equal work,
women in leadership of unions of which they are members, special provisions for
maintenance of seniority while women workers are on maternity leave, two years
maternity pay from the boss, special recognition of the demands of Black and
other minority group women." "U.S. Workers: Key to Revolution," *PL* (Aug.
1969), repr. in ibid., 339–340.

[91] "Black Workers: Key Revolutionary Force," *PL* (Feb. 1969), repr. ibid.,
277. "Because of its all-embracing character in the U.S., racism also acts as a
pattern-setter to similarly divide many different groups of workers along national
and racial lines." "U.S. Workers: Key to Revolution," *PL* (Aug. 1969), repr. ibid.,
338. In a discussion of the conflict between parents and unionized teachers in
NYC, Milt Rosen wrote, "But the nationalist deviation, which must be combat-
ted, thrives primarily because of chauvinism. Which is the main danger to the
working class, chauvinism or nationalism? We say chauvinism! If you are going
to make a one-sided error, for crying out loud, make it combatting chauvinism."

"Build a Base," *PL* (June 1969), repr. ibid., 41. He did not mention the anti-Semitism that others detected in the statements of some Black nationalists involved in the community control controversy. "The turning point came with the war. Now the Nazis stood revealed as enemies not only of the Jews but of all Americans . . . it became clear, that anti-Semitism was a kind of blind hatred that had doomed six million Jews to the extermination chambers. Everywhere there was an instinctive revulsion against ideas that had such horrible consequences." Oscar Handlin, *American Jews: Their Story* (New York: Anti-Defamation League of B'nai B'rith, 1972), 33–34. "Nor was there much concern over anti-Semitism in the first half of the 1960's. Anti-Semitism seemed to have become almost invisible." Nathan Glazer, *American Judaism* (Chicago, Ill.: University of Chicago Press, 1972), 167. In becoming communists, PL's Jewish members simultaneously took a step toward assimilation and accepted the burden of being part of an objectionable minority. Communism replaced Judaism as the cross they bore.

[92] ". . . the question of fighting racism is a principled question, a question of strategy, not tactics." "Black Workers: Key Revolutionary Force," *PL* (Feb. 1969), repr. in *RT*, 275.

[93] George Thayer, *The Farther Shores of Politics: The American Political Fringe Today* (New York: Simon & Schuster, 1967), 418.

[94] "Progressive Labor Party, Preamble to Constitution," *PL* (Mar.-Apr. 1966): 1–2.

[95] "For as long as capitalism exists, fascism will inevitably spring up out of the wreckage of liberalism." "Stopping Fascism: Allies vs Comrades," *PL* (Sept. 1976): 55. ". . . only socialism is a viable alternative to fascism." Ibid., 17. "Not only the well-known Nazi genocide toward the Jews need be cited." "The Historical Fight Against Fascism," *PL* (Apr. 1976): 20.

[96] "The fascists feed and grow fat on racism like a pig feeds and grows fat on garbage. To the extent that communists can remove racist garbage from society, to that extent the fascist pigs will be stunted in their growth," *PL* (Apr. 1976): 38. "Today, the KKK in the Marines or LA, ROAR in Boston, the U.S. Nazis in Chicago, represent the same scurvy racist potential as the original Nazis." M. K., "On the Similarities Between the U.S. and Weimar Germany," *PL* (Oct.-Nov. 1977): 7.

[97] Progressive Labor defended Marx, who came from a nonreligious, German Jewish family, against the charge that he was anti-Semitic, a charge based on his *On the Jewish Question* (1844), whose concluding sentence reads, "The emancipation of the Jews, in the final analysis, is the emancipation of mankind from Judaism." Karl Marx, *On the Jewish Question* (1844), repr. in *Writings of the Young Marx on Philosophy and Society*, eds. Loyd D. Easton and Kurt H. Guddat (Garden City, N.Y.: Doubleday & Company, 1967), 248. PL quoted these

lines from Marx to show that while he opposed Judaism, he favored rights for Jews. For believing Jews, this could be viewed as a distinction without a difference. To the extent that Jews remained committed to Judaism, which Marx made a metaphor for capitalism, they were an obstacle to socialism. Under socialism, Judaism, whose secular basis was capitalism, would evaporate. Ultimately, then, Jews would not enjoy civil rights as Jews; this was the emancipation of the Spanish Inquisition. Marx's call to emancipate mankind ideologically from Judaism was pursued diabolically in Hitler's genocidal campaign to emancipate Europe from Jews. However, PL saw Marx's Jewish origin as proof against the accusation that he was anti-Semitic, but was frustrated by the persistence of his critics: "This does not stop the experts, some of them Jewish nationalists who love to attack Jewish communists as 'self-hating Jews.' " R. O. M., "Marx: Fighter Against Racism," *PL* (summer-fall 1981): 50–52. However, if Jewish socialists and communists, following Marx, equated Judaism with capitalism, then their opposition to capitalism could involve self-hatred, atonement and an attempt to cope with anti-Semitism by identifying with a universal class. "For Trotsky, like many of his fellow Jewish revolutionaries, felt total revulsion for the Jewish past. In historian Salo Baron's words, it bordered on 'outright self-hatred, and greatly contributed to the revolution's destructive methods in dealing with the established Jewish institutions.' Trotsky believed that Zionism was doomed to failure and called its founder, Theodore Herzl (1860–1904), a 'repulsive figure' and 'shameless adventurer.' " Louis Rappoport, *Stalin's War Against the Jews: The Doctor's Plot and the Soviet Solution* (New York: The Free Press, 1990), 15. Like Trotsky, PLers had contempt for Zionists, whom they accused of collaborating with the Nazis. "Zionism: Boomerang of Racism," *PL* (Apr. 1976): 63–71. "We, in Progressive Labor Party, dedicate the publication of this pamphlet to our Arab and Jewish comrades who have recently been jailed by the fascist Israeli state." "Socialist Revolution Will Destroy Israeli Fascism" (PL pamphlet, n.d.): 3. PL's own solution to the problem of anti-Semitism was to eliminate the traditional bases for regarding Jews as an objectionable minority, i.e., by creating a world without either religions or nations.

[98] Rosen, "Dubinsky 'Strikes' Out Again!" *PL* (Mar. 1964): 19.

[99] Editorial, *CD*, 25 July 1964, 1, 5, cited in HUAC, "Subversive Activities in Riots," 898.

[100] "From July 18, 1964 to July 23, 1966, there have been no less than 20 uprisings in ghettos across America." "Black Liberation—Now!" (PL pamphlet, n.d.), 1, cited in HUAC, "Subversive Influences in Riots," 897.

[101] HUAC, "Subversive Influences in Riots," 928. See Chapter 1 of the present study for a discussion of PL's involvement in the Harlem Rebellion of 1964.

[102] Rosen, "Dubinsky 'Strikes' Out Again," *PL* (Mar. 1964): 19.

[103] Jacobs, "David Dubinsky: Why His Throne is Wobbling," in id., *The State of the Unions,* 118.

[104] Rosen, "Dubinsky 'Strikes' Out Again," *PL* (Mar. 1964): 19.

[105] Edward Lemansky, interview by the author, tape recording, New York City, 7 Aug. 1991; Robert F. Williams, *Negroes with Guns* (New York: Marzani & Munsell, 1962); "From Rob Williams," *Freedom* [PL newspaper], n.d., 1.

[106] Rosen, "Dubinsky 'Strikes' Out Again," *PL* (Mar. 1964): 19.

[107] Milton Rosen, "Johnson Honors Dubinsky's War On the Poor," *CD,* 11 June 1964, 4; "Trace History of 'Johnson-Dubinsky' Friendship," *JU,* 15 Jan. 1964, 2; "President Johnson Leads Salute to Health Center," *JU,* 1 June 1964, 3; "President's Visit High Point of Health Center Jubilee," *JU,* 15 June 1964, 3.

[108] Rosen, "Dubinsky Honors Johnson's War On the Poor," *CD,* 11 June 1964, 4.

[109] Steve Martinot, "Dubinsky Fights With Bosses—Against Workers," *CD,* 4 July 1964, 6.

[110] Walter Linder, "Dubinsky, Garment Bosses Tie Workers in Knots," *CD,* 8 Dec. 1964, 5.

[111] Walter Linder, "Dubinsky Rule Brings Garment Workers' Ruin," *CD* 17 Nov. 1964, 6.

[112] During Rosen's speech, a heckler started yelling "Commie!" in an "attempt to break up the rally," but he was silenced by a small crowd that surrounded him and called him a "KKKer." Halfway through the rally, twenty police officers broke up a confrontation between a reporter for *El Diario* and a group of Puerto Ricans who disapproved of his "hastily made up sign," which provocatively alluded to the shooting of a police officer by a rapist that he had apprehended. Mark Shapiro, "Garment Workers' Solidarity," *CD,* 1 Aug. 1964, 3.

[113] Mark Shapiro, "Garment Rally," *CD,* 8 Aug.1964, 3.

[114] "Garment Workers Cheer Attack on Dubinsky," *CD,* 29 June 1965, 2. In his keynote address to the ILGWU convention in Miami Beach, Florida, Dubinsky supported Johnson's war policy in Vietnam and military intervention in Santo Domingo. *JU,* 15 May-1 June 1965, 17.

[115] "PLP Hits the Streets," *CD,* 13 July 1965, 4.

[116] "Meredith Protest Meeting: Garment Workers Cheer Call to 'Get Out of Vietnam,'" *CD,* 21 June 1966, 5.

[117] "End of an Era: Dubinsky Retires," *JU,* 15 Mar.-1 Apr. 1966, 2; "I Have Decided to Retire," Text of Dubinsky's March 16, 1966 letter to the ILGWU General Executive Board declaring his intention to resign, repr. ibid., 17; "The Press and D. D.," *JU,* 15 Apr. 1966, 5. This article contains laudatory remarks about Dubinsky from various newspapers around the United States.

[118] "The Press and D. D.," *JU,* 15 Apr. 1966, 5.

[119] Jerry Weinberg, "Garment Center Workers March," *CD*, 4 May 1965, 3; Editors, "End the Sweatshops," ibid., 4.

[120] Ibid.

[121] Ibid.

[122] Editors, "Dubinsky's 'Plantation'—Finish the Job," *CD*, 18 May 1965, 5.

CHAPTER 5. THE MAKINGS OF A COMMUNIST TRUCKER

[1] PL borrowed the term "colonizing" from the Communist Party USA. It designated the tactic of sending students to work in industry so that they might attract workers to communism. By 1970, PL regarded colonizing as a mistake. "The Future is Bright," *PL* (June 1970), repr. in *RT*, 347–355.

[2] PL's garment organizing initially depended on the activities of three college-educated, twenty-something, White males who colonized New York City's garment trucking industry during the late 1960s: Steve Martinot, Ed Lemansky and Dave Davis. Two other PLers worked in the garment industry during this period: Bob Apter and Dave Douglas, a Trinidadian who "soon disappeared." EL, interview, 7 Aug. 1991. At various times, other PLers held jobs in garment or participated in garment street rallies.

[3] "ILGWU Local 102 Godfathered by Garment and Trucking Bosses," *CD*, 24 Jan. 1974, 7. This article was intended to revive PL's organizing efforts in the garment center, which had waned after a brief period of intense activity during the late 1960s. PL focused on the garment trucking industry but PL's insight into the strategic importance of garment trucking reflected the wisdom of hindsight. According to Edward Lemansky, one of PL's principal colonizers in the garment center, PLers wound up working in garment trucking simply because jobs were available there. EL, interview, 7 Aug. 1991. Shutting down the garment industry would have been a convincing demonstration of both workers' power and PL's power. The article was partly intended to empower Black and Hispanic workers by making them aware of their potential impact on the industry, but it also gave PLers an inspiring vision of the possible revolutionary consequences of their garment organizing. For an earlier PL statement on the strategic importance of garment trucking, see A Garment Worker, "What Makes Garment Men Slaves?" *CD*, Oct. 1967. (The male-orientation of *Challenge* articles about garment trucking is discussed below.) "Soon after leading the Bolsheviks to power in 1917, V. I. Lenin pointed to the American Negroes as constituting an 'oppressed class' which should be most helpful in extending the communist revolution to the United States." U.S. News & World Report, *Communism and the New Left*, 65. "It is not likely that the Communists in their thirty years of activity in this country would have given as much attention to the black minority had the Party not

been convinced that Negroes could ultimately be used to serve Party ends. And in the Communist's mind, the Party ends came in the course of time to be inseparable from the ends which Negroes should seek." Record, *The Negro and the Communist Party*, 296. The same could be said of the working class.

⁴ "ILGWU Godfathered by Garment Trucking Bosses," *CD*, 24 Jan. 1974, 7.

⁵ Ibid. ". . . the bosses of the industry can make a lot more money if the production of garments is split up among a lot of little shops, each one doing a certain piece of the work. . . . But to do this you need fast truckers . . . cheap truckers. So the garment industry has created an army of slaves to do its fetching and hauling for it." A Garment Worker, "What Makes Garment Men Slaves?" *CD*, Oct. 1967.

⁶ "The uneducated go there because they can't get a better job without a high school diploma. Men just out of prison go there because they can't get a better job with their record ('paying your debt to society' is just crap). Mostly, Black and Puerto Rican workers go there because, in this society, they can't get the jobs a white man can get." A Garment Worker, "What Makes Garment Men Slaves?" *CD*, Oct. 1967.

⁷ *Challenge* listed three obstacles to rebellion: "constant intimidation," "buying off the union leaders" and "the thugs, the Mafia." Ibid.

⁸ House Committee on Education and Labor, Congressman Herbert Zelenko's Subcommittee, Hearings on the Garment Industry, Federal Court House, Manhattan, New York, 24 Aug. 1962, David Dubinsky, testimony, repr. in "ILGWU President Testifies," *JU*, 1 Sept. 1962, 9.

⁹ "During the course of the House Hearings . . . Pres. David Dubinsky, in his voluntary appearance, averred that Local 102 was a 'problem child' for the ILGWU and that the situation would be looked into." "'102' Triumph at Fast Co. Bursts Sweetheart Slur," *JU*, 1 Dec. 1962, 4.

¹⁰ "ILGWU Local 102 Godfathered," *CD*, 24 Jan. 1974, 7.

¹¹ Felipe DeJesus, interview by author, tape recording, New York City, 26 Mar. 1996. He led a major strike at Figure Flattery in 1968. See Walter Linder, "ILGWU-Figure Flattery Co.," *PL* (Oct. 1968): 42–48.

¹² "ILGWU Local 102 Godfathered," *CD*, 24 Jan. 1974, 7.

¹³ In 1960, there were 154,246 women and 100,148 men working in the apparel industry. Laurentz, *Racial/Ethnic Conflict*, 278. The ILGWU estimated that by 1980, 80% of the garment work force in New York City was comprised of women. Ibid., 411.

¹⁴ A Garment Worker, "What Makes Garment Men Slaves?" *CD*, Oct. 1967. "The guys in the shops who had led the first two strikes did not take the time, IN ADVANCE, to patiently explain to the men what the fight was all about." "Garment Workers Need Plan to Win," *CD*, May 1970, 6. The male-oriented language in these articles is typical of *Challenge* articles about the male domain of garment trucking.

[15] However, *Challenge* articles about garment factory workers did address the issue of sexism. "FINALLY, THE FACT THAT THE MAJORITY of the garment workers are women, who the bosses and their capitalist system tell us 'need less,' enhances the bosses' ability to keep these wages low. By dividing men and women workers, as well as white from minority workers, the bosses and their 'aides' in the ILGWU have about the best one-two punch available to them for feathering their own nests." "Fabricate Deals—Workers Will Cut Them Apart," *CD*, 10 Jan. 1974, 11. For PLP's statement condemning sexism at its founding convention in April 1965, see "PL Constitution," *PL* (May-June 1965): 5. Soon after the convention, a *Challenge* editorial listed conditions in the garment market that should be challenged: ". . . The 'extra-special' exploitation of more than 100,000 women garment workers, who work for low pay to support children whose fathers are victims of low wages and unemployment." "End the Sweatshops," *CD*, 4 May 1965, 4.

[16] For male domination of the ILGWU, see Laurentz, *Racial/Ethnic Conflict*, 148–153. "No failure of ILGWU leaders hit home quite as strongly as their failure to wage a stronger, more concerted fight to end sexual abuse in the shops." Ibid., 148. "Jewish males exploited these women in the shops and Jewish males were responsible for policies which implicitly condoned such practices." Ibid., 153. Laurentz emphasizes the racial and ethnic aspect of the tension between Jewish men, both employers and ILGWU officials, and Black and Hispanic women who worked in the garment industry.

[17] Edward Lemansky, interview by author, tape recording, New York City, 15 Aug. 1991. Articles in *Justice* about Local 102 contracts indicate the size of pay increases but do not indicate what the union scale was for each job category. See "'102' Carts 11th-Hour Pact Bringing Raises for 2,000," *JU*, 15 Mar. 1964, 4; "'102' Renewal Talks On 300 Deadlocked," *JU*, 1 Mar. 1966, 7; and "$13 Pay Hike for 300 In '102' Pact at Gilbert," *JU*, 8 Aug. 1968, 12. *Challenge* indicated that at United Marlboro, for example, union scale was $132 for drivers, $122 for helpers and $90 for pushers. EL, "Garment Strikers Win 1st Round at United Marlboro Trucking," *CD*, Apr. 1970, 10.

[18] "By discriminating against Black people the ruling class is able to force on them a per capita income of $1,000 less per year than that of white people." PLP Black Liberation Commission, "Program For Black Liberation," *A Plan for Black Liberation* (PL pamphlet, Jan. 1969), 2. "Black rebellions are currently the most advanced expression of the class struggle." Ibid., 3.

[19] "Black, white and Puerto Rican; drivers, helpers, and rack pushers, they stood together against the boss." A Garment Worker, "City-Wide Trucking: Men Win Union Scale Demand," *CD*, Nov.-Dec. 1967, 6. "All the workers—drivers, truck helpers and rack pushers—must unite together and fight for a decent hourly rate." A Garment Worker, "Truckmen Need Unity Too," *CD*, Apr. 1968, 8.

[20] "First of all, the pay is rock bottom. . . . A man worked for spot cash only. And not much of that. . . . The hours were killing and still are." "Selman's: 40 March Down to Union Hall," *CD*, Nov.-Dec. 1967, 6.

[21] EL, interview, 7 Aug. 1991.

[22] Luce, *America's Trojan Horse*, 54–65, 67–68; EL, interview, 7 Aug. 1991.

[23] Luce, *America's Trojan Horse*, 93.

[24] Steve Martinot, "Dubinsky Fights With Bosses—Against Workers!" *CD*, 4 July 1964, 6.

[25] "The New McCarthyism . . . History of Grand Jury Persecution," *PL* (Mar. 1965): 31.

[26] Steve Martinot, "Students and Liberalism," *PL* (Oct. 1965): 20.

[27] Ibid., 16.

[28] EL, interview, 7 Aug. 1991. In 1951, Lemansky's father (whose own father had been a Menshevik, and whose uncle had been a Bolshevik), was a Teachers Union activist and was fired from his position as a teacher at New York City's Boys High School for "insubordination" after refusing to answer questions about membership in the Communist Party. When Ed figured out in 1959 that his father had been in the CP and asked him about it, his father's first response was to retort, "What are you, McCarthy?" Ed's mother only admitted her CP membership to him when she was slightly inebriated (after drinking a beer). "Alright, I was; I was," she admitted, while the "Internationale" played. By joining PL, Lemansky could both emulate and rebel against his parents. Ibid.

[29] Ibid. Twelve thousand members of the Communist Party lived in Brooklyn in the late 1940s; they had a considerable number of children, a fair number of whom probably attended Antioch, whose student body numbered between 1,200 and 1,500 when Lemansky attended in the late 1950s and early 1960s. Ibid.

[30] Ibid. Lemansky was only able to graduate from High School in New York City because his parents insisted that he sign the required loyalty oath. Some time later, five students refused to sign the oath. Three of these students were admitted to Antioch even though they did not have high school diplomas, but only one actually attended. Oberlin, Swarthmore and Reed also accepted members of this group. Ibid.

[31] Ibid. "Horace Mann was the first president of the college, which, in 1920, adopted the cooperative, or study-plus-work plan which is now used at over one thousand colleges and universities. The quarter system is used with one summer term as a regular quarter and the regular schedule calls for a five-year program. . . ." *The College Blue Book: Narrative Desciptions,* 18th ed. (New York: Macmillan, 1981), 529.

[32] EL, interview, 7 Aug. 1991. "The National Association for the Advancement of Colored People (N.A.A.C.P.), founded in 1909 . . . worked to secure

legal recognition of Negro rights through the courts; its outstanding achievement was the Supreme Court's decision of 1954 ordering the desegregation of public schools." Keesing's Research Report 4, *Race Relations in the USA*, 3. "The *N.Y. Times* reported Mar. 20 [1960] that informal organizations to support Southern Negro students in their protests against lunch counter segregation had appeared in these 21 non-Southern colleges & universities: . . . Antioch College & Wilberforce University in Ohio. . . ." Lester A. Sobel, ed., *Civil Rights, 1960–63: The Negro Campaign to Win Equal Rights and Opportunities in the United States* (New York: Facts on File, 1964), 6. "The NAACP Feb. 11 and Apr. 20 issued 2 lists of a total of 32 non-Southern communities that it said had some form of segregated schooling." Ibid. 78. The 11 Febuary list included Cleveland, Ohio.

[33] EL, interview, 7 Aug. 1991. "For years America's best-known 'bright young socialist,' Harrington, inherited the mantle of Norman Thomas and Eugene Debs. Although never the leader of a large movement, he was the only socialist after 1960 whom many Americans could identify and trust." Maxine Phillips, "Harrington, Michael," in *Encyclopedia of the American Left*, ed. Buhle, 290–292. Stephen Jay Gould taught biology, geology and history of science at Harvard University for over twenty-five years and now teaches at New York University. He has written more than a dozen books; for example, see Stephen Jay Gould, *Eight Little Piggies: Reflections in Natural History* (New York: W. W. Norton, 1993).

[34] EL, interview, 7 Aug. 1991. "While never having more than 2,000 members, the SWP has sometimes enjoyed an influence far beyond its numbers in the labor and radical movements." Paul Le Blanc, "Socialist Workers Party," in *Encyclopedia of the American Left*, ed. Buhle, 727–729.

[35] EL, interview, 7 Aug. 1991. ". . . through the summer of 1960 and into early 1961, FPCC [Fair Play for Cuba Committee] evolved at a dizzying pace, with dozens of chapters formed in major cities and smaller college towns along the coasts and across the Mid-West. In the latter case, for example, not only did local Fair Play committees draw upon the Old-Left's remaining industrial sanctuaries in Chicago, Detroit and Cleveland, but students and political novices at schools like Antioch College in Yellow Springs, Ohio, the University of Michigan in Ann Arbor, Carelton College in Northfield, Minnesota, and Indiana University in Bloomington also jumped into the fray." Gosse, *Where the Boys Are*, 144. Although the FPCC was founded by Robert Taber, a CBS reporter, and Allen Sagner, a wealthy New Jersey contractor and reform Democrat, it's growth—in six months—from three local chapters to an organization "claiming 7,000 members in twenty-seven 'adult chapters' and forty Student Councils" was spurred by Taber's covert alliance with the SWP, which "provided organizational resources that FPCC lacked." Ibid., 138–147.

[36] EL, interview, 7 Aug. 1991. See Taylor Branch, *Parting the Waters: America in the King Years, 1954–63* (New York: Simon & Schuster, 1988), 451–491.

[37] EL, interview, 7 Aug. 1991. See Thomas, *The Cuban Revolution*, 577–606; and Gosse, *Where the Boys Are*, 203–254.

[38] EL, interview, 7 Aug. 1991. "A New Left then began slowly to take root, nourished by the pacifist and socialist British New Left of the Aldermaston Marches and the *New Left Review* . . . " Jack Newfield, *A Prophetic Minority*, cited in Gosse, *Where the Boys Are*, 4.

[39] "'New Left Clubs' sprang up on British campuses, and two journals, *The Reasoner* and *Universities and Left Review*, merged in 1960 into the *New Left Review*, intended to be the intellectual expression of the New Left Clubs." Paul Buhle, "New Left," in *Encyclopedia of the American Left*, ed. Buhle, 517.

[40] EL, interview, 7 Aug. 1991. Lemansky's parents had disavowed Stalin as well.

[41] Ibid.

[42] Ibid. ". . . one does not necessarily have to wait for a revolutionary situation; it can be created." Ernesto Guevara, *Guerrilla Warfare*, trans. by J. P. Morray (1961), 111, cited in Thomas, *The Cuban Revolution*, 258. W. E. B. Du Bois, *John Brown*, (Philadelphia, Pa.: G. W. Jacobs & Company, 1909). "In February 1953, a great crowd of Chinese at Peking greeted the arriving Dr. W. E. B. Du Bois, pre-eminent black American Scholar, pioneer Pan-African, and a founder of the National Association For the Advancement of Colored People. They sang 'John Brown's Body,' with its chorus of 'Glory, glory, hallelujah . . . his soul goes marching on. . . .' It was fitting enough that Du Bois was one of Brown's biographers and spiritual descendants, founding the Niagara Movement, predecessor of the N.A.A.C.P., at Harper's Ferry." Richard O. Boyer, *The Legend of John Brown: A Biography and a History* (New York: Alfred A. Knopf, 1973), 518. Lemansky was more impressed by Brown's idea of guerrilla warfare than Guevara's. "Subtitled 'An Independent Socialist Magazine,' *Monthly Review* is known worldwide within the Left as the key source of intellectual support for Third World liberation movements; as a point of origin of much of modern Marxian political economy; and as representing the most independent-minded version of Marxism to be found anywhere in the United States during the post-World War II era." John Bellamy Foster, "Monthly Review," in *Encyclopedia of the American Left*, ed. Buhle, 483–485. For Mao Tse-tung's writings, see *SWM*, 4 vols.

[43] EL, interview, 7 Aug. 1991.

[44] For example, see Everett K. Wilson, *Sociology: Rules, Roles, and Relationships* (Homewood, Ill.: Dorsey Press, 1966).

[45] For example, see Amos H. Hawley, *Human Ecology: A Theoretical Essay* (Chicago, Ill.: University of Chicago Press, 1986).

[46] EL, interview, 7 Aug. 1991. He had not abandoned the idea of a career in sociology, and his willingness to complete six months of work as a research assistant left open the possibility of his returning to graduate study at Michigan.

[47] "PL Hits JFK Aggression Against Cuba at U.N.," *PL* (Oct. 1962): 13. "However, a man who later identified himself as Milton Rosen, chairman of an organization he called Progressive Labor, of 799 Broadway, said he had been responsible for the pro-Castro, anti-Kennedy demonstration at the end of Dr. Dorticos's speech." *New York Times*, 9 Oct. 1962, repr. ibid. The story was also reported in Cuba. *"Detienen a Norteamericanos Simpatizantes de Cuba,"* *Hoy*, 9 Oct. 1962, repr. in *PL* (Jan. 1963): 12.

[48] "Socialist Labor Group Rallies," *Columbia Daily Spectator*, 26 Oct. 1962, repr. in *PL* (Nov. 1962): 4. "Progressive Labor sponsored a demonstration in Harlem Oct. 25 and a march from 125 St. and Seventh Ave. to the UN Oct. 27." *National Guardian*, 5 Nov. 1962, repr. ibid.; "PL Organizes Against U.S. Aggression," ibid., 3–4.

[49] EL, interview, 7 Aug. 1991. See "PL Organizes Against U.S. Aggression," *PL* (Nov. 1962): 3.

[50] EL, interview, 7 Aug. 1991. See Robert F. Williams, *Negroes With Guns*; Howard Zinn, *SNCC: The New Abolitionists* (Boston, Mass.: Beacon Press, 1965); and Clayborne Carson, *In Struggle: SNCC and the Black Awakening of the 1960s* (Cambridge, Mass.: Harvard University Press, 1995).

[51] Fred Jerome was a graduate of the City College of New York, where he edited a school newspaper; he later worked for *Newsweek*. "His father, V. J. Jerome, was formerly editor of *Political Affairs*, the CPUSA's theoretical organ, and remained a member of the CPUSA until his death in August of 1965. . . . V. J. Jerome was in reality Jerome Isaac Romain, and it is jokingly rumored that the initials 'V. J.' stood for J. V. (Stalin) spelled backwards." Fred Jerome was one of the founders of Advance, a CP youth organization in New York. He visited Cuba in 1960 and after his return, lived under an alias in Atlanta, Georgia. In 1965 he met with Che Guevara at the Cuban Mission to the UN. He edited *Challenge* and *Progressive Labor*, and was a member of PL's National Committee. His brother Carl organized for PL on New York City's Lower East Side. Luce, *America's Trojan Horse*, 73–74.

[52] Lemansky, Nakashima and Apter joined forces again in the latter half of the 1960s in New York City where they were part of PL's industrial concentration in the garment industry. Larry Phelps, a member of PLM's student group at the University of North Carolina in Chapel Hill (formed in August 1962), spent a few months with PLM's tiny band in Monroe. Phelps was subsequently stabbed to death by an unknown assailant in front of PLM's Harlem headquarters. EL, interview, 7 Aug. 1991. "Chapel Hill—A small group of University of North Carolina

students is organizing a 'Progressive Labor Club' aimed at developing a 'truly revolutionary national party based on improving the condition of the workers along Marxist-Leninist lines.' . . . Most of the members, who began meeting in June, are former members of the New Left Club, a discussion group 'for anyone left of Kennedy' . . . This group and one in Atlanta are the only two in the South. It has no formal organization at present, although spokesmen have been designated. One is Dennis King, 21, a university senior majoring in history. His father, Dr. A. K. King, is head of the University's summer school. Another member is Nick Bateson, 26, a graduate student in psychology from Oxford, England. His father is English literary critic F. W. Bateson, an Oxford instructor who is now a visiting professor at Penn State. . . . King says that there are about a dozen people in the group, most of them UNC students." Gary Blanchard, "UNC Students Form Labor Club Along Marxist Lines," *The Charlotte Observer*, 2 Aug. 1962, repr. in *PL* (Sept. 1962): 12. King's series on Lyndon LaRouche, which appeared in *Our Town*, was praised by New York's Senator Daniel Patrick Moynihan and was followed by a book, Dennis King, *Lyndon LaRouche and the New American Fascism* (New York: Doubleday & Company, 1989). "The N.C. Department of the American Legion Saturday urged trustees of the University of North Carolina to investigate a Progressive Labor Club at the Chapel Hill campus." Victor K. McElheny, "University Group Termed Atheistic," *Charlotte Observer*, 23 June, 1963, repr. in *PL* (Jul.-Aug. 1963): 15.

[53] "Population: 10,882; 29.3 per cent Negro." Capus M. Waynick, John C. Brooks and Elsie W. Pitts, eds., *North Carolina and the Negro* (Raleigh, N.C.: North Carolina Mayors' Co-operating Committee, 1964), 129. Relative to Greensboro (whose population was 123,334), for example, Monroe was a small town, whose civil rights struggle, consequently, did not involve large numbers of people. Its notoriety derived from Williams' advocacy of armed self-defense.

[54] Ibid.; Williams, *Negroes With Guns*, 50; EL, interview, 7 Aug. 1991. "'In North Carolina the Union sentiment was largely in the ascendant and gaining strength until Lincoln prostrated us,' wrote a bitter unionist." James M. McPherson, *The Battle Cry of Freedom: The Civil War Era* (New York: Ballantine Books, 1988), 277.

[55] Williams, *Negroes With Guns*, 50. "The Klans were busy in the piedmont region in central North Carolina, and when the realm split apart in 1927, information came to light of night riding in various parts of the state, as well as a large number of unreported floggings in Raleigh's Wake County. . . . With the Raleigh Klan disbanded, headquarters operations were shifted to Charlotte." David M. Chalmers, *Hooded Americanism: The History of the Ku Klux Klan* (New York: New Viewpoints, 1981), 94–97. "Mr. Daniel Moore, Governor of North Carolina, announced on Jan. 2, 1966, that he had appointed a committee of representatives of State agencies to wage an active campaign against the Klan. 'The

committee intends to first prevent violence and, second, to see that every resource will be used in tracking down and bringing to justice persons responsible
for violence in North Carolina.'" Keesing's Research Report 4, *Race Relations in
the USA*, 11. For an account of the murder of anti-Klan protestors (members of
the Communist Workers Party) in Greensboro, North Carolina, 3 Nov. 1979, see
Chalmers, *Hooded Americans*, 416–423.

[56] Williams, *Negroes With Guns*, 50. "The report [NAACP's annual report
for 1961] said NAACP membership had increased to 388,347 and its 1960 income had exceeded $1 million." Sobel, ed., *Civil Rights, 1960–63*, 62.

[57] Sobel, ed., *Civil Rights, 1960–63*, 53.

[58] Williams, *Negroes With Guns*, 50–64. To underscore the White community's resistance to giving blacks access to the pool, even for one day a week,
Williams indicated that the NAACP integrated the public library in 1957 "without any friction at all" (in contrast to Virginia and other Southern states where efforts to integrate libraries led to violence). Ibid., 51. However, a 1964 Mayor's
Better Citizenship Committee report maintained that "The library remains segregated. . . ." Waynick, ed., *North Carolina and the Negro*, 130. "Citizens Fire
Back at Klan," *Norfolk, Virginia Journal and Guide*, 12 Oct. 1957, 1, repr. in
Williams, *Negroes with Guns*, 56. According to Williams, only three Negro publications reported the incident: the *Afro-American*, the *Norfolk Journal and
Guide*, and *Jet Magazine*. Ibid., 57. However, in the 17 Jan. 1959 issue of *The
Nation*, George L. Weissman wrote, "The Klansmen found a veritable fortress. A
sandbagged line of defense protected the front and flanks; a heavy chain across a
side road prevented envelopment. Steel-helmeted men with rifles and shotguns
manned the defenses and when the Klansmen fired from the cars, the fire was returned. Not conditioned to this kind of reception, the motorcade ignominiously
took off. The example of standing up to the Klan appears in large measure to
have encouraged the Indians of nearby Robeson County weeks later, to meet the
KKK units with their celebrated counterattack." George L. Weissman, *The Nation* (17 Jan. 1959), cited in Camilo De Chispa (pseud.), "The Story They Won't
Tell: Murder in Monroe," *PL* (Jul.-Aug. 1962): 2.

[59] Williams, *Negroes With Guns*, 61–67.

[60] Ibid., 66–74; Marable, *Race, Reform and Rebellion*, 62; Also see Martin
Bauml Duberman, *Paul Robeson: A Biography* (New York: Ballantine Books,
1989); and Lamont H. Yeakey, "Paul Robeson," in *The American Radical*, eds.
Mari Jo Buhle, Paul Buhle and Harvey J. Kaye (New York: Routledge, 1994),
279–286.

[61] Williams, *Negroes With Guns*, 42–49.

[62] "By debasing and demoralizing the black man in small personal matters,
the system eats away the sense of dignity and pride which are necessary to challenge a racist system. But the fundamental core of racism is more than atmos-

phere—it can be measured in dollars and cents and unemployment percentages. We therefore decided to present a program that ranged from the swimming pool to jobs." Ibid., 75.

[63] Ibid., 75–84; Carson, *In Struggle*, 42–44.

[64] Williams, *Negroes With Guns*, 75–93. Also see: De Chispa, "The Story They Won't Tell: Murder in Monroe," *PL* (Jul.-Aug. 1962): 1; EL, "'Kidnap': Frame-up!" *PL* (Mar. 1964): 1; and Marable, *Race, Reform and Rebellion*, 62–63.

[65] Williams, *Negroes With Guns*, 84–90. The *Crusader* continued publication in Cuba and was sent to the U.S. through the Fair Play for Cuba Offices in Canada. Williams' daily broadcast from Cuba to Southern blacks were known as "Radio Free Dixie." The *Monthly Review* suggested that his "apocalyptic vision of violence may be nothing more than a nightmare," but Phillip Luce alleged that the Black Liberation Front was "formed in Cuba in 1964 by black nationalists who were members of the second 'student' trip to that island." Luce, *America's Trojan Horse*, 47–49. "RAM [Republic of New Africa] was organized in winter 1963, with Williams as leader-in-exile. It began to set up front organizations, such as Black Brotherhood Improvement Association, Black Liberation Front (1964), Jamaica Rifle and Pistol Club, Black Panther Party in N.Y.C. (August 1966), and Black Arts Repertory Theater, led by LeRoi Jones." U.S. News & World Report, *Communism and the New Left*, 100. However, Luce, in a June 1964 *Progressive Labor* article, claimed, "The trip last year had a special effect on the black people that went. Many of them were at the time Black Nationalists following what might be termed a simplistic anti-white attitude. The talks we had with Robert Williams coupled with the reality of the successful Cuban attempt to destroy racism created the framework in which these young people could return to the United States and involve themselves in political activity of a broader nature than anti-whiteism." Phillip Luce, "Students to Cuba—Bury Travel Ban," *PL* (June 1964): 16.

[66] Richard Crowder, "Raleigh Conference Snubs Negro Workers' Demands," *Freedom*, 15 July 1963, 1. "Sanford [North Carolina Governor Terry Sanford] met with about 125 Negro leaders June 25 [1963] to further his appeal [to end demonstrations and negotiate], but North Carolina NAACP leader Floyd McKissick of Durham later rejected the appeal and said: We seek nothing less than complete acceptance of Negroes as full first-class citizens of North Carolina." Sobel, *Civil Rights, 1960–63*, 124.

[67] "The Spirit of Robert Williams," *PL* (Mar. 1963): 5–6.

[68] "'We appreciate all the community has done so far,' Richard Crowder president of MYAC said, 'But the help has to keep coming. After all food does get eaten, and the gas gets burned, and it has to be replaced daily or we can't

carry on our work.'" "Freedom House Opens—Center of Activity," *Freedom*, 15 July 1963, 1. "But the ministers, realizing the depth of support for the action [a school boycott for integrated education], suddenly opened the doors of their churches to the meetings. Although the people thanked the ministers for this action, many roundly condemned them for taking too long." "A Freedom Lesson Out of School," *PL* (Sept. 1963): 15.

[69] EL, interview, 7 Aug. 1991.

[70] Ibid. Seventeen freedom riders came to Monroe in 1961 in order to support the local NAACP's struggle for "fundamental demands," such as the employment of "Negroes in skilled or supervisory capacities in the City Government." [This was part of Williams' ten point program.] "The community rented a house for them which was christened 'Freedom House' in their honor." Williams, *Negroes With Guns*, 75–78. "Freedom House, at 605 Brown Street, has been established as the headquarters of the MYAC with support in the form of food and money coming from the Negro community of Union County." "Monroe Youth Organize," *PL* (Jul.-Aug. 1963): 14. Also see "Freedom House Opens—Center of Activity," *Freedom*, 15 July 1963, 1.

[71] EL, interview, 7 Aug. 1991. ". . . the present average wage for domestic workers is $12.00 to $18.00 a week, in some cases with no social security payments." "Monroe Youth Organize," *PL* (Jul.-Aug. 1963): 14; Marti Moorer, "Domestic Workers Organize League for Jobs and Justice," *Freedom*, 15 Jul. 1963, 1, repr. ibid. The Women's League was active in nearby Pageland, South Carolina. "The tooth dentist of Pageland doesn't want to be patronized by any Negroes. How do I know? Because he is still sending us around to the back door." Mrs. Georgie Blakeney, Vice President, Chesterfield County Women's League, "Just Thinking. . . ." *Freedom*, n.d. [probably late 1963], 4. Also see: M. M. Blakeney, "For a Better Life," *Freedom*, 18 Apr. 1964, 5; "Monroe Youth Organize," *PL* (Sept. 1963): 15; and "Negroes Push Boycott at Monroe School," *The Charlotte News*, 3 Sept. 1963, 2A, repr. ibid. According to Ed Lemansky, local schools were desegregated after "a couple of months," but a Mayor's Better Citizenship Committee report in 1964 indicated that Monroe's schools were still segregated. Waynick, ed., *North Carolina and the Negro*, 130. "The first of a series of Welfare Clinics was held by Freedom House on Saturday, November 16, 1963 . . . attended by 30 families from Union County. . . . Freedom House's efforts to help people get on welfare has met with some success." "Welfare Department vs People's Welfare," *Freedom*, n. d. [probably late 1963], 3.

[72] EL, interview, 7 Aug. 1991.

[73] Waynick, ed, *North Carolina and the Negro*, 129.

[74] "A Freedom Lesson Out of School," *PL* (Sept. 1963): 15.

[75] EL, interview, 7 Aug. 1991.

[76] Ibid. "Freedom House is guarded and steps have been taken to prevent white inspired violence in the Negro community. . . . News of new attacks against the MYAC reached us as we were going to press. According to our Southern Editor, several MYAC organizers have been arrested, and the Klan elements in the area have tried to murder several others." "Monroe Youth Organize," *PL* (Jul.-Aug. 1963): 15. Also see "A Freedom Lesson Out of School," *PL* (Sept. 1963): 15–16.

[77] EL, interview, 7 Aug. 1991. The weapons, a .32 calibre pistol and a 7.35 rifle, had belonged to Robert Williams. "A Freedom Lesson Out of School," *PL* (Sept. 1963): 16.

[78] EL, interview, 7 Aug. 1991; "Monroe Youth Organize," *PL* (Jul.-Aug. 1963): 15–16; "Hoods Fail in Attempt to Kill MYAC Organizers; FBI Stalls; Negroes Organizing Self-Defense," *Freedom*, 15 Aug. 1963, 1, repr. ibid., 16.

[79] Williams, *Negroes with Guns*, passim.

[80] EL, interview, 7 Aug. 1991.

[81] Ibid. According to Lemansky, many of Monroe's White citizens regarded the town as progressive.

[82] Waynick, ed., *North Carolina and the Negro*, vii, 129–130.

[83] Editorial, *Freedom*, n.d. [probably late 1963], 1. "*Freedom*, a bi-weekly four page paper has begun to come out. More than 2,000 copies of the first issue [15 July 1963] were sold in the Negro community here, and it has also been distributed around the country." "Monroe Youth Organize," *PL* (Jul.-Aug. 1963): 14. *Freedom*'s masthead read, "Break thy slavery's want and dread. Bread is Freedom, Freedom bread!" *Freedom*, 15 July 1963, 1, repr. ibid.

[84] Editorial, *Freedom*, n.d. [probably late 1963], 1.

[85] "A Freedom Lesson Out of School," *PL* (Sept. 1963): 16.

[86] Williams, *Negroes With Guns*, 117–119.

[87] EL, interview, 7 Aug. 1991; *Freedom*, n.d. [probably late 1963], 1, 3. According to Phillip Luce, Williams travelled to China at least twice and wrote "extensively in support of the Chinese doctrine of violent world revolution" and called China's first A-bomb "a freedom bomb." When he returned to the United States, Williams was the nominal leader of the Republic of New Africa, which held that cooperation between black and White radicals was impossible, but subsequently changed his position and left the group. Luce, *America's Trojan Horse*, 49–50. The Republic of New Africa "was founded in March 1968 at the Shrine of the Black Madonna (Central United Church of Christ, Detroit, Michigan). About 190 signed a declaration of independence declaring all blacks 'forever free and independent of the jurisdiction of the United States.' Robert F. Williams, then in exile in Peking to avoid arrest on kidnapping charges, was named president; H. Rap Brown was later named minister of defense." U.S. News & World Report,

Communism and the New Left, 96. However, Williams did later recognize the jurisdiction of the United States. "Black Nationalist Robert F. Williams of Detroit has been testifying in secret for two days this week before the Senate Internal Security subcommittee about his activities here and abroad. . . . When Thurmond [Senator Strom Thurmond of N.C.] asked Williams if he was a communist, Williams said, 'No, I'm a black nationalist, but I welcome the support of anyone who wants to help me, even yours.'" Saul Friedman, "Senators Hear Black Leader in Secret," *Detroit Free Press*, repr. in *'Two Steps Forward'—PLP Internal Bulletin* (22 May 1970). Also see Tracy B. Strong and Helene Keyssar, *Right In Her Soul: The Life of Anna Louise Strong* (New York: Random House, 1983).

[88] EL, interview, 7 Aug. 1991. SNCC leader Bob Moses did graduate work at Harvard during the 1950s. Carson, *In Struggle*, 46. "Wendy and her parents lived in internment camps in California in the beginning of World War II." Luce, *The New Left*, 78. "Wendy Nakashima, Jake Rosen's wife, was associated with left-wing groups at CCNY [City College of New York] and had spent a month in Cuba in 1960." Luce, *America's Trojan Horse*, 66. ". . . Wendy Nakashima, a Progressive Labor recruit from the CP." Ibid., 74. Nakashima was one of the PLMers indicted by a Manhattan grand jury in connection with the Harlem Riots of July 1964; PLM identified her as "Wendy Nakashima, 24—Vice-Pres. of CCNY PLM club. She was in Atlanta during July and most of August 1964." "The New McCarthyism. . . . History of Grand Jury Persecution," *PL* (Mar. 1965): 31. Nakashima ran as an antiwar independent for the New York State Assembly in the 69th AD. *Challenge*, which covered her candidacy, provided a brief biography. "When a year-old infant in 1941, her family among thousands of Japanese-Americans, was placed in this country's first concentration camps—'internment camps the government calls them' she says with a wry smile. She spent the next three years of her life in these camps. . . . She grew up in New York City, danced professionally, but found time to visit revolutionary Cuba in 1961. . . . When she returned she joined the Progressive Labor Movement, 'to make the same kind of change in this country.' . . . went South to fight the semi-slavery. . . . She worked in North Carolina and in Atlanta with her husband, Jake Rosen, then a Southern organizer for the P.L.M. . . . she went back to City College and immediately became involved in campus struggles there. When she was called before a witch hunting Grand Gury attempting to frame Progressive Labor in connection with the Harlem rebellion, she refused to 'cooperate.' She then served thirty days in Civil Jail for 'contempt,' refusing to 'purge' herself by answering the D.A.'s loaded questions. . . . When released, she immediately immersed herself in the problems of the people on the West Side where she lives." Frank Scott, "Anti-War Independent," *CD*, 21 June 1966, 2. Also see: "N.Y. Candidates Against Viet War," *CD*, 4 Aug 1966, 4; Wendy Nakashima, "Appeal From

Prison," *CD*, 16 Mar. 1965, 4; and Walter Linder, "Rich Man's Jury—Poor Man's Jail," *CD*, 2 Mar. 1965, 3.

[89] EL, interview, 7 Aug. 1991. "Several Waveland papers suggested that the college backgrounds of SNCC workers hindered their efforts to develop self-confident leadership among poorly educated blacks." Carson, *In Struggle*, 142.

[90] EL, interview, 7 Aug. 1991. "He usually has firm faith in the God his white neighbor worships, and is his white neighbor's equal in loyalty to the American political creed." Waynick, ed., *North Carolina and the Negro*, 9.

[91] EL, interview, 7 Aug. 1991. "In 1962, as in 1961, he [Pesident John F. Kennedy] had refused to make civil rights a focal point of his administration.... Virtually all of the civil rights activism at the time centered in the South, and there even the modest efforts of the Kennedy Administration to enforce voting rights or protect demonstrators caused the President's popularity to decline." However, after Birmingham Police Commissioner Eugene "Bull" Connor "unleashed snarling police dogs" and "high-pressure hoses and electric cattle prods" against civil rights marchers in April and May 1963, and after Alabama Governor George Wallace "defied a federal court order by personally blocking the door to prevent two Negroes from registering at the University of Alabama" in June, Kennedy delivered [a television address, 11 June 1963] an "emotional plea for 'the nation to fulfill its promise.' . . . A week later, as he had promised, Kennedy sent his new civil rights proposal to Congress. . . . To his credit, once he had firmly committed himself to the cause of civil rights, the President met with literally thousands of people to urge their support. . . . Kennedy who was skeptical about the good that the march [the March on Washinton, 28 Aug. 1963] could accomplish and concerned that lawlessness by some of the demonstrators might start a riot and seriously alienate Congress, responded to the event without enthusiasm." Jim F. Heath, *Decade of Disillusionment: The Kennedy-Johnson Years* (Bloomington, Ind.: Indiana University Press, 1975), 109–115. "President Kennedy appeared by July to have changed his mind about the march. At his July 17 press conference he categorized the march as 'in the best tradition' of peaceable assembly 'for a redress of grievances.'" Sobel, ed., *Civil Rights, 1960–63*, 102.

[92] EL, interview, 7 Aug. 1991.

[93] Ibid.

[94] Williams, *Negroes With Guns*, 88–109; EL, "'Kidnap': Frame-up!" *PL* (Mar. 1964): 14.

[95] Williams, *Negroes With Guns*, 104. They were sentenced as follows: Mallory—16 to 20 years in prison; Crowder—7 to 10 years; Reape—5 to 7 years; and Lowery—3 to 5 years. EL, "'Kidnap': Frame-up!" *PL* (Mar. 1964): 14.

[96] Ibid.

[97] Ibid.; EL, interview, 7 Aug. 1991. "William M. Kunstler, who may be identical with the William Kunstler mentioned above, is a member of the firm Kunstler and Kunstler, 511 Fifth Avenue, New York City; has been attorney for the American Civil Liberties Union; and has, in the past, acted as the legal representative of several 'freedom riders' in Mississippi." Letter from J. Edgar Hoover to Kenneth P. O'Donnell, Special Assistant to the President, 7 Dec. 1962, repr. in *Martin Luther King, Jr.: The FBI File*, eds. Michael Friedly and David Gallen (New York: Carroll & Graf, 1993), 136–137. "All seven [the Chicago Seven], together with their lawyers (William Kunstler and Leonard Weinglass), were found guilty of contempt of court and were sentenced to prison terms ranging from one day in jail to a total of four years and thirteen days on twenty-four counts in the case of Kunstler." U.S. News & World Report, *Communism and the New Left*, 170. Also see William M. Kunstler with Sheila Isenberg, *My Life As a Radical Lawyer* (New York: Birch Lane Press, 1994).

[98] EL, interview, Aug. 7, 1991. "Carmichael exclaimed, 'They don't do the kind of work we do nor do they live in the areas we live in. They don't ride the highways at night.' He asserted that for King nonviolence was 'everything' but for SNCC it had always been simply a tactic. . . . Carmichael recalled that the discussion ended when he asked those carrying weapons to place them on the table. Nearly all of the black organizers working in the deep South were armed." Carson, *In Struggle*, 164.

[99] Carson, *In Struggle*, 183. "At a fall conference in Atlanta on October 14–16, 1960, SNCC attempted to consolidate the student protest movement by establishing an organizational structure and clarifying its goals and principles. . . . Among the leftist groups represented were the Socialist party and its youth wing, the Young People's Socialist League, the newly formed SDS, the Southern Christian Educational Fund (SCEF), and the Highlander Folk School, a training school for labor organizers." Ibid., 27–28.

[100] EL, interview, 7 Aug. 1991. Jake Rosen was a graduate of the City College of New York and was married to Wendy Nakashima. He had been a member of the CP, an organizer of the American delegation to the Moscow World Youth Conference in 1957 and also led an excursion to China (for which activities he was hanged in effigy at City College). In 1960 he worked with an international youth brigade in Cuba and during the summer of 1961, he lived under an alias in Augusta, Georgia. After being expelled from the CP, he was editor of *Freedom*, PL's southern newspaper, and southern editor of *Progressive Labor*. He became a member of PL's National Committee and organized PL's founding convention in April 1965. Luce, *America's Trojan Horse*, 74–75. Also see Thayer, *The Farther Shores of Politics*, 421. According to Ed Lemansky, Rosen wrote some of the radical passages that SNCC leader, John Lewis incorporated into his speech for the March on Washing-

ton in 1963, but which he deleted under pressure from moderate civil rights leaders; and Rosen later worked with SNCC leader Stokely Carmichael on the strategy
that created the Black Panther Party in Loundes County, Alabama. EL, interview, 7
Aug. 1991. Among other things omitted from his speech, Lewis was planning to
say, "The revolution is at hand, and we must free ourselves of the chains of political
and economic slavery. The nonviolent revolution is saying: '. . . we will take matters into our own hands and create a source of power, outside of any national structure, that could and would assure us a victory.'" "What John Lewis Did Not Say,"
National Guardian, repr. in *PL* (Sept. 1963): 14. For the full text of the speech that
Lewis intended to give, see Staughton Lynd, *Nonviolence in America: A Documentary History* (Indianapolis, Ind.: Bobbs-Merrill, 1966), 482–485. "King took this
opening to doubt, correctly, that the 'scorched earth' language was in fact Lewis'.
'John, I know you as well as anybody,' he said. 'That doesn't sound like you.'"
Branch, *Parting the Waters*, 879. According to Taylor Branch, James Forman in-
serted the controversial reference to Sherman's "scorched earth" policy ("We will
march through the South, through the heart of Dixie, the way Sherman did. We
shall pursue our own 'scorched earth' policy and burn Jim Crow to the ground—
nonviolently.") into Lewis' speech, which Branch characterized as a "collective
manifesto of SNCC's early years." Ibid., 873–874. Branch does not mention Rosen
as one of the several contributors to this manifesto. However, a piece by Lewis
which appeared in *Freedom* the following year argued that the "current revolution"
was at a "very critical period. . . . If we are to achieve a nonviolent victory the non-
violent movement must become radical enough with a positive program of action
to meet the needs, the aspirations, the longings of an oppressed people." *Freedom*,
18 Apr. 1964, 6. Also see Zinn, *SNCC*, 190–215; and Marable, *Race, Reform and
Rebellion*, 81–82. "Then Carmichael held up a picture of the symbol of the Loundes Freedom Organization and said, grinning, 'You ever see a panther? He can't be
tamed, and once he gets going, ain't nothing going to stop him!' . . . In April
[1966], the Loundes County Freedom Organization with its dramatic emblem of
the black panther, was officially organized." Ed Clark, Southern Editor, "Black
Panther's Power," *PL* (Oct.-Nov. 1966): 33–37. This article may have been written
by Jake Rosen, who Phillip Luce identified as PL's Southern Editor. For another account of Carmichael's activities in Loundes County, see Carson, *In Struggle*,
162–166. PL subsequently changed its position on Carmichael, the Black Panthers
and progressive nationalism. See: Bill Epton, "Stokely's Anti-Communism Bared,"
PL (Oct. 1968): 88–98; Bill Epton, Fred Jerome and Walt Reiley, "FBI-CP-SWP
Combo Tries Baiting the Panther Trap," *PL* (Aug. 1969): 14–22; Editorial, "Not a
Black Worker in Sight: Panthers Play to Empty House," *PL* (Nov. 1969): 3–5; and
Mortimer Scheer, "Nationalism Divides Workers," ibid., 6–18. Also see David
Hilliard and Lewis Cole, *This Side of Glory: The Autobiography of David Hilliard*

and the Story of the Black Panther Party (New York: Little, Brown & Company, 1993); and Stokely Carmichael and Charles V. Hamilton, *Black Power: The Politics of Liberation in America* (New York: Vintage Books, 1967). According to Lemansky, Carmichael "almost" came to Monroe at PLM's invitation. EL, interview, 7 Aug. 1991. Coincidentally, Carmichael testified before the Senate Internal Security Committee on the same day as Robert F. Williams. See note no. 87 in this chapter.

[101] EL, interview, 7 Aug. 1991. "Recognizing that they could not forestall the type of student militancy displayed in the freedom rides, Kennedy administration officials tried to persuade civil rights groups, including SNCC, to become more involved in voter registration work, which presumably would result in less intense white opposition. SNCC and other civil rights organizations sent representatives to a meeting with Robert Kennedy on June 16, 1961, where the attorney general suggested that the energies of the freedom ride campaign be directed toward the goal of registering southern blacks who had been disenfranchised through violence, intimidation, and more subtle methods such as literacy tests and poll taxes. Kennedy assured the activists that financial support for such projects would be made available by private foundations." Carson, *In Struggle*, 38–39.

[102] Ibid., 268–269.

[103] EL, interview, 7 Aug. 1991. According to Lemansky, PLM's publications and actions, rather than Jake Rosen, promoted progressive nationalism.

[104] Ibid.; "With the 84 Americans in Cuba," *PL* (Jul.-Aug. 1964): 16–17.

[105] EL, interview, 7 Aug. 1991. Apparently, there had been problems between Laub and Martinot during PLM's first Cuba trip in 1963.

[106] EL, interview, 15 Aug. 1991.

[107] Luce, *America's Trojan Horse*, 60. Ed Lemansky, in an interview with Alberto Perez of *Prensa Latina*, said, "We condemn the illegal espionage flights and North American aggressions against Cuba." Cited in "With 84 Americans in Cuba," *PL* (Jul.-Aug. 1964): 16.

[108] EL, interview, 15 Aug. 1991; Fred Jerome, "Washington Won't Touch Birmingham Killers, Steps Up Attacks On Students, PLM," *PL* (Oct.-Nov. 1963): 1. "For over five years, in fact—before we won—the Communists, when they didn't ignore us, were political rivals of our movement." C. Wright Mills, *Listen, Yankee: The Revolution in Cuba* (New York: Ballantine Books, 1961), 106. When Joseph Newman of the *New York Herald Tribune* visited Cuba and asked what name applied to the new Cuban society, he was told that the Cuban government and Revolution "were neither 'capitalist nor Communist' but simply 'Cuban and humanist.'" Leo Huberman and Paul M. Sweezy, *Cuba: Anatomy of a Revolution* (New York: Monthly Review Press, 1960), 145.

[109] "The New McCarthyism . . . History of the Grand Jury Persecution," *PL* (Mar. 1965): 25–36.

[110] EL, interview, 7 Aug. 1991.

[111] "The Cuban workers feel great love for their revolution, and desire to protect it from foreign invasion." Bonnie Flemming, "what I saw," *PL* (Oct.-Nov. 1963): 19–21. Flemming was a twenty-year-old premedical student at the University of California at Berkeley. "And when we went to a cooperative farm in Rosario, in the heartland of Cuba, we asked an administrator of the farm why he had been appointed instead of a farmer. When we learned that this administrator was merely appointed by the Cuban Farm Bureau because, according to him, he 'could be trusted,' we had a real session." Luce, *America's Trojan Horse*, 60–61.

[112] EL, interview, 7 Aug. 1991. "Castro has misused the great confidence bestowed on him by the people. He has taken the people into alliances with the most reactionary forces on earth. His one-man paternalistic rule smacks more of feudalism than socialism." Jake Rosen, "Is Cuba Socialist?" *PL* (Nov. 1969): 52–63. "In our Party, in the past, many of us too were strongly influenced by Che . . . Our attachment was subjective and romantic." Eric Johnson, "'Strike a Pose, *Companeros:'* Guevara's Great Adventure," *PL* (May 1969): 53–63.

[113] Judy Warden, "Cuba Ban Busters Back, Face HUAC Quiz," *CD*, 29 Aug. 1964, 2. Also see the statement of the eighty-four students who traveled to Cuba. Ibid.

[114] EL, interview, 7 Aug. 1991. According to Phillip Luce, Lemansky was arrested for "trying to strangle a policeman." Luce, *America's Trojan Horse*, 95.

[115] EL, interview, 7 Aug. 1991. "As we parted, I said to him [Lemansky], 'I'd like to ring you if there are any questions.' He answers, '. . . If I'm out of jail!'" Thayer, *The Farther Shores of Politics*, 421.

[116] "Build a Base," *PL* (June 1969), repr. in *RT*, 44; EL, interview, 7 Aug. 1991."He [Lemansky] claims that he has been in jail four times, the longest term for three months. He complained that over one hundred PLP members have been arrested and convicted of various offenses. 'We weren't guilty of anything,' he said. 'This is not a persecution complex; that's just the way the game is played here.'" Thayer, *The Farther Shores of Politics*, 421.

[117] EL, interview, 7 Aug. 1991.

[118] Ibid. For a discussion of Rosen and Scheer's role in the founding of PL, see Chapter 1 of the present study. Lemansky became a member of PLP's National Committee. PL's first attempts to implement its colonizing plan were not very successful. Steve Martinot had already secured employment in a steel mill in New Jersey but was fired. Ed Lemansky got a job as a shipping clerk in a book publishing company, but Milt Rosen told him that it was politically useless and asked

him to get a job in New York City's garment market. EL, interview, 15 Aug. 1991.
[119] EL, interview, 7 Aug. 1991.
[120] Ibid.
[121] Ibid.
[122] Ibid. "'My truck was broken into and robbed while I was making a delivery, so I got fired.' That is the story told to *Challenge* by a driver for one of New York's larger garment trucking companies." "I Was Robbed . . . So I Got Fired!" *CD*, Apr. 1969, 5. At Empire Carriers, prospective employees were given lie detector tests to assess their honesty. ". . . THEY'RE STEALING OUR LABOR from us—and WE have to take the lie detector tests about stealing." A Garment Worker, "Lie Detectors Don't Test Real Thieves—the Bosses," *CD*, Aug. 1967. At another garment trucking firm, management attempted, unsuccessfully, to install a television camera to "spy on the guys in the shop." A Garment Worker, "New Squeeze By Garment Bosses," *CD*, July 1967, 9.
[123] EL, interview, 15 Aug. 1991. ". . . Lemansky, for instance, a big, strapping fellow . . . " Thayer, *The Farther Shores of Politics*, 420.
[124] EL, interview, 15 Aug. 1991.

CHAPTER 6. COMMUNIST TRUCKERS BETWEEN A ROCK AND A HARD PLACE

[1] "Garment Union Hacks Are Clay Pigeons," *CD*, 21 Feb. 1974, 10.
[2] "ILGWU President Testifies," *JU*, 1 Sept. 1962, 1.
[3] Ibid., 1–2.
[4] Ibid., 9. Local 102's papers are not available at Local 102 (now Local 132–98–102), the ILGWU (now UNITE) or the Labor Relations Documentation Center at Cornell University.
[5] House Committee on Education and Labor, Congressman Herbert Zelenko's Subcommittee, Hearings on the Garment Industrey, Federal Court House, Manhattan, New York, 23 Aug. 1962, Fred Heinken, testimony, 118–127, 138–141; Louis D'Amato, testimony, ibid., 127–133, 138–141.
[6] Jack Borofsky, testimony, ibid., 133–138, 141–151; James Crombie, testimony, ibid., 151–166.
[7] David Dubinsky, testimony, ibid., 24 Aug. 1962, 220.
[8] Ibid., 190–191, 218–221, 250–259.
[9] "Garment's Union Hacks Are Clay Pigeons," *CD*, 21 Feb. 1974, 10.
[10] "Selman's: 40 March Down to Union Hall," *CD*, Nov.-Dec. 1967, 6.
[11] Ibid.
[12] Ibid.; "Who's Our Boss?" *CD*, Jan. 1968, 3; "Union 'Tries' Selman Stewards," *CD*, Feb. 1968, 6.

[13] Ibid.; "Brothers, Join Us," (Selman's Strike Committee leaflet, n.d.), repr. in *CD*, Jan. 1968, 3. Although most garment workers were women, the overwhelming majority of workers in garment trucking were men. *Challenge* often refers to them as "truckmen" or simply the "men" or "guys," and discusses them in terms of male roles and responses. It seems that the PL garment truckers who wrote these articles were imbued with a male ethos. How this affected their organizing in garment trucking is not clear, although it may have adversely affected PL's organizing efforts among the majority of garment workers, who were women.

[14] "Who's Our Boss?," *CD*, Jan. 1968, 3.

[15] Ibid.

[16] Ibid.

[17] Ibid.

[18] Ibid.; "Union 'Tries' Selman Stewards," *CD*, Feb. 1968, 6.

[19] "Union 'Tries' Selman Stewards," *CD*, Feb. 1968, 6.

[20] "Selman's: New Steward, Old Problems," *CD*, Mar. 1968, 8. Jackson subsequently became a Local 102 business agent and played a key role in defeating PL's efforts in garment trucking.

[21] "Selman's Fired Martinot," *CD*, May 1968, 11; "Selman's Rank-and-File Fight," *CD*, June-July 1968, 14; "Selman's Bosses and Union Leaders Gang Up" (leaflet, n.d.), repr. in *CD*, June-July 1968, 14.

[22] A Garment Worker, "City-Wide Trucking: Men Win Union Scale Demand," *CD*, Nov.-Dec. 1967, 6.

[23] Ibid.

[24] Ibid. The election of Lemansky as shop steward and the workers' initially negative view of Local 102 were only reported on much later in "Wildcat at City-Wide: But Gang-Up Beats Strike to Back Steward," *CD*, Dec. 1968, 6.

[25] "Truckers Fight Boss, Pie-Cards," *CD*, Jan. 1968, 2.

[26] Ibid.

[27] Ibid. "We can only achieve our complete freedom when we remember that we cannot stop fighting—because the bosses won't stop grabbing." A Garment Worker, "The Struggle Is Only Starting," ibid., 5. "We must remember that the unions do not belong to these sellouts. Unions belong to the rank and file. The fakes, the phonies, the finks run the unions today—lets take them back." "Bad Union? Join It, THEN Fight," *CD*, Feb. 1968, 8.

[28] "At City-Wide Trucking—Business Agent Talks a Good Game, But . . . ," *CD*, Mar. 1968, 8.

[29] Ibid.

[30] "City-Wide: 'Impartial' Against Us," *CD*, May 1968, 10.

[31] Ibid.

[32] Ibid.

[33] Ibid.

[34] Ibid.; "Arbitration Helps Boss Kill Struggle," *CD*, Jan. 1969, 13.

[35] "Wildcat at City Wide: But Gang-Up Beats Strike to Back Steward," *CD*, Dec. 1968, 6; EL, "City Wide Shop Notes," (leaflet, n.p., n.d.), which included the following disclaimer: "THIS IS NOT A UNION PUBLICATION - IT HAS BEEN PRINTED AND PAID FOR BY ME [Ed Lemansky]."; EL, "Fight Back At City Wide Against Garment Center Slavery!" (leaflet, n.p., n.d.).

[36] "Wildcat at City Wide: But Gang-Up Beats Strike to Back Steward," *CD*, Dec. 1968, 6.

[37] Ibid.

[38] Ibid.

[39] Ibid.; "Government Not Neutral—Backs Bosses Against Workers," *CD*, Jan. 1969, 13. Also see EL, "Real Communists Are Poison for the Bosses: Progressive Labor Party Builds Workers' Strength," ibid., 15.

[40] EL, "Real Communists Are Poison for the Bosses: Progressive Labor Party Builds Workers' Strength," *CD*, Jan. 1969, 15.

[41] Ibid.

[42] "Again Workers See Arbitration is Bosses' Game," *CD*, Dec. 1968, 6; "Arbitration Helps Boss Kill Struggle," *CD*, Jan. 1969, 13; Ruling by Herbert H. Pensig, Impartial Chairman & Arbitrator, 22 Nov. 1968.

[43] Letter, Local 102 to Edward Lemansky, 6 Nov. 1968, detailing charges against him and asking him to answer the charges on 13 Nov. 1968.

[44] EL, "We Accuse the Leaders of Local 102," (Garment Workers Action Committee leaflet, 13 Nov. 1968).

[45] "New Garment Trucking Contract in February," *CD*, Jan. 1970, 26; "Workers at Ideal Win," *CD*, Feb. 1970, 21.

[46] A Garment Worker, "Newmark Garment Workers Win," *CD*, Mar. 1970, 11. PL later identified its organizer at Newmark as Dave Davis. See "Garment Workers Invade Sellout's 'Trial' of PLP'er," *CD*, 1 Nov. 1970, 6.

[47] A Garment Worker, "Newmark Garment Workers Win," *CD*, Mar. 1970, 11.

[48] Ibid.

[49] "One Shop Learns from Another—Strikes Spread," *CD*, Apr. 1970, 11; EL, "Garment Workers Win 1st Round at United Marlboro Trucking," ibid., 10.

[50] EL, "Garment Workers Win 1st Round at United Marlboro Trucking," *CD*, Apr. 1970, 10; "ILGWU helps boss split shop by blocking rack-pushers' $," ibid.

[51] "U-M round 2: Pickets get 20 rehired; Rack-pushers $ open," *CD*, Apr. 1970, 10; "One shop learns from another—Strikes spread," *CD*, Apr. 1970, 11.

[52] "Garment Carriers - Striker Accuses ILG," *CD*, May 1970, 6.

[53] Ibid.

[54] EL, "ILG Hack Breaks Strike," *CD*, May 1970, 6.

[55] Ibid.

[56] EL, "Action Follows Previous Battles," *CD*, 1 Nov. 1970, 6.

[57] "Garment Workers Invade Sellout's 'Trial' of PLP'er," *CD*, 1 Nov. 1970, 6.

[58] Vance Fields, "Black garment worker says go all the way," *CD*, Aug. 1970, 10.

[59] PL believed that elections for union office were irregular. See "102 Circus," *CD*, Mar. 1968, 9.

CHAPTER 7 ANATOMY OF A COMMUNIST-LED WILDCAT STRIKE

[1] Felipe DeJesus, interview by the author, tape recording, New York City, 26 Mar. 1996. For DeJesus, a "worker-led strike" was one that neither the employer or the union could manipulate.

[2] Caute, *The Year of the Barricades*, xi. Also see, George Katsiaficas, *The Imagination of the New Left: A Global Analysis of 1968* (Boston, Mass.: South End Press, 1987).

[3] Manuel Maldonado-Denis, *Puerto Rico: A Socio-Historic Interpretation* (New York: Vintage Books, 1972), 250. Also see Karl Wagenheim and Olga Wagenheim, eds., *The Puerto Ricans: A Documentary History* (Garden City, N.Y.: Anchor Books, 1973), 69, 77–78.

[4] FD, interview, 26 Mar. 1996; Maldonado-Denis, *Puerto Rico*, 3.

[5] FD, interview, 26 Mar. 1996.

[6] Ibid.; Maldonado-Denis, *Puerto Rico*, 192.

[7] Maldonado-Denis, *Puerto Rico*, 189–209.

[8] Puerto Rican political scientist and independence advocate, Manuel Maldonado-Denis, arguing that Commonwealth status changed the form of U.S. control over Puerto Rico but not its substance, disparaged the "so-called" Commonwealth as the "supreme creation in the art of political mythology." Ibid.

[9] FD, interview, 26 Mar. 1996; Maldonado-Denis, *Puerto Rico*, 274–275. "She [Puerto Rican, Sandra Rodriguez speaking in Spanish at a PL garment rally in New York] asked why so many Puerto Ricans leave their own country to come to the United States. 'Because,' she said, 'they cannot get work.'" Mark Shapiro, "Garment Rally," *CD*, 8 Aug. 1964, 3. "The massive post-war exodus has been described by one of the most prominent of Puerto Rican demographers as 'one of the greatest exoduses of population registered by history.'" Maldonado-Denis, *Puerto Rico*, 315. "The Puerto Rican migration of the 1940s and 1950s became a forerunner of other movements from Caribbean nations. Puerto Ricans, as American citizens, were not technically immigrants; they had the right of unrestricted migration to the mainland. Among the factors contributing to this large migration after

World War II was cheap air fare between New York and San Juan." Reimers, *Still the Golden Door*, 128.

[10] FD, interview, 26 Mar. 1996.

[11] Ibid. For example, when striking sugar cane workers asked for nationalist help, "the nationalists, deeply involved in the struggle for independence, progressively diminished the aspect of social justice in their propaganda." Corretjer concluded, "It was a lapse, but an unfortunate one." Juan Antonio Corretjer, *La Lucha por la Independencia de Puerto Rico* (San Juan, P.R.: *Publicaciones de Union del Pueblo Constituyente*, 1950), 64, 70, quoted in Maldonado-Denis, *Puerto Rico*, 242.

[12] FD, interview, 26 Mar. 1996.

[13] Juan Antonio Corretjer, "Puerto Rico: A Strategy for Revolution," *PL* (Oct.-Nov. 1966): 101.

[14] Mark Shapiro, "Garment Rally," *CD*, 13 July 1965, 4.

[15] FD, interview, 26 Mar. 1996.

[16] Alice Jerome, "1001 Days and Nights on the Lower East Side," *PL* (Mar.-Apr. 1966): 33–38; "Integrated Workers Affiliates with PL" (Press Statement of the Integrated Workers Club of Progressive Labor, signed by Carl Jerome, President, Maria Quinones, Secretary, and Genoveva Clemente, Treasurer), repr. in *PL* (July-Aug. 1963): 5.

[17] FD, interview, 26 Mar. 1996; Jerome, "1001 Days and Nights," *PL* (Mar.-Apr. 1966): 38.

[18] FD, interview, 26 Mar. 1996.

[19] Ibid.

[20] Ibid.

[21] Ibid.; ". . . CHALLENGE-DESAFIO reporter Felipe de Jesus." "PLP Hits the Streets," *CD*, 13 July 1965, 4; "Felipe Dejesus, Editor of DESAFIO . . ." "Garment Workers Cheer Call to 'Get Out of Vietnam!' " *CD*, 21 June 1966, 5.

[22] FD, interview, 26 Mar. 1996.

[23] "PLP Hits the Streets," *CD*, 13 July 1965, 4. Also see "Garment Workers Cheer Attack on Dubinsky," *CD* 29 June 1965, 2.

[24] FD, interview, 26 Mar. 1996.

[25] "Garment Workers Cheer Call to 'Get Out of Vietnam!' " *CD*, 2 June 1966, 5. For a defense of the ILGWU's role in Puerto Rico, see Dubinsky's testimony before Congress, quoted in *JU*, 1 Sept. 1962, 8–9.

[26] FD, interview, 26 Mar. 1996.

[27] See Chapter 6 of the present study.

[28] FD, interview, 26 Mar. 1996.

[29] Ibid.

[30] Ibid.

[31] Ibid.

[32] Ibid.

[33] Ibid.; Walter Linder, "NY Garment Workers Fight and Beat ILGWU-Figure Flattery Co.," *PL* (Oct. 1968): 43. DeJesus recalled that at peak season Figure Flattery employed as many as three thousand workers, with three hundred in the shipping department alone, but no figures this large were reported by PL at the time.

[34] FD, interview, 26 Mar. 1996.

[35] Marcelino Lopez, "Figure Flattery Sweatshop," *CD*, Oct. 1968, 12; Walter Linder, "NY Garment Workers Fight and Beat ILGWU-Figure Flattery Co.," *PL* (Oct. 1968): 43.

[36] FD, interview, 26 Mar. 1996. Linder put the average wage at $61.00 a week. Linder, "NY Garment Workers Fight and Beat ILGWU-Figure Flattery Co., *PL* (Oct. 1968): 43. The three-year contract signed by Local 32 in 1966 provided for the following minimums, effective 1 January 1968: operators, $1.85 per hour; floor workers, $1.55 per hour; shipping clerks, $68.00 per week; cutters, $90.00 per week; and markers and graders, $100.00 per week. "In '32' Bra Terms Covering 6,000," *JU*, 1 Jan. 1966, 3. The average wage (difficult to calculate without more information), although quite modest, was probably somewhat higher than Linder reported. PLer Marcelino Lopez, who worked at the plant, reported that men started at $1.75 per hour and received only modest increases thereafter, receiving a 10c per hour increase, for example, after their two-month probation ended and they became union members. Women began at $1.60 per hour. But many workers never received any pay increases because they were laid off at the end of their probationary period. Lopez, "Figure Flattery Sweatshop," *CD*, Oct. 1968, 12.

[37] FD, interview, 26 Mar. 1996.

[38] Ibid.; Linder, "ILGWU-Figure Flattery Co.," *PL* (Oct. 1968): 43; Lopez, "Figure Flattery Sweatshop," *CD*, Oct. 1968, 12; Tyler, *Look for the Union Label*, 86–89.

[39] FD, interview, 26 Mar. 1996; Linder, "ILGWU-Figure Flattery Co.," *PL* (Oct. 1968): 43; Lopez "Figure Flattery Sweatshop," *CD*, Oct. 1968, 12; Tyler, *Look for the Union Label*, 54.

[40] FD, interview, 26 Mar. 1996. Grover A. Whalen, who mediated the ILGWU's general strike in the New York City dress industry in 1933, maintained, "Under the terms of the final agreement, the sweatshop is abolished. After all these years, there is sufficient force behind this agreement to wipe the word sweatshop forever out of the American language." Quoted in "35 Years Ago: Dress Strike Turned the Tide," *JU*, 15 Aug. 1968, 11. The Figure Flattery strike began a day before this edition of Justice came out. ". . . standards have been gradually raised and sweatshop conditions which existed in the industry's early days have been eliminated." Louis Stulberg, "NYC's $ Multi-Billion Apparel Trade," *Westsider*, fall 1968, repr. in *JU*, 1 Dec. 1968, 5.

[41] FD, interview, 26 Mar. 1996. Similar conditions probably existed at other shops. For example, a letter to *Challenge* from garment truck driver Louie Wilson described an incident that he witnessed at the Ajax Dress Co. on 35th St. Wilson observed the boss "tearing into the shop yelling and screaming 'where is no. 77, where is no. 77, what is she doing to me?'" The boss, confronting the woman worker "began shaking a blue piece of material in front of the woman's nose and began screaming about an extra stitch somewhere. The spit from the boss' mouth was spraying on the woman's face." "Worker Sees Woman Humiliated in Garment Shop," *CD*, May 1969, 8.

[42] FD, interview, 26 Mar. 1996.

[43] Ibid.; Linder, "ILGWU-Figure Flattery Co.," *PL* (Oct. 1968): 44.

[44] FD, interview, 26 Mar. 1996. "Allegations of 'discrimination' levelled at the ILGWU have been effectively refuted by a group of more than 500 Cuban refugees from Castro's tyranny." "500 Cuban Refugees in '155' Laud Equal Work, Earnings Opportunities," *JU*, 15 Sept. 1962, 4.

[45] "Figure Flattery is Outstanding for the Low Salaries They Pay Workers," (SDS leaflet, n.d.), repr. in *SDS Work-In 1968* (SDS pamphlet, n.d.), 9.

[46] Ibid.

[47] "Support Figure Flattery Strikers" (SDS leaflet, n.d.), repr. in *SDS Work-In 1968* (SDS pamphlet, n.d.), 10.

[48] FD, interview, 26 Mar. 1996; Linder, "ILGWU-Figure Flattery Co.," *PL* (Oct. 1968): 44.

[49] "Support Figure Flattery Strikers" (SDS leaflet, n.d.), repr. in *SDS Work-In: 1968* (SDS pamphlet, n.d.), 10.

[50] FD, interview, 26 Mar. 1996.

[51] Ibid.; "New York City's Apparel Industry, over the years, has succeeded in establishing a model pattern for peaceful labor relations. . . . Strikes are a rarity in organized shops." Stulberg, "NYC' $ Multi-Billion Apparel Trade," *Westsider*, repr. in *JU*, 1 Dec. 1968, 5.

[52] FD, interview, 26 Mar. 1996; Linder, "ILGWU-Figure Flattery Co.," *PL* (Oct. 1968): 44.

[53] FD, interview, 26 Mar. 1996.

[54] Ibid.; Tyler, *Look for the Union Label*, 273–274.

[55] FD, interview, 26 Mar. 1996; Linder, "ILGWU-Figure Flattery Co.," *PL* (Oct. 1968): 44. "Then you have Sabby Nahami [sic], one of our business agents that is the champion of the Spanish cause, of the Spanish people's cause. Most of his time he has to spend for the Government in Latin America and the same thing here what I told you about Edward Gonzalez." House Committee on Education and Labor, Congressman Herbert Zelenko's Subcommittee, Hearings on the Garment Industry, Federal Court House, Manhattan, New York, 24 Aug. 1962, David Dubinsky, testimony, 218. For the AFL-CIO's activities in Latin America, see

Ronald Radosh, *American Labor and United States Foreign Policy* (New York: Random House, 1969); and Fred Hirsch, "Our AFL-CIO Role in Latin America" (pamphlet, n.p., 1974). For background on the Latin American labor movement, see Victor Alba, *Politics and the Labor Movement in Latin America* (Stanford, Calif.: Stanford University Press, 1968).

[56] Linder, "ILGWU-Figure Flattery Co.," *PL* (Oct. 1968): 44.

[57] Ibid. According to Linder, the workers were fired with the agreement of the union.

[58] Ibid.; "Walkout Hits Girdle Plant," *Daily News*, 21 Aug. 1968, 88.

[59] Picture in *CD*, Sept. 1968, 1; picture in *CD*, Oct. 1968, 13.

[60] Linder, "ILGWU-Figure Flattery Co.," *PL* (Oct. 1968): 44.

[61] Ibid.

[62] Ibid.

[63] ". . . whom have we been recruiting? It is mainly teachers, welfare workers and students, independents and professionals. This is good and should increase. But whom have we NOT been recruiting? Industrial workers (except in rare instances)." "Improve our Base Building," repr. in *RT*, 72.

[64] Steering Committee, Chicago Work-In, "Work-In 1968: SDS Goes to the Factories," in *SDS Work-In* (SDS pamphlet, n.d.), 2; "SDS Work-In Active in Garment Center," *CD*, Sept. 1968, 4.

[65] "Walkout Hits Girdle Plant," *Daily News*, 21 Aug. 1968, 88; Kamensky, "Work-In Supports Garment Strike," in *SDS Work-In: 1968* (SDS pamphlet, n.d.), 12; FD, interview, 26 Mar. 1996.

[66] Victor Riesel, "SDS Spreads Revolt from Campus to Labor," 25 Sept. 1968, quoted in Dennis Kamensky, "Work-In Supports Garment Strike," in *SDS Work-In* (SDS pamphlet, n.d.), 14.

[67] Ibid., 12; "Workers' Unity in Garment Strike Beats Gang-Up of Bosses and ILGWU Leaders," (leaflet, n.p., n.d.) repr. ibid., 11–12; "Arthur Goldberg— Impartial Arbitrator?" (leaflet, n.p., n.d.) repr. in *CD*, Sept. 1968, 4. "Leaflets now being prepared [for distribution in the garment center] include one on ILGWU support of Humphrey and his line of more police in the ghettos (a high percentage of the ILGWU Black and Latin American membership lives in those ghettos), and another on the keynote speech at the ILGWU national convention last spring, which was given by Lyndon Johnson." "SDS Work-In Active in Garment Center," *CD*, Sept. 1968, 4. Apparently, members of the SDS Labor Committee, Lyndon LaRouche's group, distributed leaflets and sold their newspaper, *Solidarity*, at Figure Flattery on Friday, 13 August 1968, the day after the workers had won the strike. "Some SDS-ers Leech on Garment Strikers," *CD*, Sept. 1968, 4.

[68] Linder, "ILGWU-Figure Flattery Co.," *PL* (Oct. 1968): 48; Alfred Albelli, "Millionaire Files Suit," *Daily News*, 29 Aug. 1968, repr. in *CD*, Oct. 1968, 12;

"Workers' Unity in Garment Strike Beats Gang-Up of Bosses and ILGWU Leaders," (leaflet, n.d.), repr. in *SDS Work-In* (SDS pamphlet, n.d.), 11.

[69] Jeff Gordon, "SDS: An Analysis," *PL* (Oct. 1968): 99. Also see Adelson, *SDS*. This struggle finally came to a head at SDS's next annual convention in the summer of 1969, resulting in a disastrous split in the organization.

[70] Jared Israel and William Russel, "Herbert Marcuse and His Philosophy of Copout," *PL* (Oct. 1968): 59. For a discussion of "new working class" theory, see Calvert, *A Disrupted History*.

[71] Herbert Marcuse, *One Dimensional Man*, quoted in Kamensky, "Work-In Supports Garment Strike," in *SDS Work-In* (SDS pamphlet, n.d.), 13.

[72] Ibid., 13; Linder, "ILGWU-Figure Flattery Co.," *PL* (Oct. 1968): 46; FD, interview, 26 Mar. 1996.

[73] FD, interview, 26 Mar. 1996.

[74] Ibid.

[75] Ibid.

[76] Ibid.

[77] Kamensky, "Work-In Supports Garment Strike," in *SDS Work-In* (SDS pamphlet, n.d.), 13.

[78] "All Out Fight at Figure Flattery," *CD*, Feb. 1969, 6; FD, interview, 26 Mar. 1996.

[79] Linder, "ILGWU-Figure Flattery Co.," *PL* (Oct. 1968): 46.

[80] "Support Figure Flattery Strikers" (leaflet, n.p., n.d.), repr. in "Work-In Supports Garment Strike," in *SDS Work-In* (SDS pamphlet, n.d.), 11.

[81] Linder, "Workers Beat Gang-Up of Bosses," *CD*, Sept. 1968, 2.

[82] Linder, "ILGWU-Figure Flattery Co.," *PL* (Oct. 1968): 46–47.

[83] Ibid., 47.

[84] Ibid., 42–43.

CHAPTER 8. ANATOMY OF AN ANTICOMMUNIST PURGE

[1] Linder, "ILGWU-Figure Flattery Co.," *PL* (Oct. 1968): 47.

[2] Ibid., 43.

[3] "Continue the Struggle" (leaflet, n.p., 25 Sept. 1968), repr. in "Leaflet Fig.-Flattery: Workers Action Committee Calls on ILG Rank & File," *CD*, Oct. 1968, 13.

[4] Leaflet Fig.-Flattery," *CD*, Oct. 1968, 13.

[5] Max Goldenberg, "As I View It," *Corset and Brassiere Workers Bulletin*, Sept. 1968, repr. in *CD*, Nov. 1968, 12; FD, interview, 26 Mar. 1996.

[6] Goldenberg, "As I View It," *Corset and Brassiere Workers Bulletin*, Sept. 1968, repr. in *CD*, Nov. 1968, 12.

[7] Ibid.

[8] Ibid. Goldenberg did not address any of the other issues raised by the Workers Action Committee.

[9] FD, "Figure Flattery Steward Hits ILGWU Hack," *CD*, Nov. 1968, 12.

[10] Ibid.; "Since then [1940] minimums [in Puerto Rico] were raised. . . . This applies to the corset and brassiere industry. . . . " Dubinsky's testimony before Congress, quoted in *JU*, 1 Sept. 1962, 9.

[11] Dubinsky's testimony before Congress, quoted in *JU*, 1 Sept. 1962, 9.

[12] "Many employees are Puerto Ricans . . . and currently Figure Flattery employs 800 people, expecting to increase its personnel by 200 more by the end of the year." *El Diario–La Prensa*, 11 Apr. 1968, quoted in "Figure Flattery Steward Hits ILGWU Hack," *CD*, Nov. 1968, 12.

[13] Ibid.

[14] "ALL Out Fight at Figure Flattery," *CD*, Feb. 1969, 6.

[15] "'War on Poverty' Supplies Goons for War on Poor," *CD*, Feb. 1969, 7; Pancho Lopez, "El Tiempo Backs ILGWU Sellouts," *CD*, Feb. 1969, 8.

[16] Lopez, "El Tiempo Backs ILGWU Sellouts," *CD*, Feb. 1969, 8.

[17] *El Tiempo*, 26 Dec. 1968, quoted in Pancho Lopez, "El Tiempo Backs ILGWU Sellouts," *CD*, Feb. 1969, 8.

[18] Ibid.

[19] Ibid.

[20] Ibid.

[21] "13% Raise for 6,500 in '32' Corset, Bra Pact," *JU* 1 Jan. 1969, 3. The three-year contract provided for a 7% raise in January 1969 and an additional 6% in July 1970. Effective 1 July 1970, the minimums were as follows: floor workers, $2.00 per hour; shipping clerks, $2.43 per hour; and operators, $2.30 per hour.

[22] Ibid.

[23] FD, interview, 26 Mar. 1996.

[24] *El Tiempo*, 26 Dec. 1968, quoted in Lopez, "El Tiempo Backs ILGWU Sellouts," *CD*, Feb. 1969, 8.

[25] Ibid. In addition to the editorial already discussed, a number of articles by William Rivera about the Figure Flattery Strike appeared in *El Tiempo*. *Challenge* alleged that "The bosses gave *El Tiempo* reporters free run of the shop to harass workers," and accused *El Tiempo* of printing "vicious lies about the 'nice relations' between the workers and the bosses, 'disturbed' only by 'outside agitator' DeJesus." "All out Fight at Figure Flattery," *CD*, Feb. 1969, 6. According to George Alamo, a WAC activist, these *El Tiempo* articles criticized DeJesus and other Figure Flattery workers. Alamo characterized Rivera as a "newspaper flunkey," and *El Tiempo* as a "scandal sheet." George Alamo, "Parade of Traitors at Figure Flattery," *CD*, May 1969, 8.

[26] Alamo, "Parade of Traitors at Figure Flattery," *CD*, May 1969, 8.

[27] FD, interview, 26 Mar. 1996; "Battle On at Figure Flattery," *CD*, Jan. 1969, 1; "All Out at Figure Flattery," *CD*, Feb. 1969, 6; Francisco Rosario, "An Inside View of Fig. Flattery Fight," ibid., 7; Alamo "Parade of Traitors at Figure Flattery," *CD*, May 1969, 8.

[28] "All Out Fight at Figure Flattery," *CD*, Feb. 1969, 6.

[29] Ibid.

[30] Ibid.

[31] Ibid.

[32] Alamo, "Parade of Traitors at Figure Flattery," *CD*, May 1969, 8; "War on Poverty Supplies Goons for War on the Poor," *CD*, Feb. 1969, 7; Francisco Rosario, "An Inside View of Fig. Flattery Fight," ibid.

[33] Alamo, "Parade of Traitors at Figure Flattery," *CD*, May 1969, 8.

[34] "All Out Fight at Figure Flattery,"*CD*, Feb. 1969, 6.

[35] Alamo, "Parade of Traitors at Figure Flattery," *CD*, May 1969, 8.

[36] "'War on Poverty' Supplies Goons for War on Poor," *CD*, Feb. 1969, 7.

[37] Ira Perelson, "Hundreds of NY Students Join Fig. Flattery Fight," *CD*, Feb. 1969, 28.

[38] Ibid.; "S.F. State—New High in 1 Student Rebellion," *CD*, Jan. 1969, 1.

[39] "'War on Poverty' Supplies Goons for War on Poor," *CD*, Feb. 1969, 7.

[40] Ibid.

[41] "All Out Fight at Figure Flattery," *CD*, Feb. 1969, 6.

[42] Ibid.

[43] Ibid.

[44] Francisco Rosario, "An Inside View of Fig. Flattery Fight," *CD*, Feb. 1969, 7.

[45] Ibid.

[46] Ibid.

[47] Ibid.

[48] Ibid.

[49] "All Out Fight at Figure Flattery," *CD*, Feb. 1969, 6.

[50] *CD*, Feb. 1969, 6.

[51] FD, interview, 26 Mar. 1996.

[52] Ibid.

Selected Bibliography

Note: This study is based on newspapers, periodicals, pamphlets, leaflets, internal party documents, testimony before congressional committees, and tape-recorded interviews by the author, as well as on dissertations, papers and books. The author made extensive use of his own collection of documents, borrowed additional material from Edward Lemansky of Brooklyn, New York, and found the remainder of his sources in the Tamiment Library and Robert Wagner, Jr. Labor Archives at New York University's Bobst Library, whose many resources were indispensable. All these sources are fully cited in the endnotes. The selected bibliography that follows is limited to some of the books, dissertations and papers that the author found useful.

Adelson, Alan. *SDS.* New York: Charles Scribner's Sons, 1972.

Alha, Victor. *Politics and the Labor Movement in Latin America.* Stanford, Calif.: Stanford University Press, 1968.

Allison, Graham T. *Essence of Decision: Explaining the Cuban Missile Crisis.* Boston, Mass.: Little, Brown & Company, 1971.

Anderson, Terry H. *The Movement and the Sixties.* New York: Oxford University Press, 1995.

Andors, Stephen. *China's Industrial Revolution: Politics, Planning, and Management, 1949 to the Present.* New York: Pantheon Books, 1977.

Arendt, Hannah. *The Origins of Totalitarianism.* San Diego, Calif.: Harcourt, Brace Jovanovich, 1979.

Aronowitz, Stanley. *False Promises: The Shaping of American Working Class Consciousness.* New York: McGraw-Hill, 1973.

———. *Working Class Hero: A New Strategy For Labor*. New York: The Pilgrim Press, 1983.

Asher, Robert and Ronald Edsforth, eds. *Autowork*. Albany, N.Y.: State University of New York Press, 1995.

Auletta, Ken. *The Streets Were Paved With Gold*. New York: Vintage Books, 1980.

Baldassare, Mark, ed. *Cities and Urban Living*. New York: Columbia University Press, 1983.

Barbash, Jack, ed. *Unions and Union Leadership: Their Human Meaning*. New York: Harper & Brothers, 1959.

Baritz, Loren, ed. *The American Left: Radical Political Thought in the Twentieth Century*. New York: Basic Books, 1971.

Barkin, Solomon. *The Decline of the American Labor Movement and What Can Be Done About It*. Santa Barbara, Calif.: Center for the Study of Democratic Institutions, 1961.

Bell, Daniel. *The End of Ideology: On the Exhaustion of Political Ideas in the Fifties*. 1960. Rev. ed., New York: Collier Books, 1961.

———. *Marxian Socialism in the United States*. Princeton, N.J.: Princeton University Press, 1967.

Bellush, Jewel and Bernard Bellush. *Union Power and New York: Victor Gotbaum and DC 37*. New York: Praeger, 1984.

——— and Stephen M. David, eds. *Race and Politics in New York City: Five Studies in Policy-Making*. New York: Praeger, 1971.

——— and Dick Netzer, eds. *Urban Politics: New York Style*. Armonk, N.Y.: M. E. Sharpe, 1990.

Benin, Leigh David. "Radicals in the Real World: The Social Service Employees Union and the Limits of the New Radicalism of the 1960s." Ph.D. seminar paper, New York University, 1987.

Berdyaev, Nicolas. *The Origins of Russian Communism*. 1937. Reprint translated from the Russian by R. M. French. Ann Arbor, Mich.: The University of Michigan Press, 1987.

Berezhkov, Valentin M. *At Stalin's Side: His Interpreter's Memoirs From the October Revolution to the Fall of the Dictator's Empire*. Translated by Sergei V. Mikheyev. New York: Birch Lane Press, 1994.

Bernard, Richard M., ed. *Snowbelt Cities: Metropolitan Politics in the Northeast and Midwest Since World War II*. Bloomington, Ind.: Indiana University Press, 1990.

Bernstein, Eduard. *Cromwell and Communism: Socialism and Democracy in the Great English Revolution* (in German). 1895, 1930. Reprint, translated by H. J. Stenning. New York: Schocken Books, 1963.

Bernstein, Irving. *A Caring Society: The New Deal, the Worker, and the Great Depression*. Boston, Mass.: Houghton Mifflin, 1985.

Berry, Brian J. L. *America's Utopian Experiments: Communal Havens from Long-Wave Crises*. Hanover, N.H.: University Press of New England, 1992.

Billington, James H. *Fire in the Minds of Men: Origins of the Revolutionary Faith*. New York: Basic Books, 1980.

Blackwell, William L. *The Industrialization of Russia: An Historical Perspective,* 2nd ed. Arlington Heights, Ill.: Harlan Davidson, 1982.

Blau, Francine D. and Marianne A. Ferber. *The Economics of Women, Men and Work*. Englewood Cliffs, N.J.: Prentice Hall, 1986.

Bloom, Alexander. *Prodigal Sons: The New York Intellectuals and Their World*. New York: Oxford University Press, 1986.

Bok, Derek C. and John T. Dunlop. *Labor and the American Community*. New York: Simon & Schuster, 1970.

Bookman, Ann and Sandra Morgen, eds. *Women and the Politics of Empowerment*. Philadelphia, PA.: Temple University Press, 1988.

Bouchier, David. *Idealism and Revolution: New Ideologies of Liberation in Britain and the United States*. London: Edward Arnold, 1978.

Bourne, Randolph S. *War and the Intellectuals: Collected Essays, 1915-1919*. Edited with an introduction by Carl Resek. New York: Harper & Row, 1964.

Boyer, Richard O. *The Legend of John Brown: A Biography and a History*. New York: Alfred A. Knopf, 1973.

Branch, Taylor. *Parting the Waters: America in the King Years, 1954-63* New York: Simon & Schuster, 1988.

Breines, Wini. *Community and Organization in the New Left, 1962-1968: The Great Refusal*. South Hadley, Mass.: J. F. Bergin Publishers, 1982.

Brody, David. *Workers in Industrial America: Essays on the Twentieth Century Struggle*. New York: Oxford University Press, 1980.

———. *In Labor's Cause: Main Themes on the History of the American Worker*. New York: Oxford University Press, 1993.

———, ed. *The American Labor Movement*. New York: Harper & Row, 1971.

Browder, Earl. *The People's Front*. New York: International Publishers, 1938.

Buhle, Mari Jo, Paul Buhle, and Dan Georgakas, eds. *Encyclopedia of the American Left*. Urbana, Ill.: University of Illinois Press, 1992.

———, Paul Buhle, and Harvey J. Kaye, eds. *The American Radical*. New York: Routledge, 1994.

Buhle, Paul. *Marxism in the United States: Remapping the History of the American Left*. London: Verso, 1987.

——— and Alan Dawley, eds. *Working for Democracy: American Workers From the Revolution to the Present*. Urbana, Ill.: University of Illinois Press, 1985.

Calvert, Greg and Carol Neiman. *A Disrupted History: The New Left and The New Capitalism*. New York: Random House, 1971.

Cantor, Milton. *The Divided Left: American Radicalism, 1900-1975.* New York: Hill & Wang, 1978.

Carmichael, Stokely and Charles V. Hamilton. *Black Power: The Politics of Liberation in America.* New York: Vintage Books, 1967.

Carpenter, Jesse Thomas. *Competitive and Collective Bargaining in the Needle Trades, 1910-1967.* Ithaca, N.Y.: New York State School of Industrial and Labor Relations, Cornell University, 1972.

Carr, E. H. *The Bolshevik Revolution, 1917-1923,* vol. 1. Hamondsworth, Middlesex, Eng.: Penguin Books, 1966.

———. *Twilight of the Comintern, 1930-1935.* New York: Pantheon Books, 1982.

Carson, Clayborne. *In Struggle: SNCC and the Black Awakening of the 1960s.* Cambridge, Mass.: Harvard University Press, 1995.

Caute, David. *The Great Fear: The Anti-Communist Purge Under Truman and Eisenhower.* New York: Simon & Schuster, 1978.

———. *The Year of the Barricades: A Journey Through 1968.* New York: Harper & Row, 1988.

Central Committee of the C.P.S.U. (B.). *History of the Communist Party of the Soviet Union (Bolsheviks): Short Course, 1939 Edition.* Reprint. San Francisco, Calif.: Proletarian Publishers, no date.

Chafe, William H. *The Unfinished Journey: America Since World War II.* New York: Oxford University Press, 1986.

Chalmers, David M. *Hooded Americanism: The History of the Ku Klux Klan.* New York: New Viewpoints, 1981.

Charlton, Michael and Anthony Moncrieff. *Many Reasons Why: The American Involvement in Vietnam.* New York: Hill & Wang, 1978.

Charney, George. *A Long Journey.* Chicago, Ill.: Quadrangle Books, 1972.

Cioran, E. M. *History and Utopia* (in French). 1960. Translated by Richard Howard. New York: Seaver Books, 1987.

Clark, Gordon L. *Unions and Communities Under Siege: American Communities and the Crisis of Organized Labor.* Cambridge, Eng.: Cambridge University Press, 1989.

Clecak, Peter. *America's Quest for the Ideal Self: Dissent and Fulfillment in the 60s and 70s.* New York: Oxford University Press, 1983.

Cochran, Bert. *Labor and Communism: The Conflict that Shaped American Unions.* Princeton, N.J.: Princeton University Press, 1977.

———, ed. *American Labor in Midpassage.* New York: Monthly Review, 1959.

Cohen, Marcia. *The Sisterhood: The True Story of the Women Who Changed the World.* New York: Simon & Schuster, 1988.

The College Blue Book: Narrative Descriptions. 18th Edition. New York: Macmillan, 1981.

Conlin, Joseph. *The Troubles: A Jaundiced Glance Back at the Movement of the 1960's*. New York: Franklin Watts, 1982.

Cooke, Alistair. *Alistair Cooke's America*. New York: Alfred A. Knopf, 1973.

Coony, Terry A. *The Rise of the New York Intellectuals: Partisan Review and Its Circle, 1934-1945*. Madison, Wis.: University of Wisconsin Press, 1986.

Corretjer, Juan Antonio. *La Lucha por la Independencia de Puerto Rico*. San Juan, P.R.: *Publicaciones de Union del Pueblo Constituyente*, 1950.

Coye, Molly Joel and John Livingston, eds. *China Yesterday and Today*. Toronto, Can.: Bantam Books, 1979.

Cragg, Gerald R. *Freedom and Authority: A Study of English Thought in the Early Seventeenth Century*. Philadelphia, Pa.: The Westminster Press, 1975.

Crankshaw, Edward. *Khrushchev: A Career*. New York: Viking Press, 1966.

Crowe, Kenneth C. *Collision: How the Rank and File Took Back the Teamsters*. New York: Charles Scribner's Sons, 1993.

Cummings, Bernice and Victoria Schuck. *Women Organizing: An Anthology*. Metuchen, N.J.: The Scarecrow Press, 1979.

Daniels, Roger. *Concentration Camps USA: Japanese Americans and World War II*. Hinsdale, Ill.: The Dryden Press, 1971.

Danish, Max D. *The World of David Dubinsky*. Cleveland, Ohio: The World Publishing Company, 1957.

Davis, Mike. *Prisoners of the American Dream: Politics and the Economy in the History of the U.S. Working Class*. London: Verso, 1986.

De George, Richard T. *Patterns of Soviet Thought: The Origins and Development of Dialectical and Historical Materialism*. Ann Arbor, Mich.: University of Michigan Press, 1966.

Denker, Joel. *Unions and Universities: The Rise of the New Labor Leader*. Montclair, N.J.: Allanheld, Osmun, 1981.

Derber, Charles, William Schwartz and Yale Magrass. *Power in the Highest Degree: Professionals and the Rise of the New Mandarin Order*. New York: Oxford University Press, 1990.

Dewey, John. *David Dubinsky: A Pictorial Biography*. New York: Inter-Allied Publications, 1951.

Diggins, John Patrick. *The Rise and Fall of the American Left*. New York: W. W. Norton, 1992.

Dinnerstein, Leonard. *Antisemitism in America*. New York: Oxford University Press, 1994.

Djilas, Milovan. *The New Class: An Analysis of the Communist System*. New York: Frederick A. Praeger, 1957.

———. *Conversations With Stalin* (in Serbo-Croat). Translated by Michael B. Petrovich. New York: Harcourt, Brace & World, 1962.

————. *The Unperfect Society: Beyond the New Class*. New York: Harcourt, Brace, & World, 1969.

Drachkovitch, Milorad M., ed. *Marxism in the Modern World*. Stanford, Calif.: Stanford University Press, 1965.

Draper, Theodore. *The Roots of American Communism*. New York: Viking Press, 1957.

————. *Castro's Revolution: Myth and Reality*. New York: Frederick A. Praeger, 1962.

————. *Present History: On Nuclear War, Detente, and Other Controversies*. New York: Random House, 1983.

————. *American Communism and Soviet Russia: The Formative Period*. New York: Vintage Books, 1986.

————. *A Present of Things Past: Selected Essays*. New York: Hill & Wang, 1990.

Duberman, Martin Bauml. *Paul Robeson: A Biography*. New York: Ballantine Books, 1989.

Dubinsky, David and A. H. Raskin. *David Dubinsky: A Life with Labor*. New York: Simon & Schuster, 1977.

Dubofsky, Melvyn, ed. *American Labor Since the New Deal*. Chicago, Ill.: Quadrangle Books, 1971.

Du Bois, W. E. B. *John Brown*. Philadelphia, Pa.: G. W. Jacobs & Company, 1909.

Durkheim, Emile. *Socialism* (in French). Reprint, edited by Alvin W. Gouldner from an edition originally edited by Marcel Mauss. New York: Collier Books, 1962.

Dutt, R. Palme. *Fascism and Social Revolution: A Study of the Economics and Politics of the Extreme Stages of Capitalism in Decay*. 1934. Reprint, San Francisco, Calif.: Proletarian Publishers, 1974.

Edwards, Stewart. *The Paris Commune 1871*. Chicago, Ill.: Quadrangle Books, 1971.

Eisenstein, Zillah R., ed. *Capitalist Patriarchy and the Case For Socialist Feminism*. New York: Monthly Review Press, 1979.

Evans, Sara M. *Personal Politics: The Roots of Women's Liberation in the Civil Rights Movement & the New Left*. New York: Vintage Books, 1980.

————. *Born for Liberty: A History of Women in America*. New York: The Free Press, 1989.

Fanon, Frantz. *The Wretched of the Earth* (in French). 1961. Translated by Constance Farrington. New York: Grove Press, 1963.

————. *A Dying Colonialism* (in French). 1959. Translated by Haakori Chevalier. New York: Grove Press, 1965.

Fantasia, Nick. *Cultures of Solidarity: Consciousness, Action and Contemporary American Workers*. Berkeley, Calif.: University of California Press, 1988.

Fawcett, Edmund and Tony Thomas. *The American Condition.* New York: Harper & Row, 1982.

Fink, Leon and Brian Greenberg. *Upheaval in the Quiet Zone: A History of Hospital Workers' Union, Local 1199.* Urbana, Ill.: University of Illinois Press, 1989.

Fischer, George, ed. *The Revival of American Socialism: Selected Papers of the Socialist Scholars Conference.* New York: Oxford University Press, 1971.

FitzGerald, C. P. *Mao Tse-Tung and China.* Hammondsworth, Middlesex, Eng.: Penguin Books, 1977.

Fitzpatrick, Sheila. *The Russian Revolution, 1917-1932.* Oxford, Eng.: Oxford University Press, 1984.

Foner, Philip S. *The Black Panthers Speak.* Philadelphia, Pa.: Lippincott, 1970.

———. *American Labor and the Indo-China War: The Growth of Union Opposition.* New York: International Publishers, 1971.

———. *Organized Labor and the Black Worker, 1619-1973.* New York: Praeger, 1974.

———. *Women and the American Labor Movement.* New York: The Free Press, 1980.

Form, William. *Divided We Stand: Working Class Stratification in America.* Urbana, Ill.: University of Illinois Press, 1985.

Forman, James. *The Making of Black Revolutionaries: A Personal Account.* New York: Macmillan, 1972.

Foster, William Z. *American Trade Unionism: Principles and Organization, Strategy and Tactics.* New York: International Publishers, 1947.

———. *History of the Three Internationals: The World Socialist and Communist Movements from 1848 to the Present.* New York: Greenwood Press, 1968.

Franklin, H. Bruce, ed. *From the Movement Toward Revolution.* New York: Van Nostrand Reinhold, 1971.

Freeman, Joshua B. *In Transit: The Transport Workers Union in New York City, 1933-1966.* New York: Oxford University Press, 1989.

Friedland, Roger. *Power and Crisis in the City: Corporations, Unions and Urban Policy.* New York: Schocken Books, 1983.

Friedly, Michael and David Gallen, eds. *Martin Luther King, Jr.: The FBI File.* New York: Carroll & Graf, 1993.

Frisch, Michael H. and Daniel J. Walkowitz, eds. *Essays on Labor, Community, and American Society.* Urbana, Ill.: University of Illinois Press, 1983.

Gerassi, John, ed. *The Coming of the New International: A Revolutionary Anthology.* New York: The World Publishing Company, 1971.

Geschwender, James A. *Class, Race and Worker Insurgency: The League of Revolutionary Black Workers.* Cambridge, Eng.: Cambridge University Press, 1977.

Ginger, Ann Fagan and David Christiano, eds. *The Cold War Against Labor.* 2 vols. Berkeley, Calif.: Meiklejohn Civil Liberties Institute, 1987.

Gitlin, Todd. *The Sixties: Years of Hope, Days of Rage.* Toronto, Can.: Bantam Books, 1987.

Gittings, John. *The World and China, 1922–1972.* New York: Harper & Row, 1974.

Glazer, Nathan. *American Judaism.* Chicago, Ill.: University of Chicago Press, 1972.

Gollobin, Ira. *Dialectical Materialism: Its Laws, Categories, and Practice.* New York: Petras Press, 1986.

Gornick, Vivian. *The Romance of American Communism.* New York: Basic Books, 1977.

Gosse, Van. *Where the Boys Are: Cuba, Cold War America and the Making of a New Left.* London: Verso, 1993.

Gould, Stephen Jay. *Eight Little Piggies: Reflections in Natural History.* New York: W. W. Norton, 1993.

Gould, William B. *Black Workers in White Unions: Job Discrimination in the United States.* Ithaca, New York: Cornell University Press, 1977.

Goulden, Joseph C. *Meany.* New York: Antheneum, 1972.

———. *Jerry Wurf: Labor's Last Angry Man.* New York: Antheneum, 1982.

Graham, Stephen. *Stalin: An Impartial Study of the Life and Work of Joseph Stalin.* 1931. Reprint. Port Washington, N.Y.: Kennikat Press, 1970.

Graubard, Stephen R. *Kissinger: Portrait of a Mind.* New York: W. W. Norton, 1974.

Gray, Jack, and Patrick Cavendish. *Chinese Communism in Crisis: Maoism and the Cultural Revolution.* New York: Praeger, 1968.

Green, Gil. *The New Radicalism: Anarchist or Marxist?* New York: International Publishers, 1971.

———. *What's Happening to Labor.* New York: International Publishers, 1976.

———. *The World of the Worker: Labor in Twentieth Century America.* New York: Hill & Wang, 1980.

Green, James R., ed. *Workers Struggles Past and Present: An American Reader.* Philadelphia: Temple University Press, 1983.

Grey, Ian. *Stalin: Man of History.* Garden City, N.Y.: Doubleday & Company, 1979.

Gruber, Helmut, ed. *International Communism in the Era of Lenin.* Garden City, N.Y.: Doubleday & Company, 1972.

Guarasci, Richard. *The Theory and Practice of American Marxism, 1957-1970.* Lanham, Md.: University Press of America, 1980.

Guest, David. *A Textbook of Dialectical Materialism.* New York: International Publishers, 1939.

Guevara, Ernesto. *Che Guevara Reader: Writings by Ernesto Che Guevara on Guerrilla Strategy, Politics and Revolution.* Edited by David Deutschmann. Melbourne, Australia: Ocean Press.1997 (in Spanish). Translated by J. P. Murray. 1961.

Hall, Burton, ed. *Autocracy and Insurgency in Organized Labor*. New York: E. P. Dutton, 1972.

Hall, Gus. *Working Class USA: The Power and the Movement*. New York: International Publishers, 1987.

Hamilton, Edith, and Huntington Cairns, eds. *Plato: The Collected Dialogues*. New York: Pantheon Books, 1961.

Handlin, Oscar. *American Jews: Their Story*. New York: Anti-Defamation League of B'nai B'rith, 1972.

Harrington, Michael. *The Other America: Poverty in the United States*. New York: The Macmillan Company, 1962.

Harris, Barbara J. *Beyond Her Sphere: Women and the Professions in American History*. Westport, Conn.: Greenwood Press, 1978.

Hawley, Amos H. *Human Ecology: A Theoretical Essay*. Chicago, Ill.: University of Chicago Press, 1986.

Hayden, Tom. *Reunion: A Memoir*. New York: Random House, 1988.

Hayes, T. Wilson. *Winstanley the Digger: A Literary Analysis of Radical Ideas in the English Revolution*. Cambridge, Mass.: Harvard University Press, 1979.

Heath, Jim F. *Decade of Disillusionment: The Kennedy-Johnson Years*. Bloomington, Ind.: Indiana University Press, 1975.

Hechsler, Charles C. *The New Unionism: Employee Involvement in the Changing Corporation*. New York: Basic Books, 1988.

Helfgot, Roy B. *Made in New York: Case Studies in Metropolitan Manufacturing*. Cambridge, Mass.: Harvard University Press, 1959.

Herring, George C. *America's Longest War: The United States and Vietnam, 1950-1975*. New York: Alfred A. Knopf, 1979.

Hevener, John W. *Which Side Are You On?: The Harlan County Coal Miners, 1931-1939*. Urbana, Ill.: University of Illinois Press, 1978.

Hicks, John and Robert Tucker, eds. *Revolution & Reaction: The Paris Commune, 1871*. Boston, Mass.: Massachusetts University Press, 1973.

Higgins, Hugh. *Vietnam*. London: Heinemann, 1975.

Hilliard, David and Lewis Cole. *This Side of Glory: The Autobiography of David Hilliard and the Story of the Black Panther Party*. New York: Little, Brown & Company, 1993.

Hodgson, Godfrey. *America in Our Time*. New York: Vintage Books, 1976.

Hongqi [Red Flag]. *More on the Differences Between Comrade Togliatti and Us*. Peking: Foreign Languages Press, 1963.

Hook, Sidney. *From Hegel to Marx: Studies in the Intellectual Development of Karl Marx*. Ann Arbor, Mich.: University of Michigan Press, 1962.

Hoover, J. Edgar. *A Study of Communism*. New York: Holt Rinehart & Winston, 1962.

Hopkins, George W. *The Miners For Democracy: Insurgency in the United Mine Workers of America, 1970-1972.* University of North Carolina Press, 1976.

Horne, Alistair. *The Fall of Paris: The Siege and the Commune, 1870–71.* New York: St. Martin's Press, 1965.

Hosking, Geoffrey. *The First Socialist Society: A History of the Soviet Union from Within.* Cambridge, Mass.: Harvard University Press, 1992.

Howe, Irving. *Beyond the New Left.* New York: McCall Publishing, 1970.

Huberman, Leo and Paul M. Sweezy. *Cuba: Anatomy of a Revolution.* New York: Monthly Review Press, 1960.

Hudson, G. F. *Fifty Years of Communism: Theory and Practice, 1917-1967.* New York: Basic Books, 1968.

Hunnius, Gerry, G. David Garson and John Case, eds. *Workers' Control: A Reader on Labor and Social Change.* New York: Vintage Books, 1973.

Hyland, William G., ed. *The Reagan Foreign Policy.* New York: Meridian, 1987.

Isserman, Maurice. *If I Had A Hammer: The Death of the Old Left and the Birth of the New Left.* Urbana, Ill.: University of Illinois Press, 1987.

Jacobs, Dan N. and Hans H. Baerwald, eds. *Chinese Communism: Selected Documents.* New York: Harper & Row, 1963.

Jacobs, Paul. *The State of the Unions.* New York: Atheneum, 1963.

Jacobson, Julius, ed. *The Negro and the Labor Movement.* Garden City, N.Y.: Anchor Books, 1968.

Jaworskyj, Michael, ed. *Soviet Political Thought: An Anthology.* Baltimore, Md.: The Johns Hopkins University Press, 1967.

Jenkins, J. Craig. *The Politics of Insurgency: The Farm Worker Movement in the 1960s.* New York: Columbia University Press, 1985.

Johnson, Haynes and Nick Kotz. *The Unions.* New York: Pocket Books, 1972.

Johnson, Hewlett. *The Soviet Power: The Socialist Sixth of the World.* New York: International Publishers, 1940.

Joll, James. *The Second International: 1889-1914.* New York: Harper & Row, 1966.

Kahan, Stuart. *The Wolf of the Kremlin.* New York: William Morrow & Company, 1987.

Karnow, Stanley. *Vietnam: A History.* New York: The Viking Press, 1983.

Katsiaficas, George N. *The Imagination of the New Left: A Global Analysis of 1968.* Boston, Mass.: South End Press, 1987.

Kaufman, Jonathan. *Broken Alliance: The Turbulent Times Between Blacks and Jews in America.* New York: Charles Scribner's Sons, 1988.

Keesing's Research Report 4. Race Relations in the USA, 1954–1968. New York: Charles Scribner's Sons, 1970.

Kelly, John. *Trade Unions and Socialist Politics.* London: Verso, 1988.

Kennan, George F. *Russia and the West Under Lenin and Stalin*. Boston, Mass.: Little, Brown, & Company, 1961.

Kerry, Tom. *Workers, Bosses, and Bureaucrats: A Socialist View of the Labor Movement in the 1930's*. New York: Pathfinder Press, 1980.

Kim, M. P., et al. *The History of the USSR: The Era of Socialism*. Moscow: Progress Publishers, 1974.

King, Dennis. *Lyndon LaRouche and the New American Fascism*. Garden City, N.Y.: Doubleday & Company, 1989.

Klehr, Harvey. *Communist Cadre: The Social Background of the American Communist Party Elite*. Stanford, Calif.: Hoover Institution Press, 1978.

———. *The Heyday of American Communism: The Depression Decade*. New York: Basic Books, 1984.

——— and John Earl Haynes. *The American Communist Movement: Storming Heaven Itself*. New York: Twayne Publishers, 1992.

Koch, Stephen. *Double Lives: Spies and Writers in the Secret Soviet War Against the West*. New York: The Free Press, 1994.

Koedt, Anne, Ellen Levine and Anita Rapone, eds. *Radical Feminism*. New York: Quadrangle, 1973.

Kreps, Juanita M. *Women and the American Economy: A Look to the 1980's*. Englewood Cliffs, N.J.: Prentice-Hall, 1976.

Kunstler, William M. with Sheila Isenberg. *My Life as a Radical Lawyer*. New York: Birch Lane Press,1994.

Labor Research Association. *Labor Fact Book 16*. New York: International Publishers, 1963.

La Botz, Dan. *Rank and File Rebellion: Teamsters For a Democratic Union*. London: Verso, 1990.

Lader, Lawrence. *Power on the Left: American Radical Movements Since 1946*. New York: W. W. Norton & Company, 1979.

Laqueur, Walter. *The Fate of the Revolution: Interpretations of Soviet History from 1917 to the Present*. New York: Charles Scribner's Sons, 1987.

Lasch, Christopher. *The Agony of the American Left*. New York: Alfred A. Knopf, 1969.

Lash, Scott. *The Militant Worker: Class and Radicalism in France and America*. Rutherford, N.J.: Fairleigh Dickinson University Press, 1984.

Laslett, John H. M. and Seymour Martin Lipset, eds. *Failure of a Dream? Essays in the History of American Socialism*. Berkeley, Calif.: University of California Press, 1974.

Laurentz, Robert. "Racial/Ethnic Conflict in the New York City Garment Industry, 1933-1980." Ph.D. dissertation, State University of New York at Binghamton, 1980.

Leiserson, William M. *American Trade Union Democracy*. New York: Columbia University Press, 1959.

Lenin, V. I. *Lenin on the Revolutionary Proletarian Party of a New Type*. Peking: Foreign Languages Press, 1960.

———. *V. I. Lenin: Selected Works*. (in Russian) 3 vols. Moscow: Progress Publishers, 1975.

———. *On Trade Unions: A Collection of Articles and Speeches*. Moscow: Progress Publishers, 1970.

Lens, Sidney. *The Crisis of American Labor*. New York: A. S. Barnes & Company, Inc., 1961.

———. *Unrepentant Radical: An American Activist's Account of Five Turbulent Decades*. Boston, Mass.: Beacon Press, 1980.

Lenz, Elinor and Barbara Meyerhoff. *The Feminization of America: How Women's Values are Changing Our Public and Private Lives*. Los Angeles, Calif.: Jeremy P. Tarcher, 1985.

Lerner, Max. *America As A Civilization: Life and Thought in the United States Today*. New York: Simon & Schuster, 1957.

Levy, Peter B. *The New Left and Labor in the 1960s*. Ubana, Ill.: University of Illinois Press, 1994.

Lewis, John Wilson, ed. *Major Doctrines of Communist China*. New York: W. W. Norton, 1964.

Lewy, Guenter. *The Cause That Failed: Communism in American Political Life*. New York: Oxford University Press, 1990.

Lifton, Robert Jay. *The Future of Immortality and Other Essays for a Nuclear Age*. New York: Basic Books, 1987.

Lightfoot, Claude M. *Ghetto Rebellion to Black Liberation*. New York: International Publishers, 1968.

Linden, Carl A. *Khrushchev and the Soviet Leadership, 1957-1964*. Baltimore, Md.: The Johns Hopkins Press, 1966.

Lipset, Seymour Martin. *Rebellion in the University*. Boston, Mass.: Little, Brown & Company, 1971.

Litwack, Leon. *The American Labor Movement*. Englewood Cliffs, N.J.: Prentice-Hall, 1962.

Lozovsky, A. [pseud.]. *Marx and the Trade Unions*. Westport, Conn.: Greenwood Press, 1976.

Luce, Phillip Abbott. *The New Left*. New York: David McKay Company, Inc., 1966.

———. *The New Left Today: America's Trojan Horse*. Washington, D.C.: The Capital Hill Press, 1971.

Lynd, Alice and Staughton Lynd. *Rank and File: Personal Histories by Working Class Organizers*. Boston, Mass.: Beacon Press, 1973.

Lynd, Staughton. *Nonviolence In America: A Documentary History.* Indianapolis, Ind.: Bobbs-Merrill, 1966.

Maier, Mark. *City Unions: Managing Discontent in New York City.* New Brunswick, N.J.: Rutgers University Press, 1987.

Maldonado-Denis, Manuel. *Puerto Rico: A Socio-Historic Interpretation.* New York: Vintage Books, 1972.

Mao Tse-tung. *Selected Works of Mao Tse-Tung.* 4 vols. (in Chinese). Peking: Foreign Languages Press, 1960.

Marable, Manning. *Race, Reform and Rebellion: The Second Reconstruction in Black America, 1945-1982.* Jackson, Miss.: University Press of Mississippi, 1984.

Marcuse, Herbert. *One Dimensional Man.* Boston, Mass.: Beacon Press, 1964.

Marx, Herbert L., Jr., ed. *American Labor Unions: Organization, Aims, and Power.* New York: H. W. Wilson, 1950.

Marx, Karl. *Writings of the Young Marx on Philosophy and Society.* Edited and translated by Loyd D. Easton and Kurt H. Guddat. Garden City, N.Y.: Doubleday & Company, 1967.

———— and Frederick Engels. *Selected Works.* New York: International Publishers, 1968.

Mason, Daniel and Jessica Smith, eds. *Lenin's Impact On the United States.* New York: NWR Publications, 1970.

Matusow, Allen J. *The Unraveling of America: A History of Liberalism in the 1960's.* New York: Harper Torchbooks, 1986.

McLellan, David. *Marxism After Marx: An Introduction.* London: PAPERMAC, 1980.

McLoughlin, William G. *Revivals, Awakenings, and Reform: Essays on Religion and Social Change in America, 1607-1977.* Chicago, Ill,: University of Chicago Press, 1978.

McPherson, James M. *The Battle Cry of Freedom: The Civil War Era.* New York: Ballantine Books, 1988.

Medvedev, Roy A. *Let History Judge: The Origins and Consequences of Stalinism.* New York: Vintage Books, 1973.

Mendes, Richard. "The Professional Union: A Study of the Social Service Employees Union of the N.Y.C. Department of Social Services." Ph.D. dissertation, Columbia University, 1974.

Metzger, Norman and Dennis D. Pointer. *Labor-Management Relations in the Health Services Industry: Theory and Practice.* Washington, D.C.: Science & Health Publications, Inc., 1972.

Michels, Robert. *Political Parties: A Sociological Study of the Emergence of Leadership, the Psychology of Power, and the Oligarchic Tendencies of*

Organization. 1915. Reprint, translated by Eden and Cedar Paul. New York: Dover Publications, 1959.

———. *Roberto Michels' First Lectures in Political Sociology* (in Italian). *1927.* Reprint, translated by Alfred de Grazia. New York: Harper & Row, 1965.

Miller, James. *Democracy in the Streets: From Port Huron to the Seige of Chicago.* New York: Simon & Schuster, 1988.

Millett, Kate. *Sexual Politics.* Garden City, N.Y.: Doubleday & Company, 1970.

Mills, C. Wright. *Listen, Yankee: The Revolution in Cuba.* New York: Ballantine Books, 1960.

———. *Power, Politics and People: The Collected Essays of C. Wright Mills.* Edited by Irving Louis Horowitz. New York: Ballantine Books, 1963.

———. *C. Wright Mills and the Power Elite.* Compiled by G. William Domhoff and Hoyt B. Ballard. Boston, Mass.: Beacon Press, 1969.

———. *The New Men of Power: America's Labor Leaders.* 1948. Reprint, New York: August M. Kelly, 1971.

Milton, David and Nancy Dall Milton. *The Wind Will Not Subside: Years in Revolutionary China, 1964-1969.* New York: Pantheon Books, 1976.

———, Nancy Milton, and Franz Schurmann, eds. *People's China: Social Experimentation, Politics, Entry Onto the World Scene, 1966 through 1972.* New York: Vintage Books, 1974.

Mitchell, Juliet. *Woman's Estate.* New York: Random House, 1973.

Moody, J. Carroll and Alice Kessler-Harris. *Perspectives on American Labor History: The Problems of Synthesis.* DeKalb, Ill.: Northern Illinois University Press, 1989.

Moody, Kimberly. *An Injury to All: The Decline of American Unionism.* London: Verso, 1988.

Moore, Barrington, Jr. *Injustice: The Social Basis of Obedience and Revolt.* White Plains, N.Y.: M. E. Sharpe, 1978.

Morton, Henry W., and Rudolf L. Tokes, eds. *Soviet Politics and Society in the 1970's.* New York: The Free Press, 1974.

Mosca, Gaetano. *The Ruling Class* (in Italian). 1896. Reprint, edited and revised by Arthur Livingston. Translated by Hannah D. Kahn. New York: McGraw-Hill, 1939.

Moses, John A. *Trade Union Theory from Marx to Walesa.* New York: Berg, 1990.

Murphy, Kenneth. *Retreat From the Finland Station: Moral Odysseys in the Breakdown of Communism.* New York: The Free Press, 1992.

Murphy, Marjorie. *Blackboard Unions: The AFT and the NEA, 1900-1980.* Ithaca, N.Y.: Cornell University Press, 1990.

National Advisory Commission on Civil Disorders. *Report of the National Advisory Commission on Civil Disorders.* New York: Bantam Books, 1968.

Navasky, Victor S. *Naming Names*. Middlesex, Eng.: Penguin Books, 1981.

Nelson, Truman. *The Right of Revolution*. Boston, Mass.: Beacon Press, 1968.

Newfield, Jack and Wayne Barrett. *City For Sale: Ed Koch and the Betrayal of New York*. New York: Harper & Row, 1988.

———— and Paul Du Brul. *Permanent Government: Who Really Runs New York?* New York: Pilgrim Press, 1981.

Nove, Alec. *An Economic History of the U.S.S.R.* Revised edition. Hamondsworth, Middlesex, Eng.: Penguin Books, 1982.

O'Neill, William L. *Coming Apart: An Informal History of America in the 1960's*. Chicago, Ill.: Quadrangle Books, 1971.

————, ed. *American Society Since 1945*. Chicago, Ill.: Quadrangle Books, 1969.

Oppenheimer, Martin. *White Collar Politics*. New York: Monthly Review Press, 1985.

Oxford Analytica. *America in Perspective*. Boston, Mass.: Houghton Mifflin, 1986.

Parenti, Michael. *The Anti-Communist Impulse*. New York: Random House, 1969.

Parmet, Robert S. *Richard Nixon and His America*. Boston, Mass.: Little, Brown & Company, 1990.

Payne, Robert. *The Rise and Fall of Stalin*. New York: Avon Books, 1966.

Pfaff, William. *The Wrath of Nations: Civilization and the Furies of Nationalism*. New York: Simon & Schuster, 1993.

Phillips, William, ed. *Partisan Review: The 50th Anniversary Edition*. New York: Stein & Day, 1985.

Polenberg, Richard. *One Nation Divisible: Class, Race, and Ethnicity in the U.S. Since 1938*. New York: Penguin, 1980.

Powers, Richard Gid. *Not Without Honor: The History of American Anticommunism*. New York: The Free Press, 1995.

Progressive Labor Party. *Revolution Today: U.S.A: A Look at the Progressive Labor Movement and the Progressive Labor Party*. New York: Exposition Press, 1970.

Rabinowitch, Alexander. *The Bolsheviks Come to Power: The Revolution of 1917 in Petrograd*. New York: W. W. Norton, 1978.

Radosh, Ronald. *American Labor and United States Foreign Policy*. New York: Random House, 1969.

Rappoport, Louis. *Stalin's War Against the Jews: The Doctor's Plot and the Soviet Solution*. New York: The Free Press, 1990.

Ravitch, Diane. *The Great School Wars: New York City, 1805-1973: A History of Public Schools as Battlefield of Social Change*. New York: Basic Books, 1974.

Record, Wilson. *The Negro and the Communist Party*. New York: Atheneum, 1971.

Reimers, David M. *Still the Golden Door: The Third World Comes to America.* New York: Columbia University Press, 1985.

Reynolds, Larry T. and James M. Henslin, eds. *American Society: A Critical Analysis.* New York: David McKay, 1973.

Reynolds, Morgan O. *Power and Privilege.* New York: Universe Books, 1984.

Rosenblum, Gerald. *Immigrant Workers: Their Impact on American Labor Radicalism.* New York: Basic Books, 1973.

Rowbotham, Sheila. *The Past Is Before Us: Feminism in Action Since the 1960s.* Boston, Mass.: Beacon Press, 1989.

Ruth, Robert Douglass. "A Study of the Factors Affecting Teacher Attitudes and Participation in the New York City Decentralization Controversy." Ph.D. dissertation, Duke University, 1974.

Sagan, Carl and Richard Turco. *A Path Where No Man Thought: Nuclear Winter and the End of the Arms Race.* New York: Random House, 1990.

Sale, Kirkpatrick. *SDS.* New York: Random House, 1973.

Schell, Orville. *Mandate of Heaven: A New Generation of Entrepreneurs, Dissidents, Bohemians, and Technocrats Lays Claim to China's Future.* New York: Simon & Schuster, 1994.

Schub, David. *Lenin: A Biography.* Baltimore, Md.: Penguin Books, 1966.

Schulkind, Eugene, ed. *The Paris Commune of 1871: The View From the Left.* New York: Grove Press, 1974.

Seale, Bobby. *Seize the Time: The Story of the Black Panther Party and Huey P. Newton.* New York: Vintage Books, 1970.

Seifert, Roger V. *Teacher Militancy: A History of Teacher Strikes, 1896-1967.* London: The Falmer Press, 1987.

Selsam, Howard. *What is Philosophy? A Marxist Introduction.* New York: International Publishers, 1939.

———. *Philosophy in Revolution.* New York: International Publishers, 1957..

Shaffer, Lynda. *Mao and the Workers.* Armonk, N.Y.: M. E. Sharpe, 1982.

Shefter, Martin. *Political Crisis/Fiscal Crisis: The Collapse and Revival of New York City.* New York: Basic Books, 1985.

Shirokov, M. *Textbook of Marxist Philosophy* (in Russian). Leningrad Institute of Philosophy, 1937. Reprint. Chicago, Ill.: Proletarian Publishers, 1978.

Sitkoff, Harvard. *The Struggle for Black Equality, 1954-1980.* New York: Hill & Wang, 1981.

Skocpol, Theda. *States and Social Revolutions: A Comparative Analysis of France, Russia, and China.* Cambridge, Eng.: Cambridge University Press, 1979.

Smith, Hedrick. *The New Russians.* New York: Random House, 1990.

Smith, Tony. *Thinking Like a Communist: State and Legitimacy in the Soviet Union, China, and Cuba.* New York: W. W. Norton, 1987.

Sobel, Lester A., ed. *Civil Rights, 1960-63: The Negro Campaign to Win Equal Rights and Opportunities in the United States.* New York: Facts on File, 1964.

Spero, Sterling D. and Abram L. Harris. *The Black Worker: The Negro and the Labor Movement.* New York: Atheneum, 1974.

Stalin, Joseph. *Foundations of Leninism* (in Russian). 1939. Reprint, New York: International Publishers, 1970.

Starr, John Bryan. *Continuing the Revolution: The Political Thought of Mao.* Princeton, N.J.: Princeton University Press, 1979.

Stimpson, Catharine R., et al., eds. *Women and the American City.* Chicago, Ill.: University of Chicago Press, 1981.

Stone, I. F. *The Haunted Fifties: 1953-1963.* Boston, Mass.: Little, Brown, & Company, 1989.

Strauss, Leo and Joseph Cropsey, eds. *History of Political Philosophy.* Chicago, Ill.: Rand McNally, 1963.

Strong, Anna Louise. *The Rise of the Chinese People's Communes.* Peking: New World Press, 1959.

Strong, Tracy B. and Helene Keyssar. *Right in Her Soul: The Life of Anna Louise Strong.* New York: Random House, 1983.

Susman, Warren I. *Culture As History: The Transformation of American Society in the Twentieth Century.* New York: Pantheon Books, 1984.

Sustar, Lee. "Black Militancy and Labor Struggles: The Postal Strike of 1970." Ph. D. seminar paper, New York University, 1987.

Szelenyi, Ivan, ed. *Cities in Recession: Critical Responses to the Urban Policies of the New Right.* London: Sage Publications, 1984.

Taft, Philip. *United They Teach.* Los Angeles, Calif.: Nash Publishing, 1974.

Tan, Chester C. *Chinese Political Thought in the 20th Century.* Newton Abbot, Devon, Eng.: David & Charles, 1972.

Taylor, A. E. *Plato: The Man and His Work.* Cleveland, Ohio: Meridian Books, 1956.

Teodori, Massimo, ed. *The New Left: A Documentary History.* Indianapolis, Ind.: Bobbs-Merrill, 1969.

Thayer, George. *The Farther Shores of Politics: The American Political Fringe Today.* New York: Simon & Schuster, 1967.

Thomas, Hugh. *The Cuban Revolution.* London: Weidenfeld & Nicolson, 1986.

Tompson, William J. *Khrushchev: A Political Life.* New York: St. Martin's Griffin, 1997.

———. *Quotations From Chairman Mao Tse-Tung.* Peking: Foreign Languages Press, 1972.

Tsipko, Alexander S. *Is Stalinism Really Dead?* translated from the Russian by
    E . A. Tichina and S. V. Nikheev. San Francisco, Calif.: Harper San Francisco,
    1990.
Tyler, Gus. *The Labor Revolution: Trade Unions in a New America.* New York:
    Viking Press, 1967.
———. *The Political Imperative: The Corporate Character of Unions.* New
    York: The Macmillan Company, 1968.
———. *Look for the Union Label: A History of the International Ladies' Gar-
    ment Workers' Union.* Armonk, N.Y.: M. E. Sharpe, 1995.
Ulam, Adam B. *The Bolsheviks: The Intellectual, Personal, and Political History
    of the Triumph of Communism in Russia.* New York: Collier Books, 1968.
Unger, Irwin. *The Movement: A History of the American New Left, 1959-1972.*
    New York: Harper & Row, 1974.
U.S. News & World Report. *Communism and the New Left.* Wash., D.C.: Books
    by U.S. News & World Report, 1970.
Vaksberg, Arkady. *Stalin Against the Jews.* Translated by Antonina W. Bouis.
    New York: Alfred A. Knopf, 1994.
Viorst, Milton. *Fire in the Streets: America in the 1960's.* New York: Simon &
    Schuster, 1979.
Wagenheim, K. and Olga Wagenheim, eds. *Puerto Ricans: A Documentary His-
    tory.* Garden City, N.Y.: Anchor Books, 1973.
Walzer, Michael. T*he Revolution of the Saints: A Study of the Origins of Radical
    Politics.* New York: Atheneum, 1974.
———. *The Company of Critics: Social Criticism and Political Commitment in
    the Twentieth Century.* New York: Basic Books, 1988.
Waynick, Capus M., John C. Brooks and Elsie W. Pitts, eds. *North Carolina and
    the Negro.* Raleigh, N.C.: North Carolina Mayors' Co-operating Commit-
    tee, 1964.
Weber, Max. *Weber: Selections in Translation.* (in German) Edited by W. G.
    Runciman. Translated by Eric Mathews. Cambridge, Eng.: Cambridge Uni-
    versity Press, 1978.
Weitzman, Joan. *City Workers and Fiscal Crisis: Cutbacks, Givebacks, and Sur-
    vival, A Study of the New York City Experience.* New Brunswick, N.J.: Rut-
    gers University Press, 1979.
Wetter, Gustav A. *Dialectical Materialism: A Historical and Systematic Survey
    of Philosophy in the Soviet Union.* New York: Frederick A. Praeger, 1958.
Williams, Robert F. *Negroes with Guns.* New York: Marzani & Munsell, 1962.
Williams, William A. *Contours of American History.* Cleveland, Ohio: The
    World Publishing Co., 1961.
Wilson, Everett K. *Sociology: Rules, Roles, and Relationships.* Homewood, Ill.:
    Dorsey Press, 1966.

Wittfogel, Karl A. *Oriental Despotism: A Comparative Study of Total Power.* New Haven, Conn.: Yale University Press, 1957.

Wolfe, Bertram D. *Three Who Made a Revolution: A Biographical History.* New York: Dell Publishing Company, 1964

———. *An Ideology in Power: Reflections on the Russian Revolution.* New York: Stein & Day, 1969.

Woodis, Jack. *New Theories of Revolution: A Commentary on the Views of Frantz Fanon, Regis Debray and Herbert Marcuse.* New York: International Publishers, 1972.

Young, Nigel. *An Infantile Disorder? The Crisis and Decline of the New Left.* Boulder, Colo.: Westview Press, 1977.

Zaroulis, Nancy and Gerald Sullivan. *Who Spoke Up? American Protest Against the War in Vietnam, 1963-1975.* Garden City, N.Y.: Doubleday & Company, 1984.

Zeitlin, Morris. *American Cities: A Working Class View.* New York: International Publishers, 1990.

Zieger, Robert H. *American Workers, American Unions, 1920-1985.* Baltimore, Md.: The Johns Hopkins University Press, 1986.

———. *The CIO, 1935-1955.* Chapel Hill, N.C.: University of North Carolina Press, 1995.

Zinn, Howard. *SNCC: The New Abolitionists.* Boston, Mass.: Beacon Press, 1965.

———. *Postwar America, 1945-1971.* Indianapolis, Ind.: Bobbs-Merrill, 1973.

Index

Abrams, Irving, 124
Acion Patriotica Unitaria, 149
Alamo, George, 177–178, 180
Aldermaston, 104
Amalgamated Clothing Workers of
America, 76
American capitalism, 42–43, 44–45, 62
American exceptionalists, 42
American Jewish Committee, 86
American labor movement:
AFL, 85, 123
AFL-CIO, 8, 72, 161
and anticommunist crusade, xiv, 8
CIO, 98, 123
insurgency in, xiv
in New York City, xv. *See also* New
York City
PL's assessment of, xii, xiv, 7–10
and socialism, 7–10, 75
*See also For an Alternative Labor
Policy*
American workers, xii–xiii, 8–9, 44,
48–49, 54, 58, 65, 165, 188–189,
194–196. *See also* Blacks: work-
ers; Hispanic workers; revolution
and reform; women workers
Anderson, Vivian, 17
Antioch College, 102–105, 192
Apter, Bob, 106, 113

anticommunist crusade, xi, xiv, xvi, 8,
85, 121, 188
Anti-Defamation League, 164
Anti-Fascist War. 30
anti-imperialism, xii, 34, 43. *See also*
May Second Movement
antinationalism, 37, 43
antirevisionism, ix, xi. 19, 24–25, 32,
39–43, 188–190
anti-Semitism, x, 85–88
antiwar movement, 44–45, 58. *See also*
May Second Movement; SDS;
Vietnam War
arbitration, 128, 132–134, 137–138
Arecibo, Puerto Rico, 147–148
Atlanta, Georgia, 114, 116

Ballinger, Skip, 182
Barbash, Jack, 74
Barrett, James, 110
Bay of Pigs, 104, 181
Berger, Sam, 137
Betances, Ramon Emeterio, 147–148
Black and Latin American League,
182
Blacks:
civil rights, 44, 62. *See also* Monroe,
North Carolina; SNCC
nationalism, 18, 63–64, 116

319

Harlem Rebellion, 16–18, 45, 62, 89, 91, 117, 151, 189. *See also* Epton, William
Harlem Solidarity Committee, 94
Harlem Unemployment Council, 96
Harrington, Michael, 12, 104, 175
Havana, Cuba, 113, 117. *See also* Cuba
Hawley, Amos H., 105
Hazard, Kentucky miners' strike, 11–12, 45, 102, 189
Head Start, 182
Heinkin, Fred, 124
High School of Fashion Industries, 91
Hill, Herbert:
  on Black and Hispanic garment workers, 79, 83–84, 89, 93–94
  congressional testimony of, 82–84
  and Holmes Case, 80
  on ILGWU's importance, 72
  See also anti-Semitism; Dubinsky, David: congressional testimony of; garment industry: congressional investigation of; ILGWU: discrimination in; Jacobs, Paul; NAACP; Rosen, Milton: congressional investigation of garment industry
Hispanic workers, x, xv–xvi, 63, 79, 158, 179, 191–192. *See also* DeJesus, Felipe
Hitler, Adolf, 20
Hogan, Frank, 16, 124
Holocaust, 88
Holmes Case, 80, 83
Hospital and Nursing Home Workers. *See* Local 1199
Houghton, Jim, 96
House Committee on Education and Labor, 80, 82, 122
House Committee on Un-American Activities (HUAC):
  and Buffalo CPUSA, 5
  and Harlem Rebellion, 18, 89, 117
  and Progressive Labor Movement, 13, 127

  and Student Committee for Travel to Cuba, 13, 102, 117–118
  See also anticommunist crusade; Willis, Edwin E.

Ideal Garment Trucking, 139
idealism, 24–25
immigrants, 74
Integrated Workers, 150
International, 26
International Committee Against Racism, 49–50, 60
International Ladies' Garment Worker' Union:
  charges against by Hill, Herbert, 82–87
  congressional investigation of, 80–82, 122–126
  criticism of, 76–79, 92–94, 135, 178–179, 182, 191
  discrimination in, x, xvi, 82–84
  dress industry contract, 90–91
  importance of, xvi, 72–73
  Jewish leadership of, x, 79, 191
  jobbers' and contractors' association contract , 88–91
  and Liberal Party, 72, 74, 164
  Local 10, 75, 80, 83–84, 176
  Local 22, 161
  Local 32, 156–157, 159, 161–162, 167, 170, 172, 176–177, 180, 184–186, 193
  Local 60–60A, 82–84
  Local 66, 93
  Local 89, 83–84
  Local 102, 101, 120, **122–146**, 186, 192
  1909 general strike, 156
  policy on minimum wage, 76, 78, 152, 155
  progressivism of, 73, 82
  regulatory force in, 90
  rift with NAACP, 83, 87
  Tyler, Gus, in defense of, 84–85
  See also Dubinsky, David; garment industry; Hill, Herbert; Jacobs, Paul; Rosen, Milton; Tyler, Gus

For Product Safety Concerns and Information please contact our EU
representative GPSR@taylorandfrancis.com
Taylor & Francis Verlag GmbH, Kaufingerstraße 24, 80331 München, Germany

www.ingramcontent.com/pod-product-compliance
Lightning Source LLC
Chambersburg PA
CBHW071404090426
42737CB00011B/1347